The Ethnographic Experiment

Pacific Perspectives
Studies of the European Society for Oceanists

Series Editors: Christina Toren, University of St Andrews, and Edvard Hviding, University of Bergen

Oceania is of enduring contemporary significance in global trajectories of history, politics, economy and ecology. The books published in this series explore Oceanic values and Oceanic imaginations, documenting the unique position of the region – its cultural and linguistic diversity, its ecological and geographical distinctness, and always fascinating experiments with social formations. This series thus conveys the political, economic and moral alternatives that Oceania offers the contemporary world.

The Ethnographic Experiment

A.M. Hocart and W.H.R. Rivers in Island Melanesia, 1908

◆●◆

Edited by Edvard Hviding and Cato Berg

berghahn
NEW YORK · OXFORD
www.berghahnbooks.com

First edition published in 2014 by
Berghahn Books
www.berghahnbooks.com

©2014, 2016 Edvard Hviding and Cato Berg
First paperback edition published in 2016

Library of Congress Cataloging-in-Publication Data

The ethnographic experiment: A.M. Hocart and W.H.R. Rivers in island
Melanesia, 1908 / Edited by Edvard Hviding and Cato Berg. -- First edition.
     pages cm. -- (Pacific perspectives: studies of the European society for
Oceanists) (Percy Sladen Trust Expedition to Melanesia)
     ISBN 978-1-78238-342-0 (hardback) -- ISBN 978-1-78533-339-2 (paper-
back) -- ISBN 978-1-78238-343-7 (ebook)
     1.   Ethnology--Solomon Islands--History. 2.   Ethnology--Solomon
Islands--Fieldwork. 3.   Participant observation--Solomon Islands.
4.   Solomon Islands--Social life and customs. 5.   Rivers, W. H. R.
(William Halse Rivers), 1864-1922--Travel--Solomon Islands. 6.   Hocart,
A. M. (Arthur Maurice), 1884-1939--Travel--Solomon Islands. I. Hviding,
Edvard.
     GN671.S6E47 2014
     305.80099593--dc23

                                                                    2013044575

British Library Cataloguing in Publication Data
A catalogue record for this book is available from the British Library

ISBN 978-1-78238-342-0 (hardback)
ISBN 978-1-78533-339-2 (paperback)
ISBN 978-1-78238-343-7 (ebook)

Contents

◆●◆

Figures and Tables

◆●◆

Figures

Tables

Preface

———— ◆●◆ ————

This book is the outcome of a long-term collective effort by all authors to bring to the forefront of anthropology's history a poorly known and often ignored, but in our view ground-breaking, instance of early anthropological fieldwork. Whereas A.M. Hocart and W.H.R. Rivers are both, in distinct and different ways, recognised as prominent and influential scholars in the development of twentieth-century anthropology, it is not so widely known that as early as in 1908 they carried out prolonged fieldwork together in the Melanesian islands of the south-west Pacific. The fieldwork, known in some circles as the Percy Sladen Trust Expedition to the Solomon Islands, was centred on the western parts of that archipelago, particularly the small but historically significant island of Simbo in the New Georgia group, but also taking in the inter-island character of social and cultural life around New Georgia. Rivers carried out further survey work in the islands of Vanuatu, then the New Hebrides.

As anthropologists whose own long-term research is focused on the Western Solomons, the editors of this book have both found it somewhat surprising that the pioneering fieldwork carried out by Hocart and Rivers in 1908 has been given so little attention by historians of anthropology and by biographical writers. This seems all the more remarkable given that the early work in the Solomon Islands by Hocart and Rivers constitutes one of the first, if not *the* first, examples of modern anthropological fieldwork employing methods of participant observation through long-term residence among the people studied. Indeed, it may be argued that those very methods were in part founded by the two fieldworkers back then in 1908. For scholars of Melanesian anthropology and Pacific studies, the published and unpublished materials from the Percy Sladen Trust Expedition of 1908 provide a unique, rich and ethnographically grounded view of Pacific peoples at a critical historical moment of transition from pre-colonial indigenous sovereignty in the broadest sense to colonial suppression by the British Empire, encapsulation by the global commodity economy, and massive Christian conversion. The insights that the fieldwork of these two intellectually broad-minded scholars provide on remote Pacific societies, and into turn-of-the-century European thought, makes a re-appraisal of the work they carried out in 1908 significant for understanding complex trajectories in Pacific and colonial history as well as the history of ideas.

Acknowledgements

——— ◆●◆ ———

In 2008 we invited a small group of colleagues whose research has engaged closely with Hocart's and Rivers's materials from Island Melanesia to meet in Bergen, in order to celebrate the centennial of the Percy Sladen Trust Expedition through days of lively discussion. While that informal event was funded and hosted by the Bergen Pacific Studies Research Group at the Department of Social Anthropology, University of Bergen, the subsequent stages of our work towards the completion of this book have also been facilitated by the University of Cambridge, represented by St John's College, the Cambridge University Library and the Museum of Archaeology and Anthropology (MAA). We gratefully acknowledge the assistance given in this regard by Tim Bayliss-Smith of St. John's College and Nicholas Thomas of the MAA. The latter institution has been a close collaborative partner through the duration of this book project, and as its Director, Nicholas Thomas has encouraged much interaction between the book's chapters and the museum's collections. Nick also came up, inspirationally, with the 'experimental' title for this book. Tim Bayliss-Smith has facilitated, and been a very active partner in, explorations of the Haddon Papers at the Cambridge University Library and of sources of information in lesser known repositories.

The collective research process of which this book is a part is grounded in the international research programme 'Pacific Alternatives: Cultural Heritage and Political Innovation in Oceania', generously funded by the Research Council of Norway from 2008 to 2012 (Grant no. 185646). At Berghahn Books our thanks go to Ann DeVita, Molly Mosher and Charlotte Mosedale for their patience and careful guidance, and to Marion Berghahn for her enthusiastic reception of the book proposal. At the University of Bergen we are grateful to cartographer Kjell Helge Sjøstrøm of the Departments of Geography and Social Anthropology, for producing all the book's maps, and to Ane Straume and Camilla Aa. Jensen of the Bergen Pacific Studies Research Group for editorial work on all chapters. Our sincere thanks go to all the book's contributors for the constant inspiration and dedicated effort they have given to this collective project of discovery and writing. Above all, on behalf of all contributors, we express our sincere gratitude to so many Solomon Islanders and ni-Vanuatu for their kind assistance and support during many years of fieldwork on their islands.

Edvard Hviding and Cato Berg
Bergen, October 2013

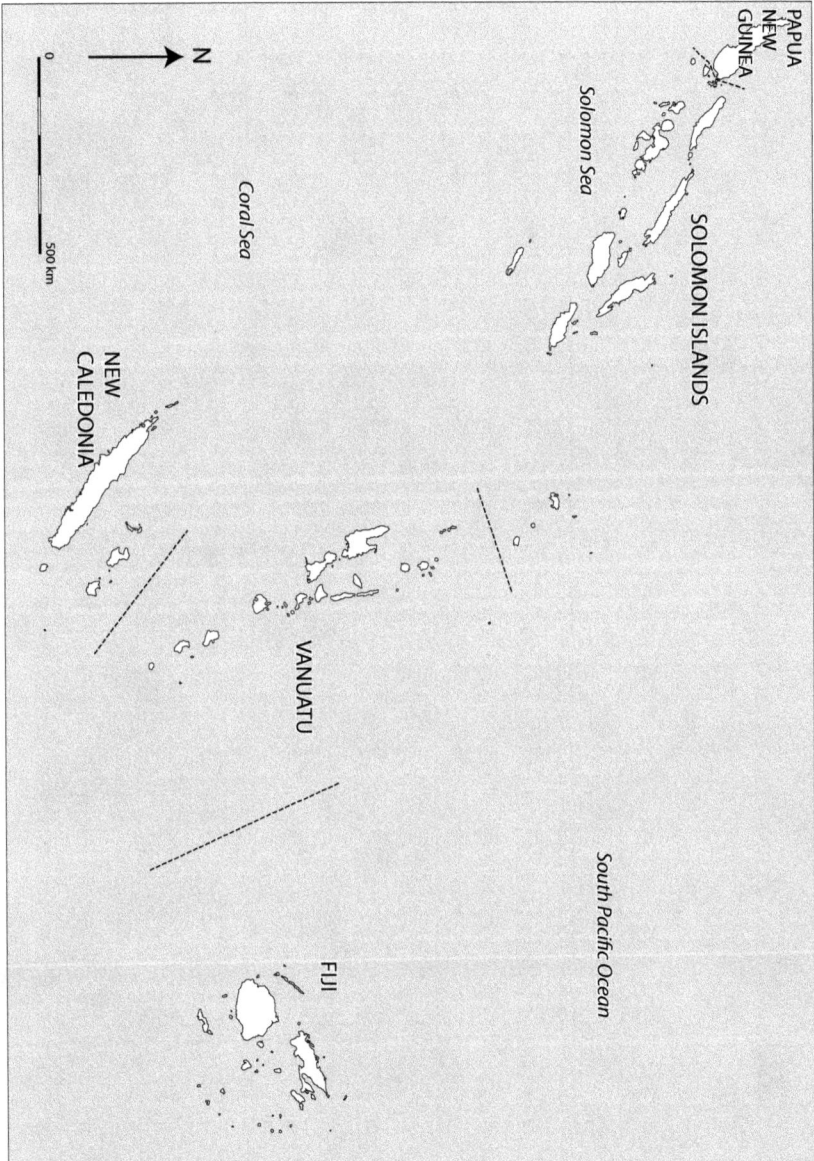

Island Melanesia: the geographical context of the Percy Sladen Trust Expedition (map by K.H. Sjøstrøm, University of Bergen).

Introduction

The Ethnographic Experiment in Island Melanesia

◆●◆

Edvard Hviding and Cato Berg

Anthropology in the Making: To the Solomon Islands, 1908

In 1908, three British scholars travelled, each in his own way, to the south-western Pacific in order to embark on pioneering anthropological fieldwork in the Solomon Islands. They were William Halse Rivers Rivers, Arthur Maurice Hocart and Gerald Camden Wheeler. Rivers (1864–1922), a physician, psychologist and self-taught anthropologist, was already a veteran fieldworker, having been a member of the Cambridge Torres Strait Expedition for seven months in 1898 (Herle and Rouse 1998), after which he had also carried out five months of fieldwork among the tribal Toda people of South India in 1901–2 (see Rivers 1906).

The Torres Strait Expedition was a large-scale, multi-disciplinary effort with major funding, and had helped change a largely embryonic, descriptive anthropology into a modern discipline – reflective of the non-anthropological training of expedition leader Alfred Cort Haddon and his team, among whom Rivers and C.G. Seligman were to develop anthropological careers. During the expedition, Rivers not only engaged in a wide range of observations based on his existing training in psychology and physiology, but also increasingly collected materials on the social organisation of the Torres Strait peoples, work that ultimately resulted in him devising the 'genealogical method' for use by the growing discipline of anthropology, with which he increasingly identified.

The 1908 fieldwork in Island Melanesia which is the focus of this book was on a much smaller scale than the Torres Strait Expedition, but it had a more sharply defined anthropological agenda.[1] Building on his development of the genealogical method, and no doubt on epistemological innovations brought forth by his encounters with the Torres Strait Islanders (and subsequently the Toda), Rivers had secured funds from the Percy Sladen Trust in London for 'a journey to the Solomon Islands for the purpose of making investigations in anthropology'.[2] His main research agenda was the scientific investigation, through substantial ethnographic fieldwork, of the wealth of 'kinship systems' of the Pacific islands, and as such it represented the cutting edge of the budding discipline of social anthropology.

A look at the background for this scholarly initiative is instructive. Being an important foundation of the fieldwork that commenced in 1908, the 1898 expedition to investigate the Melanesian islanders of the Torres Strait has also in general terms been considered a landmark in the development of a new anthropology. In her social history of the development of British anthropology, Kuklick (1991: 133–34) notes that '[t]he intellectual pedigree of modern British social anthropologists conventionally – and with considerable justification – begins with the members [of the Torres Strait Expedition]'. Fredrik Barth goes a step further by arguing that the Torres Strait Expedition in fact had some important consequences for the development of anthropology that were not really recognised by its leader, the zoologist Haddon, who kept insisting that the expedition's major achievement was that of bringing 'trained scientists to make their observations in situ':

> Rivers and Seligman and, for that matter, Haddon himself were not scientists trained in anthropology with any expert skills in identifying phenomenal forms and accumulating systematic observations in the discipline. They were, on the contrary, amateurs in anthropology with some scientific training in *other* disciplines. What had happened was that the little island communities in the Torres Straits had *imposed* on them the new organisation of primary data by locality and the realisation of the complexity and internal connections of each local form of life. Rivers and Seligman were exposed to an intensive training experience in these respects and thereby became ethnographers of a new kind. (Barth 2005: 13–14, original emphasis)

In Rivers's own description of the genealogical method he states that this anthropological tool was initially devised for the practical purpose of 'studying as exactly as possible the relationship to one another of the individuals on whom we were making psychological tests' (Rivers 1900: 74). However, he soon found that the systematic collection of genealogies allowed for the deeper study of 'many sociological problems'. It appears that he was side-tracked from his more narrow original intentions of studying colour perception among Torres Strait Islanders, becoming fascinated with what he called 'social and vital statistics', and the broader value of such material for deducing patterns in totemism, ritual and social organisation. Rivers's 'discovery' of what he believed was a more accurate method for obtaining information through ethnographic fieldwork was to have profound implications on the emerging anthropology of the time, and could not be overlooked, even by its critics (see Berg, this volume).

Clearly, the research agenda Rivers devised for the new expedition to the islands of Melanesia in 1908 amounted to an ethnographic experiment, whereby emerging anthropological theory and method would be brought to bear on, and tested through, encounters with so far undocumented examples of social life under circumstances of what we call today 'alterity'. In the early-twentieth-century Solomon Islands, British imperial influence was still modest, and the archipelago could be approached by an anthropological fieldworker as a scene where resilient, so far autonomous local societies faced accelerating, unpredictable intervention from the forces of Empire, Christianity and money. In a two-page letter of application to the Percy Sladen Trust, Rivers expressed particular interest in what he believed – in the mind-set of an earlier, evolutionist anthropology – must be locally existing, surviving examples of ancient 'maternal' systems, to be found on the ground in the Solomons:

> I should endeavour while in the Solomons to obtain as complete an account as possible of the sociology and religion of the natives of two districts, one in which there is still a definite maternal system of society, and one in which this has been replaced by a system of father-right, my chief objective being to study the mode of transition between these two states of social organisation. In addition I should hope to study the psychology of the natives, and especially their senses, by experimental methods.
>
> The shorter periods in the Polynesian islands would be devoted to obtaining the systems of kinship, on which subject I could obtain the information I need in a few weeks.
>
> I may mention that in the subjects to which I should pay especial attention, the works of Codrington and others on the people of Melanesia give very little information.[3]

Obviously cast in the evolutionary mode still characteristic of the anthropology of the day – 'maternal' societies being inevitably replaced by ones of 'father-right' – the fieldwork Rivers envisaged was also to be both comparative and experimental. His reference to Anglican missionary cum ethnographer R.H. Codrington is of significance, as Rivers may indeed have relied more on this source than he would admit (see Kolshus, this volume). Author of an early classic study, *The Melanesians: Studies in their Anthropology and Folk-Lore* (Codrington 1891), this pioneer had decades of experience from the islands, but Rivers evidently aimed to explore dimensions of Melanesian social life so far not covered by such early descriptive efforts, and, moreover, to do so using a strong theoretical platform, through a combination of brief visits to many field locations and longer-term residence in a few.

Evidently, Rivers wanted to make the most out of his Pacific expedition, and he took the longest possible journey to the Solomons. He travelled westwards across the Pacific Ocean and in the course of about four months visited Hawaii, Fiji, Tonga and Samoa. On board the Anglican Melanesian Mission's ship the *Southern Cross*, he visited a number of islands in Vanuatu (then the New Hebrides) and the eastern Solomons. Meanwhile, his two junior expedition partners made their way to Australia, from where they caught a steamer out to the Solomons. Hocart (1883–1939) was the youngest of the three, having recently studied Greek, Latin, philosophy and ancient history at Oxford, and subsequently psychology in Berlin. Wheeler (1872–1943) had a science doctorate from the University of London, and had engaged in the emerging social anthropology of the time through studies with the Finnish anthropologist Edvard Westermarck (who later also taught Bronislaw Malinowski) and had authored *The Tribes and Intertribal Relations in Australia* (Wheeler 1910).

Aspects of the biographies and intellectual trajectories of the three scholars, and the nature and circumstances of the fieldwork they carried out in 1908, are examined later on in this chapter. At this stage, let it be noted that it was both anthropology and anthropologists that were in the making during the Percy Sladen Trust Expedition to the Solomon Islands.[4] An expedition it was, but no simple empirical quest for the discovery of something unknown. It was to be a sustained effort of ethnographic, cross-cultural experiment, through direct encounter, involving residence and long-term interaction with Pacific islanders whose existence was undergoing rapid transformation. It was also another prominent example of how, to follow Barth's observation, local realities imposed radically different understandings on the ethnographers. As encounter, the fieldwork was to be a mutual experiment in which initiative was simultaneously ethnographic and indigenous.

How were the expedition's participants prepared for such experimentation? Regarding their academic qualifications, Wheeler's desk-based anthropological study of Australian materials (Wheeler 1910) was overshadowed by the fact that Rivers had published a massive monograph from substantial fieldwork in India (Rivers 1906). Rivers had made a name for himself as an ethnographic practitioner and – largely through

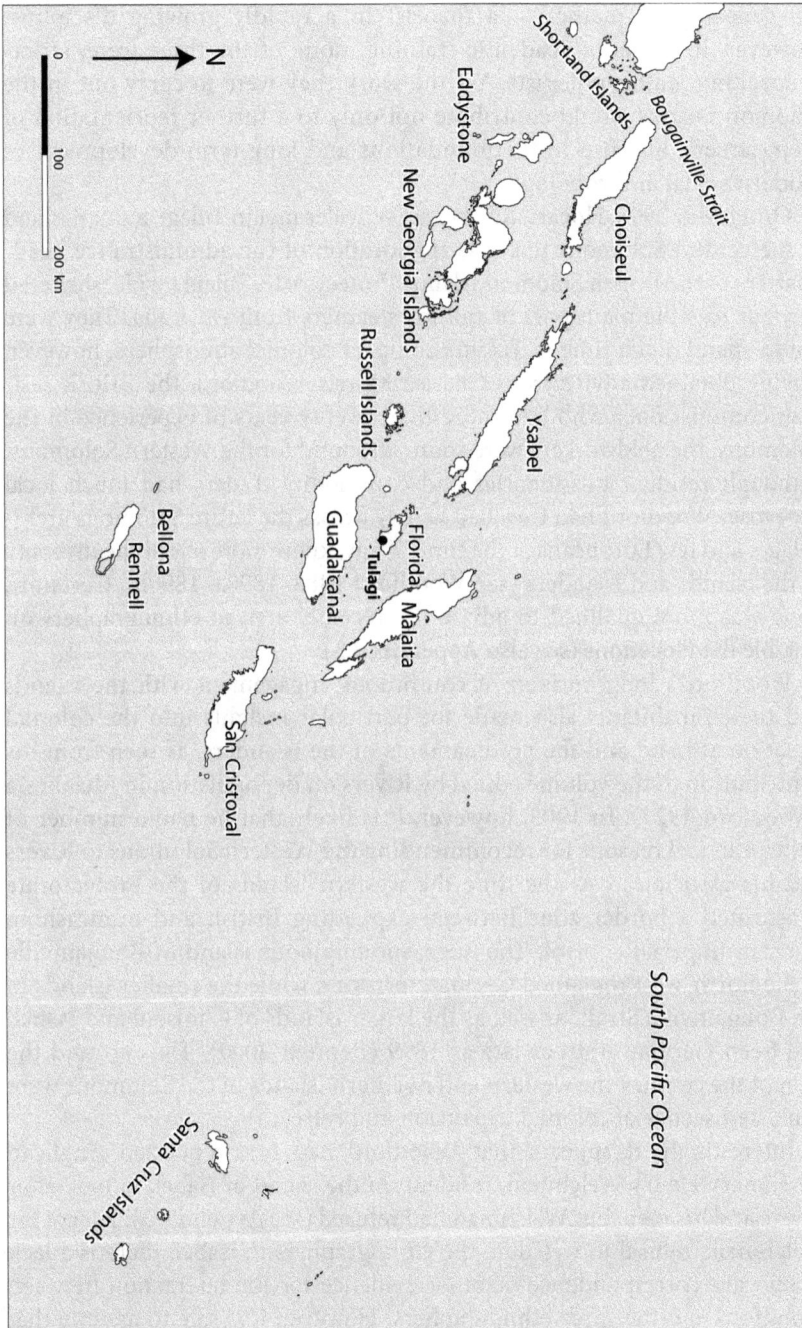

Figure 0.1: The British Solomon Islands Protectorate in 1908, with colonial-era island names (map by K.H. Sjøstrøm, University of Bergen).

the genealogical method – a theorist in a rapidly growing discipline. However, in terms of academic training, none of the three were, strictly speaking, anthropologists. Yet the work they were to carry out in the Solomon Islands would contribute not only to a further reorientation of their careers, but also to the foundations and long-term development of modern social anthropology.

On 11 May 1908, Hocart, Rivers and Wheeler met in Tulagi, a small island in the central Solomons that was the location of the administrative headquarters of the British Solomon Islands Protectorate. Tulagi's wide, sheltered harbour was the main port of call for steamers from Australia. They were not to spend much time in Tulagi's compact colonial atmosphere, however. Having obtained advice from Charles Morris Woodford, the British resident commissioner who had more than twenty years of experience in the Solomons, the fieldworkers were soon outbound for the Western Solomons. Although resident missionaries and commodity traders had much local expertise, Woodford had travelled widely across the entire Solomons archipelago, and few Europeans at the time, if any, knew more about the diversity of the islands and islanders (see Woodford 1888, 1890a, 1890b). Certainly, none was more qualified to advise the recently arrived ethnographers on suitable field locations (see also Appendix 3.3).

Woodford's long horizon of continuous engagement with the islands and their inhabitants also made for particular insights into the colonial situation at hand and the predicaments of the islanders, as seen from his contribution to the volume edited by Rivers on depopulation in Melanesia (Woodford 1922). In 1908, however, it is likely that he had a number of quite practical reasons for recommending the Western Solomons to Rivers and his associates.[5] At the time the western islands of the Protectorate constituted a border zone between expanding British and diminishing German imperial control. The huge, mountainous island of Bougainville to the north-west remained German territory, while the smaller islands in the Bougainville Strait, as well as the larger islands of Choiseul and Isabel, had been German until as late as 1899 (Bennett 2000). Thus around the turn of the century the western and northern islands of the Solomons were contested scenes of colonial expansion and retreat.

Interestingly, it appears that Woodford had first requested Anglican missionary Henry Welchman, resident on the island of Isabel, to look after Rivers and his men, but Welchman had refused (see Appendix 3). Except for Welchman's refusal to welcome the ethnographers to Isabel, there is a lack of relevant correspondence or other evidence for the interaction between Woodford and the three ethnographers. However, it is safe to assume that Woodford saw some usefulness in a substantial British scholarly presence in the imperial border zone of New Georgia. He and Rivers would also both have been aware of the fact that the major scholarly ethnographic effort in the British Solomon Islands Protectorate so far had focused on the eastern islands, where Codrington had already set the stage for what would be a continuous sequence of anthropologically interested Anglican missionaries. In short, from Woodford's perspective the New Georgia islands would have been seen as both imperially remote and anthropologically undocumented, in general need of more British attention, and therefore in more than one sense a good location for Rivers and his co-researchers.

Rivers, Hocart and Wheeler obtained local transport from among the plethora of mission boats and traders' vessels that plied the archipelago and passed through Tulagi's busy port. They embarked on a westwards sea journey of approximately 400 kilometres to the most remote parts of the New Georgia group, a dense cluster of large and small islands, some high and volcanic, others low and coralline, an ecologically and culturally complex archipelago where some of the world's largest coral lagoons allow for sheltered travel and a strongly maritime way of life. The progression of the expedition was rapid. By 14 May the three were already settled on the small island of Simbo, referred to then by some islanders as Narovo or Madegusu, and by European navigators as Eddystone. That rocky island, an outlying part of the New Georgia archipelago with thermal springs and volcanic fissures emitting sulphurous steam, had been a favourite port of call for early European traders and American whalers from the late eighteenth century. On the highly competitive scene of inter-island relationships in New Georgia, where warfare, enmity, alliances and exchange were in continuous flux, the Simbo people had long maintained a regionally powerful role far surpassing the relative size of their island and its population. Right up until the time of the Percy Sladen Trust Expedition, Simbo people had retained a double-sided reputation as welcoming to Europeans, yet ferocious and successful inter-island warriors and headhunters. While the practices of overseas raiding and headhunting were characteristic of all of New Georgia, Simbo had long stood out as a particularly agreeable place for Europeans to trade, local warlike practices notwithstanding. The log of the Scottish trader Andrew Cheyne gives a particularly vivid glimpse of encounters and interactions, both tense and productive, between islanders and European visitors (Cheyne 1971: 303–7).

Just a few years prior to the arrival on Simbo of Rivers and his associates, a measure of 'pacification' had been established across the Western Solomons. Ocean-going war canoes had been destroyed by colonial police, and punitive actions by gunboats of the Royal Navy combined with local agency had caused quite a rapid cessation of warfare, headhunting and attacks on European traders. By 1908, only a very few renegade warriors were left in the Western Solomons. Missionaries (mainly Methodists, who arrived in Roviana Lagoon in 1902) were establishing footholds in an increasing number of islands and localities, and islanders were drifting into a copra-based colonial economy. The local perception of changing times was acute. It was into this atmosphere of rapid and radical socio-political transformation in the islanders' lives that the three British fieldworkers stepped. At Simbo they must surely have been welcomed by Fred Green, a resident European trader, who would have brokered contacts with local men of influence. The anthropologists' equipment was landed, tents were pitched, informants were identified and approached, and scholarly investigations were launched among the people of Simbo. Fieldwork was under way.

Rivers and his two junior associates had few professional predecessors in the area. In the New Georgia islands, only sketchy ethnographic work had been carried out, by missionaries, wealthy adventurers, Royal Navy officers and other navigators, resulting alternately in quite sensational descriptions of local customs or in arid inventories of such customs based on the Royal Anthropological Institute's field manual *Notes and Queries on Anthropology*.[6] Further to the north-west, however, in and around the Bougainville Strait, scholars from other European intellectual traditions had been at work for some time. In 1903, German entomologist and collector Carl Ribbe had published a book documenting his 'two years among the cannibals of the Solomon Islands', with meticulous descriptions of local customs and ethnographic objects (as well as an appendix of physical measurements of islanders) from the Bougainville Strait, with some attention also given to Vella Lavella and Roviana in New Georgia (Ribbe 1903). While Ribbe was no professional ethnologist, the German presence to the north-west of New Georgia was decidedly professional at the time of the arrival of Rivers, Hocart and Wheeler, in that R.C. Thurnwald, who had studied anthropology and sociology in Berlin and Vienna, was already carrying out fieldwork in the Bougainville Strait and on Bougainville itself. Wheeler would later team up with Thurnwald. After a month's residence and work on the little island of Simbo, Rivers wrote in a report to the Percy Sladen Trust that 'circumstances [had] not been very favourable so far':

[T]he south-east season has been very late in setting in and in consequence we have had a great deal of rain; the people are very reticent and were at first very suspicious; the whole district is very unsettled, and all three members of the expedition have already had fever, but in spite of this we have done very well. The social organisation has been worked out to a great extent, though there is still much detail to fill in; we have collected a large amount of physical, technological and linguistic material and during the last week, we have begun to make a good deal of progress in the investigation of magic and religion, and the prospects for future work here now look very hopeful.[7]

Whereas Wheeler was to leave after about two months and travel north for independent fieldwork in the Shortland Islands, Rivers and Hocart spent almost four months of intensive fieldwork as residents on Simbo. They then travelled on a vessel owned by Fred Green for a month's 'survey work' in a number of villages on the nearby island of Vella Lavella, before Rivers left the Western Solomons altogether at the end of September. He returned to the Anglican Melanesian Mission's ship the *Southern Cross* and retraced his route of investigations on the outbound journey, in the central and eastern Solomons and the New Hebrides. Meanwhile, Hocart continued fieldwork in the Western Solomons on his own for the rest of the year. After Vella Lavella, he worked in Roviana Lagoon for six weeks; there he made the most out of already established relationships with Roviana men he had met on Simbo. He interacted with the powerful groups of Nusa Roviana and the adjacent mainland around Munda, but adopted a remarkably broad geographical scope for his ethnographic research, following vernacular definitions of 'Roviana' as 'the south west coast of New Georgia from Konggu Mbairoko ... to the island of Mbaraulu'.[8] Hocart then returned to Simbo for a couple of weeks to 'follow up clues picked up elsewhere' (Hocart 1922: 71). Finally, in December Hocart spent two weeks on the island of Kolobangara (also referred to as Duke, or in Hocart's spelling, Nduke), before returning to Simbo for the last time, leaving on 1 January 1909.

Although Wheeler's fieldwork was to be by far the most extensive, it was Rivers and Hocart who were to become the more famous scholars, though this was in their later incarnations and not as a result of any reputation garnered from their fieldwork in the remote Solomons in 1908. However, as noted in the chapters in this volume by Bayliss-Smith and Hviding, it is likely that neither Rivers – the famous psychiatrist (who pioneered the treatment of shell-shocked soldiers during the First World War) and founder of modern social anthropology – nor Hocart – the prolific anthropological writer, comparativist and largely unrecognised 'intransigent genius' (Needham 1970: xvii) who influenced Lévi-Strauss and Dumont – would have managed such achievements without their experiences in Melanesia in 1908. Against this background, and because the published and unpublished materials left by Hocart and Rivers give unique opportunities for examining how the fieldwork was carried out and how anthropological knowledge was built, this book focuses on those two and not Wheeler. It must be remembered, though, that Wheeler undoubtedly has the honour of having carried out one of the first long and remotely located periods of fieldwork in the history of modern social anthropology, under what must have been very challenging circumstances.

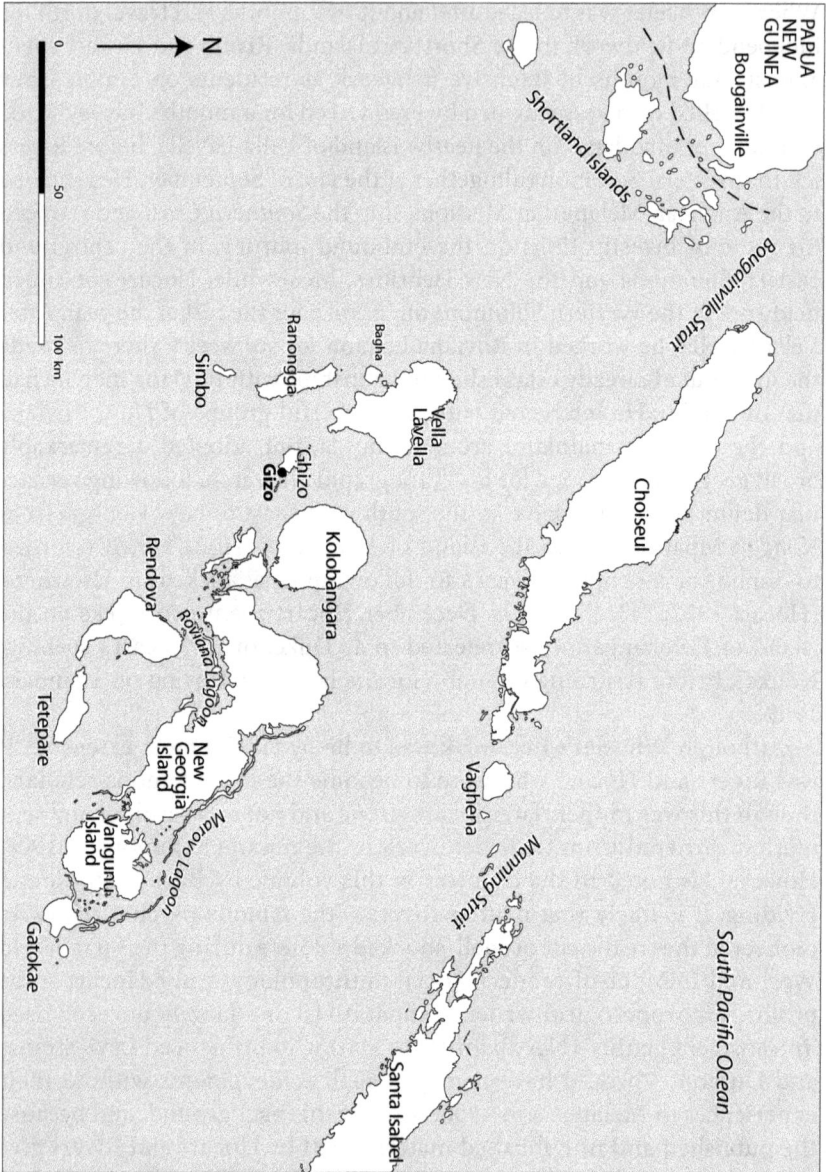

Figure 0.2: The western and northern parts of the Solomon Islands, including locations at which Hocart, Rivers and Wheeler carried out fieldwork in 1908 (map by K.H. Sjøstrøm, University of Bergen).

Centennial Reappraisals

In this introductory chapter, the work of the Percy Sladen Trust Expedition to the Solomon Islands is approached with regard to what we see as its prominent, but neglected, place in the history of anthropology and related disciplines. We outline the historical and ethnographic contexts for the fieldwork and provide an account of the institutional circumstances of the expedition. Attention is given to the local conditions the pioneer ethnographers faced in 1908: a situation of intense change with social upheaval, new economic arenas, disease, depopulation and colonial subjugation.

The contributors to this volume approach the 1908 fieldwork as representing, in one way or another, a profound cross-cultural encounter. Although not widely known, and barely discussed even in biographies of Rivers and Hocart, the fieldwork carried out during the expedition stands out as an early example of modern ethnographic research involving residence among and continuous interaction with the people studied, hallmarks of advanced anthropological method later claimed by Malinowski in his famous treatise on fieldwork in the opening chapter of *Argonauts of the Western Pacific* (Malinowski 1922: 1–25). However, except for the initiative that has resulted in this book, the centennial of the Percy Sladen Trust Expedition of 1908 went by quite unnoticed. Its path-breaking achievements have long since faded into obscurity, quite unlike the first expedition in which Rivers played an important part, that to the Torres Strait in 1898, the centennial of which was elaborately marked (see Herle and Rouse 1998).

The reasons why biographers, as well as historians of anthropology, have not given much weight to the 1908 fieldwork are not entirely clear, but some suggestions can be given. Compared to Malinowski's extraordinarily long fieldwork in the Trobriands, and the degree to which he relied on the acquired ability to speak the vernacular language, the work in the Western Solomons by Rivers and Hocart was destined to be seen as inferior in terms of both its duration and the level of linguistic competence achieved. Quite simply, while Malinowski (and his students and successors) explicitly aimed at very long periods of fieldwork and at learning local languages, a strategy that became a standard for modern fieldwork in social anthropology, Rivers and Hocart spent only six months in the Western Solomons, and relied largely on the Melanesian Pidgin of the day, with some vernacular competence in the collection of myths, magical formulae and other texts. As the scope of anthropological methodology developed very rapidly in the early twentieth century, pioneering early work like that of Rivers and Hocart fell by the wayside as more spectacular performances were achieved, and duly reported, from the time of Malinowski onwards.

Furthermore, since no well-organised publication plan arose from the Western Solomons fieldwork (see below), the significance and originality of the work that was carried out in 1908 all but faded from view. Rivers's two-volume magnum opus *The History of Melanesian Society* (Rivers 1914a) was itself so densely packed with ethnographic materials gathered through survey work on brief visits to many other Melanesian island localities (see Kolshus, this volume) that the major 'intensive' research effort at Simbo and elsewhere in New Georgia hardly stood out. While in his post-fieldwork report to the Percy Sladen Trust, Rivers presented the ambition of publishing '[a] book by Mr Hocart and myself on 'The Western Solomon Islands', probably in two volumes',[9] this never eventuated, and the ways of the two fieldworkers parted after Simbo.

On leaving the Solomons, Hocart took a post as a schoolmaster in Fiji, and while thus employed received a fieldwork scholarship from Oxford University. He remained in the Pacific until 1914, and in between work 'as head-master of a native school' (Hocart 1929: 3) at Lakeba in the Lau islands he carried out ethnographic fieldwork in Fiji, Samoa, Tonga and several small islands including Rotuma and Wallis – a scholarly achievement that would support his broadening comparativist agenda. Rivers returned to England after his slow journey back through the islands of Melanesia, and took up research and teaching at Cambridge. The First World War saw Hocart on active service in France, while Rivers (who had briefly revisited Melanesia in 1914/15) developed his pioneering psychiatric approach to treating shell shock. Wheeler, meanwhile, did not embark on a career in academia after his year of fieldwork in the Solomons. In 1926 he published a monograph on Mono-Alu folklore, a massive descriptive account of myths, stories and songs from the Shortland Islands and southern Bougainville (Wheeler 1926), but his definitive monograph on Mono-Alu society was never published. Concurrent with the untimely death of Rivers in 1922, Hocart launched a series of long, descriptive ethnographic articles in the *Journal of the Royal Anthropological Institute* (Hocart 1922, 1925, 1929, 1931b, 1935, 1937; see Hviding, this volume). The definitive book on the Western Solomons from the Percy Sladen Trust Expedition was never to eventuate.

This volume is grounded in long-term research experiences from exactly those areas of Island Melanesia where Rivers and Hocart worked in 1908. It has emerged from many years of collaborative work by the contributors, who have between them carried out fieldwork in almost every corner of the New Georgia group where Rivers and Hocart did their work, and in parts of Vanuatu where Rivers worked on his own. The authors have also carried out extensive archival studies on the materials from the 1908 expedition, including the examination of fieldnotes, correspondence and other documents left by Rivers and Hocart, and of objects and photographs. Combining perspectives from anthropology, archaeology, history and human geography, and benefiting from several contributors' command of vernacular languages, the book examines from multiple perspectives the cross-cultural, many-stranded interactions that developed in the course of the expedition between the specific historical situations of the scholars and of the people and places under study.

There are significant general implications of this multidisciplinary study of a particularly interesting instance of early-twentieth-century anthropological fieldwork. In terms of the history of ideas, understandings can be developed of the Western historical, political and cultural circumstances of the time concerning the study of other worlds, other people and the exotic. Together, the following chapters aim to achieve such understanding through a perspective that combines an awareness of the prevailing early-twentieth-century views that informed this particular ethnographic experiment with an ethnographically grounded understanding of the local circumstances at hand in 1908. It is here that fieldwork by the volume's contributors carried out in the late twentieth and early twenty-first centuries becomes particularly valuable. In cases where Rivers and Hocart interviewed named Solomon Islanders, the actual situation more than a hundred years ago can in some cases be traced to a high level of detail – from the philosophical, moral, ideological presuppositions informing the ethnographers' questions, to the social and political positions and practical motivation of the responding 'informants'.

If, as Herle and Rouse (1998: 1–7) and others have argued, modern British social anthropology was invented during the Cambridge Torres Strait Expedition in 1898, the discipline truly gained strength through the scholarly venture that unfolded in Island Melanesia in 1908. Hocart, in particular, developed methods of participant observation on Simbo, and both ethnographers accounted for this methodological innovation, albeit indirectly. In a wider, not strictly anthropological perspective, their deep cross-cultural experiences in the Solomon Islands influence later work: the original contributions made by Rivers to the treatment of shell-shock victims during the First World War; the politically radical position taken, also by Rivers, on the fate of colonised peoples regarding the depopulation of Melanesia, which he saw as caused in part by excessive colonial intervention; and the sweeping comparative approaches developed in Hocart's studies of kingship and caste, acknowledged by Dumont (1980) as a vantage point for his theoretical writings on hierarchy.

Some of the methodological innovations seen in the Solomons were founded in the fieldwork Rivers had already carried out in the Torres Strait.

Lessons and approaches from that fieldwork were refined by Rivers in 1901/2 during his field study of kinship and ritual among the Toda of southern India. But the dedicated and massively productive ethnographic quest of the two scholars on Simbo, based, as it must have been, on the creative interplay between the established scholar and his younger counterpart – and on the fact that neither of them had a specific training in nineteenth-century evolutionary anthropology but could draw on wide intellectual backgrounds – must be seen as an independent cornerstone in the history of anthropology. Of particular significance is their shared research strategy of following local beliefs, practices and organisational forms along comparative dimensions from Simbo outwards through survey work elsewhere in the Western Solomons, and their capacity (particularly notable in Hocart's case) for situating informants' statements socially in terms of local structures of knowledge and power – thus foretelling in a significant way the tenets of post-structuralist and postmodern social theory (Hviding, this volume).

Separate Worlds, Connected Careers: Influences of the Fieldwork

The influences of the everyday circumstances of the 1908 fieldwork on the intellectual lives and personal outlook of Rivers and Hocart must have been profound, and as such had potential ramifications for the way in which anthropology and related disciplines developed. As Langham (1981) notes, the history of the social sciences in the early twentieth century could have been quite different if the massive amount of ethnographic material from New Georgia had been published, particularly in monograph form, and if the careers of Rivers and Hocart had followed the conventional path of academics at the time (see also Dureau, this volume).

At stake for Rivers and Hocart during their fieldwork were central early-twentieth-century questions about magic, rationality, metaphysics and the person. Two gentlemen of the late Victorian era were thrown into a still vital and powerful mixture of Melanesian sorcery, witchcraft and spiritual agency and intervention. They lived among everyday practitioners of ancestor worship, who became so accommodating that they actively drew their European residents into those domains by eagerly interpreting for them the strange experiences they might have, to the extent of opening a channel through a spirit medium for conversations between Simbo ancestors and the ethnographers, albeit after 'ten sticks of tobacco as an inducement':

> At last there was a whistling: it was Onda's ghost; the way they knew who it was, was by calling out the names of deceased persons till the ghost whistled 'yes'. After the first whistling there was a long interval and a discussion about the White Men

from England. Onda said, 'Why do the White Men want to come? I can't see (? recognise) them; I have never seen a White Man'. 'The White Men want to hear the spirits speak', said [the medium] Kundahite. (Hocart 1922: 94, original parentheses)

Some of these challenging insights into altogether different life-worlds clearly influenced another largely forgotten strand of Rivers's intellectual record: his lively and exploratory lecture series to the Royal College of Physicians of London, later published as *Medicine, Magic and Religion* (Rivers 1924).

This intellectually fertile, and mentally challenging, aspect of the Simbo fieldwork has been explored through fiction in Pat Barker's best-selling Regeneration trilogy (Barker 1991, 1993, 1995), in which Rivers the wartime psychiatrist is a central character. In the final volume, *The Ghost Road* (Barker 1995), these explorations take the form of conjectural but evocative accounts of what the fieldwork experiences on Simbo may have been like, and how for Rivers they may have influenced his every-day medical work. Several chapters in *The Ghost Road* are devoted to a dramatisation of the fieldwork (grounded, as it were, mostly in Hocart's published materials). Barker connects narratives of mental and medical challenges faced by Rivers as an army captain developing ways to deal with shell-shocked patients at Craiglockhart War Hospital in Scotland to glimpses of the field experiences from Simbo.

For example, Rivers, while experimentally treating a patient whose paralysis of the legs is caused by psychological trauma, is described as pondering over the relationships between medical treatment and 'magical solutions', responding to the well-educated patient's queries about witch-doctors, seventeenth-century witch-finders and the designation of 'shell shock' as 'hysterical symptoms … paralysis, deafness, blindness, muteness'. The psychiatrist's mind wanders off to recollections of a particular category of debilitating illness on Simbo. The condition of *nggasin*, 'caused by an octopus that had taken up residence in the lower intestine', was intentionally attributed by Rivers to himself, with the aim of experiencing the treatment – a true ethnographically experimental situation. The Simbo healer set to work on Rivers, who claimed *nggasin*-like symptoms, but after examination concluded to the ethnographer: 'You no got *nggasin*'. Back in Scotland, finalising the day's treatment of his paralysed patient, Rivers thinks of him: 'But *you* have' (Barker 1995: 47–52). Intense experiences from participant observation in which even the ethnographer's body is offered for use by local practitioners of medicine and magic are brought to bear on First World War patients whose symptoms defy rationality and the medical mainstream.

Furthermore, in Barker's narrative the horrors of trench warfare as conveyed by patients to Rivers are played off against surreal nightmarish invocations of Melanesia. In one passage, Rivers is portrayed reading disturbing news in the morning paper about a particularly dreadful battle in France, and as his mind drifts off to the Solomons, juxtaposition is immediate in Barker's narrative:

> He took his glasses off, put them on the bedside table and pushed the tray away. He meant only to rest a while before starting again, but his fingers slackened and twitched on the counterpane and, after a few minutes, the newspaper with its headlines shrieking about distant battles slipped sighing to the floor.
>
> Ngea's skull, jammed into the *v* of a cleft stick, bleached in the sun. A solitary bluebottle buzzed in and out of the eye sockets and, finding nothing there of interest, sailed away into the blue sky.
>
> On his way down to the beach to bathe, Rivers paused to look at the skull. Only a month ago he'd spoken to this man, had even held his hand briefly on parting. No wonder the islanders wore necklaces of *pepeu* leaves to guard themselves against *tomate gani yambo*: the Corpse-Eating Spirit. (Barker 1995: 203–4)

In this volume, the cross-cultural intellectual and practical dimensions of the fieldwork experience on Simbo in 1908 are analysed for the very first time in the concrete sense of how they may have raised prominent mental challenges for the two scholars, grounded as they were in late-nineteenth-century Western thought. The impact of the fieldwork on Rivers's career (and psyche) explored in Barker's *Regeneration* novels has been further examined by Bayliss-Smith (this volume). For Hocart, we know that after the 1908 expedition he continued to engage with a wide range of anthropological themes, first over many years in Fiji with visits to other Pacific archipelagos, later in Ceylon, and increasingly in engagement with non-fieldwork materials which he tended to read in the applicable languages, for example Sanskrit. The fact that Hocart did not obtain a tenured position in a university until shortly before his death (he was appointed to a professorship in sociology in Cairo as late as 1934) only seems to have spurred him on to creativity and greater comparative diversity, and to publish widely on different topics within evolutionary anthropology, history, archaeology and political philosophy. Hviding (this volume) proposes some alternative paths of influence for Hocart in mainstream anthropology had his career been different.

In the Field: Trajectories of the Percy Sladen Trust Expedition

We have already argued that the Percy Sladen Trust Expedition was one of the very first modern anthropological field projects whereby European scholars carried out intensive investigations through long-term residence among a non-European people, largely unsupported by an extensive colonial apparatus. It is also significant that on the island of Simbo, where most of the fieldwork was carried out, there had been regular interaction with Europeans, but there was not yet a missionary presence. As the initiator and leader of the expedition, Rivers brought his own eclectic and imaginative scholarly diversity to an encounter with islanders not yet significantly affected by colonialism and Christianity, influences that had already been strong in the Torres Strait. In 1908, Rivers was a well-established scholar of multiple vocations, holding a lectureship in experimental psychology at Cambridge, and since 1902 a fellowship at St John's College. Qualified first as a medical doctor, he had practised as a ship's surgeon and then taken special training as both a physician and a psychologist, before moving into anthropology in the Torres Strait and among the Toda. Hocart was obviously recruited to carry out much of the mainstream ethnographic documentation. Circumstances relating to the participation of Wheeler in the expedition are less clear, but correspondence between Rivers and the trustees of the Percy Sladen Memorial Fund (discussed below) indicates that Hocart was funded by the grant to Rivers from the Fund, whereas Wheeler joined at a later stage, with support from the University of London, the Royal Geographical Society and a Royal Society Government grant. The following account of the expedition's beginnings is based on the original correspondence between Rivers and the Percy Sladen Memorial Trust Fund.[10]

On 30 May 1907, Rivers sent a letter of grant application (supported by a letter of recommendation from A.C. Haddon) to the Percy Sladen Memorial Trust Fund. This small institution was set up by the widow of marine biologist Percy Sladen (1849–1900) in his memory, intended to support research in 'the earth and life sciences', in particular fieldwork in remote locations. We have previously quoted from the application letter from Rivers, in which he outlined in concise terms an innovative experimental approach to a somewhat dated evolutionary agenda.

In his subsequent application form, dated 13 June 1907, Rivers's handwritten text presented the research agenda even more succinctly: 'the chief aim [in the Solomon Islands] being to study the nature of social organisation based on maternal descent and the mode of its transition to paternal descent'. The application makes clear the envisioned budget for the fieldwork: '£300 which would be devoted to defray travelling expenses, photography, payments to natives as guides, interpreters, etc. and any exceptional\personal expenses such as camping outfit. It is expected that the total expenditure (including personal expenses) would be between £500 and £600, the additional amounts coming from my income as Fellow of St John's College, Cambridge'.

In another hand, the note '£400 granted' was added to the form. A letter of gratitude followed immediately, Rivers stating that he 'will be glad to call it the Percy Sladen Trust Expedition'. From his previous research,

Rivers already had a strong record of fieldwork in remote places. In the above-mentioned letter of recommendation, Haddon expressed that he had 'no hesitation in stating that [Rivers] is an ideal observer – patient, sympathetic, and absolutely efficient and honest'. Haddon went so far as to conclude that '[Rivers's] recent memoir on the Todas is, in my opinion and in that of others, the very best socio-religious study of a native tribe that has yet been made by any field observer', and that '[t]he Trustees [of the Percy Sladen Fund had] the opportunity of sending into the field the best qualified Englishman' (Appendix 3).

As preparations for the expedition proceeded, Rivers informed the trustees of the Percy Sladen Memorial Fund in October 1907 that A.M. Hocart ('of Exeter College, Oxford') was 'very anxious' to go with Rivers to the Solomon Islands. Hocart had been strongly recommended by W. McDougall (who was part of the Torres Strait Expedition with Rivers) and R.R. Marett (an early Oxford anthropologist). Rivers suggested that Hocart be incorporated into the expedition, and that he should stay behind in Melanesia after Rivers returned to England to continue work 'either in the Solomons or in Woodlark Island'. Rivers applied to the Fund for a supplementary grant of £300 for Hocart's participation; the trustees awarded £100. In December, Rivers boarded the trans-Atlantic steamer R.M.S. *Adriatic*, and while at sea wrote to one of the trustees explaining that Hocart's doctor had given him a health report that 'made it very doubtful whether he ought to go to the Solomons'. Having looked for a replacement, Rivers had 'found a Mr. G.C. Wheeler, a pupil of Westermann [Westermarck] ... who is a very capable man who is very anxious to go', but he added that 'Mr Hocart after a more favourable report from his doctor is also very anxious to go so I have arranged to take them both'. Rivers saw this as a fine opportunity for expanding the geographical scope: 'If both are able to come, the amount of work done by the expedition ought to be very much increased, and I hope after a preliminary time together that we may separate and work out different districts'.

As described above, Rivers, Hocart and Wheeler met in Tulagi in May 1908, and were soon on their way to the New Georgia Islands, then a little-known western corner of the British Solomon Islands Protectorate, whose inhabitants still retained some of their infamous reputation for large-scale inter-island warfare, mass killings, slavery and head-hunting. The intention had been from the start to do collaborative fieldwork, dividing tasks among the three. The original list of this division of labour can still be found in the Haddon Papers in Cambridge, a collection that includes the remains of Rivers's materials and correspondence.[11]

After about two-and-a-half months on Eddystone (Simbo), Wheeler took River's challenge to 'separate and work out different districts'. He departed and travelled north-west to the Shortland Islands and the

Bougainville Strait, working there by himself for nine more months. Wheeler was known as a master of many languages, a facility evident in his knowledge of the Mono-Alu language as used in his monograph, and still appreciated by modern-day Mono-Alu speakers, some of whom have read the book. Wheeler's work is itself worthy of follow-up study. His long fieldwork in the Bougainville Strait was unique for its time. His monograph on Mono-Alu folklore (Wheeler 1926) and his massive unpublished volume on the 'sociology' of the area constitute a remarkable ethnographic corpus (see below). French anthropologist Denis Monnerie (1995, 1996, 1998, 2002) has carried out a major re-study based on Wheeler's materials, and his assessment of Wheeler's monograph is worthy of note:

> In his introduction to this classic work, Wheeler laid the foundations of analyses concerning the distribution, the combinations and the transformations of mythical and folk literature themes in Oceania. On this last point, i.e. the transformations of mythical themes, he defined a very modern approach which foreshadowed that of Claude Lévi-Strauss in *Les Mythologiques*. (Monnerie 2007)

Wheeler's publication record shows a spate of short descriptive pieces not long after the fieldwork, mainly in German journals (Wheeler 1911, 1912a, 1912b, 1912c, 1912d, 1913a, 1913b, 1913c, 1914a, 1914b), reflecting the relationship he developed in the field with R.C. Thurnwald, followed by a long absence of publications until *Mono-Alu Folklore* (Wheeler 1926), and nothing afterwards. After Wheeler's death in 1943, his wife typed up most of the 'sociology' manuscript, amounting to approximately 1,275 pages, the section on religion alone amounting to over 400 pages. With the support of Wheeler's wife and son in 1953, G.P. Milner of the School of Oriental and African Studies (SOAS) sought to persuade the Royal Anthropological Institute to publish the manuscript, but to no avail. It is clear that Wheeler's fieldwork was more detailed and extensive by far than the work in the Solomons of either Hocart or Rivers. Had it been published soon after the research was completed, Wheeler may well have been considered today as one of the founders of anthropology in Melanesia, but his impressive research results still remain largely unknown and unread.[12]

While Wheeler independently developed his own long-term research agenda in the Bougainville Strait and was not to return to his one-time research partners, Rivers and Hocart divided the work in Simbo between them, as seen from the introduction the first part of Hocart's first article stemming from the fieldwork on Simbo:

> Our joint work was apportioned according to subjects, Dr. Rivers taking kinship, social organisation, ghosts, gods, and other subjects, while I took death, fishing,

warfare; a few subjects, such as the house, were joint. When working alone I took over the whole. Of course, these divisions were rather artificial and we constantly overlapped, and either was constantly gathering material that belonged to the other. We constantly kept one another informed. It follows that the material of either of us published separately must be incomplete, but publication has already been so long delayed that it is better to publish only a fragment than withhold valuable material any longer. I am therefore publishing as a first instalment my own information on 'the Cult of the Dead' as practiced in Eddystone; it is sufficiently full to be of use, and indeed gives the essentials. The subject of chieftainship was not properly mine, but my later visits cleared up a certain number of obscurities, so that it can be used at least as an introduction; the chapters on Death and on Skull-houses can be considered as complete, barring, perhaps, a few details. Ghosts were more thoroughly investigated by Dr. Rivers, but the fragments I have collected can usefully be included here to complete the subject. The gods also come within Dr. Rivers's province, but the essential part, the ritual, did not come out till my second visit, so that the bulk of the information will be found here ... The reader, however, should bear these facts in mind if he is inclined to criticise the incompleteness of the material. (Hocart 1922: 71)

This exemplifies a general pattern for Hocart's sparse accounts of the fieldwork: in all respects he remains purely descriptive, simply communicating what actually happened and how it was organised by Rivers and himself. Nowhere does he elevate accounts of the fieldwork to a Malinowskian level of methodological reflection and generalisation. In a related vein, the few remarks Rivers made about the fieldwork are limited to comments on the 'intensive' and 'survey' genres, and provide little if any general methodological argument beyond contrasting the potentials of the two genres. The lack of such reflection by both Hocart and Rivers on the potential contribution to the development of anthropological method of their fieldwork, even years after it took place, indicated that they did not see themselves as the experimental ethnographic pioneers we argue that they in fact were.

Returning now to the 'division of labour', it seems that Hocart actually did a lot of the kinship research himself, since the genealogies to be found in archives are largely written in his hand.[13] On close examination there are annotations that link genealogies recorded by Hocart and the materials Rivers produced, such as 'see Rivers 123'. Of the genealogical materials that remain, only those from Vella Lavella are entirely in Rivers's own hand. We may speculate as to why Hocart ended up doing a lot of the work that was supposed to be Rivers's own speciality. Obviously, we cannot know whether there may have been duplicates that were lost after Rivers's death. It could be that Rivers recognised Hocart's skill with genealogical work, and left this time-consuming task to him as part of his training as an ethnographer and as the junior partner in the fieldwork. We may also speculate that Rivers left the actual recording of genealogies to Hocart while he himself got busy with what he saw as the main analytical ambition for that type of work, namely the unravelling of 'meanings' in the relationship systems. Rivers's preoccupation with physical anthropology may also have been time-consuming, and might be yet another reason for him to have left genealogical work to Hocart in Simbo. In Vella Lavella, Rivers seems to have done both of these tasks by himself (see Berg, this volume).

The Percy Sladen Trust Expedition resulted in a diverse corpus of published and unpublished works, whose ethnographic richness has been of considerable significance to generations of anthropologists working in the region and elsewhere. Although of uneven theoretical significance, the results of the expedition have shaped a range of lasting theoretical themes and research questions concerning the history and anthropology of Island Melanesia, and more generally concerning human social organisation. The following chapters bring to light original materials not been previously analysed, such as Rivers's original genealogies, photographs taken and objects collected during the expedition (Berg; Thomas, this volume), and informants' drawings of contemporary scenes in New Georgia (Hviding; Thomas, this volume).

At this stage we wish to examine the long and somewhat idiosyncratic post-expedition publication record. Wheeler's publications between 1911 and 1926 have been discussed above; here we deal with the publishing strategies of, first, Rivers and then, Hocart.[14] A modest file of correspondence between the two and the Percy Sladen Memorial Trust between 1909 and 1920 shows that there was no strong agenda of collaborative work. We have noted that while Rivers was at work in Cambridge and then during the First World War as an army psychiatrist in England and Scotland, Hocart worked as a schoolmaster in Fiji (with intermittent fieldwork) and then saw wartime service in France. Already in 1909, Rivers wrote to the Trust and outlined an ambitious agenda involving several 'books on the Western Solomons and on kinship'.[15] In March 1912 he wrote to the Trust noting that a 750–page book – 'the first part of the work of the Expedition to the Solomon Islands' – that is, *The History of Melanesian Society* (Rivers 1914a) – had been accepted by Cambridge University Press, and that he had 'made a good deal of progress with the second book on the Solomon Islands which [he was] doing in conjunction with Mr Hocart'.[16] Later that year he gave an update, apologising for the delay but notifying the Trust that the first volume of the 'full account' was finally being submitted to the Press, and that 'the bulk of the second volume' would be taken up by 'theoretical discussion' of the 'nature of Melanesian society'.[17] In that letter there is no reference to any collaboration with Hocart, and it seems that the envisaged co-authorship of a book on the Western Solomons was no longer part of Rivers's plans. Was communication with Hocart, then still in Fiji, too difficult? Did Rivers deem Hocart's research interests incompatible with his own grand theoretical agenda? We do not know. In any event, war intervened. In 1920, it was Hocart who wrote to the Trust, explaining how, in 1908 he 'accompanied Dr Rivers to the Solomons on the Percy Sladen Trust Expedition. The publication of the reports [has] been delayed by my appointment to a post out there, then by the war. Now that I have a considerable part ready for publication it is difficult to get it published'.[18] Noting that he planned a first publication through the '[M]emoirs of the Anthropological Association of America' of 150 pages, and that in the somewhat longer run he would also bring to publication visual materials of 'about one hundred plates, two maps, and ten to twenty drawings', he applied for the cost of printing those materials. This was rejected by the Trust, whose representative W.A. Herdman added a handwritten note to Hocart's letter asking 'why should we subsidise the U.S.?' It was probably Rivers who came to Hocart's rescue following his election to the presidency of the Royal Anthropological Institute (RAI), enabling Hocart to launch in 1922 on his long series of descriptive papers in the RAI's own journal.

To summarise, the joint fieldwork by Rivers and Hocart did provide the foundations for Rivers's monumental opus *The History of Melanesian Society* (Rivers 1914a). Although the two volumes of that work have later been judged as inadequate in terms of theory and come to be seen as characterised by piecemeal, scant ethnography, it is hard to argue against the overall quality of the project as the first-ever comparative work on central Melanesian concepts of social organisation, leadership and cosmology. Hocart's later career in historical anthropology and cultural history included monographs on such diverse topics as kingship in comparative perspective (1927), the history and ethnography of the Lau group of Fiji (1929), and the archaeology of the Temple of the Tooth in Kandy, Ceylon (1931a). It is unlikely that these diverse works, widely read by scholars of comparative religion and the human sciences, would have seen the light of day without their author's foundational experiences from early anthropological fieldwork in the Western Solomons.

Fieldwork as Conjuncture

In the opening paragraph of *The History of Melanesian Society*, Rivers outlined his established perspective on ethnographic method, which in the present context is worth quoting at some length, despite its persistent turn-of-the-century evolutionist distinction between 'low' and 'civilised' forms of culture:

There are two chief kinds of ethnographical work; one, intensive, in which the whole of the culture of the people, their physical characters and environment are examined as minutely as possible; the other, survey-work in which a number of peoples are studied sufficiently to obtain a general idea of their affinities in physique and culture both with each other and with peoples elsewhere. There is one feature of low forms of culture which makes these two kinds of work essentially different. In civilised culture we are accustomed to distinguish certain definite departments of social life which can to a large extent be kept apart, but among those people we usually speak of as primitive, these departments are inextricably interwoven and interdependent so that it is hopeless to expect to obtain a complete account of any one department without covering the whole field. In consequence, however deeply one may attempt to go in survey-work, the information gained must inevitably be incomplete and can never possess the accuracy which an intensive study would have given. Another feature of survey-work which has the same effect is that the proper valuation of the evidence of witnesses is impossible. (Rivers 1914a, i: 1)

Next, Rivers goes on to specify how this methodological distinction relates to the fieldwork carried out in 1908 by Rivers and his two associates:

The work of the Percy Sladen Trust Expedition to the Solomon Islands falls into two distinct parts; intensive work done by Mr. A.M. Hocart and myself in the western Solomon Islands and by Mr. G.C. Wheeler in the islands of Bougainville Straits, to be recorded in other volumes; and survey-work, done by myself during the journey to and from the Solomon Islands, which is the subject of the present book. (Rivers 1914a, i: 1)

By 1908, 'ethnography' as such had for quite some time been a part of colonial agendas, in terms of the need to know more about colonial subjects. The Royal Anthropological Institute's *Notes and Queries* 'manual' was still handed out to colonial administrators, missionaries bound for exotic places and travellers in general, the results being analysed afterwards in British universities. Conventional ethnographic fieldwork was not yet established as essential to obtaining information, a fact which makes Rivers's and Hocart's efforts something of a novelty at the time. Malinowski's extensive field research in the Trobriands between 1914 and 1918 is conventionally regarded as marking the beginning of modern (British) social anthropology as a discipline founded in the ethnographic authority provided by long-term fieldwork, based on the method of participant observation. But six years before Malinowski's arrival in the Trobriands, Rivers and Hocart lived independently on Simbo, pitching their tent away from the house of the resident European trader, and pursuing a broad range of investigations through interviews and interactions, and by the carefully planned observation of many ceremonial events. Not unexpectedly, there is evidence that Rivers, as a veteran of fieldwork under challenging circumstances in Melanesia, influenced Malinowski in the latter's decision to embark on fieldwork in the region.[19]

We have noted that in 1908 the islanders of New Georgia still retained elements of their fierce reputation among travellers, missionaries and colonial officials. Inter-island raiding, headhunting and the taking of slaves had in fact seen intense escalation as late as the latter half of the nineteenth century, as the availability of steel tools had made the construction of war canoes much simpler and faster, and as access to firearms had become regular (McKinnon 1975; Hviding 2014). At the time of Rivers's and Hocart's fieldwork, the inhabitants of Simbo had not been exposed to direct missionary activity, but significant parts of New Georgia were already under the influence of the Methodist Mission, which was established in Roviana Lagoon in 1902. The Simbo people of the time had relatives and friends who were already attending church, and Hocart and Rivers would have been acquainted with some members of the Methodist clergy, notably Revd R.C. Nicholson, who was the resident head of the mission station at Bilua on Vella Lavella.[20]

But the history of inter-island warfare, alliance and enmity was not so distant in 1908, the year when the last heads – of both white men and Melanesians – were taken in New Georgia, by renegade warriors who had refused to adapt to the new regime of the *Pax Britannica*. Be that as it may, the two pioneer ethnographers appear to have found no difficulties in staying with people who had only a few years before been recurrent targets of British naval 'gunboat diplomacy' dedicated to end the endemic warfare and headhunting of the Western Solomons.

There is a general point to be made here about anthropological fieldwork as being by necessity a conjuncture between the ways in which ethnographer and informant are situated, in their own specific contexts of history, culture and power. Hocart's introductory remarks to his first publication arising from the 1908 expedition may help us visualise fieldwork as event, and methodology as social interaction, and the relevant parts are therefore quoted at some length:

Methods.

Our work was done through interpreters. Their pidgin was of the most rudimentary description, but as our knowledge of the language improved, their scanty English was richly supplemented with native words. We were frequently able to understand what was said before it was interpreted. Prayers and some stories were taken down word for word and constitute an effective check on interpreted material.

Working through interpreters is certainly not ideal, and it is to be hoped that field-workers will in the future undergo a linguistic training and seek to work in the vernacular; but this is not given to all, and it is a great mistake to imagine that because interpreted work is not the best, it therefore is not good.

Our interpreters were mostly poor; but one of them, Njiruviri … turned out in the end to be not only the best interpreter, but head and shoulders the best informant. It is a pity that, being in possession of much secret lore, he carefully disguised his knowledge and was therefore long wasted as a mere channel of communication, when he could have been used as an original scholar and thinker. The eldest son of the chief who controlled the most important cults in the island, debarred by being a hunch-back from great physical activity, he had devoted himself to thought and learning. His knowledge was not only vast, but most accurate: reluctant to give away the secret formulae, he was mercilessly conscientious in repeating them once he had been induced to do so. He knew exactly how much he knew, and always distinguished his theories from facts. Had he been a European he would have ranked high among the learned, and an account of the island based on his evidence alone would still be invaluable.

Kundakolo … was discovered early and was a great contributor. His knowledge was vast, but his memory was not as good as it had been; he was also a dreamer with a peculiar imagination, as could be seen by his drawings. He also was conscientious and never claimed to know what he did not. He owned all the great lore of his village and we were constantly referred to him.

Leoki … was the best narrator and expositor of any; in fact he was the only one who seemed able to tell a story, though he fell far below the Rovianese. He contributed chiefly tales and a few legends, until, running short, he decided to unfold one of the most important rituals of the island, the cult of the gods. He was thoroughly accurate and aware of his limitations. In fact it may be said that an informant who romances is very rare indeed, when a careful check is kept and they know it, for they are very mindful of their reputation.

All these belonged to the same village of Narovo. Keana, my interpreter during my last visit, belonged to Simbo and thus put me in touch with some Simbo material. He was intelligent and not afraid to correct misconceptions under which the other allowed us to labour for months. It was he who threw most light on chieftainship. He was good at explaining such matters, but he was anything but conscientious, and when it came to long formulae his chief thought was boiling everything down.

Rinambesi was the oldest man in the island, was noble in Karivara, and the father of one of the chiefs of Ove. His knowledge was not proportionate to his age or station, and his memory was not good, but with his son and grandson he made some interesting contributions.

Such were our chief informants. Scarcely a native who came to see us but contributed something, for not one but possessed at least a remedy. (Hocart 1922: 71–73)

This account is noteworthy for the way in which Hocart details the diversity of informants, the varied distribution of knowledge among them, and the cumulative contributions each main informant made to the ethnographic experiment of the two fieldworkers. The final sentence, although somewhat contrived in expression, conveys a very significant dimension of this ground-breaking fieldwork: an impressive muster of interpreters and key informants, headed by the hunchback whose name is correctly spelled Ziruviri (a man who in many cases is reported by Hocart to have had well-grounded 'theories' on topics of ethnographic interest), provided solid foundations for the gathering of ethnographic knowledge. But there was also a fairly wide engagement in the anthropological work by the Simbo people in general. This foreshadows Malinowski's tenets regarding the fieldworker's ideal immersion in the local community, and also explains the consistent endeavour, particularly by Hocart (see Hviding, this volume), to position the information volunteered according to who provided it, from what social position and with what degree of cultural specificity.

On the other hand, Hocart's retrospective methodological statement notwithstanding, there is little to be learned from the published and unpublished materials left by Rivers and Hocart about the actual, practical aspects of their fieldwork. Little if anything is communicated by either of the two on how they organised the practicalities of their everyday life. The iconic tent is briefly mentioned, there is passing reference to food (canned and local), a low reliance on resident Europeans is implied, and a careful examination of fieldnotes, typescripts and publications provides clues to mobility during the fieldwork. But candidness about what actually took place and what practical challenges had to be met is absent from the materials of the two fieldworkers, and it seems to remain in the realm of the dramatist and novelist – as in Pat Barker's case – to visualise any trials and tribulations faced during this founding exercise in long-term fieldwork. What we know more about, is the fate of the expedition's analytical ambitions as formulated by Rivers.

Struggles with Social Organisation in New Georgia

The 'New Georgia[n] Group' as encountered by Rivers and Hocart constituted – as it still does – a great interactional field of peoples, languages, traditions, objects and ideas extending over a north-west/south-east axis over some 200 kilometres, encompassing twelve major islands from tiny Simbo to the 'mainland' of New Georgia, and three great lagoons of which two are enclosed by raised barrier reefs – all of which is connected through a maze of waterways, channels and stretches of open sea. In an even wider inter-island sense, the everyday horizons of New Georgians also included major overseas locations on the large islands of Choiseul, Isabel and Guadalcanal. While such geographical scale is evident from the repertoire of tales collected and published by Hocart, in theoretical and methodological terms it would be the complexities of inter-island kinship that posed the greatest challenges (as well as inspiration) for the pioneer ethnographers, who arrived on the scene with the genealogical method and the aim of finding 'mother right', yet quite unprepared to handle the nature of kinship throughout most of New Georgia.

Their initial confusion when confronted by the pre-eminently bilateral kinship systems of New Georgia (or perhaps rather the confusion faced by Rivers in his capacity as the recognised kinship theorist) came from the pre-planned research programme of excavating 'original' mother-right societies in 'districts in which there is still a definite maternal system of society'.[21] Theoretically as well as empirically, this plan was founded in the evolutionary approach of kinship studies at the time, as derived more or less directly from L.H. Morgan (1877). Kinship theory at the time had a strong evolutionary cast, seeing the original state of humankind in terms of 'mother-right societies', bound to be replaced by 'father-right' systems at a later stage.[22] The search by Rivers for mother-right societies was a rather conventional one in terms of the intellectual mode of the era, although his choice of Melanesia is less clear. Rivers perhaps wanted to explore a part of the world that at the time was still deemed 'archaic' and that had not been covered under Morgan's original comparative kinship programme. What was clearly remarkable for the era, however, was that Rivers ventured into one of these 'archaic' societies himself. The methodological problems and analytical confusion that arose during fieldwork among New Georgians, who mostly organised their lives through bilateral kinship (Hviding 2003), may also have resulted in a certain reduction of the systems to their absolute core, generating a search for uniqueness of kin terms rather than a quest for inter-island compatibility. While Rivers had, through the genealogical method, established what became (and still is) a predominant mode of methodology in kinship studies, he still lacked a more sophisticated theoretical programme that could handle unexpected outcomes of the ethnographic experiment that unfolded in 1908.

While the genealogical method had been explained by Rivers (1900), the initial article on that method did not have the same impact as a later contribution he made to the fourth edition of *Notes and Queries on Anthropology* (Rivers 1912). Also influential in this regard is his volume *Kinship and Social Organisation* (Rivers 1914b). Whereas the article from 1900 gave a condensed outline of the method developed and used in the Torres Strait, the description Rivers gave in *Notes and Queries* was richer and more programmatic, amounting to a full methodological outline for a prospective anthropology of kinship. In 1912 Rivers had the benefit of several fieldwork periods and localities to draw upon.

During the months he spent with Hocart in the Western Solomons, Rivers collected kinship materials from most parts of New Georgia, and he was able to build up massive data sheets concerning social relations extending far beyond the island of Simbo. It is important to note that the fieldwork, based in a practical sense on Simbo, was not confined to a 'single island' approach – partly because Simbo people's sociality was inter-island in scope and not at all restricted to their own island (Bayliss-Smith; Dureau; Hviding, this volume). Whereas Hocart did on his own accumulate considerable kinship materials in Roviana and Nduke (Kolobangara) while Rivers was travelling elsewhere, Rivers confined his collecting of genealogies to the islands of Simbo and Vella Lavella.

As for the analytical deployment of these large data sets, most of them were used, together with additional ones from Vanuatu, to generate the comparative models used in *The History of Melanesian Society*. In addition, the genealogies Rivers collected in Vella Lavella were used later to substantiate the depopulation hypothesis he proposed for Melanesia (Rivers 1922; Bayliss-Smith 2006; Bennett, this volume). But his grasp of the Vella Lavella materials at the level of social organisation is relatively poor, which is remarkable as that island is actually one of the few possible 'mother right societies' Rivers and Hocart could have encountered in the Solomons (Berg, this volume). It is curious that Rivers never pondered the importance of the relationship between mother's brother and sister's son in Vella Lavella. Although he did describe it terminologically, he never attempted to deduce anything at a structural level about this potentially very significant observation. Probably, the massive work of completing the vast comparative two-volume work dominated his intellectual capacity at the time, even more so owing to his having abandoned the original theoretical framework for the volumes. As Berg (this volume) also argues on the basis of the vast comparative material Rivers and Hocart collected, perhaps the people of Vella Lavella did not really stand out that much at the time from their New Georgia neighbours. People of Vella Lavella do not differ physically from them, and their material culture and general way of living must have seemed for both Hocart and Rivers fairly similar to that found in other parts of New Georgia where they worked. Rivers in fact gave no weight to the regional linguistic anomaly, whereby a non-Austronesian language is spoken in Vella Lavella, only commenting that the kinship system of the island seemed to be a further simplification of the general New Georgia model. We may also speculate here as to the influence of interpreters and of the trader Fred Green in colouring perceptions of Vella

Lavella as simply a variant of the general New Georgia type. No matter what the reason was, Rivers concluded from faulty premises, and missed out altogether on this particular 'mother right' society.

As for later critiques of Rivers's original kinship programme, it is important to note that the flaws in his analyses were largely connected to a lack of understanding of the most basic systemic levels. Examining the theoretical agendas and empirical findings of Rivers regarding Simbo, Scheffler (1962) and Hviding (2003) have discussed the ways in which both he and Hocart confounded the two concepts of *taviti* (relation through bilateral kinship) and *butubutu* (cognatic descent group). This, and the failure to find the regionally singular matrilineal clans of Vella Lavella, had severe ramifications for the understanding developed during the 1908 fieldwork more generally, as seen from the provisional assessment made by Rivers on the social organisation of the New Georgia islands in a report to the Percy Sladen Trust soon after the fieldwork:

> The people of the Western Solomons were found to have a very high type of social organisation, and all the institutions usually regarded as characteristic of Melanesia, such as female descent, the dual organisation and the secret societies were found to be absent. There was no trace of a clan organisation nor of totemism. The system of kinship was of a simple kind, almost as simple as that of Polynesia, and marriage was regulated entirely by kinship. Descent was entirely in the male line and there was a singular absence of any customs which might be regarded as survivals of mother-right.[23]

In Berg's chapter, the concept of *toutou* (matrilineal clan) in Vella Lavella is examined, and it is noted how reciprocal terminological relationships are still remarkably consistent with most everyday kinship practice on the island today, which lends credibility to the persistent accuracy of Rivers's genealogical method. In the chapter by Rio and Eriksen, the wider entanglements of method and fieldwork are addressed with reference to the brief work by Rivers on kinship in the island of Ambrym, Vanuatu, a soon-to-be famous location in the development of kinship theory.

At the end of the day, it seems almost uncanny how the methodologies Rivers and Hocart applied in the fieldwork in New Georgia appear not to have enabled them to come to grips with the (admittedly) complex and oftentimes unpredictable processes of group formation in the islands. With the benefit of hindsight, it seems today that it would be near impossible to make ethnographic inquiries in New Georgia without discovering the enduring significance of the largely cognatic *butubutu* concept (Hviding 2003). It is, then, as if the kinship-related research by Rivers and Hocart represented an anthropological era prior to the structural-functionalism of

British social anthropology and its firm focus on corporate groups. Perhaps ironically, the approach of Rivers and Hocart also seems to connect more closely to recent post-structuralist tenets in which 'kinship' and 'descent' are replaced by open-ended notions of 'relatedness' (e.g. Carsten 2000), with politico-jural groups less in focus compared to the central concerns of British social anthropology from later in the 1920s and well into the 1950s.

The Chapters

The eight chapters that follow examine the successes and failures of the Percy Sladen Trust Expedition. There are many levels and cross-cutting connections in such a collective examination. The history of anthropology and related fields carries with it the implication that early scholarship is, inevitably, heavy on shortcomings, and the scholarly legacy of Rivers, in particular, has been subject to its share of such judgements. In contrast, Hocart's intellectual legacy in terms of the Solomon Islands fieldwork is one more of neglect than of outright dismissal. The realities discussed in this book are complex and equivocal as the contributors examine the expedition's enduring contributions, unrecognised successes, and more or less resounding failures.

One crucial point is a degree of inherent dissonance in the collective reappraisal we make of Hocart's and Rivers's work, which brings forward both the strengths and limitations of the fieldwork and its lasting impact on the history of anthropology. It certainly also fleshes out current debates among scholars as to the lasting value of early fieldwork. At a general level, and as the chapters proceed and weave their interconnected arguments, the reader will note that reappraisals of Hocart's work are generally more positive than those of Rivers's. The collective argument of the book is, however, more complex. As argued here, and by Dureau, the factual contribution of our anthropological ancestors can now be appreciated in more generous ways than twenty years ago, when postmodern approaches ruled the ground and early anthropology had faded in value, not least owing to what was seen as its entrenchment in colonialism and its grounding in now unfashionable theories.

For instance, chapters by Dureau, Hviding, Berg, Rio and Eriksen, and Kolshus approach the materials from the expedition in an almost forensic manner. Reappraisals of the ethnographic materials reveal both analytical strengths and direct misrepresentations, and provide glimpses of the social organisation and practices they sought to understand but grasped insufficiently. We also gain important insights into the fieldwork personae of Hocart and Rivers through the chapters by Dureau, Hviding, Bayliss-Smith and Thomas. This goes beyond standard biographical work, as we catch glimpses of how the two evolved as persons and scholars through their immersion in fieldwork. The importance of the fieldwork experience on these two late-Victorian gentlemen scholars can hardly be exaggerated. This was a particular moment in colonial history where Hocart and Rivers had the opportunity to record materials on pre-Christian religion while also supplementing this by taking photographs and collecting objects – an opportunity lost to later ethnographers owing to the rapidly changing world of many Pacific islanders. This quality of the moment is what the chapters engage: particular encounters between ethnographers and islanders, and the concerted outcomes of such events.

Although the failures of the grand theoretical schemes developed by both Rivers and Hocart are there to be seen and can hardly be contested, the chapters also put forward a collective argument about the enduring value of the fieldwork materials. If there is no such enduring value, how may we account for the imminently recognisable value of the materials from 1908 for present-day scholars active in Island Melanesia? The shortcomings of the expedition are, of course, also obvious, but after all this was fieldwork, ethnographic description and anthropological analysis in an early incarnation, and it may be suggested that many of the field methodologies now so well known to anthropology by necessity had to be invented on the spot in 1908, as seen in Hviding's analysis of Hocart's structured comparison of inter-island materials. Chapters by Berg and Thomas also compare little known materials such as genealogical notes, photographs and objects in order to illuminate important methodological aspects of Rivers's work, while chapters by Rio and Eriksen and Kolshus point to what went wrong for Rivers in terms of research methodology and generalisation. It may be strange that Rivers in particular is more remembered for where he went wrong than what he did right. In that regard, the chapters by Bayliss-Smith and Bennett provide a strong middle ground where Rivers's scholarly, medical, philosophical and political contributions are analysed both in terms of their enduring significance and shorter-lived success.

In Chapter 1, Christine Dureau discusses how anthropologists draw upon the fieldnotes, manuscripts and publications of earlier ethnographers as part of conceptualising socio-cultural change and continuity. She provides a context for a combined appraisal of Rivers's and Hocart's contributions in the history of anthropology. From her unique position as an anthropologist who has carried out long-term fieldwork on the very island that was the locality of Rivers's and Hocart's fieldwork, Dureau is appreciative of their research, but critical of the many shortcomings in their materials and analysis. She notes the tendency to consider the cultural and political placement of such earlier anthropologists in ways that make the analysis of the work of such anthropological 'ancestors' highly critical, focusing on matters of representation, colonial power and imperial emplacement. Although important in its own right, such critique tends to be moralistic, 'othering' the 'ancestral figures' who have preceded present anthropologists in their field sites, so the latter may present themselves as their antitheses: neither colonial nor imperial. Dureau's chapter explores how we can represent earlier fieldworkers without recuperating old progressivist histories of the discipline, and she critically reconsiders and qualifies her own earlier treatment of Hocart and Rivers in this light. Dureau's questions go beyond earlier fieldworkers to include those agents, such as missionaries, who are 'awkward' subjects of historical anthropological analysis when our goal is to understand them as cultural beings without losing sight of their political placement and activity. Thus, Dureau's chapter discusses the early ethnographers as situated subjects, both in the field and in their texts. This is a particularly important exercise since Dureau pursues this in a 'post-postmodern time'. As the field of social anthropology has changed, so it has become easier to look with more sympathetic eyes on the collected works of Rivers and Hocart without losing sight of their shortcomings.

In Chapter 2, Edvard Hviding discusses how, as an ethnographer of quite another part of the Western Solomons (Marovo Lagoon, to the east), he came to Hocart's fieldnotes and published corpus after having carried out his own first long-term fieldwork, and gradually realised that these accounts, considered by conventional criteria to be manically descriptive and more than a little chaotic, constitute a remarkable background for analysing inter-island relations in the history of Island Melanesia. Connecting his own work in Marovo Lagoon with the work by Hocart in 1908, Hviding develops an examination of continuities and discontinuities in the Western Solomons in a regional sense, and shows how comparative interpretations of pan-New Georgian patterns of core cultural concepts and social phenomena can be made from the twin vantage points of Simbo in the far west and Marovo in the far east. Hviding argues for an appreciation of Hocart's sophisticated approach to the fundamentally inter-island nature of apparently 'local' phenomena in New Georgia, and shows how materials from Simbo in 1908 connect in surprising ways to oral history from Marovo. Discussing aspects of Hocart's methodology and epistemology, and the opportunities his materials give for comparison in time and space from the 1908 'snapshot' they contain of New Georgians situated between the pre-colonial and the colonial, Hviding seeks to reconstruct the ethnographic moment of 1908 in terms of how the New Georgians interacted with and educated their two British visitors. This chapter truly brings out the ethnographic encounter between Hocart and the islanders.

Hocart's remarkable fieldwork, which today would be aptly titled multi-sited methodology, spanned several islands in New Georgia. He consistently compared islands and customs, and recorded disparate versions of myths and ritual. Hviding rightly argues that this approach may actually reflect a world view Hocart himself derived from working among islanders whose cosmology was (and is) inter-island in nature.

In Chapter 3, Cato Berg traces how the 'genealogical method' as developed by Rivers was applied in his collection of genealogical material in Vella Lavella. This kinship methodology provided one of the first theoretical and methodological frameworks for dealing comparatively with kinship and descent since Morgan (Fortes 1969). However, the genealogical method has also been targeted by critical voices, even from Rivers's own students and friends, although, as Berg notes, some recent commentators have been more generous towards Rivers. In this chapter, a background is provided for Rivers's mode of kinship inquiry, and his use of the method in one village in the Solomons in 1908 is analysed extensively. It is shown how Rivers's work on demography and death rates on Vella Lavella relied on an application of complex kinship data, not merely statistics, collected along the coast of the island. Berg retraces parts of Rivers's recording of genealogical material through using his own fieldwork materials from Vella Lavella's north-western corner and his extensive analysis of remaining original materials by Rivers held in the Haddon Papers, housed in the Rare Manuscripts Collection of Cambridge University Library. Although Rivers received funds from the Percy Sladen Trust to search for what he believed were ancient 'mother right' societies to be found in this part of Melanesia, he never actually realised that Vella Lavella was one of the few matrilineal societies in New Georgia, thus a prime example of just the type of social organisation he was looking for. Despite this significant lapse by Rivers, Berg's reanalysis allows for a new appraisal of the scientific value of Rivers's fieldwork in terms of Melanesian history, as a source of cultural heritage in the Western Solomons, and as a remarkable window onto a certain village on Vella Lavella in 1908.

Chapter 4 extends the geographical scope beyond the Solomons to look into a particular excursion made by Rivers into another locality in Island Melanesia. Knut Rio and Annelin Eriksen explore the journey Rivers made after leaving the Western Solomons, travelling on the mission ship *Southern Cross* from island to island in the eastern Solomons and the New Hebrides (now Vanuatu) – what Rio and Eriksen refer to as 'a journey through evolutionary time'. Working mostly on the ship, interviewing informants who came on board at ports of call and using missionary interpreters, Rivers broke the ground for *The History of Melanesian Society*. Rio and Eriksen then examine the return of Rivers to the New Hebrides in 1914, focusing on his particular interest in kinship on the island of Ambrym, a form of kinship that Rivers placed in an evolutionary scheme as a fossil of earlier forms of Melanesian social organisation. Based on their own long-term fieldwork on Ambrym, Rio and Eriksen revisit Rivers to assess his very early ethnographic contribution to debates about Ambrym social organisation, later made famous through long-lasting debates involving an extraordinary succession of distinguished participants, including A.B. Deacon, C.G. Seligman, A.R. Radcliffe-Brown, C. Lévi-Strauss, P. Josselin de Jong, H. Scheffler and R. Needham. As several contributors to this book point out, the Percy Sladen Trust Expedition was notable for its participant's failure to understand connections between observed social 'rights' and actual group formation. Rivers never cracked the code of Ambrym kinship, although the clues are to be found even in his own material. Unlike previous discussions that to some extent only identify the failures of Rivers's analysis, this chapter also discusses the possible reasons behind Rivers's mistakes in the context of his survey work in that part of the Pacific.

In Chapter 5, Thorgeir Kolshus further broadens the context of this book by discussing Rivers's wide-ranging 'extensive survey work' in Mota and Tikopia. Kolshus gives a close analysis of Rivers's two key informants who provided much of the material on these and other islands in the south-east Solomons and Vanuatu. Rivers the ethnographer developed a close working relationship with his two important informants; a collaboration that also skewed the outcome of the fieldwork and the reporting by Rivers on social organisation and religion. Although being sympathetic to the 'survey' project developed by Rivers, Kolshus also reveals some of the inadequacy of Rivers's methodology, developing views expressed by Raymond Firth on Rivers's analysis of social organisation on Tikopia. In fact, Firth did not find Rivers's material of much use for his own long-term fieldwork on Tikopia from 1928 onwards. Kolshus examines the close relationship between Rivers and the Melanesian Mission, not least in terms of how he was dependent on the mission for assistance throughout his travels. Kolshus also shows how the inadequacies and inconsistencies of 'survey work' resulted in much speculative research. Unlike the assessments in earlier chapters of the research carried out in the Western Solomons, this chapter demonstrates that Rivers stretched his rather thin data too far, a tendency that Kolshus argues comes from inherent flaws of Rivers's survey work.

In Chapter 6, Tim Bayliss-Smith notes how Rivers was one of the first scholars to draw attention to the ongoing depopulation of the Melanesian islands, and to question the still-dominant 'extinction discourse' of the time that saw 'vanishing races' as a regrettable but inevitable consequence of Western imperialism and geo-political domination. Bayliss-Smith explores how Rivers's imaginative use of the genealogical data he and

Hocart collected in the Western Solomons constitutes a pioneer study in historical demography, providing insights that are still unmatched anywhere in Melanesia in the nineteenth and early twentieth century, apart from Fiji. However, shortfalls are also identified in the demographic study. Explanations given by Rivers for the phenomena that he documented are less impressive, and Bayliss-Smith argues that Rivers's achievement in applying the genealogical method to historical demography should not blind us to flaws in his interpretation of social processes. His suggestion that Simbo women were too apathetic to conceive, to give birth or to nurture healthy infants lacks any ethnographic foundation, and Rivers's dismissal of disease factors is a curious blind-spot in view of his own medical background. By the time of his death in 1922, Rivers had developed a new theory of society from his reading of Freudian psychology and from his own experiences as a wartime psychotherapist treating cases of 'shell shock' among soldiers and airmen. He believed that following the pressures of war and from the power of suggestion, post-war Europe was experiencing a state of what he called 'universal psycho-neurosis'. Bayliss-Smith argues that when seeing the psychological impact of colonialism as a form of shell shock, Rivers could entertain speculations about Solomon Islands demography and a rationale for the depopulation of the islands that was ongoing in 1908. This chapter brings out the effect that intensive fieldwork had on the personality of Rivers, and how it changed him in the years to come. Rivers continued to revisit his experiences – particularly in Simbo – for the rest of his life.

In Chapter 7, Judy Bennett extends the context of the 1908 fieldwork into pan-Pacific, even global, scenes of colonial history. She examines Rivers's claim for the 'psychological factor' as a major cause of depopulation in Melanesia and the Pacific more generally, observing how his ideas were taken up in colonial circles and beyond. As depopulation had been almost synchronous with the advent of Europeans in the Pacific, a strong causal association was suggested with the social, economic and political impact of Europeans on indigenous people. Bennett shows, however, that almost simultaneously with the publication of Rivers's influential collection *Essays on Depopulation in Melanesia* (Rivers 1922), practitioners of Western biomedicine and the newly constituted League of Nations increasingly focused attention on the links between depopulation and introduced diseases. Soon the medical model was triumphant over Rivers's 'psychological factor', but a range of agents including literary critics, administrators, planters, anthropologists and medical doctors still used Rivers's position to defend their positions or to advance their disciplines and causes.

In Chapter 8, Tim Thomas throws light upon perhaps the most neglected outcome of the Percy Sladen Trust Expedition, namely the artefacts and photographs that Rivers and Hocart collected and took in the Western Solomons. These now form part of the collections of the Cambridge University Museum of Anthropology and Archaeology. Previously thought to be a mere afterthought of the expedition, the objects and photographs were, Thomas convincingly argues, an integral part of Rivers's scientific programme. However, as Thomas demonstrates, the fate of the collection of objects and photographs is directly connected to Rivers's theoretical change of position from evolutionism to diffusionism, as demonstrated in his 1911 address to the British Association for the Advancement of Science. Rivers lost faith in his material culture data and abandoned any plans to utilise them in any scientific manner. Thomas notes how Rivers was convinced that material culture was the first aspect of change in colonial circumstances, and as such the least valuable in any scientific description of social change. The chapter also contains a valuable Appendix listing the various categories of objects that Rivers and Hocart collected, and provides also novel information on the photographs taken during the expedition.

The Ethnographic Experiment

To offer some concluding remarks, let us revisit the title of this book. To what extent did the Percy Sladen Trust Expedition to Island Melanesia constitute an 'ethnographic experiment'? The concept of 'experiment' does not necessarily ring that well within the social sciences today, but for this book it is a word carefully chosen for all its implications about the ethnographic work that Hocart and Rivers undertook in 1908. We argue that the Percy Sladen Trust Expedition was an experiment in the true meaning of the word, in terms of its original methodology, the complexity of the research and its successes and failures, and the personal implications of the fieldwork for the fieldworkers.

The two fieldworkers had a rather loose program of research, at least when we consider the original aim of unearthing 'mother-right societies' in a state of 'survival'. Although Rivers had honed his skills as an ethnographer of kinship systems in the Torres Strait, and had successfully published the first methodological programme for that specific line of research, he had to revise his methods in the Solomon Islands when faced with realities that were probably quite different from those he had expected. A recently developed methodology was brought along for the fieldwork; empirical realities intervened; and the methodology had to be adjusted in order for the emerging ethnographic materials to make sense. This experimental approach to field ethnography also had a lasting effect on the personal life of Rivers. It is very interesting that he almost never revisited the Torres Strait or the Toda in his later writings, but instead tended to emphasise his experiences in the Solomon Islands, and Simbo in particular. This attests to the strong affect the months of 'intensive' fieldwork had on him, as also exemplified in several chapters of this book. To that extent, the example of Rivers predates postmodern anthropology and its strong emphasis on the subjective experience and cooperative nature of research.

The experimental aspects of the expedition also come out well in the constant revision of socially positioned ethnographic information seen in Hocart's published papers, unpublished manuscripts and fieldnotes.[24] As discussed in several of the following chapters, Hocart became deeply submerged in the societies of the Western Solomons at the time, and through dedicated, ethnographically productive practice he devised a method of multi-sited ethnography, eighty years before the term became anthropologically fashionable. Hocart's constant quest for comparative data is demonstrated by his solitary travels when Rivers worked elsewhere. In that sense, the ethnographic experiment was even more fundamental for Hocart, untrained as he initially was in anthropology and without any previous field experience. The quality of his ethnographic materials, out-standing even by today's standards, is a worthy memorial to him in the records of the social sciences.

The following chapters will make clear that the expedition of 1908 was an 'experiment' that had its measure of success, but one that could also have yielded much more than it did. As it happened, Rivers and Hocart had stumbled upon two very different islands – Simbo and Vella Lavella – whose ethnographic characteristics could have provided them with laboratory-like circumstances for experimentation, had the research effort only been further developed. Although well connected socially, Simbo and Vella Lavella in fact were (and are) island societies with utterly different languages and highly contrasting systems of social organisation. This, coupled with many shared characteristics of culture and ecology, should have made the two islands ideal case studies in an 'experimental' sense. If Rivers and (particularly) Hocart had been able to carry out much longer fieldwork and taken into account archaeology and linguistics (neither of which was available at the time), the expedition's repertoire of ethnographic 'experiments' might have yielded extremely interesting results. For example, some simple insights into the difference between Austronesian and non-Austronesian languages could have provided an important comparative orientation for the study of social organisation. In 1908, this potential was not fully realised. As true pioneers of fieldwork, Rivers and Hocart had the privilege of creating modern meth-odology on the spot, but also the misfortune of implementing an ethno-graphic experiment before its time.

Acknowledgements

We are grateful to two anonymous reviewers for their comments on this chapter. Our sincere thanks go to Tim Bayliss-Smith for close and critical readings of several versions, for many important ideas and suggestions throughout, and for locating, providing access to and transcribing long-forgotten files of correspondence involving Rivers and Hocart.

Notes

1. Non-specialist readers may perhaps wonder why the term 'Island Melanesia' has such prominence in the book, given that the part of the world called Melanesia is geographically characterised above all as consisting of islands, large and small. However, Island Melanesia has a long and continuing currency as a distinct term for the groups of islands 'to the east and southeast of New Guinea, [today referred to as] the Bismarck archipelago, the Solomon Islands, Vanuatu and New Caledonia', whose inhabitants, 'now and in the past, have always been … island dwellers' (Spriggs 1997: 1). At the same time, the cultural diversity of this region was something that was becoming apparent even at the time of the 1908 expedition. As Spriggs (1997: 2) puts it, 'Island Melanesians are simply the people who happen to live there'.
2. Letter from Rivers to the Trustees, Percy Sladen Memorial Fund, 30 May 1907, Linnean Society Archives, London (hereafter LSA).
3. Rivers to the Trustees, Percy Sladen Memorial Fund, 30 May 1907, LSA.
4. In this book we follow Rivers in his designation of the research as the Percy Sladen Trust Expedition, a label suggested by him in a letter of gratitude to the Trustees of the Percy Sladen Memorial Trust Fund after he had been granted £400 for the expedition (Rivers to the Trustees, Percy Sladen Memorial Trust, 13 June 1907, LSA).
5. Letter from Welchman to Woodford, Mara Na Tabu, 30 March 1908, '[R] e local matters; refusal to act as the Bishop's "Commissary"; refusal to look after Rivers', C.M. Woodford, 'Papers on the Solomon Islands and other Pacific Islands, 1879–1927', Pacific Manuscripts Bureau, Australian National University, Canberra, PMB 1290, ref. 2/59, 2/60. See also Appendix 3.
6. For contrasting examples of naval and missionary reports on New Georgia, see Somerville (1897) and Goldie (1908).
7. Letter from Rivers to A.W. Kappel, secretary to the trustees, Percy Sladen Memorial Trust, from Simbo, 14 June 1908, LSA. Reproduced as Appendix 1.1 (this volume).
8. Hocart, 'Roviana – Topography, Districts, Chiefs', unpublished manuscript, Turnbull Library, National Library of New Zealand, Wellington.

9. Rivers, 'The Western Solomons', typewritten report sent from St John's College, Cambridge, to A.W. Kappel, 'Clerk to the Trustees' of the Percy Sladen Memorial Trust, 4 May 1909, LSA. Reproduced as Appendix 1.3 (this volume).

10. See Rivers to the Trustees, Percy Sladen Memorial Fund, various dates, 1907, LSA, and Appendix 3.

11. See Haddon Papers, Cambridge University Library, Cambridge, envelopes 12009, 12046, 12084.

12. Wheeler, G.C. n.d. Untitled MS, approximately 1200 pp., referred to in Wheeler (1926) under the title 'Sociology'. School of Oriental and African Studies Library, London. Microfilm.

13. See Hocart, 'Genealogies Eddystone, Roviana, Kolombangara', unpublished manuscript, Turnbull Library, National Library of New Zealand, Wellington.

14. See also Hviding (this volume) for the latter.

15. Rivers to the Percy Sladen Memorial Trust, 2 May 1909, LSA, 'W.H.R. Rivers' file.

16. Rivers to the Percy Sladen Memorial Trust, 29 March 1912, LSA, 'W.H.R. Rivers' file.

17. Rivers to the Percy Sladen Memorial Trust, 23 October 1912, LSA, 'W.H.R. Rivers' file.

18. Hocart to the Percy Sladen Memorial Trust, 19 May 1920, LSA, 'W.H.R. Rivers' file.

19. Michael Young notes in his intellectual biography of Malinowski how in late 1913 and early 1914 Rivers and three other prominent representatives of the developing discipline of British anthropology 'lobb[ied] behind the scenes to find him funding for fieldwork' (Young 2004: 245). This was prior to the departure by most of them, along with more than three hundred other British scholars, to Australia for the eighty-fourth meeting of the British Association for the Advancement of Science. According to Young, 'Haddon, Seligman and Marett each played a significant part and, together with Rivers, they seemed to have persuaded Malinowski that he should work in Melanesia. Rivers would have favoured the Solomons or the New Hebrides; Haddon and Seligman, New Guinea' (Young 2004: 245). The large group of British scholars departed for Australia in June 1914, and by the time they arrived in Australia in August war had been declared. As far as Malinowski is concerned, the rest is history (and anthropological folklore).

20. Nicholson (1922) later published a biography of one of his most promising converts, Danny Bula, in which some of the ethnographic remarks he made were clearly influenced by the later diffusionist programme of Rivers and employed by him in *The History of Melanesian Society* (Rivers 1914a) after his abandonment of evolutionist theory.

21. See Rivers to the Trustees, Percy Sladen Memorial Fund, 30 May 1907, LSA.
22. The assumption that in the Solomons archipelago 'maternal' systems were likely to co-exist with those of 'father right' would have been valid from a reading of the ethnographic materials available at the time, but it is not clear exactly on what evidence Rivers built his comparative proposal. Certainly, too little was known at the time about social organisation in New Georgia and other islands in the western Solomons to guide him to what became the expedition's field locations. It was probably Woodford's advice that steered the ethnographic newcomers in the Solomons to the western islands.
23. Rivers, 'The Western Solomons', typewritten report sent from St John's College, Cambridge, to A.W. Kappel, 'Clerk to the Trustees' of the Percy Sladen Memorial Trust, 4 May 1909, LSA. Reproduced as Appendix 1.3 (this volume).
24. Christine Dureau, who has worked most closely with Hocart's unpublished materials, estimates that he produced some 1,500 pages of original fieldnotes in 1908, totalling over 100,000 words. She notes, though, that Hocart's fieldnotes are discontinuous, with many pages missing from the collection held at the Turnbull Library in Wellington. Some can be found in the collection of Rivers's papers housed among the Haddon Papers in Cambridge, and others seem to have been discarded as Hocart wrote up his manuscripts.

References

Barker, P. 1991. *Regeneration*. London: Viking Press.
———— 1993. *The Eye in the Door*. London: Viking Press.
———— 1995. *The Ghost Road*. London: Viking Press.
Barth, F. 2005. 'Britain and the Commonwealth', in *One Discipline, Four Ways: British, German, French, and American Anthropology* (The Halle Lectures), F. Barth, A. Gingrich, R. Parkin and S. Silverman, 3–59. Chicago: The University of Chicago Press.
Bayliss-Smith, T. 2006. 'Fertility and Depopulation: Childlessness, Abortion and Introduced Disease in Simbo and Ontong Java, Solomon Islands', in *Population, Reproduction and Fertility in Melanesia*, S. Ulijaszek (ed.), 13–52. Oxford: Berghahn.
Bennett, J.A. 2000. 'Across the Bougainville Strait: Commercial Interests and Colonial Rivalry, c. 1880–1960', *Journal of Pacific History* 35: 67–82.
Carsten, J. (ed.). 2000. *Cultures of Relatedness: New Approaches to the Study of Kinship*. Cambridge: Cambridge University Press.
Cheyne, A. 1971. *The Trading Voyages of Andrew Cheyne, 1841–1844*, (ed.) D. Shineberg. Canberra: Australian National University Press.
Codrington, R.H. 1891. *The Melanesians: Studies in their Anthropology and Folklore*. Oxford: Clarendon Press.

Dumont, L. 1980. *Homo Hierarchicus: The Caste System and its Implications.* Chicago: University of Chicago Press.

Fortes, M. 1969. *Kinship and the Social Order: The Legacy of Lewis Henry Morgan.* Chicago: Aldine.

Goldie, J.F. 1908. 'The People of New Georgia. Their Manners and Customs and Religious Beliefs', *Proceedings of the Royal Society of Queensland* 22(1): 23–30.

Herle, A., and S. Rouse (eds). 1998. *Cambridge and the Torres Strait: Centenary Essays on the 1898 Anthropological Expedition.* Cambridge: Cambridge University Press

Hocart, A.M. 1922. 'The Cult of the Dead in Eddystone of the Solomons', *Journal of the Royal Anthropological Institute* 52: 71–112, 259–305.

_____ 1925. 'Medicine and Witchcraft in Eddystone of the Solomons', *Journal of the Royal Anthropological Institute* 55: 229–70.

_____ 1927. *Kingship.* London and Oxford: Oxford University Press.

_____ 1929. *Lau Islands, Fiji.* Honolulu: Bernice Bishop Museum.

_____ 1931a. *The Temple of the Tooth in Kandy.* London: Published for the Government of Ceylon by Messrs. Luzac & Co.

_____ 1931b. 'Warfare in Eddystone of the Solomon Islands', *Journal of the Royal Anthropological Institute* 61: 301–24.

_____ 1935. 'The Canoe and the Bonito in Eddystone', *Journal of the Royal Anthropological Institute* 65: 97–111.

_____ 1937. 'Fishing in Eddystone', *Journal of the Royal Anthropological Institute* 67: 33–41.

Hviding, E. 2003. 'Disentangling the *Butubutu* of New Georgia: Cognatic Kinship in Thought and Action', in *Oceanic Socialities and Cultural Forms: Ethnographies of Experience*, I. Hoëm and S. Roalkvam (eds), 71–113. Oxford: Berghahn.

_____ 2014. 'War Canoes of the Western Solomons', in *The Things We Value: Culture and History in Solomon Islands*, B. Burt and L. Bolton (eds), 103–15. Canon Pyon: Sean Kingston Publishing.

Kuklick, H. 1991. *The Savage Within: The Social History of British Anthropology, 1885-1945.* Cambridge: Cambridge University Press.

Langham, I. 1981. *The Building of British Social Anthropology: W.H.R. Rivers and his Cambridge Disciples in the Development of Kinship Studies, 1898-1931.* Dordrecht: Reidel.

McKinnon, J. 1975. 'Tomahawks, Turtles and Traders: A Reconstruction in the Circular Causation of Warfare in the New Georgia Group', *Oceania* 35(4): 290–307.

Malinowski, B. 1922. *Argonauts of the Western Pacific: An Account of Native Enterprise and Adventure in the Archipelagoes of Melanesian New Guinea.* London: Routledge and Kegan Paul.

Monnerie, D. 1995. 'On "Grand-mothers", "Grand-Fathers" and "Ancestors": Conceptualizing the Universe in Mono-Alu (Solomon Islands)', in *Society and Cosmos in Oceania*, D. de Coppet and A. Iteanu (eds), 105–33. Oxford: Berg.

_____ 1996. *Nitu, les vivants, les morts et le cosmos selon la société de Mono-Alu (Iles Salomon)*. Leiden: Centre for Non-Western Studies.

_____ 1998. 'Oceanian Comparison Reconsidered: The Mono-Alu Problem', *Social Anthropology* 6(1): 91–107.

_____ 2002. 'Monnaies de Mono-Alu (Iles Salomon): Valorisations, discontinuités et continuités dans les objets et les relations sociales en Mélanésie', *L'Homme* 162: 59–85.

_____ 2007. 'Gerald Camden Wheeler (Biographical details). British Museum Collection Online Database. Retrieved 10.01.2011 from: http://www.britishmuseum.org/research/search_the_collection_database/term_details. aspx?bioId=34307

Morgan, L.H. 1877. *Ancient Society*. New York: Henry Holt & Co.

Needham, R. 1970. 'Editor's Introduction', in A.M. Hocart, *Kings and Councillors: An Essay in the Comparative Anatomy of Human Society*, R. Needham (ed.), xiii–xcix. Chicago: University of Chicago Press.

Nicholson, R.C. 1922. *The Son of a Savage: The Story of Daniel Bula*. London: Epworth.

Ribbe, C. 1903. *Zwei Jahre unter der Kannibalen der Salomo-Inseln: Reiseerlebnisse und Schilderungen von Land und Leuten*. Dresden-Blasewitz: Hermann Bayer.

Rivers, W.H.R. 1900. 'A Genealogical Method of Collecting Social and Vital Statistics', *Journal of the Anthropological Institute* 30: 74–82.

_____ 1906. *The Todas*. London: Macmillan.

_____ 1912. 'A General Account of Method', in *Notes and Queries on Anthropology*, 4th edition, B.W. Freire-Marreco and J.L. Myres (eds), 124. London: Royal Anthropological Institute.

_____ 1914a. *The History of Melanesian Society*, 2 vols. Cambridge: Cambridge University Press.

_____ 1914b. *Kinship and Social Organisation*. London: Constable.

_____ (ed.). 1922. *Essays on the Depopulation of Melanesia*. Cambridge: Cambridge University Press.

_____ 1924. *Medicine, Magic and Religion*. London: Kegan Paul, Trench and Trübner.

Scheffler, H.W. 1962. 'Kindred and Kin Groups in Simbo Island Social Structure', *Ethnology* 1(2): 135–57.

Somerville, H.B.T. 1897. 'Ethnographical Notes in New Georgia, Solomon Islands', *Journal of the Royal Anthropological Institute* 26: 357–413.

Spriggs, M. 1997. *The Island Melanesians*. Oxford: Blackwell.

Wheeler, G.C. 1910. *The Tribe, and Intertribal Relations in Australia*. London: John Murray.

_____ 1911. 'A Note on the Telei Speech of South Bougainville, Solomon Islands', *Zeitschrift für Kolonialsprachen* 1: 290–304.

_____ 1912a. 'Mono (A Speech Sample of a Melanesian Language Spoken in the Bougainville Straits, Western Solomon Islands)', *Le Maître Phonétique* 1/2: 12–14.

_____ 1912b. 'Sketch of the Totemism and Religion of the People of the Islands in the Bougainville Strait (Western Solomon Islands)', *Archiv für Religionswissenschaft* 15: 24–58, 321–58.

_____ 1912c. 'A Text in Mono Speech (Bougainville Strait, Western Solomon Islands)', *Zeitschrift für Kolonialsprachen* 3: 63–76.

_____ 1912d. 'Two Tales in Mono Speech (Bougainville Strait)', *Man* 12: 21–24.

_____ 1913a. 'Nine Texts in Mono Speech (Bougainville Strait, Western Solomon Islands) with Translation and Notes', *Mitteilungen des Seminars für Orientalische Sprachen zu Berlin* 16: 66–113.

_____ 1913b. 'Six Tales from the Bougainville Strait, Western Solomon Islands', *Anthropophyteia* (Leipzig) 10: 262–80.

_____ 1913c. 'A Text in Mono Speech (Bougainville Strait, Western Solomon Islands)', *Anthropos* 8: 738–53.

_____ 1914a. 'An Account of the Death Rites and Eschatology of the People of the Bougainville Strait', *Archiv für Religionswissenschaft* 17: 64–112.

_____ 1914b. 'Totemismus in Buim [sic] (Süd-Bougainville)', *Zeitschrift für Ethnologie* 46: 41–44.

_____ 1926. *Mono-Alu Folklore (Bougainville Strait, Western Solomon Islands)*. London: Routledge.

Woodford, C.M. 1888. 'Explorations of the Solomon Islands', *Proceedings of the Royal Geographical Society* 10: 351–76.

_____ 1890a. 'Further Explorations in the Solomon Islands', *Proceedings of the Royal Geographical Society* 12: 393–418.

_____ 1890b. *A Naturalist among the Head-hunters: Being an Account of Three Visits to the Solomon Islands in the Years 1886, 1887 and 1888*. London: G. Philip.

_____ 1922. 'The Solomon Islands', in *Essays on the Depopulation of Melanesia*, W.H.R. Rivers (ed.), 69–77. Cambridge: Cambridge University Press.

Young, M. 2004. *Malinowski: Odyssey of an Anthropologist*. New Haven: Yale University Press.

1

Acknowledging Ancestors

The Vexations of Representation

◆●◆

Christine Dureau

A theorist is a child of his own times, or rather a brother of his own, and the child of former ones.

—A.M. Hocart

Ancestral Issues

How to write about W.H.R. Rivers's and A.M. Hocart's 1908 Percy Sladen Trust Expedition to the Solomon Islands? The mere title of their undertaking – an expedition – evokes a journey into a recently pacified area aboard a colonial mission yacht in order to investigate a social evolutionist project on 'mother-right' societies, as Rivers called them (see also Hviding and Berg, Berg, Rio and Eriksen, this volume). On one hand, the expedition is a case of colonial and social evolutionist anthropology, with implications of cultural and racial ranking. On the other hand, it was an under-appreciated contribution to the development of participant-observation fieldwork and anthropology's focal shift from social evolution to social organisation. Either way, our disciplinary imperative to place people in their social, cultural and temporal worlds requires more than stereotype.

This is not simple. Describing early anthropologists as people of their time risks dismissing awkward questions about the discipline's colonial roots and eliding the ways in which they were more than people of their time. The problem, then, is one of wending a way between hagiography and defamation, acknowledgement and dismissal. In a context of contemporary concern with representation and anxiety about what it means to be an anthropologist, it is relatively easy to 'use and distance' – exploiting their materials while hedging that usage with disclaimers about their shortcomings. As one who has repeatedly drawn upon Hocart's and Rivers's Solomons corpus, I find myself increasingly uneasy with such approaches.

This chapter rehearses some of these issues with reference to Rivers's and Hocart's research on Simbo,[1] issues that scholarly politics render inseparable from questions of how to regard them, themselves. I take my own anthropological biography as partially standing for the experiences of a particular generation of Antipodean anthropologists, and begin with two anecdotes about my encounter with postmodernist anthropology.

In 1988, after some two years absence from university, I commenced doctoral studies. Visiting the university bookshop, I found a window display of Clifford and Marcus's *Writing Culture* (1986), which I soon heard other anthropology postgraduates discussing and was encouraged to read. When I did so, like others, I was plunged into profound uncertainty about a discipline that I had regarded as the left, critical one (cf. Roseberry 1996: 5).

Then, in the early 1990s, midway through my doctoral fieldwork, I attended the annual conference of the Australian Anthropological Society (AAS) at which one paper analysed an early–mid-twentieth-century government anthropologist. It made important arguments about anthropology's relationship with colonial administrations, and its location in a world in which access and funding often depend on those whose policies we oppose (see also Kuklick 1991; Pels 2008). The paper was convincing, and its concerns remain with me, but as I listened to the discussion of governance, representation and careers, I became uncomfortable about another kind of representation – specifically of the dead anthropologist in question. During questions, I tentatively suggested some contextualisation: beyond the knowledge/power issues and the textual residua of his advice on government policy, why was this man a government anthropologist? What was his sense of anthropology, its relationship to colonialism, and the place of his research in the lives of those about whom he made recommendations? Are dead anthropologists no more than the texts they leave behind, as later reinterpreted? Such questions of how to contextualise scholarly practice continue to discomfort me.[2] So does the answer I received: 'I don't know what you want to do with these people – celebrate them … ?' Indeed, what to do with them? And how to use their materials, a question not just about their methodological and theoretical credibility, but of their authors' political being.

My life as an anthropologist has been lived largely in the context and wake of critiques represented by *Writing Culture* and the presentation just mentioned, in the context of Rivers's and Hocart's ethnographic materials juxtapositioned with my own research, as a citizen and resident of two settler societies, and in silently contemplating the issues I address here. My primary concerns are with Hocart's and Rivers's fieldwork relationships and methods, their representational practices and the ethics of how to treat them. I address their work partly via reflections on alternate disciplinary histories, in an era of 'transformations within anthropology that have shifted perspective and emphasis from the "primitive" to the "post-colonial"' (Knauft 1999: 3), and partly by considering how contemporary Christian Tinoni Simbo (people [of] Simbo) deal with the difficulties of appraising their own ancestors. In both cases, our forebears undertook foundational work upon which we rely in the present, although we now reject their premises and practices. Tracking from modernist to post-modernist to post-postmodern anthropology, I outline how a pre-1980s disciplinary history might have treated Rivers and Hocart before critically deconstructing their work. I then address these opposed approaches by reference to Simbo conceptualisations of their ancestors as 'good sinners', before asking how to regard Hocart and Rivers in post-postmodern times.

Admiring Histories

Rivers and Hocart verge on prominence in disciplinary histories, almost but never quite among the greats. They are generally represented as brilliant anthropologists, somewhat out of step with their times, whose potential contributions to the discipline were averted by their abrupt, early deaths – Rivers at 58 in 1922; Hocart at 53 in 1939 – and by their problematic academic trajectories – Rivers into the cul-de-sac of diffusionism, and Hocart into maverick interests and prolonged difficulties in securing an academic position. Sapir (2006: 72) captures something of both of them in characterising Rivers as 'brilliant and unconvincing'.

Stocking observes of Rivers that he was 'maltreated in the disciplinary memory – attacked, misappreciated, neglected, repressed' (Stocking 1995: 199–200). He and others have suggested that Rivers's contributions to methodology and theories of social organisation are 'obscured' by the ways in which Radcliffe-Brown and Malinowski are credited with developing approaches and techniques that he pioneered, such as prolonged intensive fieldwork. Certainly, Rivers saw the New Georgia research as an instance of this (Stocking 1995; Urry 1972; Langham 1981; Barth 2005). Somewhat like Stocking's point about Rivers's legacy, Lucien Scubla describes Hocart's contribution as ignored by a triumphant structural-functionalism, whose practitioners abandoned the 'accumulated wisdom' of 'their predecessors [relegating them] to the prehistory of the discipline' (Scubla 2002: 360). Influencing Sahlins, and a neglected precursor of Lévi-Strauss and Dumont, his credibility is only secondarily attested through his contribution to their work (Scubla 2002).

Against concerns about their neglect, Hocart and Rivers can incite hagiography.[3] Richard Slobodin's (1997) biography of Rivers apparently aspires to represent a Renaissance figure of psychology and ethnology. Arthur Kleinman, one of the foremost medical anthropologists of our time, characterises Rivers as his model anthropologist, a polymath and 'exemplar of remaking moral experience by living a moral life', who constantly reinvented himself in order to best engage the issues of his time (Kleinman 2006: 201). For Scubla, Hocart's death symbolised anthropology's theoretical decline, and he was one of 'a few exceptional souls [who] escape the general dumbing down'. He suggests that renewed attention to Hocart's work would have an effect on anthropology akin to 'the prodigious rise of the physico-mathematical sciences' following the 'rediscovery of the works of Archimedes' (Scubla 2002: 361, 374).

More measured accounts note the quality of Rivers's and Hocart's fieldwork, Stocking depicting them as, 'by present standards, quite competent ethnographers' (Stocking 1995: 119). He characterises Hocart as 'the most complete anthropologist' of his time, highlighting his extensive fieldwork and celebrating the 'unusually sensitive' research of one who, '[t]rying to understand the native culture "from within" … [was] quite remarkably "reflexive"' (1995: 232).

In Rivers's case, appreciation of his research qualities is augmented by acknowledgement of his influence on the consolidation of fieldwork through his contributions to successive editions of *Notes and Queries*, and as one who used his Cambridge position to train a generation of fieldworkers (Stocking 1995; Urry 1972; Barth 2005). Against the repeated characterisation of Rivers as establishing the legitimacy of participant observation, Barth grants Hocart that credit, suggesting that Rivers's 'most enduring effect … resulted from his painstaking conceptual work on social organization' (Barth 2005: 16), which grew out of his efforts to deal with his Melanesian materials. Given such acknowledgements of Rivers's and Hocart's innovations, what, then, of their Solomons work?

The development of fieldwork around 1900 reflected a growing concern with 'facts'. Rivers recognised that facts alone were less important than 'the manner in which they were collected', hence his stress on prolonged fieldwork in the interests of scientific accuracy (Urry 1972: 50, 52). At this 'rather shadowy' point in disciplinary history, when social evolutionism was in decline and structural-functionalism had not yet emerged (Urry

1972; Langham 1981; Stocking 1995: 14), Rivers was a central figure in bridging the two. Indeed, at about the time of the Solomons fieldwork, he 'was teetering on the great divide between the nineteenth-century tradition of explanation in terms of survivals and ... the typical twentieth-century form of explanation in terms of the presently functioning social order' (Langham 1981: 84; see also Urry 1972).

In New Georgia, Hocart and Rivers continued the colour testing that Rivers had pursued in the Torres Strait Islands in 1898, and Rivers collected material with his genealogical method. They worked largely through interpreters, but Hocart, in particular, developed considerable linguistic understanding. Although they divided the research, they were aware that this approach had shortcomings. As Hocart noted of the division of labour on Simbo – 'Dr Rivers taking kinship, social organization, ghosts, gods, and other subjects, while I took death, fishing, warfare; a few subjects, such as the house, were joint' – 'these divisions were rather artificial' (Hocart 1922: 71–72). They also took different skills and interests to New Georgia. One was testing his theories and practising a methodology developed elsewhere; the other, on his maiden fieldwork, was 'inclined ... to a very different style of fieldwork from [Rivers] ... rather than asking detailed questions, he listened' (Stocking 1995: 221).

Rivers's and Hocart's fieldwork must have been generally harmonious. Fred Green, a trader resident and married on Simbo, suggests in a letter to Rivers that they had left 'many friends behind you both White and Black'. Green describes Hocart as 'still in raptures with [Simbo] ... and [longing] to be with the savages again', stressing his rapport with Tinoni Simbo.[4] Their engagement with New Georgia went beyond a passion for fieldwork, suggesting an appreciation for native capacities and cultures at odds with contemporary colonial attitudes. This was particularly so of Hocart. Shortly after his Solomons research, for example, he criticised Methodist missionaries in Fiji for their 'distant & superior reserve which riles me more than all the straightforward abuse of a Solomon Island trader'.[5] For Rivers (1926: 39), Simbo understandings of death disproved scholarly characterisations of primitive thought as 'prelogical', one instance of a career-long assumption of 'minor differences yet basic similarities' in human perception (Bayliss-Smith, this volume). In later years, Hocart, more vehemently, protested Eurocentric perceptions of native illogic and irrationality. Typically:

> What I object to is the suggestion that the savage (if there is such a thing) stands quite apart in his inability to answer a difficult question ... or in his tendency to invent an explanation ... Put the same sort of question to any intelligent European ... and he will either have no answer, or else invent some reason. (Hocart 1935: 343)

His example is of how he and his Fijian informant, drawing on their own explanatory frameworks, had different explanations for the origins of a cave they were discussing.

We ought not overdo this celebration. Hocart clearly thought his own understanding superior; he was, then, reflective for his time. Overall, though, within the constraints of their perception and political position, their fieldwork can be celebrated for its humane approach and its opposition to Eurocentrism and colonial insensitivity.

I also admire the quality of their fieldwork, especially as revealed in Hocart's practice. His New Georgian writing is highly empirical. In some respects, it reads like the nineteenth-century collection of facts-upon-facts that he later rejected (e.g. Hocart 1933). In other respects, it speaks to Rivers's ideal of the systematic collection of well-contextualised facts, itself reflecting his insistence on careful analysis of evidence over deduction or speculation (Langham 1981: 125–26). The links between ethnographic work and generalisation are explicit and detailed, albeit threatening to drown anyone not specifically interested in the small island of Simbo. These accounts contain limited theoretical development, although their influence is discernible in Hocart's later, more analytical, works, his most developed Simbo papers (Hocart 1922, 1931) prefiguring his theories of divine kingship and ritual violence. Further, the expedition materials have contributed to later theoretical developments. To cite two examples, Rivers's Simbo-based kindred continues to inform kinship theory (e.g. Hviding 2003) and Roger Keesing's (1984; see also Dureau 2000) crucial reconceptualisation of Melanesian *mana* depends on Hocart's many translations of Simbo prayers, with their closing invocations to the ancestors, *mu mana tu* ('you be efficacious').

From the perspective of a later fieldworker interested in social change, the redundancy in Hocart's materials is remarkably helpful. Consider the issue of leadership. During my first fieldwork, I was struck by the extent of contention about *baŋara* (sing., pl., leaders, chiefs). Some insisted that these were patrilineally inherited positions, although *baŋara* genealogies suggested both tendencies to sister's son succession and the adoption of outsiders if no one within the lineage was appropriate to the position, implying the significance of competence over heredity. Others disputed the principles and protocols of succession, enactments and entitlements of respect to *baŋara* and the grounds for moral evaluation of contemporary office-holders. One of the few things common to the various positions, including those who insisted that there has always been a paramount chieftainship (Solomon Islands Pijin: *paramaon cif*), was the avowal that their vision reflected 'ancient Simbo custom' (*na hahanana Simbo podelai kame rane sosoto*, lit. 'Simbo ways beginning long ago'). Different understandings of the *binaŋara* (leadership, chieftainship) – more or less hereditary, appointed or popularly proclaimed, degrees of achieved versus ascribed authority, the extent and kinds of mutual obligation between *baŋara* and followers – inflected many aspects of social life. To give one minor example, was Ami, having given birth only a few weeks earlier, required to pay compensation for walking across a pathway that led past a *baŋara*'s house several metres away? Was her walking there and reluctance to pay a sign of the deterioration of *kastom*? Or did the *baŋara*'s demand signify hunger for respect or the greediness characteristic of the present, to be understood in contradistinction to times when *baŋara* attracted respect by virtue of the powerful nurturance they extended to their followers?

The sheer array of contending claims raised questions about how to understand historical shifts and continuities on Simbo in the context of contemporary scholarly arguments about social coherence and fragmentation. Simbo seemed to encapsulate new critiques of a homogenising ethnography that had been overly focused on order and regularity. Or perhaps the untidy social claims about the *baŋara* demonstrated the social unravelling caused by a century of rapid historical changes? Certainly, widespread nostalgic accounts and older people's reminiscences implied the latter.

Hocart's observations on 'chieftainship' (e.g. Hocart 1922, 1931) reveal a flexible institution that broadly structured local society without the hard and fast rules of leadership that an intervening anthropological generation had assumed. He opens a discussion of 'chieftainship' with a distinction between 'chiefs proper' and 'influential persons … [or elders]' before revealing dissent regarding who is properly counted as a chief, and the slipperiness of defining *baŋara*, 'some universally acknowledged, others doubtful'. Consider his account of Sinalaŋa:

> The consensus of opinion is against Sinalanga having been a chief; Mbiu declared he was a commoner holding prestige with the white men; one denied at first that he was a chief then admitted he was 'a little bit'. It was alleged that he had frightened some people into obedience by means of his 'devildevil'. Perhaps he was an energetic and ambitious commoner who aspired to the chieftainship, and only failed to found a line because he had no successor strong enough to assert himself against the belief in the family's evil eye whether sincere or originating in the calumnies of his enemies. Perhaps, too, he may have been a chief whose title is not acknowledged owing to this same evil eye.[6]

Hocart's account is messy, adding to the complexity of how Tinoni Simbo conceive and debate individuals' entitlements or obligations, intractable in the face of efforts to clearly delineate rules of leadership. His materials suggest, then, that Simbo political office has long been situational, conforming to elements of both and neither contrasts in the big man-chief typology. To my mind, it substantially contributes to understanding aspects of Simbo history and sociality. The relatively consistent uncertainty about *binaŋara*, for example, stands in notable contrast to the radical change to *baere*, 'friendship'.[7] In 1908, this included a formal exchange relationship between two people, sometimes at the instigation of the *baŋara*, as well as referring more generally to friendship. By the 1990s, *baere* as an exchange relationship was obsolete, the term still referring to friendship but, in the context of contemporary sexuality and marriage, it also referred to lovers' necessarily discrete relationships.

Individually, these two topics communicate considerable detail about particular aspects of change. But it is the simultaneous breadth and detail of Hocart's data that lend the greatest understanding. Thus, the broad continuities in *binaŋara* alongside the reconstitution of *baere* and other changes and continuities (in marriage, religious logic, household constitution and so on) demonstrate how historical forces differentially affect different aspects of social life. In a sense this is a truism, but the juxtaposition of Hocart's materials to more recent social practices and concerns makes it impossible to render a simplistic account of social change. Given the rather narrower focus of the Percy Sladen Trust Expedition, this is a remarkably rich resource.

Hocart's material also speaks to later criticisms of the 'writing at arm's length' that distances readers from the people upon whom ethnographies are based (Spencer 2001: 448). In 'Cult of the Dead...', for example, Hocart (1922) includes accounts of variable practices and the tracks of individual Tinoni Simbo remain clear.

If I have stressed the value of Hocart's materials, this is at least partly because they are extensive and detailed, and the available mix of fieldnotes, topical manuscripts and published articles enables me to draw upon ethnographic details while engaging his interpretations. In Rivers's case, I am more dependent on his published works, his archival materials on Simbo being much more limited in quantity and focus.

The materials have also been valued by some Tinoni Simbo, who regarded them as a repository of otherwise lost knowledge. A number of people regarded Hocart's manuscript vocabulary as a potential baseline dictionary, and in 1992 'The Cult of the Dead' (1922) was submitted to a court case involving a major land dispute (but see Pels 2008: 288). Beyond these more formal values, the individuals depicted in Hocart's articles on Simbo had personal value for people who were related to them, and they were quickly incorporated into accounts of family histories.[8]

Aside from the locally ascribed value of their published works, it is hard not to appreciate Hocart and Rivers for their methodological contributions, the lasting value of carefully collected historical ethnographic data, for their convivial approach to those with whom they undertook research, and for the contribution of that research to anthropology. So goes one version of the Percy Sladen Trust Expedition. It suggests the value of an approach that admits the contexts in which they lived and wrote, the arguments in which anthropology was engaged at the time, and entails a generosity of spirit that practices the relativism that today we aspire to extend to all of our research subjects.

Deconstructing Ancestors

A postmodernist approach suggests that understanding Rivers and Hocart as anthropologists of their time entails contextualising them as practitioners of a discipline grounded in the colonial.[9] Given the uncertainty as to what 'postmodern' refers to – even a leading postmodernist theorist like Ihab Hassan struggles to articulate this, while striving to delineate a post-postmodern perspective (Hassan 2003; see also di Leonardo 1991: 21–27; Matthewman and Hoey 2006) – it is as well to outline how I use the term. For my purposes, 'postmodernism' refers to a broad intellectual movement challenging the premises and validity of positivist-oriented social sciences by pointing to their enmeshment in networks of culture and power. *In toto*, this diverse movement challenges the status and knowability of truth (Knauft 1994: 126).

Postmodernist anthropology raised diverse questions about anthropological stresses and suppositions. Among its elements were critiques of aspirations to an objective social scientific anthropology; demands for reflexive accounts of fieldwork; an insistence on the double partiality of ethnographic truths (Clifford 1986); the highlighting of inequality and fragmentation in contradistinction to earlier treatments of social and cultural homogeneity; characterisations of anthropology as colonial; and questions about ethnographic research in postcolonial contexts. And, in innumerable forms, representation was problematised, particularly in reference to Said's account of the Orient as a discursive construction, which was extrapolated to anthropology as a form of colonial or imperial knowledge-production (Knauft 1994, 1999; Spencer 2001; Trencher 2002; Bunzl 2005; Graeber 2006; Burke and Prochaska 2007). As Bruce Kapferer (2007: 73) notes, virtually everything taken to define anthropology has 'either been seriously challenged or rejected'. Many anthropologists were left 'grappling not only with what they can say they know, but how to say it at all' (Trencher 2002: 212) or who they could speak about. A simplistic account of postmodern critiques of anthropology goes something like the following.

Clifford and Marcus's *Writing Culture* (1986) published to 'immediate extraordinary effect' (Spencer 2001: 443), symbolises a disciplinary 'crisis' and 'auto-critique'. It was a watershed volume (Spencer 2001: 444; Trencher 2002), a culmination of converging critiques and innovations, including feminist theory, post-structuralism and the literary turn (di Leonardo 1991; Spencer 2001; Trencher 2002)[10] *Writing Culture*, an icon of post-modernism for many anthropologists, thus signified dispersed concerns about, and facilitated criticisms of, anthropology's place in colonisation, imperialism and knowledge/power relationships. Commentators on the discipline suggested that anthropology had at least two crucial roles, practical and representational.

Highlighting anthropology's colonial roots suggested a discipline of applied advice and implicit justification. Indeed, from the 1890s, 'not a moment when moral critique of colonial empire was a likely standpoint from which to launch a career in anthropology' (Stocking 1995: 372; see also 381; Urry 1972; Kuklick 1991: 182–241; Pels 2008), anthropologists like Rivers (1917) advocated anthropology's relevance to responsible colonial government.[11] Evans-Pritchard, as every undergraduate knows, studied the Nuer at the behest of the Anglo-Sudan colonial administration; in some places, trainee colonial officers were required to take anthropology courses, and some colonial administrations employed government anthropologists (Kuklick 1991: 197, 202). Anthropological theory and colonial interest coincided, too. The structural-functional focus on political structure, for example, mirrored British interests in indirect rule. Yet many historians of the discipline see anthropologists as relatively insignificant colonial actors, fitting awkwardly into colonial echelons, their research regarded as too esoteric for their employers' needs, and their theoretical advances grating against colonial officers' more self-serving social evolutionist models (e.g. Kuklick 1991: 182; Stocking 1995).

More significantly, representational practices necessitated critical re-interpretation of texts in terms of 'their literary devices and tropes, and an examination of their embeddedness within the very structures and relations of … colonial power' (Roseberry 1996: 7; see also Bunzl 2005: 191). A disciplinary focus on difference – tribes, strange and challenging practices, peoples of darker hues – discursively manufactured both the distance that anthropologists thought they were rejecting and a field of knowledge/power, with natives as objects of expertise.

Postmodernist anthropology was differently inflected in different places (Spencer 2001; Trencher 2002; Goldsmith 2005). Trencher (2002), for example, claims a particular salience to the 'literary turn' in US cultural anthropology. In settler societies with recent acrimonious histories of colonial dispossession, contention and resistance, like Australia and New

Zealand, postmodernist and postcolonial theory merged, leading some to see anthropology 'as representative of all that is truly bad about research' (Smith 2006: 11).

In Australia and New Zealand in the 1990s, Pakeha[12] anthropologists like myself felt a real urgency and intensity to calls for disciplinary reform. We, keen-eyed would-be anthropologists, criticised colonialism; many of us had been attracted to anthropology because it gave us a language with which to refute racism and ethnocentrism. Now we learned that the discipline we had passionately embraced was deemed a colonial exemplar *par excellence* (Stocking 1995: 368; cf. Kuklick 1991: 292–93; Spencer 2001; Trencher 2002; Pels 2008). Some of my peers vehemently rejected such concerns. Others rejected anthropology as unsalvageable and headed to the suburbs of sociology (cf. Scheper-Hughes 1992: 26–29). Still others, with more or less intensity and righteousness, engaged concerns about writing's relationship to power, accepting demands for greater self-consciousness about research and interrogation of the anthropological archive, including undertakings like the Percy Sladen Trust Expedition.

Hocart and Rivers arrived in New Georgia a few years after pacification, at a point at which 'the ebbing tide of mid-Victorian liberal optimism was [being] overtaken by the cresting wave of empire' (Stocking 1995: 98; cf. Kapferer 2007). Members of the Oxbridge elite, they were engaged in one of innumerable colonial 'will-to-know' projects (Richards 1992). Given this context, the key questions concern the nature of their research, rather than the quality of their ethnographic materials.

Their approach could be seen as arrogantly imperialist, emblematic of the poststructuralist ironic play on subjects and objects – newly subject people, subjected to the ethnographer's objectifying gaze and rendered objects of research, their subjectivity moot. New Georgians were subjected to research for Rivers's thesis on mother-right, known in its terms, and compelled to cooperation. Rivers and Hocart several times refer to terse, surly Tinoni Simbo, who apparently resented their presence, but, as Kuklick notes, anthropologists 'in the colonial era … were recognized as members of the ruling class – and their inquiries were likely to be answered' (Kuklick 1991: 192; see also Pels 2008). Hocart and Rivers pressed on with their research against obvious resistance – people trying to mislead them about the times of mortuary rituals, for example. Hocart recounts tricking an old man into revealing information about a ritual, and then coercing an informant into giving information: '*armed* with his hint I was able to *extract* the most important rite of the day out of the *unwilling* Njiruviri' (Hocart 1922: 87, my emphases).

Against images of them as reflective, humane scholars, ethnocentric interpretations are hardly uncharacteristic. Rivers's (1914: 253) response to the inclusiveness of Simbo's classificatory kinship terminology was to see it as an impoverished nomenclature. Hocart squandered a unique chance to investigate Simbo's reported female *baŋara* (*baŋara maqota*), dismissing them as glorified cooks, not only misunderstanding the significance of food, but reflecting prevailing assumptions about women in his own and 'savage societies'.

Their approach and attitude, then, was comfortably masculine-imperial. If Rivers later criticised the insensitive pacification, it was the manner rather than fact that was at issue. His essay on depopulation reeks of Melanesian inadequacy: Tinoni Simbo cannot cope with life now that they are denied the headhunting 'which took an all-pervading part in [their] lives' (Rivers 1922: 101). So traumatised are they that, unable or unwilling to reproduce, they face extinction. The diffusionism informing Rivers's approach was compatible with the era's heightened imperialism: in Rivers's model, contact was tragically progressive because it brought inferior people under the rule of superior ones, 'forcing the former to adopt a more civilized mode of behaviour' (Kuklick 1991: 257; see also 261–62). In developing an argument for the restoration of 'old interests' among Tinoni Simbo and other Island Melanesians, Rivers (1922: 107–8) evokes the 'white man's burden', placing a civilising, therapeutic, imperative on the administration to 'preserve enough [old customs and traditions] to maintain interest while removing all those features which conflict with the ideals of modern civilisation'. For those Melanesians who used to be headhunters, he suggests the 'substitution of a porcine head for a human head', and 'the introduction of canoe races' as 'efficacious' means for 'maintaining interest and zest in life'.

Hocart and Rivers were a relatively benign pair, patronising, rather than criticising, and generally getting along with people, despite their manifest association with the colonial government. If they travelled as guests of the colonial Anglican Melanesian Mission (to whom the proceeds of Rivers's last volume were donated), this was a tolerant mission, respecting indigenous culture and committed to autonomous conversion (Hilliard 1978). But this relative benignity is an issue: not that they advocated or advised violent colonisation, but that in their very liberalism, their will to a benevolent colonialism, they contributed to its rationalisation (cf. Bayliss-Smith, Bennett, this volume). Perhaps anthropologists ultimately had little impact on the direct rule of colonial societies; perhaps others wrote profoundly ethnocentric and racist tracts; but in promoting humane treatment, anthropologists accepted the relationships that required such compassion. Rivers's and Hocart's benignity, then, should neither be overstated nor taken as the final point.

Such is another account of the expedition.

If postmodernism challenged histories of an anthropology arising from the darkness of racism, evolutionism and ethnocentrism, it has itself been criticised on various grounds. Of particular relevance is 'temporal ethno-centrism', whereby earlier anthropologists are judged by the canons of a postcolonial anthropology concerned to relocate the discipline in a more inclusive future. While such retrospective accounts might contribute to the decolonisation of, and more subtle reflection on, the discipline, they also easily lead to damnation and self-justification. Such accounts are often characterised by cavalier treatments of reputations and the use of '"emotive evidence" which calls on feelings rather than arguments to lead readers to accept an assertion' (Reyna, quoted in Trencher 2002: 214).

As Knauft and others have observed, 'critical engagement is easily sacrificed to rhetorical condescension' (Knauft 1994: 133), the ethical transmogrifying into the moralistic, a form of self/other construction that speaks to situations in the now more than to practices in the then. Such presentations can also proffer emotional and ethical insurance. Highlighting, say, Hocart's or Rivers's shortcomings might reassure a novice anthropologist that she had transcended her racist, colonial cultural background in her own research and writing. Less innocently, such things can also offer a kind of professional insurance, as we strive to convince our readers that we have achieved that transcendence.

My sense is that some who insisted on doing fieldwork in the immediate wake of *Writing Culture* dealt unfairly with people like Hocart and Rivers: we 'othered' them. In the classical techniques of othering, writers develop the implicit formulation, 'they are what we are not'. Rivers characterises Tinoni Simbo as incapable of dealing with progress – implicitly Rivers is modern; someone describes the Oriental as irrational – implicitly, that person is rational. I describe Rivers as a colonial paternalist – I am not. I describe Hocart as sexist – my feminist reinterpretation achieves validity in eschewing his. If I describe their writings as symbolically violent, somehow mine are not. The implication is that the authors of such accounts have repudiated the sins of those they criticise. So, if Evans-Pritchard accepted a colonial commission to record the social organisation of the Nuer, who manifestly resented his presence, Rosaldo's (1986) rhetorical style suggests that he would have refused to undertake that research. I do not mean that such accounts necessarily are motivated by righteousness. Rosaldo's argument, for example, highlights disciplinary issues by discussing individual scholars. Still, the tone and presentist stance of such arguments can leave an impression of *ad hominem* attack, often on safely dead precursors. In addressing disciplinary histories, then, our questions of representation must include those of how to represent other authors. It is in this context that I return to the Simbo that I partially share with Rivers and Hocart.

Ancestral Ambivalence

People throughout the now largely Christian Pacific have faced questions of how to regard their own ancestors, significant aspects of whose ontologies and epistemologies they now reject. A kind of destruction paradigm is one mode of response to pagan antecedents – converts destroying artefacts and spurning cultural practices as heathen in testament to Christianity's transformative effects. Alternatively, or as part of such responses, ancestors may be represented as 'devils' or 'sinners'. Others have dealt with the challenge of intimate relationship to those problematic ancestors by, for example, post-mortem baptism, incorporating the indigenous into the Christian (e.g. White 1991), or developing theologies of pagan religion as incipiently Christian.

At first glance, Simbo attitudes evoke the more negative of these possibilities, the ancestors being widely treated as temporal, social and religious 'others' to today's Christians. People repeatedly described their ancestors as 'people of the darkness', sometimes as 'crazy' (*tuturu*, 'insane, crazy, irrational, stupid') heathens: they pounded puddings at the shrines (*tabuna*) and thereby worshipped devils, they were headhunters, they were sexually lax. As such, they were people of the darkness, people of the time of sin: 'Let me tell you about the ancestors, Christina [...]. We are Christian, we are people of the light, not like the people of the past (Pijin: *taem bifoa*), not like the people of the darkness'.

However, beyond the ubiquitous discourse of light triumphing over darkness, for many people the ancestors presented an irresolvable contradiction as both heathens, whose ways should be rejected, and as people of 'love', who should be emulated. Social critique often took the form of celebrating these heathen, devil-worshipping ancestors as founders of moral sociality, including the persistent ideal of generosity/love which stands in bitter counterpoint to the selfishness of contemporary Christians (Dureau 2005). Against the quotidian talk of past darkness, then, runs a contrary theme of ancestral models for how to behave.

I repeatedly asked people about their ancestors' theological status, and received diverse responses. Very few followed the then bishop in characterising them as proto-Christians. A few described them as 'people of sin and that's that'. Many replied, 'I do not/cannot know' (*Qeke nonogaia*). And sometimes I heard that the ancestors were 'good sinners of the time of darkness' (*tinoni sini zoŋadi pana totoso rodomo*), or 'good sinners before Christianity'. Such responses partly express nostalgia for an impossibly better past, but they also sum an awareness of situational morality: 'They did not know, the ancestors; they did not know Jesus (*Zisu*). They could not'. As such, they were good within the context of their times; people who did their best in the circumstances, who were, perforce, sinners because by present definition people of those times were so.

Simbo difficulties with their ancestors are somewhat like my own. We share the problem of being judged by reference to those who came before – as in stereotypical depictions of anthropology as colonial or the media's persistent portrayals of western Solomon Islanders as headhunters. Of greater pertinence for this chapter is the mutual conundrum of how to treat these founding figures. Certainly, there are limits to the suggestion that early anthropologists, as beings of colonial darkness, be treated as some Tinoni Simbo treat their ancestors. The most obvious limitations are those of relative proximity and emotional engagement. Simbo ancestors are literal kin, defining who Tinoni Simbo may be: they stand as legal markers of rights to land, residence and resources; they were the great-grandparents, grandparents and, for a few, parents of people still alive. The changes experienced on Simbo have also been much more consequential than those occasioned by transient academic styles. And there is, of course, the question of autonomy, with anthropologists largely able to choose their careers and the places where they work. More subtle are questions about the different values entailed in our respective evaluations. Tinoni Simbo at this point are adamant Christians with an established and relatively fixed truth. Contemporary anthropology, by contrast, relativises truths and often deconstructs 'truth'.

Beyond such differences, though, I highlight a matter of attitude. Tinoni Simbo feel themselves richer for having their ancestral past to draw upon. Many people displayed subtle, reflexive awareness of the temporal, cultural and social worlds in which their ancestors lived, ambivalently accepting the contradictions of their relationships with those ancestors whose truths they reject. Many reflectively acknowledged that there is no singular truth, refusing righteousness and noting that they would have participated in the ancestors' world had they lived then. This is not just a matter a mixed acceptance and rejection but of a spirit of engagement with troubling forebears. People admitted the contradiction inherent in their evocation of 'good sinners', acknowledging it as an imperfect compromise, arising from the fact that one cannot know how to make such judgements. This is a tolerant approach to the ancestral problem, coming from people who subscribe to a (moderate) fundamentalist world-view, and one that sits markedly against the intolerance of some scholars who decry intolerance.

Vexatious Representations

My point in drawing this limited analogy is to highlight Tinoni Simbo's stance on the value of ambivalence. An anthropological approach to anthropologists should do what good anthropologists do: seek to understand 'people who lived in worlds which, though continuous with, were rather different from [their] own' (Stocking 1995: xvii). This is not as simple as it first seems. Contextualising them and their approach temporally, acknowledging that we can escape our cultural worlds to only a limited extent, an anthropological truism, raises that awkward spectre of cultural relativism, the defence of the indefensible. Within the discipline, historical contextualisation can become, or seem, apologetic.

Writing of right-wing Christian fundamentalists, Susan Harding ironically observes that 'it seems that anti-orientalizing tools of cultural criticism are better suited for some "others" constituted by discourses of race/sex/class/ethnicity/colonialism' than of others (Harding 1991: 375). Scholarly presuppositions, she suggests, thwart 'scrupulous interpretation [of] those deemed ... problematic' (Harding 1991: 376). Harding found anthropologists assuming that if she were studying fundamentalists, she must be one herself. Her argument is evocative of my problem of representing awkward ancestors without finding myself implicitly bypassing the facts of colonial roots, apologising via the discourse of time or being interpreted as doing so.

Harding's notion of 'the repugnant cultural other' neatly encapsulates how earlier anthropologists have sometimes been treated in recent decades. Further, as she notes of her fundamentalists – for whom she certainly does not apologise – such distasteful others are disciplinary stereotypes, hovering around a kernel of empirical validity. As this suggests, as important as colonial history has been to the development of anthropology (Asad 1973: 18–19), the colonizing anthropologist complicit with colonialism is a discursive product of our efforts to deal with that history. Along with cynicism about efforts at contextualisation, then, we need a balancing cynicism about that cynicism.

I have highlighted elements of Hocart's and Rivers's approaches to Simbo to demonstrate the ease with which one may appreciate or assassinate ancestors.[13] But which is the truth: the sexist, insensitive Hocart and paternalist, objectifying Rivers, or the perceptive, reflexive, engaging pair? Both and neither. Each characterisation captures something of two somewhat remarkable scholars, of their unthinking, assumed dominance and cultural awfulness, and their humane awareness that they were dealing with human beings. Each too neatly boxes them in approved or disapproved slots. Certainly, anthropologists cannot just be seen as people of their time, given that the discipline imposes an obligation of reflection on its practitioners and the lingering effects of our texts.

Pondering the Rhodes-Livingstone Institute anthropologists who worked on the Zambian Copperbelt, James Ferguson asks whether they were 'great radicals bravely battling racism and colonialism? Or were they arrogant colonial racists, denigrating and condescending to the natives ... ? In these terms the question is misposed. A more adequate approach to the matter requires a better understanding of the position [they] occupied within colonial society' (Ferguson 1999: 28).

So: let us imagine Rivers and Hocart on Simbo. Victorian and Edwardian middle-class sons of churchmen, disembarking at an island famed for savagery, a reputation that Hocart, at least, had little experiential reason to reject. Yet, in the face of their cultural truths, they engaged with people. A decade before Malinowski, both perceived the importance of learning the vernacular, and Hocart did it very well. They developed considerable rapport and, for their time, were relatively relativist.[14] Further, if they were also ethnocentric, I do not discern racism in their writings. Hocart, particularly, confronted ethnocentrism, albeit ethnocentrically. Thus, in a characteristic passage on Simbo logic, he asserts that outsiders 'have no right to impute to them muddle-headedness until we have made every effort to find out what the underlying theory of action is. This is not easy, for they are mostly inarticulate' (Hocart 1937: 40). The phrase 'they are mostly inarticulate', implicitly conflating articulateness with competence in European conceptualisation, jumps out at today's reader. It is unjust, though, to alight critically upon this phrase without acknowledging Hocart's evident intent to criticise stereotypes of native people's capacities.

Certainly, I suspect that Hocart was more self-challenging than a contemporary anthropologist who expresses less overtly problematic viewpoints. The challenges of cultural and putatively racial difference for him were far greater than for me. I had years of training in cultural relativism, I knew there were no races, that cultural practice was not heritable; I had been immersed in anti-imperialist literature. And I was greeted by kind and gregarious people, members of a society that had remade itself in the decades since Hocart and Rivers arrived in the devastating aftermath of pacification. By contrast, for them race was real (Stocking 1982: 112–22),[15] and their culture hegemonically imperialist. Neither of them tub-thumping imperialists, Rivers, albeit allusively, criticised pacification; Hocart repeatedly insisted that Melanesians deserved respect, as did Rivers, if less adamantly and with a greater degree of self-interest.[16]

None of this renders the two heroic, but it suggests the need to recognise them as at least somewhat extraordinary people who refused the easy paths of imperial apologetics and racism. If merely presenting them as people of their time does not do justice to the issues, it also does not do justice to them. It underplays Hocart's engaged, sociable fieldwork and commitment to indigenous perspectives, and Rivers's methodological and theoretical brilliance.

With the hindsight bestowed by my realisation of my limited ability to grasp Simbo mores and meanings, to overcome my ethnocentrism and social ineptitude, or to somehow conduct fieldwork that transcended the global inequalities represented by an affluent European in a poor postcolonial society, I have become more ambivalent about Rivers's and Hocart's shortcomings. I am inclined to treat them as exotic informants, interlocutors and colleagues, albeit colleagues I do not desire to emulate.

Memmi characterises colonial French philosophers as 'colonizers of good will'. He acknowledges that '[t]heir generosity was unquestionable; so, unfortunately, was their impotence, their inability to make themselves heard', while noting that goodwill would not exempt them from the consequences of their colonial being (Memmi 2003: 11). Similarly, Ferguson regards Rhodes-Livingstone Institute anthropologists as 'colonial liberals', largely unwilling to challenge the system, while feeling uncomfortable with it. 'In their relations with the conservative white establishment, they were decidedly "progressive" … [but their enterprise] was, in the end, part of the colonial establishment' (Ferguson 1999: 32).

Something similar describes Hocart and Rivers, enacting their rights as metropolitan imperial citizens to impose themselves residentially, gatecrash death rituals, harass old men and write as they would. They were liberals interested in the welfare of natives, but able to reconcile their freedom of research with Tinoni Simbo's unfreedom and, in Rivers's case, to recommend colonial policy. At the time, liberalism was becoming more favourable to state oversight of welfare. Rivers's 'psychological factor' (Rivers 1922) can be understood in this vein: an account of '[natives] powerless to protect themselves from all manner of threats to their welfare' (Kuklick 1991: 111; cf. Bayliss-Smith, Bennett, this volume). Hocart shows greater sensitivity to matters of cultural domination. Working as a schoolmaster in Fiji shortly after the Solomons fieldwork, he strove to run his school in accord with indigenous practice and, at the other end of his career, sought to train Egyptians in anthropology (Evans-Pritchard 1939), highly inclusive practices for the time and afterwards.

What about Rivers's prescription of pig-hunting and canoe-racing therapy and Hocart's dismissal of *baŋara maqota* – were these not plain old Edwardian paternalism and sexism, as I suggested in my earlier work? Well, in part, yes. Yet countering with a celebration of how Simbo has managed Europeans very well for two centuries or with a gynocentric account of society would do little to respect the lives and possibilities available to Tinoni Simbo in 1908 either. If sexual stratification was not as Hocart understood it, and women as social actors could achieve high status, in fact no female *baŋara* could gain the fame and authority of male *baŋara*, and Hocart's scattered data were central to what I could reconstitute of women's historical lives. Rivers's explanation of depopulation in terms of a kind of colonial 'shell shock' suppresses more empirically valid causes in the interests of his psychological theory (Bayliss-Smith, this volume), and his recommendations now seem ludicrous. Still, his account of the experiential consequences of colonisation anticipates Fanon's (2008) later arguments.

The anthropological perspective lies in an attitude, a frame of mind that recognises and accepts the interplay of sameness and difference, and questions what we know of our world. I find in Rivers and Hocart something of that frame of mind. It is easy to trivialise their safe relativism and disdain the paternalist mode in which it is expressed ('mostly inarticulate', 'living for headhunting'). But they demonstrate an anthropological understanding of co-humanity and, irrespective of their problematic concept, 'native', they recognised natives as people constrained and enabled by their circumstances. It matters that they allowed Tinoni Simbo to be more than the 'erstwhile savages' that permeated Methodist discourse about the Western Solomons for decades to come,[17] and continues to inform popular images of the Solomons.

Acknowledging Ancestors

To return to my anecdote about the AAS conference: how do we write about our anthropological ancestors without resorting to hagiographic histories or damning them to the darkest depths of reputational hell? Kapferer (2007) represents anthropology as an inherently Enlightenment project. As both and neither science and humanities subject, it encapsulates the 'intrinsic science/non-science rift' endemic to Enlightenment thought, incorporating its modes of understanding ranging from extreme positivism to extreme subjectivism. Anthropology contains within it:

> ... the conservative and oppressive, the Dark side of the Enlightenment ... as well as the revolutionary, indeed liberating, possibilities of Enlightenment thought and practice: the Enlightenment as throwing up its own potentials of critique as well as the suppression of such critique. The Enlightenment as instrumental in the orders of imperial expansion and ... colonial domination is ... also a force in their resistance. (Kapferer 2007: 75–76)

In a post-postmodern era, anthropology is positioned to transcend the cruder binaries arising from concentrating unduly on one of these trajectories. Hocart and Rivers could never have imagined the terms in which I have criticised them. It was a historical impossibility – politically, culturally and psychologically – for them to develop critiques of the kind that anthropologists can now write. For such reasons and because of my aware-ness of my – and my generation's – conceptual and political limitations, I advocate a triple stance of exploitation, critique and generosity.

By exploitation, I mean that Rivers's and Hocart's corpus can and should be used. As Kapferer notes, 'an ethnographic study is never completed and is always open to possibilities not even dreamed … continually a potential source of new understanding' (Kapferer 2007: 84). Their materials con-stitute a miniscule, but significant, part of anthropology's contribution to understanding humanity, standing against centuries of representational violence directed at New Georgians, an instance of how anthropological work can stand out against the normal run of knowledge, despite being marked by the tropes of its time.

By critique, I refer to the ongoing need for re-evaluation, and a vigilantly critical eye on ourselves as ethnographers and on a discipline that aspires to encompass humanity, challenging our ethnocentric ways, without losing sight of the liberating aspects of its imperative. Such re-evaluations, as Kapferer, notes, refuse to suppress 'valuable information regarding human creative possibility' (Kapferer 2007: 91–92 n.9; see also Knauft 1999: 15) while equally refusing to condone the conditions of its collection or to be confined to the world-views and interpretive limitations of its collectors.

And generosity? Hassan calls for the reinstatement of 'certain ideas, certain words … that we have forgotten in academe … words like truth, trust, spirit … reciprocity and respect, sympathy and empathy' (Hassan 2003: 6). In particular, he suggests the need to find shared truths in a world of escalating essentialisms without reinstalling overarching 'truth'. It is in this context that he advocates an 'aesthetic of trust', the essential element to these shared truths, including 'the trust of intellectual courtesy' (Hassan 2003: 7). Hassan's call, phrased at several points in remarkably anthropo-logical terms, parallels my sense of the need for hermeneutic generosity in approaching our forebears, for imaginative sympathy, participant observa-tion in the minds of the past, a projection of ourselves, *sans* hindsight, into their research environments. This is what anthropologists of anthropology have intended in seeking to understand how 'viewpoints since criticized or rejected might once have seemed reasonable to reasonable men and women' (Stocking 1995: xvii). It is also what Tinoni Simbo mean when they describe their ancestors as 'good sinners'.

Many Tinoni Simbo acknowledge the difficulties of knowing how to evaluate their ancestors, given the contradictions entailed in celebrating the demise of heathenism and lamenting the losses represented by its defeat. So, too, trying to deal with Hocart and Rivers, I flounder – willing to extract useful material for my own work, unwilling to endorse their knowledge/power practices and acknowledging them as 'reasonable men' of an era that they transcend to an extent without achieving the impossible dream of escaping their cultural and social (and political) being, let alone the chimera of innocent research. Their western Solomons materials demand acknowledgement as provocative works of fine ethnographic observation, characterised by humane approaches by the standards of their time. Echoing Tinoni Simbo's acknowledgement that the past is a problematic time whose people, who enacted their dark ways, were their own kin, I am inclined to regard Rivers and Hocart as 'good imperialists of the time before reflexivity': as founders/ancestors of some good things that we should not lightly discard. Extraordinary for their time, they were inescapably of that time. Neither celebratory history of the lost saviours of anthropology, nor damnation of demon ideologues is as appropriate as recognising a pair of anthropologists who have enriched and frustrated my understanding of that nebulous thing, humanity.

Hocart's statement about theorists and their times in my epigraph can be diversely understood. It can be read as suggesting the limited ability of any of us to transcend the times in which we find ourselves. It can imply that individuals exemplify the best of their time or embody the sins of an era: colonial anthropologist = colonial mentality = colonising; heathen ancestor = heathen morality = sinful. It can evoke the situations in which individuals find themselves and to which they must respond: caught in escalating warfare, men become warriors; born in evolutionist times, an anthropologist responds to evolutionism. Hocart's observation also evokes kinship: the sorority (to bring him into this time) of collegial mutuality and generational egality; the intergenerational inheritance of riches or negative consequences. And it suggests inheritance: of vintage ethnographic materials bequeathed to the future, necessarily marked by their time. Analogous metaphors of kinship and descent apply on Simbo, connecting people to land where ancestors planted nut trees, laid down shrines or walked their founding travels, and to a heritage of ancestors who victoriously displayed their victims' skulls as testament to their political domination of others.

His metaphor evokes the entailments and constraints of descent, too. Our choices about our ancestors are constrained. As on Simbo, the ancestors are held to have shaped the land, so in anthropology our predecessors have inescapably founded our intellectual world. To an extent, though, we can choose our ancestors or how to treat them – retaining or dropping their names from genealogies, celebrating them as the founders of all that is good about a society or discipline, denigrating them as dark sinners or colonisers. We can make choices about whether and how to remember them. Simbo has a long history of selective memorialisation. An ancestor implored or venerated in prayers remained a member of the social collective. They could also be discarded, fading from collective memory and social life, the fate of all but the greatest. Some names persist in genealogies, many more are forgotten with the adoption of Christianity. So, too, intellectual histories – like Simbo ancestors, scholars may fall from grace with changing moral, political or conceptual times, or they may be granted a place in disciplinary memory. In terms of my present awareness, Hocart and Rivers trouble me in many ways, but I find myself appreciating them as ancestors entitled to my respect.

Acknowledgements

My warm thanks to Cato Berg and Edvard Hviding for initiating the intellectually stimulating process that resulted in this chapter and book. Versions of the chapter were presented at the anthropology seminar at the University of Auckland in May 2011 and to its social anthropology writing group (Marama Muru-Lanning, Julie Park, Chris Shore and Susanna Trnka) in 2012. I thank these colleagues for their critical insight, collegial engagement and productive suggestions for revision. Mike Goldsmith generously read it and commented on key points, and Judith Huntsman shared her extensive knowledge of the history of anthropology and with her usual grace encouraged me to rein in some of my more egregious oversimplifications. Finally, I thank two anonymous referees for their perceptive, sensible and, hopefully, effective suggestions.

Notes

1. Simbo is the present-day name of the place that Hocart and Rivers variously referred to as Eddystone or Mandegusu (variably spelt, meaning 'four districts'). In 1908, 'Simbo' referred to an islet, one of the four districts that is now referred to as Nusa Simbo. My own research on Simbo was conducted over some twenty-two months between 1990 and 1992.

2. There is also the question of what a particular anthropologist represents. An era? An entire discipline throughout its history? A particular theoretical moment?

3. Kuklick is a marked exception, perceiving a scholarly concern to preserve Rivers's reputation in face of 'aspects of [his] work that have fallen out of scholarly regard' (Kuklick 1991: 179 n.112).

4. Letter from Green to Rivers, undated, Haddon Papers, Cambridge University Library, Cambridge (hereafter C/HP), env. 12018. Letter from Green to Rivers, 25 November 1909, C/HP, env. 12018.

5. Letter from Hocart to Rivers, 16 April 1909, C/HP, env. 2018.

6. Hocart, 'Chieftainship', unpublished manuscript, Arthur M. Hocart Papers, MS-Papers-0060-14. Alexander Turnbull Library, National Library of New Zealand, Wellington.

7. Hocart, 'Mbaire', unpublished manuscript, Arthur M. Hocart Papers, MS-Papers-0060-14. Alexander Turnbull Library, National Library of New Zealand, Wellington.

8. Sometimes they also became foci for contemplating social practice. Ziruviri (Njiruviri in Hocart's orthography), Hocart's key informant, for example, had a hunched back. When I showed his image to an old woman in one village, a few unmarried youth clustering around to look were initially interested in his face painting until she said dismissively, 'He was *qao* [referring to any, however slightly, disabled person]; he could help Mista Hoka [Hocart]; he had nothing [significant] to do'. This stimulated one young man to muse on the ironies of someone born into an important position and excluded from it, only to find a lasting 'name' in the highly valued literate accounts; in turn, this led to a discussion of contemporary disability and the loneliness of those who were unable to marry or assume important social positions because of their physical imperfections, side-tracking into issues of memory, the relationship of the ancestors to contemporary society and other topics.

   I was asked about Hocart several times. A few said that their parents or grandparents told them about 'Mista Hoka, who went about [wearing a loincloth] like everyone else', but this was often linked to claims of a more recent woman anthropologist going naked on Malaita and may be apocryphal. Still, the image of a participant-observing Hocart has its appeal. People seemed unaware of Rivers. I tend to assume that the differential interest reflected the dissemination of Hocart's Simbo articles in the *Journal of the Royal Anthropological Institute*.

9. Pels sees anthropology as so deeply rooted in colonialism that 'the anthropology of colonialism is also an anthropology of anthropology' (Pels 2008: 281).

10. The volume's significance is indicated by the number of later titular references to it: see Abu-Lughod (1991), Behar and Gordon (1995), and James, Hockey and Dawson (1997) for example.

11. Hocart opposed applied anthropology in the colonies (Kuklick 1991: 186–87).

12. *Pakeha* is a Maori term in common New Zealand usage, referring largely to New Zealanders of European descent, and thereby highlighting the origins of contemporary national inequalities in a history of colonial relationships. Self-identification as Pakeha can be a self-conscious acknowledgment of these facts. As an Australian now long-resident in New Zealand, and in the absence of an Australian equivalent, I use it in reference to both of my settler society incarnations.

13. Not just ancestors, of course, but dead people are sufficiently distant in time to provide examples of awful anthropology (or the awfulness of anthropology). In this context, it is notable that several colleagues have told me that their fieldnotes are to be suppressed or destroyed when they die.

14. Kuklick argues that diffusionists, of whom 'Rivers was … the most eminent spokesman', regarded relativism as 'nonsensical' (Kuklick 1991: 123).
15. See Stocking (1995: 216) for Rivers's non-refutation of the race concept, despite the evidence of his TSI colour testing.
16. See Kolshus (this volume) on Rivers dedicating *The History of Melanesian Society* to two of his islander helpers.
17. Revd J.F. Goldie deployed the trope of 'erstwhile savagery' throughout his half century as chairman of the Methodist Mission, and it recurs in almost competitively rhetorical accounts well into the twentieth century. Even in the 1990s, too many of my own kin insisted on calling Tinoni Simbo 'the natives', 'the blacks' and 'former cannibals (*sic*)', refusing to speak of them as 'people'. There are also more important issues than representation *qua* representation (Comaroff and Comaroff 1991: xiv; Knauft 1994). As Graeber (2006: 11) notes, the implications of Evans-Pritchard's Nuer fieldwork pale against the aerial bombardment to which they were subjected.

References

Abu-Lughod, L. 1991. 'Writing against Culture', in *Recapturing Anthropology: Working in the Present*, R.G. Fox (ed.), 137–62. Santa Fe, NM: School of American Research Press.

Asad, T. 1973. 'Introduction', in *Anthropology and the Colonial Encounter*, T. Asad (ed.), 9–20. London: Ithaca Press.

Barth, F. 2005. 'Britain and the Commonwealth', in *One Discipline, Four Ways: British, German, French, and American Anthropology*, F. Barth, A. Gingrich, R. Parkin and S. Silverman, 3–57. Chicago: University of Chicago Press.

Bayliss-Smith, T. 2006. 'Fertility and the Depopulation of Melanesia: Childlessness, Abortion and Introduced Disease in Simbo and Ontong Java, Solomon Islands', in *Population, Reproduction and Fertility in Melanesia*, S. Ulijaszek (ed.), 13–52. Oxford: Berghahn.

Behar, R., and D.A. Gordon (eds) 1995. *Women Writing Culture*. Berkeley: University of California Press.

Bunzl, M. 2005. 'Anthropology beyond Crisis: Toward an Intellectual History of the Extended Present', *Anthropology and Humanism* 30(2): 187–95.

Burke, E., and D. Prochaska. 2007. 'Rethinking the Historical Genealogy of Orientalism', *History and Anthropology* 18(2): 135–51.

Clifford, J. 1986. 'Introduction: Partial Truths', in *Writing Culture: The Poetics and Politics of Ethnography*, J. Clifford and G. Marcus (eds), 1–26. Berkeley: University of California Press.

Clifford, J., and G. Marcus (eds). 1986. *Writing Culture: The Poetics and Politics of Ethnography*. Berkeley: University of California Press.

Comaroff, J. and J. Comaroff 1991. *Of Revelation and Revolution Volume one: Christianity, Colonialism, and Consciousness in South Africa.* Chicago: University of Chicago Press.

di Leonardo, M. 1991. 'Gender, Culture, and Political Economy: Feminist Anthropology in Historical Perspective', in *Gender at the Crossroads of Knowledge: Feminist Anthropology in the Postmodern Era*, M. di Leonardo (ed.), 1–48. Berkeley: University of California Press.

Dureau, C. 2000. 'Skulls, *Mana* and Causality', *Journal of the Polynesian Society* 109(1): 71–98.

——— 2005. 'Keeping for Giving, Keeping for Keeping: Property Taboo on Simbo', in *A Polymath Anthropologist: Essays in Honour of Ann Chowning*, C. Gross, H.D. Lyons, and D.A. Counts (eds), 139–46. Auckland: Department of Anthropology.

Evans-Pritchard, E. E. 1939. Arthur Maurice Hocart: 1884–March 1939. *Man* 39: 131.

Fanon, F. 2008 [1952]. *Black Skin, White Masks*, trans. C.L. Markmann. London: Pluto Press.

Ferguson, J. 1999. *Expectations of Modernity: Myths and Meanings of Life on the Zambian Copperbelt*. Berkeley: University of California Press.

Goldsmith, M. 2005. 'Culture in Safety and in Danger', *Anthropological Forum* 15(3): 257–65.

Graeber, D. 2006. 'Beyond Power/Knowledge: An Exploration of the Relation of Power, Ignorance and Stupidity', Malinowski Memorial Lecture, 25 May. London School of Economics. Retrieved 25.10.2013 from: http://www2.lse. ac.uk/publicEvents/events/2006/20060328t1456z001.aspx

Harding, S. 1991. 'Representing Fundamentalism: The Problem of the Repugnant Cultural Other', *Social Research* 58(2): 373–93.

Hassan, I. 2003. 'Beyond Postmodernism: Toward an Aesthetic of Trust', *Angelaki* 8(1): 3–11.

Hilliard, D. 1978. *God's Gentlemen: A History of the Melanesian Mission, 1849–1942*. St Lucia: University of Queensland Press.

Hocart, A.M. 1922. 'The Cult of the Dead in Eddystone of the Solomons', *Journal of the Royal Anthropological Institute* 52: 71–112, 259–305.

——— 1929. 'Modern Critique', *Man* 29: 138–43.

——— 1931. 'Warfare in Eddystone of the Solomon Islands', *Journal of the Royal Anthropological Institute* 61: 301–24.

——— 1933. *The Progress of Man: A Short Survey of His Evolution, His Customs and His Works*. London: Methuen.

——— 1935. 'The Purpose of Ritual', *Folklore* 46(4): 343–49.

——— 1937. 'Fishing in Eddystone Island', *Journal of the Royal Anthropological Institute* 67: 33–41.

Hviding, E. 2003. 'Disentangling the *Butubutu* of New Georgia: Cognatic Kinship in Thought and Action', in *Oceanic Socialities and Cultural Forms: Ethnographies of Experience*, I. Hoëm and S. Roalkvam (eds), 71–113. Oxford: Berghahn.

James, A., J. Hockey and A. Dawson (eds) 1997. *After Writing Culture: Epistemology and Praxis in Contemporary Anthropology.* London: Routledge.

Kapferer, B. 2007. 'Anthropology and the Dialectic of Enlightenment: A Discourse on the Definition and Ideals of a Threatened Discipline', *Australian Journal of Anthropology,* 18(1): 72–95.

Keesing, R.M. 1984. 'Rethinking *Mana*', *Journal of Anthropological Research* 40(1): 137–56.

Kleinman, A. 2006. *What Really Matters: Living a Moral Life amidst Uncertainty and Danger.* Cary, NC: Oxford University Press.

Knauft, B. 1994. 'Pushing Anthropology Past the Posts: Critical Notes on Cultural Anthropology and Cultural Studies as Influenced by Postmodernism and Existentialism', *Critique of Anthropology* 14(2): 117–52.

———— 1999. *From Primitive to Postcolonial in Melanesia and Anthropology.* Ann Arbor: University of Michigan Press.

Kuklick, H. 1991. *The Savage Within: The Social History of British Anthropology, 1885-1945.* Cambridge: Cambridge University Press.

Langham, I. 1981. *The Building of British Social Anthropology: W.H.R. Rivers and His Cambridge Disciples in the Development of Kinship Studies, 1898-1931.* Dordrecht: Reidel.

Matthewman, S., and D. Hoey 2006. 'What Happened to Postmodernism?' *Sociology* 40(3): 529–47.

Memmi, A. 2003 [1965]. *The Colonizer and the Colonized,* 3rd ed. London: Earthscan.

Pels, P. 2008. 'What Has Anthropology Learned from the Anthropology of Colonialism?' *Social Anthropology* 16(3): 280–99.

Richards, T. 1992. 'Archive and Utopia', *Representations* 37: 104–35.

Rivers, W.H.R. 1914. *The History of Melanesian Society,* Vol. 1. Cambridge: Cambridge University Press.

———— 1917. 'The Government of Subject Peoples', in *Science and the Nation,* A.C. Seward (ed.), 302–28. Cambridge: Cambridge University Press.

———— 1922. 'The Psychological Factor', in *Essays on the Depopulation of Melanesia,* W.H.R. Rivers (ed.), 84–113. Cambridge: Cambridge University Press.

———— 1926. *Psychology and Ethnology.* London: Kegan Paul, Trench and Trubner.

Rosaldo, R. 1986. 'From the Door of His Tent: The Fieldworker and the Inquisitor', in *Writing Culture: The Poetics and Politics of Ethnography,* J. Clifford, and G. Marcus, (eds), 77–97. Berkeley: University of California Press.

Roseberry, W. 1996. 'The Unbearable Lightness of Anthropology', *Radical History Review* 65: 5–25.

Sapir, E. 2006 [1945]. 'Anthropology and Sociology', in *Anthropology in Theory: Issues in Epistemology,* H.L. Moore and T. Sanders (eds), 68–76. Oxford: Blackwell.

Scheper-Hughes, N. 1992. *Death Without Weeping: The Violence of Everyday Life in Brazil*. Berkeley: University of California Press.

Scubla, L. 2002. 'Hocart and the Royal Road to Anthropological Understanding', *Social Anthropology* 10(3): 359–76.

Slobodin, R. 1997 [1978]. *W.H.R. Rivers: Pioneer Anthropologist, Psychiatrist of 'The Ghost Road'*, rev. edn. Stroud: Sutton.

Smith, L.T. 2006. *Decolonising Methodologies: Research and Indigenous Peoples*, 9th ed. London: Zed.

Spencer, J. 2001. 'Ethnography after Postmodernism', in *Handbook of Ethnography*, P. Atkinson, A. Coffey, S. Delamont, J. Lofland and L. Lofland (eds), 443–52. London: Sage.

Stocking, G.W. 1982 [1968]. *Race, Culture, and Evolution: Essays in the History of Anthropology*. Chicago: University of Chicago Press.

———— 1995. *After Tylor: British Social Anthropology 1881–1956*. Madison: University of Wisconsin Press.

Trencher, S. 2002. 'The Literary Project and Representations of Anthropology', *Anthropological Theory* 2(2): 211–31.

Urry, J. 1972. '"Notes and Queries on Anthropology" and the Development of Field Methods in British Anthropology, 1870–1920', *Proceedings of the Royal Anthropological Institute of Great Britain and Northern Ireland* 72: 45–57.

White, G.M. 1991. *Identity through History: Living Stories in a Solomon Islands Society*. Cambridge: Cambridge University Press.

2

Across the New Georgia Group

A.M. Hocart's Fieldwork as Inter-island Practice

◆●◆

Edvard Hviding

Ethnography, Hocart Style: Cautious Methodology and Descriptive Overload

In circles beyond Pacific anthropology (e.g. Stocking 1995: 119; Barth 2005: 15–18; see also Dureau, this volume) it is recognised that the fieldwork carried out by A.M. Hocart and W.H.R. Rivers in the Solomon Islands in 1908 was of extraordinary quality for its time, that it was – through Hocart's original developments of field methodology – a founding instance of what came to be called participant observation, and that it provided important ethnographic materials for Rivers's two-volume magnum opus *The History of Melanesian Society* (1914). Nevertheless, the fieldwork itself – easily the first example of what modern anthropological method as many stranded, participatory cross-cultural encounter and practice was destined to become – has remained obscure in the history of the discipline, despite the considerable yet contested space later occupied by both protagonists in that history. While Hocart and Rivers are remembered each in his own way, it is not for the fact that they lived and worked together on a small Melanesian island, with side trips to other localities within the New Georgia group of islands, for much of a year very early in the twentieth century. In fact, most of the detailed descriptive materials from the extraordinary ethnographic experiment of the Percy Sladen Trust Expedition remained unpublished until 1922 – significantly, the year of Rivers's premature death. It was then that Hocart published the first article in what was to be a fifteen-year series of detailed descriptive accounts of the people of 'Eddystone' in the *Journal of the Royal Anthropological Institute* (Hocart 1922, 1925, 1931, 1935, 1937).

As discussed by Hviding and Berg (this volume), Hocart must have embarked on this publication project in 1920 (after the Percy Sladen Trust had rejected his request for funding for publication in the United States, and before he moved to Ceylon in 1921). We do not know whether there had been any prior communication between the two one-time fellow fieldworkers specifically about Hocart's publishing agenda, although we do know that the two met at the meeting of the British Association for the Advancement of Science in Bournemouth in September 1919, at which point in time their scholarly interests seem to have strongly diverged (Bayliss-Smith, this volume). In 1909, Rivers had stated optimistically in a brief report to the Percy Sladen Trust that there were plans for '[a] book by Mr Hocart and myself on "The Western Solomon Islands", probably in two volumes'.[1] But that massive joint work never eventuated, and in the introduction to his first *JRAI* article Hocart observed that 'the material of either of us published separately must be incomplete, but publication has already been so long delayed that it is better to publish only a fragment than withhold material any longer' (Hocart 1922: 72).[2] As if to compensate for a co-authored monograph that was never to be, Hocart's five *JRAI* articles about the Western Solomons (the first one in two parts) range very widely in terms of topics and present rich empirical materials in monographic fashion. But unlike the theoretically ambitious character of Rivers's major publication after the expedition (Rivers 1914), Hocart's texts are intensely descriptive, and not a few readers might classify them as idiosyncratic, light on theory and characterised by information overload – certainly when viewed from the perspective of twenty-first-century scholarly publishing.

These dense articles may indeed seem too confused and incoherent for the preferences of some. Not so for others: those who have ethnographic or everyday experience of the New Georgia group are likely to recognise the apparent confusion within Hocart's texts as precisely indicative of well-known patterns of life in these geographically dispersed but cultural- ly and socially well-connected islands. As Dureau (this volume) remarks, Hocart's texts are characterised by a 'redundancy [that] is remarkably helpful'. In the introduction to 'Medicine and Witchcraft in Eddystone of the Solomons', Hocart himself gives a rationale for his style which places considerable demands on the interested reader: 'I have refrained as far as possible from all comment, even on obscurities in the [vernacular] texts ...

the translations are for the general reader; the specialist should learn the language and read them in the original' (Hocart 1925: 229).[3]

For all the information overload, there are also passages of profound reflection in Hocart's *JRAI* series. In a brief discussion about the difficulty of finding out with any certainty the nature of the jurisdiction, rank and so forth of the many village-level chiefs encountered at Simbo, he commented that 'here we are not dealing with hard facts, hard and fast conceptions, such as are possible in handicrafts and in speculation, but fluid customs, elusive emanations of tact and experience' (Hocart 1922: 77). These are some of the foundations of how what I here propose to call Hocart's 'cautious field methodology' came to be so novel, and why the methodological approach itself is perhaps the greatest legacy of his work in the Solomons. Hocart largely refrained from over-generalising, followed the leads and initiatives of his informants, and mostly avoided references to such a unit of homogeneity as 'the Simbo', unlike the generalising impulse shown in later famous ethnographers' confident and authoritative portraits of 'the Trobriand Islanders', 'the Nuer' and so forth. While the latter uses of 'ethnographic authority' have been scrutinised by postmodernist critiques that question this very authority (e.g. Rosaldo 1986), it was the proponents of such an approach that gained power as social anthropology developed as a discipline. Meanwhile, Hocart's ability to acknowledge, understand and represent the inter-local worlds of the people among whom he lived, quite possibly the strongest example of the lasting value of the 1908 fieldwork, was forgotten. It took almost a hundred years for his contribution as an important founder of anthropology's hallmark method of participant observation to be recognised, albeit briefly, by Fredrik Barth, one of the greatest fieldworkers of modern social anthropology (Barth 2005: 15–16).

Connections and Encounters in the 'New Georgia Group'

The Western Solomons and the New Georgia group, of which the small island of Simbo (the 'Eddystone' of Hocart and Rivers) is the outlying south-western part, constitute a unique geographical formation in the Solomon Islands archipelago, in that a large number of mainly high volcanic islands, some fringed by huge sheltered lagoons, are clustered unevenly together in ways that facilitate maritime mobility among them.[4] In an assessment of early encounters between the islanders of Simbo and passing European ships, Nicholas Thomas (2010: 57) argues that at the time of contact with Europeans, and their ships and political economy, the people of Simbo did not constitute any sort of circumscribed 'island society'. Instead, the islanders lived lives that were 'truly archipelagic', with overseas travel and inter-island relationships being fundamental to cultural beliefs and social, political and economic practice.

The very locations of the 1908 fieldwork, although centred on Simbo, in fact had a profoundly inter-island quality. The Simbo informants told stories of wide geographical scope, and vexatious questions of cultural difference in the face of assumed coherence were taken up frequently by the ethnographers, particularly Hocart. His concern and sometimes exasperation over disagreement over what at base seemed to be shared perceptions, between informants from Simbo and, for example, Roviana, and even among people on Simbo (some of whom were not from that island), emerge regularly in his notes and publications. For the New Georgians, such apparent disagreement would have been no mystery, as core cultural themes were, and still are, known to exhibit considerable diversity across and even within the islands. This reflects what I propose to call vernacular paradigms of 'here but not there', alternately 'here but also there'. It is a form of complexity that must have taken Rivers and Hocart by some surprise, but which soon caused rapid methodological development.

Just 120 years before the Percy Sladen Trust Expedition, the New Georgia Islands were uncharted and unknown to Western navigators. On 31 July 1788, the Royal Navy convict transport *Alexander*, homeward bound from Botany Bay, met with the island of Makira in the south-eastern Solomons, and from there took a north-westerly course along the southern coast of most of the Solomons archipelago, unable to find passage northwards into open ocean until reaching, on 8 August, what later became known as the Bougainville Strait. Believing that the mountainous coasts followed during a week's sailing indicated one continuous land mass, Lieutenant Shortland, who was in command of the *Alexander*, charted the ship's passage and gave the name 'New Georgia' both to this 'large tract of land' and to the adjacent land mass on the other side of the 'Treasury Isles' through which a passage to the north was found (Stockdale 1789; Dureau 2001). It is significant that the *Alexander* also experienced several hours of substantial contact with islanders, precisely at Simbo. On 6 August:

> ... some canoes were seen with Indians in them, who came close up to the ship without any visible apprehension. Ropes were thrown to them over the stern, of which they took hold, and suffered the ship to tow them along; in this situation they willingly exchanged a kind of rings which they wore on their arms, small rings of bone, and beads of their own manufacture, for nails, beads, and other trifles, giving however a manifest preference to whatever was made of iron. Gimlets were most acceptable, but they were also pleased with nails, and pieces of iron hoops. They dealt very fairly, not betraying the least desire to steal or to defraud. (Stockdale 1789, quoted by Dureau 2001: 133)

It was also 'understood from the natives that they called the island from which they came Simboo'. Dureau (2001: 132) has analysed this encounter in terms of how the local responses described by Shortland evoke 'an assertive solicitation of further engagement'. Even at the time of what may have been their first encounter with Europeans, the people of Simbo were not unwilling to engage with newcomers in useful ways.

Lieutenant Shortland's 'New Georgia' grew increasingly smaller during the nineteenth century as traders, whalers and other navigators travelled throughout the major islands of the Solomons group and contributed to the gradual elaboration of his first coastal chart. On 12 December 1803, fifteen years after Shortland's visit, the American whaling ship *Patterson* (six months out of Providence, Rhode Island) passed 'the islands mentioned in the chart under the term of nameless Isles', and in the night, 'while running along the largest and most eastward of the nameless Isles saw a light on the shore – from this circumstance we suppose it to be inhabited although there was no other appearance which would induce one to suppose it'.[5] There were evidently expectations that night of encountering 'natives'. Judging from positions given in the log of the *Patterson*, the 'nameless Isles' were the islands of Rennell and Bellona. Passing between them into open sea and sailing fast on a strong north-easterly breeze, next day they saw 'the land of New Georgia bearing down from N. to N.N.E.', and on 14 December, Captain Aborn of the *Patterson* had seen enough to conclude that '[t]he land called by the general name of New Georgia is made up of a range of Islands neartogether [*sic*] and running from N.W. to S.E. it is in general very high and mountainous – the clouds frequently hang nearly halfway down the mountain – I think from its situation it must be a very fine country'. This conclusion established New Georgia once and for all as an island group. The following day, Aborn found his ship becalmed and 'nearly surrounded by a number of Islands which surprised us considerably as our charts do not agree with the situation of the lands'. To intensify this perhaps unnerving experience, 'at 7 AM upwards of thirty canoes full of men (nearly 200) came alongside from the westernmost island which they called Simboo'. However, they were 'entirely unarmed – one spear being the only weapon we saw – after preparing ourselves in some manner /in case of an attack/ proceeded to trade with them giving them bottles, knives, nails, Iron Hoops &c in exchange for Cocoa nuts, Trinkets, Plantains &c – they are a very handsome set of men'. Captain Aborn's log gives a detailed and fascinating account of the two days during which the *Patterson* lay becalmed off Simbo, and intensive interaction and trade took place with the inhabitants. This may be the first sustained period of interaction between any people of New Georgia and Europeans.

Visits by whaling ships continued, and from the 1840s traders also called regularly at Simbo, which had developed a reputation for friendly trade and obtained a role as a contact point for trade more widely in New Georgia. When Scottish trading captain Andrew Cheyne arrived at 'New Georgia' on 1 February 1844, he steered straight for 'Eddystone Island' where he was 'boarded by three Englishmen living on the island, who brought the two principal chiefs with them' (Cheyne 1971: 303). By then, working relations between the Simbo people and agents of the global political economy were, it appeared, well established. After the rapid establishment on Eddystone of a station for the collection and storage of bêche-de-mer, on 3 February Cheyne 'made all sail for New Georgia, to fill up our water and trade for tortoise-shell' (Cheyne 1971: 304). After a remarkably slow passage, '[o] n the evening of the 5th [the ship] arrived at New Georgia' (Cheyne 1971: 305). It is clear that Cheyne perceived 'New Georgia' to be the large land some 70 kilometres east of Simbo.

By the time of the Royal Navy's extensive survey of the Western Solomons in the 1890s, the view was that 'New Georgia consists of a group of islands, closely adjoining, roughly occupying an east-south-east direction for about 80 miles ... The largest island has no general native name' (Somerville 1897: 358). That the main island later referred to simply as 'New Georgia' has no native name is certainly correct; it is composed of a number of named districts. The navigators' name of 'The New Georgian Group' persisted, and was also employed by Hocart in his first published work of detailed ethnography (Hocart 1922: 73), although his geographical scope was limited in its eastwards extent, not including the large district of 'Ulusaghe', later known as Marovo, with which the 'Eddystone' people maintained relations of enmity and sometime alliance.

Understanding Diversity: Death, Life and Colonialism in the New Georgia Islands

In his first article on the ethnography of Eddystone, Hocart addressed the inter-island multiplicity of perspectives among the inhabitants of the New Georgia group:

> It was afterwards explained that the Ganongan practice was followed in some details; in Eddystone only a chief's jaw is tied; in Ganonga it is done for great and small; the tying of small rings on the forehead is not done at all in Narovo. A Lungan objected to burial in the ground because a buried man can't eat pudding, whereas if the head is in a skull-house he can. (Hocart 1922: 91)

This precisely conveys how ethnographic observations of burial customs on Eddystone Island in 1908 necessitated the connection, by both ethnographer and informants, of the apparently 'local' to cultural repertoires beyond that island, in this case the larger neighbouring island of Ranongga (rendered as 'Ganonga') to the north, of which the district of Lungga ('Lunga') is part. The many stages of a funeral up to 'the soul's departure' (Hocart 1922: 93) – stated by the 'best informants ... as [taking place after] thirty-six nights', at which time the soul of the deceased also travels over the sea by setting off for Sonto, the land of the dead to the north-west – form a centrepiece in Hocart's comprehensive descriptive account of the 'cult of the dead' in Eddystone.

Five deaths occurred on Eddystone while Hocart and Rivers lived there in 1908, and although the two fieldworkers were only able to fully observe and follow one of the associated sequences of funerary gatherings, all the deceased – three men, one widow and one new-born child, whose deaths occurred during May to July 1908 – presumably departed for Sonto to meet with the 'ghosts' from 'Eddystone, Ganonga Island, Vella-Lavella, Choiseul' (Hocart 1922: 95). In this manner, the spirits of the dead from all those islands in the western and north-western parts of the Solomons converge on Sonto, which must lie in Bougainville or by the Bougainville Strait, 'for Bougainville men are described as Sonto men, and armlets from the Shortlands as Sonto armlets. There is a volcano there' (Hocart 1922: 95).

The inter-island nature of life in the Western Solomons emerges from these early field materials most of all by way of the dead, who lead a mirror existence of that of their living descendants, an existence in which the mobility and mixture of individuals from different islands seem like an amplified version of everyday life in New Georgia. Hocart conveys how the dead of the islands of the north-western Solomons travel further north-west to Bougainville and settle there, where they 'sleep in the daytime and go about at night ... There they work and plan; Sonto men tell how they have heard, but not seen, the ghosts working; old men have seen them building canoes and cutters' (Hocart 1922: 95). Actually, the north-west-erly travel of the dead is a common pattern in the Solomon Islands; for example, most peoples of northern Malaita associate the 'land of the dead' with the small island of Ramos between Malaita and Isabel, where the dead 'lead a life much like that of living humans: they live in villages, raise taro and pigs' (Keesing 1982: 110).

As an anthropologist with a long-term engagement in the old region of Ulusaghe at the far south-eastern end of the New Georgia group, I am particularly interested in the ancestors of mainland New Georgia, Marovo Lagoon, Vangunu and Gatokae.[6] Those ancestors have their strongest over-seas connection to the land of the dead of the Ulusaghe people, which is, predictably, also located to the northwest: but for them it is not faraway Sonto, but the district of Ove on Simbo (Hviding 1996: 236–37). While in New Georgia all the dead depart and travel in what we call a north-westerly direction, that travel conforms to vernacular geographical concepts. In the Marovo language, this direction is referred to as *jorovoani* – 'where the sun sets'; in local cartography it also defined as 'down'. How appropriate it seems for the dead to depart their homes and travel down towards where the sun sets, which in terms of local histories of migration (supported by research in Oceanic prehistory) is also the direction from which people in the Solomons once came to their islands. Hence the dead of Marovo leave to go and live 'down' at Ove, a far from hospitable place of sulphurous fumes and hot volcanic springs.

Through the ancestors of Marovo and their obvious connections to Simbo, these two geographical extremes of the New Georgia group are my points of departure and fields of investigation. The particular observation I wish to highlight concerning the ethnographic research carried out in 1908 by Rivers and Hocart relates to certain qualities I see in the latter's published and unpublished fieldwork materials. My text therefore includes substantial quotes from Hocart's own writings in order to convey some of the essence of his texts. It is my argument that a deficiency in Hocart's published articles of descriptive ethnographic 'coherence' does not reflect bad methodology, but rather demonstrates a close involvement and deep rapport with the islanders and their own life worlds, in ways that were as yet unheard of in 1908 (see also Dureau, this volume).

If we look at a map of the Solomon Islands, we see the positioning of the New Georgia Islands in the context of the larger Solomons archipelago (see Figure 2.1). Unlike any other part of the Solomons archipelago, the New Georgia group is a compact, only partially dispersed gathering of smaller and larger islands, grouped together in an irregular fashion that conveys natural histories of volcanic activity and coral-reef building. These forces have generated a complex spatial context for human activity in the New Georgia group, which is perhaps borne out most forcefully by the almost total reliance of New Georgians on maritime travel for interaction beyond the village. The sea is the main road, or in the vernaculars, the 'path' (Hviding 1996: 165–66). New Georgians have sometimes been referred to as better paddlers than walkers; Hocart had the impression that they travelled quickly on water, but that '[t]heir legs are inadequate, probably because they never go by land if they can go by sea' (Hocart 1922: 74), a direct reference to the overwhelmingly maritime cast of everyday life in these islands.

It was quite an extraordinary combination of converging circumstances that Hocart and Rivers encountered at Simbo in 1908, which they had to manage both methodologically and practically. In 1908 the islanders still maintained many elements of their religious beliefs and medicine, so that magic and witchcraft remained as everyday practice. On the other hand,

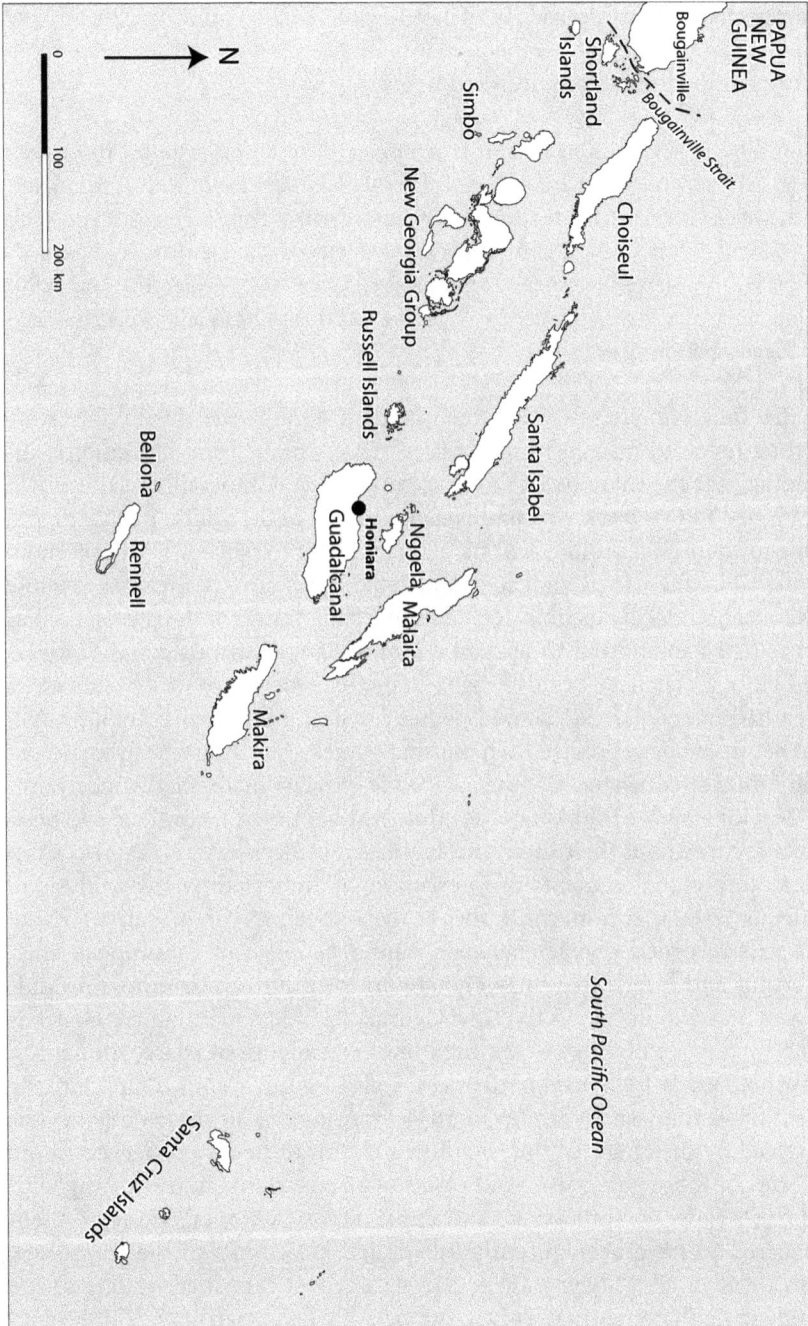

Figure 2.1: The Solomon Islands archipelago (map by K.H. Sjøstrøm, University of Bergen).

warfare had all but ceased, inter-island politics appeared moribund, and the predominant local perspective was that times were not good at all, as conveyed in Hocart's unpublished notes:

> British rule has put an end to head hunting and all the 'big fellow *kaikai*' [large-scale feasts] that were connected with it, and has thus reduced the chief to a station little above that of the commoner; as Gumi remarked with regret: 'Formerly they had big chiefs; now it is all over'. Tiro Ite is somewhat indignant at the change: '[F]ormerly the chiefs ordered their men to cut canoes and went out together; that was before my time; now it is not done: the chiefs are dullards (*tuturu*) and like commoners (*tinoni homboro*)'.[7]

In that time of rapid transition, the islanders of the Western Solomons were getting involved instead in agendas of trade, colonialism and empire, including – at the margins of those agendas – the ethnographic experiment examined in this book. The ambivalent attitude of the Simbo people of that time to their own culture and its place in history resulted, I believe, in an astute willingness to provide long and detailed accounts to the strange white visitors about local customs deemed soon to be things of the past as well as genealogies amounting to tales of social ontology.[8] In this context, Rivers and Hocart may have been strange not because they were white – for white men had interacted with Simbo people for over a hundred years already – but because they expressed such unusual interests at a time when the present and future circumstances of the local were growing increasingly uncertain.

Not long before the visit of the ethnographers, New Georgians had been quite secure about their local and regional positions, as well as in control over more global contexts of interaction, as indicated by the analysis of Dureau (2001), summarised above, by a sequence of narratives about the first recorded contact between Simbo people and a European ship. Peaceful and inquisitive early encounters with Europeans notwithstanding, in pre-colonial times the New Georgia Islanders maintained what was seen by outside observers as a high level of endemic warfare, thought to pose an equally high level of danger for visiting Europeans. I have already mentioned the visit to Simbo in 1844 by Andrew Cheyne. While he was received by the chiefs of the island in a civil way, he also observed in the villages of those chiefs 'the wall plates of a large canoe house strung with human heads, of both sexes, and apparently of all ages. Many of them appeared to have been recently killed, and the marks of the tomahawk were seen in all' (Cheyne 1971: 303–4). He was informed by one of the resident Englishmen that only a few days earlier, warriors of Simbo had returned from a 'war expedition' with 'no less than ninety three human heads' (Cheyne 1971: 304).

After peaceful interaction during the earlier years, from the 1880s onwards relationships between islanders and visiting Europeans became more violent. Even as late as 1908, punitive actions were carried out in the Western Solomons by Royal Navy gun vessels in reprisal for the killing of Europeans (see Bennett 1987: 527–29). By that time, headhunting had all but ceased throughout New Georgia, after a combination of colonial repression and indigenous initiative (Hviding 1996: 109–13), and Methodist missionaries had become well established in Roviana Lagoon, soon expanding throughout the Western Solomons and in competition with agents of Seventh-day Adventist faith. On Simbo, some aspects of old religion was still being practised, but judging from informants quoted by Hocart there was a widespread local belief that those customs were fast becoming obsolete. Hocart commented how the 'activities of chiefs had mostly ceased with head-hunting', and their main informant Ziruviri complained: 'No one is mighty now: they are all alike, they have no money; they cannot go head-hunting; they all "stop nothing" [Melanesian Pidgin: 'lead passive, uneventful lives']' (Hocart 1922: 79).

Methodology in the Making: Approaching 'Eddystone' and 'New Georgia'

As an ethnographer of another part of the Western Solomons, I did not give much attention to the ethnographic materials of Hocart and Rivers until after my first long-term fieldwork in Marovo Lagoon during 1986/87. Granted, their work in 1908 did form a part of my wider horizon of knowledge, but back in Norway after my fieldwork, and with no access to the unpublished manuscripts left by Hocart, my engagement with these anthropological ancestors was restricted to brief forays into Hocart's published articles. My main concern at the time was with Marovo Lagoon, which in 1986 was still largely undocumented anthropologically, except for a Victorian attempt (armed with *Notes and Queries on Anthropology*) by Lieutenant H.B.T. Somerville of the Royal Navy's survey ship HMS *Penguin*. While engaged in extensive hydrographical surveys of the New Georgia area between July 1893 and February 1895, which included long periods of camping with small parties of seamen in several coastal villages around Marovo Lagoon among local people still not 'pacified', Somerville collected a wide range of ethnographic materials, including hundreds of ritual and everyday objects now kept at the Pitt-Rivers Museum in Oxford. He published a comprehensive article on the ethnography of New Georgia in the *Journal of the Royal Anthropological Institute* (Somerville 1897).

In the longer run, I engaged more closely with Hocart's published corpus on 'Eddystone' as well as with the unpublished materials as part of my expanding immersion into the wider inter-island field of the New Georgia group. Anthropological work in New Georgia cannot be confined to single islands, simply because people's lives and beliefs are not. There is acute awareness among New Georgians of the existence of themselves in the local as being fundamentally constituted by the non-local. This is about more than just an outwards-oriented world-view; it involves the fundamental idea that localised phenomena are produced in continuous dialogue between the endogenous and exogenous. Any anthropologist working anywhere in the New Georgia group is faced with the prominent local notion that 'everything' may actually have come from 'somewhere else' – a 'here but also there' paradigm that consistently implies non-local origins, and considerable local appetite for that which is foreign or 'from overseas'.

From this I have come to realise that Hocart's published and unpublished works constitute, in ways not widely recognised, an extraordinary background for analysing inter-island relations in the history of Island Melanesia. The complexity of this history is exemplified particularly well by the tangled and twisted archipelago of New Georgia and its lagoons and outlying islands, wherein Simbo and Marovo form the outermost perimeters, but are closely connected through life and death. The inter-island cosmology of New Georgians also includes their immediate major single-island neighbours of Choiseul and Isabel to the north. There are opportunities offered by Hocart's materials for examining continuities and discontinuities in the Western Solomons from a regional perspective, through which these islands are conceived of as a rather special corner of the Solomons archipelago. To me, as an ethnographer of Marovo Lagoon, Hocart's materials allow for comparative interpretations of pan-New Georgian cultural concepts from the twin vantage points of my own fieldwork from 1986 onwards in Marovo to the far east, and the early twentieth-century fieldwork of Rivers and Hocart in Simbo to the far west.

Vernacular conceptualisations of space and direction are important in this regard. A number of specific east–west, up–down, sunrise–sunset connections are reflected in important traditions across the New Georgia group. In Marovo, it is widely held that *Canarium* nuts, which are so important locally, originally came from Simbo. According to one iconic tale, the nuts were brought to Marovo from Simbo by a very helpful domesticated fruit bat named Vekuveku (Hviding 1995: 3–25). But the ultimate connection is the final one: when people of old Marovo died, they went to Ove on Simbo. Still today, in thoroughly Christian postcolonial Marovo, the expression *la pa Ove* ('go to Ove') remains a euphemism for death. I mentioned how the dead of Simbo were reported to Hocart as always departing for Sonto, further down towards the Bougainville Strait and beyond. Hocart's study of the 'cult of the dead' included reports about much interaction amongst the 'ghosts' of the dead of Simbo, Ranongga, Vella Lavella and Choiseul in their shared land at Sonto. They interacted with each other – and some even cooked copra in Bougainville in order to sell it to the ghosts of white traders (Hocart 1922: 95). The dead of Marovo, however, went to Simbo. One might speculate how the dead who left Marovo and travelled to Simbo, usually in a stone canoe piloted by older ancestral spirits, experienced their new 'life' at Ove, being invisible to the living people of Simbo but relating and interacting among themselves as ancestral beings. Probably, as Hocart reports for their fellows in Sonto, they would have to 'sleep in the daytime and go about at night' (Hocart 1922: 95). In New Georgia, as in the Solomons more widely, one people's land of the dead is another people's territory and the contemporary cultural landscape of everyday life.

How to deal with such intense connectivity beyond any single island locale? I wish to highlight Hocart's singularly well-adapted methodological approach to the inter-island nature of ostensibly local phenomena – a pattern that he must have found at times to be exasperatingly complex. As this chapter proceeds, I shall show how Hocart's 1908 materials from Simbo connect to oral histories from Marovo, and I shall discuss aspects of Hocart's methodology and epistemology with regard to the opportunities his materials give for comparison in time and space. It is significant that Hocart's snapshots and deeper portraits are of New Georgians who were in 1908 situated between the pre-colonial and the colonial, and who were acutely aware of their predicament. Simbo people talked to Hocart about the old ways; they were nostalgic and not a little concerned that things were no longer as they used to be. We have seen how informants commented that formerly great men were no longer active; there was nothing much to do, and there was depression in the land. The early twentieth century was a sombre stage in the history of Tinoni Simbo (see Dureau, this volume), and so the way in which they received their two ethnographically minded visitors was most certainly influenced by the specific historical situation they lived in.

The account of the fieldwork given by Hocart in his first major ethnographic publication (Hocart 1922: 71–73; see also Hviding and Berg, this volume) enables us to visualise fieldwork as event and methodology as social interaction. Hocart's account conveys some of the essential grounding of fieldwork in ways that invite discussion about postmodern methodologies, and not simply in terms of postmodernist critiques of anthropology. Hocart was thorough and consistent in naming his informants and positioning them socially, situating and attributing their statements, qualifying one statement made by someone with another made by someone else, and so forth. And so the apparent incoherence that characterises Hocart's published articles on Simbo – a certain measure of ethnographic overload – is actually the end product of a constant process of checking, validating, comparing and qualifying, always referring to something that may be different among somebody else or somewhere else. Such is the nature of things in the New Georgia group, but Hocart's grasp of the fact seems to be in clear recognition that knowledge is unequally distributed and politically or otherwise controlled – thus foreshadowing critiques in the 1980s of the notion of culture as collective phenomena (e.g. Keesing 1987).

As discussed in the Introduction, the New Georgia 'group' was elusive for a long time in the cartographic terms of Western imperialism. The untidy gathering of small and large islands of which both Simbo and Marovo are part was not always self-evident as a 'group' in European views. By 1908, however, certain definitions had been established after more than a century of European contact with, and nautical charting of, the islands. It all started with Lieutenant Shortland's grand proposal that 'New Georgia' was a massive continuous landmass embracing most of the Solomons archipelago, and it culminated in the Royal Navy's extensive surveys during the 1890s, from which it was firmly concluded that 'New Georgia consists of a group of islands, closely adjoining, roughly occupying an east-south-east direction for about 80 miles' (Somerville 1897: 358). In his first published ethnographic account, Hocart gives his own contribution to the 'coming-into-being' of the New Georgia group, taking his lead from the work of navigators over a hundred years. He presents the New Georgia group in its twentieth-century sense, also providing a sketch map adapted from British Admiralty charts:

> Eddystone Island belongs to that group of the Solomons which I shall call the New Georgian, because New Georgia is the largest island, and appears to have been the political centre, at least that part of which is called Roviana (Rubiana of the charts). The other islands are Randuvu (Rendova on the charts), Montgomery Islands or Tetepare, Nduke (Kulambangara on the charts), Gizo, Vella-Lavella and Ganonga (Ronongo on the charts). (Hocart 1922: 73)

As indicated by the names in parentheses, Hocart himself attempted to correct the idiosyncratic spelling of island names on nineteenth-century nautical charts and navigation guides. He conveyed, but not in an entirely consistent way, what he believed to be the correct vernacular versions of these names, and went beyond the Royal Navy's reluctance to name the largest island of the group anything more specific than 'Main Island' (Somerville 1897: 358), suggesting that it should be called 'New Georgia', a name that has remained on maps and charts to this day. However, Hocart's attempt at vernacularisation was only partial, as his sketch map of the constituent locales of the 'New Georgian Group' missed its extensive eastern parts – Marovo Lagoon with the large islands of Vangunu and Gatokae. Only in his fieldnotes and published accounts of Simbo oral history do those eastern parts emerge under their proper New Georgian district name of Ulusaghe (e.g. Hocart 1922: 292; 1931: 304).[9]

There is a tension here between the imperialist cartographic preference for distinct, circumscribed, named islands, and the local topological means of reference that applied less to entire islands than to variously defined districts. The large island that came to be called 'New Georgia' had never been referred to by one name in the vernaculars of the area, instead being composed, in circular direction from the west, of the districts Roviana, Kusaghe, Kalikolo, Ulusaghe, Nono and Kalivarana (see Figure 2.2). For Hocart, this density of populated districts, each with its social, cultural and economic characteristics, must have posed a continuous challenge as the horizons of fieldwork expanded outwards from Simbo.

The Ethnography of Inter-island Cosmology

At this stage, it goes without saying that the New Georgia group has a long history of inter-island exchanges involving people, objects, practices and beliefs. Kinship, which is open-ended and bilateral throughout most of New Georgia, is at the core of this history (Hviding 2003). And so in their genealogical work, masterminded by Rivers, the two ethnographers were bound to try to follow the New Georgia area's never-ending complexity of bilateral kinship, whereby 'everybody is potentially related to everybody else', as is emphatically stated by New Georgians themselves. The genealogical method, therefore, did not turn out to be a clear-cut, unequivocal thing in New Georgia, as later critics have pointed out (Scheffler 1962; Berg, this volume). Neither Hocart nor Rivers managed to identify something so essential to New Georgia sociality as the *butubutu*, a pan-New Georgian, all-pervasive concept that refers to lineages, descent groups, kindreds and just about any social category or group formation involving relationships between parents and children and among siblings (Scheffler 1962; Hviding 2003). From my own work on the history of the New Georgian *butubutu*, I find it improbable that this concept and its associated social forms were absent in 1908.[10] Perhaps even more striking is the fact that in solidly matrilineal Vella Lavella they did not find the 'mother right' or 'maternal descent system' so central to the Percy Sladen Trust Expedition's aims as stated by Rivers (Berg, this volume). But, despite their shared lack of understanding and analysis of the structural levels of kinship in New

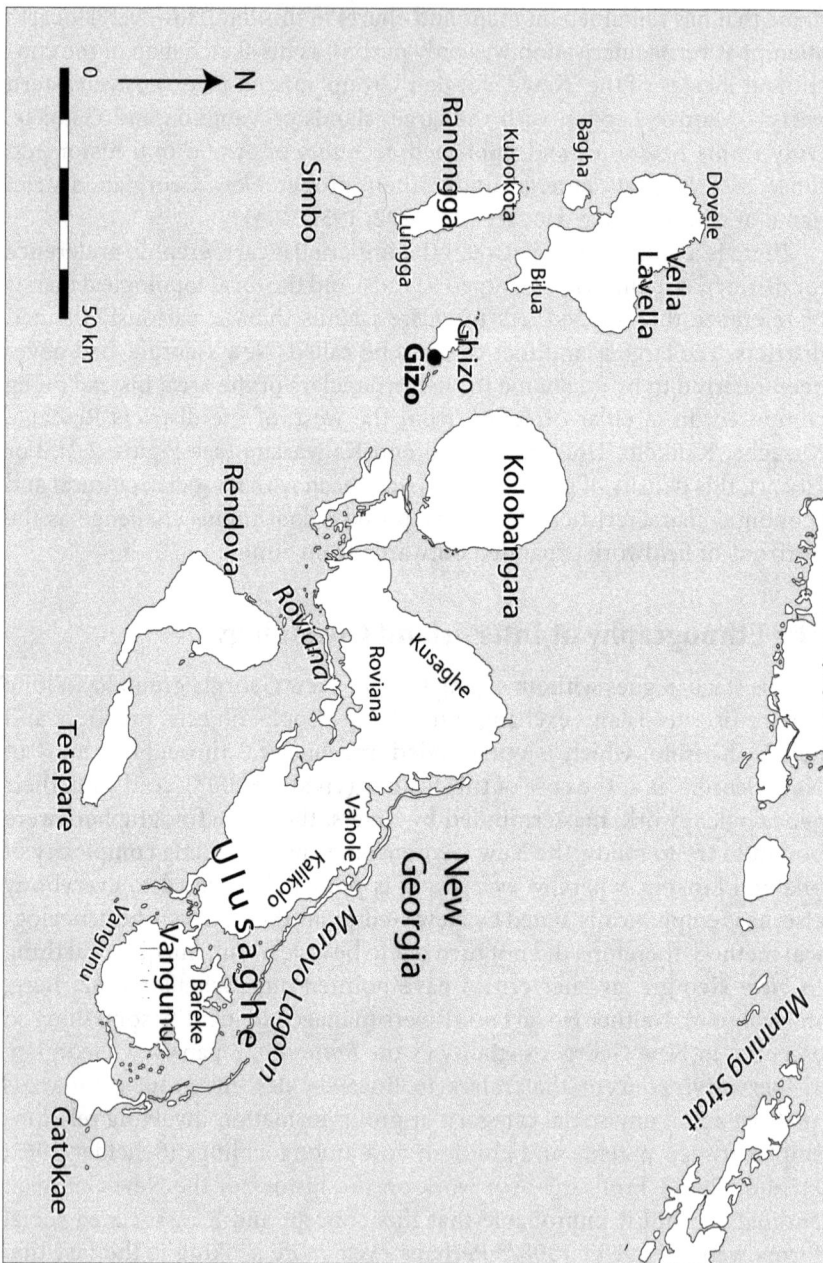

Figure 2.2: The New Georgia group, with vernacular district names (map by K.H. Sjøstrøm, University of Bergen).

Georgia, the ethnographic effort was far from weak as far as the mapping of social relationships was concerned.

Rivers and Hocart attended funeral gatherings, which then as now were events at which people from a number of islands travelled to the locality of the deceased, as a demonstration of genealogical connections (referred to, for example, in the Marovo language as *sinoto*, 'accumulated attachments'). The practice of giving speeches that reveal and explain the genealogical connections among those present remains a common feature at funerals in New Georgia. On these highly charged occasions, Hocart and Rivers recorded information about everyone attending, including their connections to places at Simbo and beyond. It may perhaps be argued that the grounding of the two ethnographers in an old ethnological paradigm in which religion was paramount but kinship less well developed directed them first to ritual occasions, but that this initial methodological emphasis generated such a wealth of genealogical information that kinship was brought to the forefront. The complexity and variability of New Georgian kinship as embodied in the *butubutu* eluded them, however, despite Rivers's grounding in a quest for matrilineality and patrilineality, and his already accomplished founding of the genealogical method. No doubt the bilaterality of New Georgian kinship (outside of Vella Lavella) confused them, given that Rivers had posed the expedition's fundamental quest as that of the transition from the matrilineal to the patrilineal.

As the ethnographers moved around and used the vessels of traders and missionaries to reach neighbouring islands, their comparatively high degree of maritime mobility simply mirrored the style of mobility among local people (mainly men). A fortuitous methodological initiative in an encounter with a knowledgeable informant vividly portrays the wide archipelagic knowledge horizons – or inter-island cosmology – of the New Georgians of the time. In the Rivers collection held at Cambridge there are some fascinating pencil drawings made by an informant from Roviana Lagoon named Ango (see also Thomas, this volume), which in sharp naturalistic pen depict maritime scenes and ceremonial dances.[11] The drawings are so rich in information as to be worthy of a chapter of their own, but here I will just make some brief comments.

On the drawings are seen war canoes and tuna-fishing canoes (as well as a few locally owned European whaling boats), named seaways, islands and village locations, marine creatures (named sharks in particular), dance scenes and ceremonial settings, and more. On all the drawings are writings in the Roviana language by what must have been a literate Methodist convert (probably the artist Ango himself, since missionaries had been active in Roviana for six years at the time). In somewhat laboriously written capital letters, war-canoe fleets are named with reference to home ports and their destinations are given, and many other illustrated elements are revealed in rather pedagogical fashion for those who are familiar with New Georgia's geography, vernacular languages and local customs. One drawing (Figure 2.3) has a particularly dense combination of pen artistry and writing, with a call-and-response sequence addressing what may be recent paths of travel for a particular canoe crew.[12] The seascape depicted has spatial references in the 'upwards' (easterly) direction to 'Zela' (a sheltered cove on the exposed coast of the northern tip of New Georgia) and in the 'downwards' (westerly) direction to 'Vela' (a vernacular rendering of Vella Lavella). Among the nine locations named in as many lines of call-and-response are Tadoki (in the Gerasi area of Ulusaghe), Kololuka (the open sea between the islands of Kolobangara and Vella Lavella), Vaghena (an island just south-east of Choiseul), Lauru (Choiseul itself) and 'Veala' (an alternative rendering of Vela or Vella Lavella) – a collection of places separated by up to 120 kilometres of open sea and exemplifying the range of destinations in and beyond New Georgia between which regular travel took place for many different purposes. In this sense, too, it becomes clear that the New Georgia group was no confined locality; the mental maps of its inhabitants ranged widely across the sea.

Considering the ways in which the islands of the New Georgia group – big and small, clustered and dispersed in diverse geographical ways – necessitated travel for marriage, exchange, warfare and more, Rivers and Hocart found themselves in fortuitous circumstances in terms of collecting comparative materials. Not only could they mimic the islanders' mobility, but they could also rely on a steady stream of long- and short-term visitors from other islands living among Simbo people. Travel in New Georgia also involved, as it still does, the buying, selling, import and export of material items and repertoires of knowledge, including a few reported examples in history of purchasing an entire language. For example, it is reckoned that the Marovo language, spoken now throughout Marovo Lagoon and on the easternmost island of Gatokae, was once purchased from the people of Kalivarana further west. Present-day discussion within and among the dozen or so linguistic groups of the New Georgia group continues to focus, at times obsessively, on differences and similarities of knowledge and practice, sometimes objectified in general Melanesian ways as *kastom* (Keesing and Tonkinson 1982). Usually such discussion is seen simply as an expression of genuine interest in 'other people's ways', taking place in contexts of little actual cultural difference as such beyond language, and concerned instead with concrete repertoires of detailed knowledge about the localised environments of land and sea.

Throughout New Georgia, there is an emphasis on the constructed and assembled nature of localised customs, in the sense of important cultural

Figure 2.3: Drawing made in 1908 by Ango of Roviana (by permission of the Cambridge Museum of Archaeology and Anthropology).

elements having arrived from overseas and being made available for local adaptation. Conversely, there is not so much concern in New Georgia about matters of 'cultural copyright' and local privilege over specific domains of knowledge, a trend that appears to reflect historical patterns of a relative lack of secrecy in the realms of magic and ritual. Traffic in knowledge and practice for a fee, as theft or as gift seems to be constitutive of both inter-island relationships and local distinctiveness in the history of New Georgia. Hocart's writings exemplify this truly inter-island quality of knowledge and discourse concerning matters of cultural specificity and generality. Stories recounted and explained by his Simbo informants were as likely to involve faraway places and peoples as to be local in their scope.

A good case in point is the large repertoire of prayers and spells that were recorded by Hocart and included in his published works, sometimes translated into English in the running text, but in some articles appended as specimens of vernacular language. One single prayer may range across several islands, including the areas of open sea that connect them. A good example given in English translation is a prayer (*varavara*) that encompasses many places in Vella Lavella, Simbo and Ranongga, the people there, and the 'straits' between those islands (see Hocart 1922: 109–10). The prayer is envisaged as travelling throughout these localities, across the seas and into the forests, with typical birds and plants involved as intermediaries of transport. Several stories accompanied by drawings from their narrators portray themes and narratives of pan-New Georgian scope. Thus the 'Eddystone world' as encountered by Rivers and Hocart was constructed locally from many non-local sources. Instead, overseas places and peoples, two-way connections between them and Simbo, and circular travels involving series of localities on several islands were all constitutive of the versions of local realities that were communicated to the inquisitive pioneer ethnographers.

The apparent heterogeneity of genre and inconclusiveness of argument that characterises Hocart's published articles are thus not representative of methodological shortcomings but rather an end result of encounters between the protagonists of the Percy Sladen Trust Expedition and New Georgian world-views of spatial connectivity. If the late Epeli Hau'ofa, distinguished scholar and Oceanic philosopher, had engaged at some depth with the research by Hocart and Rivers in 1908, he would have found some unexpected justification here in the heart of Island Melanesia for his radically alternative, by now well-known view of Oceania as an interconnected 'sea of islands', 'a large world in which peoples and cultures moved and mingled, unhindered by boundaries of the kind erected much later by imperial powers' (Hau'ofa 1994: 153–54). Hau'ofa's anti-insular view of Pacific societies emphasised the boundless potential of interaction and connection among Pacific islanders, where the seas between islands do not separate people but are 'highways rather than barriers' (Lewis 1972: 15). Studies in support of Hauʻofaʻs Oceanic vision have been concerned mainly with the truly scattered Pacific archipelagos of Polynesia and Micronesia – the most prominent example being the work of historian Paul D'Arcy (2006) – but I will argue that the sea-oriented Western Solomons model of archipelagic interconnections in cosmology and social and economic life is an important additional contribution to pan-Pacific perspectives (see also Hviding 1996). On this matter, the Percy Sladen Trust Expedition can be seen as more than an ethnographic experiment; its massive effort implicitly outlined vernacular Oceanic cosmologies that were not fully understood until almost a century later.

It is as if almost every phenomenon examined by Hocart on Simbo was presented by his informants in a fundamentally extra-local perspective. For every local entity there is, it seems, an overseas parallel somewhere in wider New Georgia – even to the extent of linking the easternmost and westernmost parts of the group, such as in the following statement, typical of the inter-island naming of places: 'The gods of Tiroto stole water from Tiroto in Ulusage and brought it in a leaf ... to Tiroto in Narovo' (Hocart 1922: 280). There are, obviously, two places named Tiroto – one at Narovo on Simbo, and one far 'up' in Ulusaghe (old Marovo). The connection is of a cosmological nature, considering that Tiroto is the main freshwater spring on Simbo (and the current source of piped water across the island). The water on Simbo thus came from Marovo, adding to a significant element of reciprocal connections between islands. Water was stolen (by the gods of Tiroto) from well-watered Ulusaghe and carried to Simbo (where there was no water), whereas *Canarium* nuts were stolen (by a domesticated fruit bat) from Simbo and carried to Marovo Island in Ulusaghe (where there were no nut trees).

Another inter-island character documented by Hocart is the Flying Chief, *Bangara pu Tatava*. Through tales told and a drawing made by a seventy-year-old man named Kundakolo, Hocart conveyed to us the legend of 'Ngangai and the Flying Chief', containing lessons about mobile agency, fundamental to the understanding of social distinctions among the various groups in Simbo:

That is why the people of Narovo, excepting Panullu, were a bush folk till quite recently, knowing not how to build canoes to catch fish, and their rapes caused constant trouble with their neighbours.

Kundakolo has illustrated the legend of Ngangai and Flying Chief ... [T]o the left stands Konga, an island near Vila in the strait between Nduke and Lokuru (Arundel Island in the chart); the trees upon it are *kikindova* and *mbirimbiri*; the large tree is *ragana*. Ngangai is represented as an octopus; Flying Chief, with a long snake-like body, is 'journeying in the air' (*nggi soana pa nullu*); he carries a spear in one hand and a basket in the other.

'Ngangai come and kill the *eau* (clam) that wants to kill us', said the men of Nduke. Ngangai went by sea; Flying Chief flew in the air and they arrived in Kongga and rested there. Then Ngangai dived down to find the *eau*, and with his four tentacles (literally, hairs), caught the eau and killed it. The rings carried by Flying Chief are the pay given by the men of Nduke. (Hocart 1922: 281)

The full scope of the inter-island world of New Georgians comes out in another story, focused on Ghaghe, an island at the western end of Isabel, by the Manning Strait. Separated from any part of New Georgia by at least 100 kilometres of ocean, the Manning Strait between the large islands of Choiseul and Isabel was a famous hunting ground for New Georgians, who would go there to raid western Isabel (or in some cases eastern Choiseul) for heads while also collecting turtles for their shell from the low sandy islands in the strait. Upon return to New Georgia, they could sell the turtle shell to European traders and use the heads for their own purposes. The island of Ghaghe is 200 kilometres from Simbo as the pigeon flies, and the story is in fact not about Simbo but about the people of faraway Ulusaghe. In this particular case they are the marauding 'salt-water' people of the Gerasi district in northern Marovo, who are to this day reckoned as being partly of Isabel origin. Here, then, is the tale of the Parrot of Ghaghe:

The men of Ulusage went out to sea; they arrived in Gage: '*Kilo*' said this parrot; the conger jumped out and ate the canoe, ate them all up. 'Alas! we are stricken, our men are perishing.' 'Go, then, Sagulele, to sea', said Kolombisu and Najarara. 'All right', said Sagulele, and went to Ysabel. 'Come, Ngaluvulu, and kill the conger; the canoes are perishing, the men are perishing'. 'All right', said Ngaluvulu, and he went and arrived in Gage. 'Come, go and get the Two Lanono', said they. Sagulele departed, he went down to Vela: 'The canoes are perishing, the men are perishing; come then you Two Lanono and kill the *suata*'. 'Good', said the Two Lanono, 'let us go'. So they came to Gage, and now they were three. 'If I cry *kilo*, come out and bite him', said the parrot. They came out and bit the conger that it died. They bit it into small pieces, and put the fragments on the land, where they were changed into stone; there are a lot of stones in Gage; these are the fragments of the *suata*. Ngaluvulu changed into stone, and the stone is now in Gage. The Two Lanono went back to Vela.

The name of the Karu Lanono means literally the two logs on which the canoe rests; they are sacred (*tambu*) sharks in Veala; they go before the canoes of the Roviana and Ngerassi people on their way to Vagena, and fight other kinds of sharks.

Kundakolo's drawing of the legend … excited great indignation among the people of Roviana; they were unanimous that he was wrong (*koha*): Ngaluvulu should be on the other side of the picture, nor should he take any part in the carnage, for he arrived too late; finally the two fishes called *makoto* are missing who decoyed the conger out of its hole. Nguambule at my request drew what he considered to be the truth. (Hocart 1922: 291–92)

This tale is remarkable for its spatial scope, which ranges from Ulusaghe in the far east down to Vella Lavella in the far west, mediated by the Manning Strait and Isabel to the north and north-east. It is also notable for the way in which the ethnographer gets entangled in a heated exchange of opinions among informants from different places. His main Simbo informant Kundakolo's depiction of the tale in a drawing does not amuse the Roviana people, who have major reservations against both plot and representation. Hocart ends up asking his Roviana informant Guabule to draw another version for him, according to 'truth' as seen from Roviana. Place-based information rules. There is a strong momentum of representing a multitude of perspectives from various islands, on what is ostensibly one and the same story and involves a number of significant beliefs and phenomena of regionally validity. Let me propose some general points about the New Georgia-wide comparative contributions contained in Hocart's materials.

There is a lot of information on rather poorly known aspects of the New Georgian ritual complex, in which there were (and are) significant similarities across the islands. One example is the way in which certain rituals revolve around puddings made from a mixture of pounded *Canarium* nuts and root crops such as taro and yams. Any reader of Hocart's notes and articles will recognise brief descriptions of ritual processes such as 'then they make puddings'. There are rich materials in Hocart's writings about inter-island warfare and alliance, and the various ways in which people connect as friends and foes across the sea. Good illustrations are also given of a key dimension in the performance of religious practice: that priests in New Georgia, the main ritual functionaries who mediated between the dead and the living, were commonly of foreign origin. Hocart (1922: 105) lists four out of five priests from the districts of Narovo, Ove, Karivara and Simbo as being captives or migrants from Isabel or Vella Lavella. That the repertoire of local Simbo remedies against illness also has significant non-local elements, brought by overseas settlers or otherwise imported, is exemplified by Hocart's report about a Simbo–Isabel connection concerning 'a series of charms [that] … are not yet part of the lore of Eddystone. They really belong to the Manning Straits. The disease is produced by an animal exactly in the manner described to me by one Sopalehe of Bugotu' (Hocart 1925: 257).

Thus even a small island like Simbo was very diverse. People from overseas lived with, and even performed crucial mortuary rituals for, the people of Simbo. Moreover, spirit beings of many kinds communicated with the living and intervened in their lives in supportive or obstructive ways. On one particular occasion on 1908, the spiritual beings from 'the land of the ghosts' also included the visiting ethnographers in their field of interest. In a remarkable passage, the ghost of Onda (an uncle of Hocart's informant Kundaite, who performed the summoning of the dead after having been 'induced' by the ethnographers through a gift of ten sticks of tobacco) announces its arrival by a whistle, after which 'there was a long interval and a discussion about the White Men from England. Onda [the visiting 'ghost'] said, "Why do the White Men want me to come? I can't see (? recognise) them; I have never seen a White Man". "The White Men want to hear the spirits speak", said Kundaite' (Hocart 1922: 94).

Hocart gives excellent explanations of the different ways of represent-ing the dead at shrines, a question of diversity that remains something of a mystery to archaeologists working in the Western Solomons. He may have oversimplified the issue, but there seems to be a pattern echoed in local conceptualisations that the dead were represented at shrines ideally in the form of an actual skull or – if the skull should be unavailable for various reasons – by an upright stone or an image carved in wood or stone. This is a truly pan-New Georgian phenomenon, recognisable at most shrines throughout the islands. There was a diverse population of dead at every major shrine: 'In Uelai we saw a head carved in stone and representing a native of Ontong Java [a large outlying Polynesian atoll north of the main Solomons]; although a foreigner he was represented by a stone because he was "good-fellow man" and worked hard for the chief in Uelai' (Hocart 1922: 92).

The observed diversity of burial practices also inspired interesting dis-cussions by Hocart on 'ethnological' variation, for example in the different standard styles of skull houses (Hocart 1922: 103–5). In 1908, such shrines were still maintained – but they were in transition, in that thatched elements were being replaced by sheets of corrugated iron. Styles remained distinct for different island localities, however. Hocart describes how, at Simbo, skull houses were constructed like a simple half roof, while at Roviana they were constituted by a fully gabled roof, and at Vella Lavella they were enclosed coffin-style caskets lifted above the ground on stilts. Such discussion exem-plifies a general reluctance in Hocart's writing to generalise, and instead a willingness to make room for the diversity of the specific and the distinct – in other words, a strong and conscious focus on thematic variations which perhaps constitute the core dynamic of Melanesian cultural diversity.

The Simbo of 1908 was, then, a small Melanesian island only in absolute size, otherwise large and embedded in contexts of great diversity. Since Lieutenant Shortland's passing visit in the *Alexander* in 1788, the island had been known to navigators and colonialists as Eddystone. Locally, 'Simbo' was used to refer only to part of it, while the proper name for the entire island was Madegusu ('four localities'). Hocart, who used Madegusu himself, noted that, '[t]o the white men and the natives of Roviana and Nduke the whole island is known as Simbo, after the third named district' (Hocart 1922: 76). With its four districts – Narovo, Ove, Simbo and Karivara – the island as a whole was viewed as a composite place even to the extent of having a historical distinction between bush people and coastal people, which seems remarkable for such a small island, although widespread on the larger islands of the Solomons. As indicated above in the tale of the Flying Chief, the former bush people of Simbo were described to Hocart (first during a visit to Roviana, after he and Rivers had lived three months among such people without ever knowing about their past) as inept and clumsy with 'dissolute ways'. They spoke another language, and were always after women to rape – a habit that caused wars. By 1908, they were in much better shape, they had become somewhat civilised, had intermarried with salt-water people and learnt how to fish, and they were really not as bad anymore – their speech could even be understood (Hocart 1922: 76–77).

It would seem that the realities at hand that were imposed on Hocart through the sustained ethnographic encounter made him reluctant to generalise even island-wide. As for the Simbo as a whole, he noted how 'Ove and Karivara have a different form of prayer', and he quoted his informants' claims that this in fact amounted to 'another speak'. As for this special 'speak', he continued:

> In Simbo, no one knows it, so they get Pore of Karivara to recite it; the Ove dead go to Tusingai, those of Karivara to the cave on Patukio. In neither case does it make any difference whether a pig is killed or not. Not everyone in Narovo knows that the soul goes to a different place according to whether a pig is killed or not. Two of our informants appeared not to know. (Hocart 1922: 89)

'Here but also there'. 'Here, but not there'. 'This one but not that one'. 'So-and-so says that it is so-and-so, but so-and-so says that it is not so'. Such sensitivity to diversity demonstrates sophisticated fieldwork methodology, with ambitions to take into account cultural diversity and social complexity. Hocart not only positioned informants in society, he also positioned statements and narratives according to the positioning of the informant, and he positioned the narratives in their cross-culturally charged inter-island context. Did he develop such methodological sophistication because the people of New Georgia already thought in such terms? The encounter between islanders whose cosmologies were decidedly pluralist and an ethnographer whose intellectual background was extraordinarily diverse certainly was a fertile field.

One issue of apparent inconsistency raised by Hocart was that some people at Simbo carried out certain mortuary rituals twenty-two nights after death, while others followed the ways of the Ranongga people across the sea and did it after twenty nights. Sometimes this discrepancy was an issue at Simbo, sometimes it was not. Along these lines we may consider the complications of how to deal ethnographically with *akesage*, the ritual of the eighteenth day, as explained by Hocart:

> The eighteenth day is *Akesage*, from *ake* to carry in the arms, and *sage* up. It is the day on which the skull is put in the skull-house, a proceeding called *vatome tomate* or 'putting in the dead'.
>
> All informants but one gave eighteen nights as the period. In point of fact Ngea's was held on June 10th, which makes sixteen, but they may have conspired to hasten it in order to elude us, for they feigned ignorance of the time it was to be held, until it was actually over. Irana's was held after twenty-two nights, but his people were following the Ganongan reckoning of twenty days; so they were only two days out. (Hocart 1922: 90)

The lengthy discussion on these complications on Simbo is followed by a brief reference to 'Lungan' customs. The information on Lungga in Ranongga (Hocart 1922: 101–2) is, however, deemed an insufficient description by Hocart, since his informants from that part of the large neighbouring island were considered 'young and ignorant'. He did, nevertheless, make the interesting observation that in Lungga they 'make taro puddings, for they have no sweet yams'. In any other locality around New Georgia but Simbo (where they have no taro) it would be those who have only yams and not taro who would be seen as the disadvantaged ones! To add to this complexity, a couple of pages of 'Ranongan customs' follow (Hocart 1922: 102–3), based on Hocart's perception that '[t]wo Ganongan [Ranonggan] informants proved much better'. The Ranongan customs are compared with those of Eddystone as contrasting in certain significant ways, and the methodological validity of conclusions about inter-island cultural difference is argued rather specifically:

> Another important difference with Eddystone is that [at Ranongga] they have feasts every ten days. This is one of the best established parts of our work, for owing to the liability of such inquiries into dates to misunderstandings we went through a second time with counters, and finally Lembu made a counting string of a thousand knots with small intervals after ten knots; with this he explained the whole system. (Hocart 1922: 103)

Here are methodological combinations and epistemological convergences in which the ethnographers expand the validity of their cross-cultural observations about neighbouring islands by combining their own counting methods with those of a trusted local. Yet, for all the attention to the methodological challenges of inter-island phenomena, Hocart often appears to have concluded on such diversity from hearsay, or at the most from a single observation or statement. The question remains as to whether he tended to identify the localised distinctiveness of customs in a certain part of New Georgia with insufficient regard for the actual spatial and temporal fluidity of 'regional' customs that he highlights elsewhere. Sometimes he makes a comment like 'in Roviana they don't do it that way'. And so it is 'here', yes, but not necessarily 'over there'.

Through a dialogue with Hocart's ethnography of fishing-related rituals (Hocart 1935, 1937), I have been able to explore some enduring aspects of engagement with the sea in Marovo Lagoon, in which present-day fishermen recite prayers to God before jumping into the water, in ways that are strikingly similar to the fishing spells and requests for ancestral help recorded by Hocart for Simbo. Now as then, in Marovo as at Simbo, it is about the state of *mana* that will give protection against the dangers of the sea, notably sharks, but often with reference to the 'coldness' of the sea hindering human activity on and under the water. There are strong echoes in the raw texts collected by Hocart. Most are insufficiently rendered by him in the vernacular, but the tone of the spells comes across nevertheless, connecting to the present-day Christian Marovo way of engaging with certain godly powers for protection underwater or in the sea.

At this stage I wish to address a truly remarkable encounter in time and space. It is about connections of both inter-island and inter-temporal nature, and it deals with a Simbo 'war' with Ulusaghe, which is given a full description in Hocart's article on warfare in Eddystone. Hocart's recording concerns a successful raid to Vahole, via the island of Vikenara, involving seven war canoes and 100 muskets, and during which many people were killed, including several chiefly women. The journey and its exploits are recounted:

[F]our new canoes were made in Simbo; so Muke Mbelanono, the chief, proclaimed a raid (*vinaria*) upon Choiseul. He sent a ring to Rembo, chief of Narovo, to obtain the loan of his men.

'Let all the men of Narovo go with Muke', said that chief, so they went; but Rembo stayed at home. Ove and Karivara also sent their 'boys'. From Simbo came four canoes, one belonging to Njura, one to Hekoto, one to Hola, and one to Muke; the other three districts supplied one apiece; that of Narovo belonged to Atolo. They were assembled in Nyou, near Tapurai, when Pogoso of Narovo, who had been to Ulusage [Ulusage includes Ngerasi; the natives always speak of this war as against Ulusage], spoke to Muke, saying: 'Do not go to Choiseul nor to Ysabel. I know Ulusage; there is one island thickly populated, with no village in the neighbourhood: I will lead you thither'. 'Is that so?' said Muke, 'Yes', said Pogoso, 'I know a passage: let us attack that island: Choiseul is too far away'. 'Very good', said Muke, 'let us go to Ulusage'. They set out with the *vovoso* charm from Koluka on board. They proceeded to Makila in Gizho, where now stands the government wharf; thence to Vila and Teme in Nduke; then crossed over to Kusage, where they called at Mase, Matahite and Njela. At the latter place they stopped while Pogoso went on with one canoe to reconnoitre. They reached Vahole, where they found an island with people on it; it was night; they left their canoes on the beach while one man went to inspect the houses; he found the people all asleep. Pogoso took a piece of ivory-nut leaf and one young coconut, and put them into the canoe [They would be both proofs that the place was inhabited; the leaf coming from the thatch; coconut palms always indicate a village]. 'Let us return', said he, 'there are men here'. They went back to report. 'Hullo, Muke', said Pogoso. 'Hullo, Pogoso. Have you seen men?' 'Yes, I have seen them; they are not away from home'. 'Is that true?' 'I would not lie to a chief. You wanted to go to Choiseul, but I told you to come here'. At sunset they left Njela and reached Vikevikenara at five o'clock, just before dawn. 'We shall go at daylight, when men see us', said Muke. So they waited. Now Vikevikenara consists of two islands. Muke and Mulemata, both chiefs of Simbo, were in one, while a company stayed in the other. Presently a canoe came past Muke's island on its way home from Wandakana. 'Are you ready?' said Muke. 'Let us kill them'. He fired, the canoe was broken, and the women began to swim, but they were caught and killed. The other party, Njoni among them, heard the report. 'Muke has taken a canoe', they said, and hastened to join him. 'We have killed five, let us turn back', said Muke. But they refused, and wanted to go on to the island (Vanole?). Then came another canoe; it had a sail and a fair wind; the six women who manned it, two chief's wives among them, sang as they went. The Eddystonians made ready their muskets and fired a hundred at once, and broke the canoes. The women were dragged ashore and killed, except the two chief's wives. 'We have killed eleven, let us go home', said Muke. 'All right', they said, and returned to Simbo. One prisoner was given to Hana, who married her, and one to Tie, who used her as a prostitute. The men of Ngerasi were angry, and the chiefs of Roviana, who were on friendlier terms with both, told Muke he must now be at war with Ngerasi (*kana*). 'Very good', said Muke, 'let us fight it out (you me *kana* now)'. So Eddystone was at war with Ngerasi, and they could not visit each other. The people of Narovo, expecting a counter raid, built houses in the bush about Ogogo. But in the meantime the British protectorate had put a stop to head-hunting, so that Ngerasi never took its revenge. The government, however, demanded the prisoners, and, meeting with a refusal, imprisoned Muke. The Deputy Commissioner raided the island, burnt down houses, and searched for Hana, but he always escaped. At last

Hingava, chief of Munda, in Roviana, was induced to use his influence, and Hana surrendered the prisoners to him. (Hocart 1931: 304–5)[13]

One hundred years later we can track a still familiar 'path' of maritime travel in northern Marovo Lagoon, near the Gerasi area of northernmost Ulusaghe, which follows the raised barrier reef's outer edge until reaching the rocky, densely forested barrier island of Vikenara, then traverses the barrier reef over the wide shallow passage of Kororo and enters the lagoon area of what is defined as the western or 'sunset' edge of the territory of the Vahole people. In front of the canoe traveller at this stage is a small island referred to as Tusu Kaka – Cockatoo Island, also known by the very old, not well-understood name Hagolohiu. It is a low, thickly forested coral island fringed with mangroves. According to Vahole traditions, this is where a substantial number of Vahole people were massacred in the late nineteenth century by firearms-carrying warriors of Simbo. It is held that the latter killed both women and men, and that they abducted at least one woman. According to local traditions about what is known as the 'massacre of Vikenara' (*eongo pa Vikenara*), this was a major blow to the Vahole people, who were allies of the Gerasi. Lieutenant Somerville described how, against the advice of his Marovo friends, he visited 'a small islet in a rather remote part of the lagoon which unlike all other islands that were covered with bush was overgrown with coconuts' (Somerville 1897: 391–92). He was told that the island had a *hope* – a taboo – pronounced over it and the surrounding coast after some twelve years before (which would have been 1881 or 1882) the 'Rubiana boys' had arrived at this island, on which there was a small village, and had taken every head in the place. Given that Somerville did part of his surveying in the 'rather remote' Gerasi area, the place he describes is very likely to be Tusu Kaka. The reference to Roviana ('Rubiana') rather than Simbo is probably an artefact of poor communication, since no other massacres are on local record for this area.

In recognition of those killed in the massacre of Vikenara, the coconut groves on Tusu Kaka were allowed to decay. The island is now densely overgrown with low coastal forest and has not been settled, nor even visited, since that nineteenth-century disaster befell the Vahole. On one occasion in 1987, a Belgian yacht was seen anchored in the shelter of Tusu Kaka, and was approached and boarded by a customary spokesman of the Vahole. The couple on the yacht were politely requested to move to a non-prohibited area close to the lagoon shore of the adjacent barrier island. I was in the Vahole spokesman's canoe at the time, and when we returned from Gerasi the next morning the yacht was gone. Such is the present power of past taboos, and such is another enduring connection between Simbo and Ulusaghe, and between Hocart's fieldwork and mine.

Fieldwork Innovations: Simbo, 1908 and Beyond

There is a general point to be made about anthropological fieldwork being a conjuncture between the ways in which ethnographer and informant are situated, in their own specific contexts of history, culture and power. In this sense, interactions between the Simbo people and the visiting ethnographers took the form a particular historical 'structure of conjuncture' amounting to 'a system of relationships destined to affect the further course' (Sahlins 1985: xiv, 139) of both Simbo society and culture and anthropological practice. Quite simply, the ethnographic experiment was carried out at a time when the two needed each other. In 1908, stories about ancestral worship, medicine and witchcraft, inter-island warfare, the ritualised high-seas hunt for skipjack tuna, and the crafts of canoe-building and everyday fishing were told to the ethnographers by a Melanesian people who had perhaps become self-conscious in a new way, as massive changes were underway and seemed likely to make irrelevant much of that knowledge and practice in which Rivers and Hocart were so interested. It is possible, although Hocart and Rivers did not record it as such, that the two Englishmen became/were seen as scribes destined to record and convey the stories of the Simbo people, as the latter were no longer so certain about their place in the inter-island world nor in the world at large.

The close dialogue that I have been fortunate to develop across the New Georgia group with the results of the Percy Sladen Trust Expedition, most particularly with Hocart's materials, suggests to me that the fieldwork of 1908 was fundamentally multi-island and inter-island, even while grounded in only a few specific locations, mainly Simbo. Hocart seems to have captured a Melanesian world based on an ever-flowing regional transferability of persons, concepts and things, echoing a more general pattern referred to by Freud as the 'narcissism of minor differences' and applied more recently by Simon Harrison to Melanesian contexts in which neighbouring groups exaggerate their distinctiveness from each other and, paraphrasing Freud, 'attach disproportionate significance to those few features that differentiate them' (Harrison 2006: 2). In the New Georgia group it may on occasion seem that it is only language that distinguishes one people from another, and group distinctiveness is generally of an 'ethnolinguistic' nature, whereby a distinct ethnic group is referred to by the name of its language rather than that of the island on which they live (although some Western Solomons languages – for example, Simbo – are also named after islands). In Hocart's lively, idiosyncratic, sometimes confusing accounts from Eddystone, the intensively active processes of differentiating group identification on inter-island levels come across forcefully for those prepared for immersion in the often bewildering detail of his writing. Perhaps this potential comes across most fruitfully if the reader – anthropologist or other – has long-term experience from another corner of the New Georgia group, so that they can say, 'that is how they do it in Simbo', and so connect in time and space.

Bruce Kapferer has argued that village-based, and thus by definition myopic, fieldwork believed to dominate the history of anthropology is but an illusion, well-suited to postmodern critiques but far from the reality reflected of generations of anthropological practice: 'The village is more a place to reside and a point from which the anthropologist moves out along the lines of social relations' (Kapferer 2000: 28). Certainly, the two gentlemen at work on the small island of Eddystone in 1908 were far from village bound and myopic. Their ethnographic experiment appears to have been both ontologically grounded and epistemologically founded in a view of the local world as far reaching and being as much exogenous as endogenous in its social, cultural and material reproduction.

However, in an anthropology that became increasingly 'scientific' through the influential careers of Malinowski, Radcliffe-Brown and others, and that increasingly pursued 'hard and fast' models of structure based on ethnographies of distinct 'societies' and 'systems', and delimited social groups connected to delimited territories, Hocart and the New Georgians had no place. Moreover, the New Georgians, pacified, colonised and Christianised, were soon burdened by an image among scholars and 'ethnologically' inclined missionaries that they had little left in the manner of 'customs', and were thus anthropologically uninteresting. In the 1940s, linguist Arthur Capell attempted a brief survey of existing scholarly work on the islands of the Western Solomons, claiming that 'very little [seemed] to have been published' (Capell 1944: 20), thus conveniently ignoring Hocart's *JRAI* series of articles.

Hocart's cautious field methodology, perhaps postmodernist some generations before the term was invented (see also Dureau, this volume), was created in that critical conjuncture in 1908 between his intellectual agenda (grounded in his diverse training in Latin, Greek, ancient history, philosophy, psychology and phenomenology) and the New Georgians' pluralist cosmology of ever-flowing regional transferability. Both the ethnographer and the islanders were positioned in a historical situation with specific challenges. While the islanders went on with their increasingly globalised lives (and in due course proved that far from all was lost), the ethnographer himself would re-emerge in different future incarnations, first as an ethnographer of the Lau islands of Fiji, then as a historically oriented comparativist theoretician preoccupied with kingship and hierarchy, destined to be more influential in certain circles, including structuralism and the study of hierarchy (see Hocart 1929, 1970; Scubla 2002; Rio and Smedal

2009; Hviding and Berg, this volume). Only at a much later stage would analyses of pluralist cosmologies re-emerge in Melanesian anthropology, and not until the end of the twentieth century would New Georgia (again) be the scene of intensive anthropological study.[14]

In 'Polyphony is not Cacophony', one of many brief but incisive and playful interventions in his pamphlet project *Waiting for Foucault*, Marshall Sahlins invokes an observation made by Hocart from his long engagement with Fiji subsequent to the Solomon Islands fieldwork, concerning a 'dictum that in Fiji two contradictory statements are not necessarily inconsistent' (Sahlins 2002: 27). Sahlins quotes Hocart's argument that '[the statements] appear to us contradictory … because we do not know, without much experience, the point of view from which each is made' (Sahlins 2002: 27). After his first fieldwork, during which he was for months surrounded by the consistently plural and potentially contradictory statements of islanders at Simbo, Vella Lavella, Roviana, Kolobangara and elsewhere across the New Georgia group, it comes as no surprise that Hocart should be well prepared to see consistency in apparent contradiction.

Acknowledgements

I am grateful to two anonymous readers for very useful critical comments on this chapter. Tim Bayliss-Smith, Cato Berg and Christine Dureau have provided close readings of several versions as the chapter has developed, and Karen Leivestad, Annelin Eriksen and Knut Rio have provided important comments on particular sections. A version was presented in 2012 to the Melanesia Research Seminar at the British Museum, and I am grateful to that audience for wide-ranging discussion.

Notes

1. Rivers, 'The Western Solomons', typewritten report sent from St John's College, Cambridge, to A.W. Kappel, 'Clerk to the Trustees' of the Percy Sladen Memorial Trust, 4 May 1909, LSA. Reproduced as Appendix 1.3 (this volume).

2. The first part of Hocart's article 'The Cult of the Dead' did not take Rivers's death on 4 June 1922 into account, as it was published in the January/June issue of the journal. In the second part, published in the July/December issue, Hocart refers in the introduction to 'the late Dr. Rivers' (Hocart 1922: 229). Since Rivers died unexpectedly, it cannot be surmised that Hocart hastened the start of his publication of Simbo materials for any reason connected to Rivers – after years of military service following work as a schoolmaster in Fiji, Hocart himself had in 1921 taken up residence in Colombo, as director of the British Archaeological Mission to Ceylon. It is likely that the

inception of a dedicated publication agenda for the Simbo materials was a fully independent decision made by Hocart, but some assistance along the way may have been given by Rivers, who was in 1920–21 president of the Royal Anthropological Institute (see Hviding and Berg, this volume).

3. A note on language and spelling is necessary, as this chapter contains a large number of place names in several Solomon Islands vernaculars, as well as vernacular terms included in quotations from Hocart. As Hocart himself noted, '[the] work was done through interpreters' (Hocart 1922: 72) – islanders who spoke the emergent form of Melanesian pidgin – and there is some inconsistency in the spelling of place names and vernacular terms throughout Hocart's materials. I have, however, retained the spellings as they are in quotations from published work. Elsewhere, I have standardised relevant spelling according to the conventions used for the languages of New Georgia (Hviding 1996: xxvii–xxix). Two particular features need attention. One is the universal 'pre-nasalisation' of voiced consonants whereby *b, d*, etc. may sound like, and are often rendered as *mb, nd*, etc. While some pre-nasalisations are so indicated in Hocart's writings, I have elsewhere refrained from this usage in favour of the conventional *b, d*, and so forth. Another is the diversity of 'g' sounds represented in New Georgian languages by the forms *g, gh, ngg, ng*, and *n̠*. This is even more complicated given that the church denominations in the Western Solomons have adopted two different sets of symbols based on original Bible translations. Hocart deals with this diversity in idiosyncratic ways, and I have not seen any reason to correct what is evidently faulty spelling in the texts quoted. Elsewhere in the text (mainly in place names) I have applied conventional spellings as *ng* (English 'singer'), *ngg* (English 'finger') and *gh* for the Melanesian 'soft g' as in 'Ulusaghe'. The only confusing exception is the island of Gatokae, whose initial G is pronounced as *ngg*, as with Ranongga, but whose inhabitants insist on the capital G. For inevitable reasons grounded in the Bible translations of the two church denominations that have dominated the Western Solomons since the early twentieth century (Methodists and Seventh-Day Adventists), the orthography standardised for this chapter is somewhat different from the Methodist-derived Simbo-based orthography used by Dureau in her chapter.

4. The island Simbo, or 'Eddystone', in fact was – and is – a combination of distinct places, only one of which was – and is – Simbo, the name that is used for the entire island today. The multi-local quality even of such a small island (some 8 kilometres from north to south) is also indicated by the alternative vernacular name of Madegusu.

5. J. Aborn, 'Log of Whaling Ship *Patterson*, Capt. Jonathan Aborn. Departure from Providence, 19 July, 1803. Return to Boston, 22 August, 1804'. Microfilm, Pacific Manuscripts Bureau, Australian National University, Canberra, PMB 770. All subsequent quotes from the *Patterson* visit in this paragraph are from this source.

6. I use 'ancestor(s)' in the widest sense gender-wise to refer to any men and women to whom living descendants claim and recognise a relationship. With a few exceptions, kinship in the Western Solomons is bilateral and descent is cognatic, and so any genealogy reckoned locally and rendered to twentieth- or twenty-first-century anthropologists will include a mixture of male and female links. Hence the gender-neutral use here of 'ancestor'.

7. A.M. Hocart, 'Chieftainship', unpublished manuscript, Arthur M. Hocart Papers, MS-Papers-0060-14. Alexander Turnbull Library, National Library of New Zealand, Wellington.

8. See Dureau (this volume) for a long-term view of local attitudes to the past; see also Berg (this volume) and Bayliss-Smith (this volume).

9. Ulusaghe, a term that was in active use during the 1908 fieldwork, is the old vernacular designation for the south-eastern parts of the New Georgia group, including the high islands of Gatokae and Vangunu and most of eastern New Georgia, as well as the main body of the wide lagoon that is formed by a double-raised barrier reef extending north and west from Gatokae. In other words, it is what is usually defined as Marovo Lagoon, and includes large parts of the administrative division of the Western Province called Marovo. However, whereas 'Marovo' – after the small island of that name located by the north coast of Vangunu right in the centre of the lagoon – was introduced by early European navigators who interacted with the people of that island, and subsequently applied the name to the entire lagoon area, 'Ulusaghe' remains a strong reference to a district of the past. It represents a traditional contrast to other major districts of the New Georgia, particularly Roviana, and it is significant that the name itself is present in the Roviana language and means 'above-and-ascending', denoting the district's geographical location in the 'upwards' direction from Roviana. For everyday purposes though, the people of Ulusaghe refer to themselves as Tinoni Marovo ('Marovo people'), and are so referred to by neighbours and others overseas.

10. The absence of references to *butubutu* in the expedition's combined results is striking. Only once in Hocart's unpublished manuscripts is the concept mentioned: 'The expression *mbutumbutu mbangara* means a descendant or a line of chiefs' (Hocart, 'Chieftainship', unpublished manuscript, Arthur M. Hocart Papers, MS-Papers-0060-14. Alexander Turnbull Library, National Library of New Zealand, Wellington). It is of course possible that New Georgians in 1908 were less preoccupied with descent and corporate kin groups than before, given the very recent collapse of the prestige-goods economy that generated much inter- and intra-group dynamics. It is also clear that the corporate landholding version of the *butubutu* has gained currency from the late twentieth century, as industrial logging made the rainforest on *butubutu*-held customary land into a valuable commodity, and as disputes over contested land rights escalated (Hviding and Bayliss-Smith 2000). But the generational depth of genealogical

materials I have collected concerning *butubutu* throughout Marovo and in New Georgia more widely disprove any argument that the *butubutu* as a descent-based land-holding group is a recent phenomenon.

11. Cambridge Museum of Archaeology and Anthropology, MAA 2010.441 – 2010.446: Six drawings, Solomon Islands. Source: Haddon, A.C. (donor); Rivers, W.H.R. Transfer from the Haddon Papers, Manuscripts Room, Cambridge University Library, November 2010. Haddon Papers Envelope 12014. I am grateful to Nicholas Thomas for providing me with these drawings, and to Anita Herle for an update of their MAA collection details.

12. Cambridge Museum of Archaeology and Anthropology, MAA 2010.446. The 'call-and-response' is not of the kind where a first speaker 'calls' and receives a response from those 'called', but rather one in which the 'caller' poses both question and answer. The standard form for all the nine lines can be translated as 'So where is it you have been? – At [named place] is where you have been'. This form represents a genre in stylised hierarchical speech in New Georgia where an authoritative narrator addresses a person or a group in the form of a question and then provides the answer without letting the addressee(s) speak.

13. The two bracketed passages in the quotation are Hocart's own explanatory footnotes.

14. For one study of pluralist cosmologies, see Scott (2007) on poly-ontology among the Arosi and Makira. For more recent studies of the New Georgia group, see e.g. Hviding (1996) and Aswani (2000); in addition to these works, there is also an increasing number of so far unpublished PhD dissertations.

References

Aswani, S. (ed.) 2000. 'Essays on Head-hunting in the Western Solomon Islands', *Journal of the Polynesian Society* (special issue) 109(1).

Barth, F. 2005. 'Britain and the Commonwealth', in *One Discipline, Four Ways: British, German, French, and American Anthropology: The Halle Lectures*, F. Barth, A. Gingrich, R. Parkin and S. Silverman (eds), 3–57. Chicago: University of Chicago Press.

Bennett, J.A. 1987. *Wealth of the Solomons: A History of a Pacific Archipelago, 1800–1978*. Honolulu: University of Hawaii Press.

Capell, A. 1944. 'Notes on the Islands of Choiseul and New Georgia', *Oceania*, 17: 20–29.

Cheyne, A. 1971. *The Trading Voyages of Andrew Cheyne, 1841–1844*, ed. D. Shineberg. Canberra: Australian National University Press.

D'Arcy, P. 2006. *The People of the Sea: Environment, Identity, and History in Oceania*. Honolulu: University of Hawaii Press.

Dureau, C.M. 2001. 'Recounting and Remembering First Contact on Simbo, Western Solomon Islands', in *Cultural Memory: Reconfiguring History and*

Identity in the Postcolonial Pacific, J.M. Mageo (ed), 130–62. Honolulu: University of Hawaii Press.

Harrison, S. 2006. *Fracturing Resemblances: Identity and Mimetic Conflict in Melanesia and the West*. Oxford: Berghahn.

Hau'ofa, E. 1994. 'Our Sea of Islands', *The Contemporary Pacific* 6: 148–61.

Hocart, A.M. 1922. 'The Cult of the Dead in Eddystone of the Solomons', *Journal of the Royal Anthropological Institute* 52: 71–112, 259–305.

———— 1925. 'Medicine and Witchcraft in Eddystone of the Solomons', *Journal of the Royal Anthropological Institute* 55: 229–70.

———— 1929. *Lau Islands, Fiji*. Honolulu: Bernice P. Bishop Museum.

———— 1931. 'Warfare in Eddystone of the Solomon Islands', *Journal of the Royal Anthropological Institute* 61: 301–24.

———— 1935. 'The Canoe and the Bonito in Eddystone', *Journal of the Royal Anthropological Institute* 65: 97–111.

———— 1937. 'Fishing in Eddystone', *Journal of the Royal Anthropological Institute* 67: 33–41.

———— 1970 [1936]. *Kings and Councillors: An Essay in the Comparative Anatomy of Human Society*, ed. R. Needham. Chicago: University of Chicago Press.

Hviding, E. 1995. *Vivinei tuari pa Ulusaghe: Stories and Legends from Marovo, New Georgia, in Four New Georgian Languages and with English Translations*. Bergen: University of Bergen; Gizo: Western Province Division of Culture.

———— 1996. *Guardians of Marovo Lagoon: Practice, Place, and Politics in Maritime Melanesia*. Honolulu: University of Hawai'i Press.

———— 2003. 'Disentangling the *Butubutu* of New Georgia: Cognatic Kinship in Thought and Action', in *Oceanic Socialities and Cultural Forms: Ethnographies of Experience*, I. Hoëm and S. Roalkvam (eds), 71–113. Oxford: Berghahn.

Hviding, E., and T. Bayliss-Smith. 2000. *Islands of Rainforest: Agroforestry, Logging and Eco-tourism in Solomon Islands*. Aldershot: Ashgate.

Kapferer, B. 2000. 'Star Wars: About Anthropology, Culture and Globalisation', *Journal of the Finnish Anthropological Society* 26(3): 2–29.

Keesing. R.M. 1982. *Kwaio Religion: The Living and the Dead in a Solomon Island Society*. New York: Columbia University Press.

———— 1987. 'Anthropology as Interpretive Quest', *Current Anthropology* 28(2): 161–76.

Keesing, R.M., and R. Tonkinson (eds). 1982. 'Reinventing Traditional Culture: The Politics of Kastom in Island Melanesia', *Mankind* (special issue) 13(4): 297–301.

Lewis, D. 1972. *We, the Navigators: The Ancient Art of Landfinding in the Pacific*. Canberra: Australian National University Press.

Rio, K.M., and O.H. Smedal. 2009. 'Hierarchy and Its Alternatives: An Introduction to Movements of Totalization and Detotalization', in *Hierarchy: Persistence and Transformation in Social Formations*, K.M. Rio and O.H. Smedal (eds), 1–63. Oxford: Berghahn.

Rivers, W.H.R. 1914. *The History of Melanesian Society*, 2 vols. Cambridge: Cambridge University Press.

Rosaldo, R. 1986. 'From the Door of His Tent: The Fieldworker and the Inquisitor', in *Writing Culture*, J. Clifford and G.E. Marcus (eds), 77–97. Berkeley: University of California Press.

Sahlins, M.D. 1985. *Islands of History*. Chicago: University of Chicago Press.

——— 2002. *Waiting for Foucault, Still*. Chicago: Prickly Paradigm Press.

Scheffler, H.W. 1962. 'Kindred and Kin Groups in Simbo Island Social Structure', *Ethnology* 1(2): 135–57.

Scott, M.W. 2007. *The Severed Snake: Matrilineages, Making Place, and a Melanesian Christianity in Southeast Solomon Islands*. Durham, NC: Carolina Academic Press.

Scubla, L. 2002. 'Hocart and the Royal Road to Anthropological Understanding', *Social Anthropology* 10: 359–76.

Somerville, H.B.T. 1897. 'Ethnographical Notes in New Georgia, Solomon Islands', *Journal of the Royal Anthropological Institute* 26: 357–413.

Stockdale, J. (ed). 1789. *The Voyage of Governor Phillip to Botany Bay; with an Account of the Establishment of the Colonies of Port Jackson and Norfolk Island; Compiled From Authentic Papers … to which are Added the Journals of Lieuts. Shorthand, Watts, Ball and Capt. Marshall with an Account of Their New Discoveries*. London.

Stocking, G.W. 1995. *After Tylor: British Social Anthropology, 1888–1951*. Madison: University of Wisconsin Press.

Thomas, N. 2010. *Islanders: The Pacific in the Age of Empire*. New Haven: Yale University Press.

3

The Genealogical Method

Vella Lavella Reconsidered

◆●◆

Cato Berg

Method through Time

The genealogical method as developed by W.H.R. Rivers has been praised as a milestone of anthropological inquiry, having provided one of the first frameworks for dealing systematically with kinship and descent. But since its inception, the genealogical method has also been targeted by critical voices, even from Rivers's students and colleagues (Hocart 1915; Radcliffe-Brown 1952). Some recent commentators have been more generous towards Rivers (e.g. Scheffler 1985; 2000), both in terms of concepts and method. In the following, I seek to give a brief background to Rivers's mode of inquiry in the field of kinship, as it was initially conceived in the Torres Strait Islands and later honed in his work among the Toda (Rivers 1906). I then take a close look at his use of the method during the Percy Sladen Trust Expedition, in the island of Vella Lavella in the Western Solomons. As a form of ethnographic practice, the genealogical method simultaneously combines fieldwork technique, theory and even ethics. In this respect, the vantage point provided by the method subsumes important aspects of what the discipline of anthropology is about. The collection of genealogical data is thus a cornerstone in the history of the discipline itself, although its overall significance has remained contested, as seen, for example, in recent work by Carsten (2004) and Bamford and Leach (2009).

It is, however, beyond the scope of this chapter to fully assess the various discussions and debates that have unfolded over a century about the merits and misfortunes of the genealogical method, and about the wider contestation of kinship studies. Instead, I aim to demonstrate some aspects of how the method was applied by Rivers, based on his original materials, and to compare certain empirical materials from the Percy Sladen Trust Expedition of 1908 with contemporary materials from my own field research in the same localities. I will also consider some general points concerning method that stem originally from Rivers. For me, engaging with Rivers's original materials has been an exercise based on my experiences of on-the-ground research issues focused on a conflict over land, timber and logging operations in north-west Vella Lavella. Ironically, this type of scene seems to display the most lasting impact of Rivers's *History of Melanesian Society* (1914a) in what was once his fieldwork locale, for that book was used by the British Solomon Islands Protectorate's second Land Commission in the 1950s to build a model of kinship-based land rights and inheritance systems for the Western Solomons, with the resultant recommendation that local land tenure principles should adapt a system of unilineal descent (Allan 1957). This anthropologically informed colonial initiative continues to inform land disputes heard in the courts of the contemporary Solomon Islands (Berg 2008).

Theorising the Genealogical Method

Rivers himself described the path of discovery which involved obtaining social statistics through a 'genealogical method' in his accounts from the Cambridge expedition to the Torres Strait in 1898. The method was subsequently used by him in fieldwork among the Toda in India (see Rivers 1906), and he developed and applied his genealogical tool to the full extent during fieldwork in the Solomon Islands and elsewhere in Island Melanesia in 1908. In a famous article from 1900, Rivers laid out the programme for collecting what he calls 'social and vital statistics' (Rivers 1900: 77). 'Social statistics' are used to infer marriage practices, totemic relations, name taboos and so forth, whereas 'vital statistics' can be used to deduce such things as reproductive qualities in marriages – an interesting point since Rivers had at that time become preoccupied with what later became the main use of materials from Vella Lavella: his depopulation hypothesis (Rivers 1900: 81; 1922).

In light of the fieldwork carried out during the Percy Sladen Trust Expedition, what is most noteworthy about the methodological approaches taken by Rivers and Hocart was that, in defiance of 'armchair anthropology', they let their theories be continuously developed by the empirical materials they gathered in various locations. This was exactly the opposite of the approach for which Godelier (1988: 72) and others have criticised a much earlier perpetrator, namely Rousseau: that exotic ethnographic facts collected randomly (or perhaps rather strategically and selectively) were put to use to illustrate what was at the time largely 'Western theory'. Although Rivers fell under the spell of diffusionism for some time, his writings show that he took into account 'exotic' people's reports on phenomena that were at the time discussed under this or that theoretical 'heading'.[1]

In 1908, anthropology was in its early years as an ethnographically grounded discipline that generated its own theories. Although Rivers has been criticised for a simplistic adaptation of concepts of 'pedigree' in his genealogical method and kinship studies (e.g. Bouquet 1993; see also Holy 1996), it was hardly a coincidence that he 'invented' kinship studies on-site in the Torres Strait, not at his desk in Cambridge.

That Rivers resorted to the imagery of pedigrees or family trees when he recorded and drew genealogies may not have been so wayward after all, as it seems his informants had no problems with adapting or formulating their own kinship relations along such lines. Genealogical charts in Rivers's published and unpublished materials may in fact well represent what were people's own depictions of their own kinship systems. We should recall that Rivers always had as his starting point a single individual, and how he went from there can easily be seen in the ways in which lines of relatives are portrayed in the unpublished manuscripts from the Percy Sladen Trust Expedition. If we take as our vantage point the idea that such lines depict local notions of kinship in, for example, Vella Lavella, then Rivers can be seen to have cleverly created and modified the genealogical method through the collection of empirical data.

Thus, the genealogical method was perhaps as much founded initially in Torres Strait Islanders' own models of kinship, and later honed and perfected through subsequent fieldwork. This interesting relationship between ethnography and model-making is also seen in Deacon's analysis of kinship in Ambrym (Deacon 1927), where he learned the repetitive cycle of marriage and remarriage between kin from an informant's visualisation in a sand drawing (see Rio and Eriksen, this volume), and in the concept of the person in New Caledonia as presented in the work of Leenhardt (1979), with its attentiveness to people's own models.

The contribution Rivers made to anthropology and kinship theory was thus substantially beyond what is conventionally attributed to him in terms of method. The sympathetic reappraisal by Scheffler (1985; 2000) of Rivers's influence, mostly through the published lectures in *Kinship and Social Organisation* (1914b), is a case in point. According to Scheffler (1985: 2), Rivers not only drew a sound distinction between 'kinship' and 'descent', but also supplied much of the theoretical vocabulary used by kinship theorists to this day. For instance, it was Rivers, not one of his kinship-focused successors at Cambridge, Meyer Fortes, who grappled initially with the notion of 'descent'. As Scheffler (1985: 2) notes, Rivers took the concept of descent as it was commonly used in the English language and suggested it should only be used in a much more narrow sense, namely to distinguish between matrilineal and patrilineal kin from the perspective of becoming a member of a group. This distinction further led Rivers to separate certain bundles of rights, such as those derived from unilineal descent, from those emerging from kinship relations, which he held to be universal and necessarily bilateral. Rivers further introduced the concepts 'succession' and 'inheritance', which are vital to understanding the manner through which a person becomes a member of 'society' (Scheffler 1985: 2). Familiar to any social and cultural anthropologist, these concepts may be better known from the work of another of Rivers's successors, A.R. Radcliffe-Brown (1952), who used these distinctions to establish the concepts of *jus in rem* and *jus in personam*.

Many of these questions have been debated elsewhere, and it is beyond the scope of this chapter to go into them further (but see Hviding and Berg, this volume). Instead, I wish to draw attention to another more specific facet of Rivers's kinship programme arising from his fieldwork in the Western Solomons in 1908. It is far from well-known that the work by Rivers on demography and death rates in Vella Lavella (Rivers 1922) relied on his application of complex kinship data, not merely statistics, collected along the coast of that island. Although Rivers had received funds from the Percy Sladen Memorial Trust to search for what he believed were ancient 'mother right' societies in this part of Melanesia, he did not realise that Vella Lavella was one of the few matrilineal societies in the New Georgia Islands, and was in fact a prime example of precisely the type of social organisation he was looking for. Despite this significant lapse by Rivers, the reanalysis of his materials which I carry out here permits a reappraisal of their relevance and value as a remarkable record of a certain village of Vella Lavella in 1908.

Rivers and Vella Lavella: Encounters over 100 Years

I carried out archival work in the Cambridge University Library in 2008, and had the chance to examine Rivers's original fieldnotes, with a specific focus on kinship diagrams and genealogies from most of the villages of Vella Lavella. The materials constituted a window into conditions on the island exactly 100 years ago, and their historical value could be assessed against my own field materials from 2001. Although I was familiar with most of the published materials from Rivers's scholarly career, in particular *The History of Melanesian Society* (Rivers 1914a), in 2008 I had the chance to go through first-hand data sets from what was arguably not only one of the few ethnographic accounts of Vella Lavella, but also the first one ever produced. The only substantial published account by Rivers of that island is found in a brief, largely comparative sub-chapter in *The History of Melanesian Society*, and is limited to a note on kinship terminology and relational terms of address as recorded in 1908. This was well before Christian missions gained widespread influence in Vella Lavella, not to speak of later developments on the island involving global capitalism, large-scale logging and mineral prospecting. What caught my attention in Cambridge was the minute detail with which Rivers had recorded kinship terminology and genealogies. This converged with my own work in significant ways, given my core interest in how kinship is politicised today through fierce village disputes surrounding logging ventures.

Considering that Rivers and Hocart only spent about a month in Vella Lavella (following about four months in Simbo), how good is the material, and what does it contain? We have to take into account that at the time, although researching a fairly simple kinship system based on seniority and gender, Rivers was working through specific informants and interpreters, accumulating, cross-checking, verifying and rejecting information as the work proceeded. This can be seen on sheets where the kinship terminology has been recorded, then crossed out, and then re-recorded – a process repeated perhaps three or four times in many cases. This uncertainty appears to have been the case particularly for affines, a category that Rivers never really came to grips with. This shortcoming was a major part of the largest flaw of the Vella Lavella fieldwork, namely the failure by Rivers (and Hocart) to see that the people of the island were in fact organised in localised matriclans – a 'society organised through mother right'. At Simbo, where kinship is and was bilateral and descent cognatic, Rivers and Hocart could not have found such a system – but on Vella Lavella, where it was present, they could have, but did not, find it.

Returning briefly to the issue of the politicised contestation of land and kinship, the question may be asked how far advanced this had become in 1908. Jackson (1978) comments that when the protectorate's first Lands Commission held its hearings, ten years after Rivers and Hocart had visited New Georgia, a large number of cases from Vella Lavella were heard. For instance, in north-west Vella Lavella, the pioneer Methodist missionary J.F. Goldie alone had managed to privately alienate from the customary tenure system some 6,000 acres belonging to the kin group at Mudimudi (Bennett 1987: 253–54; Berg 2008). This particular instance of land alienation lies at the origins of the extended case I shall examine below. Revd

Goldie would hardly have been able to alienate so much land in the more central mission localities of Roviana Lagoon, where the chiefs of the day were already experienced parties in land dealings, both with the rising colonial administration as well as with more or less shady expatriate traders, some long resident in the Western Solomons. Customary land managers in the Bilua district of southern Vella Lavella were also quite experienced, as there had been several land deals involving European traders since about 1890, especially at Liapari and Liangai in the far south.

It is interesting to note that Goldie's private land deal at Mudimudi ultimately got him into trouble with the Mission Society in New Zealand, so that he had to later sell the plot on.[2] In fact, as seen in the letters of R.C. Nicholson, the resident Methodist missionary at Bilua, local people at the time were aware not only of the value of land in terms of copra production, but also of past misdealing concerning land.[3] In her analysis of late nineteenth- and early twentieth-century traders and copra planters in New Georgia, Bennett (1987: 109) notes that certain tracts of land were alienated quite early by traders such as Frank Wickham and Peter Pratt, in part encouraged by the colonial administration as a means of 'pacifying' trouble spots through copra production. But for Vella Lavella specifically, McKinnon (1972, 1975) describes how relationships with the traders were partly monopolised by important local chiefs, and unlike at Roviana and Kolobangara, larger-scale alienation of land in Vella Lavella did not to take place until the advent of missionaries in the early twentieth century.

Returning now to Rivers, his ethnographic materials and his use of them, he did complete aspects of his evolving theoretical programme, as seen in *The History of Melanesian Society*. However, while the essay he had published in 1900 on the genealogical method outlined an analytical programme for ethnographically grounded kinship studies, his monumental two-volume book on Melanesia was an ambitious comparative attempt to reconstruct original kinship structures for the region, interspersed and woven together with any manner of brief information on ritual, totemism and leadership, to name just a few topics. Rivers did not pursue a more sophisticated agenda of kinship studies and theoretical refinement, although much can be glimpsed in his collection *Kinship and Social Organisation* (Rivers 1914b), especially with regard to the tenets of kinship common at the time and their wider implications for society. The absence of more sophisticated analysis suggests that Rivers may have gone astray or been otherwise intellectually occupied. As Langham (1981) has noted, Rivers also missed out on the six-class system in Ambrym later analysed by Deacon (1927; see also Rio and Eriksen, this volume). Clearly, Rivers was deeply engaged in other topics in the Solomons, and the sheer scope of the survey work he undertook in addition to the in-depth fieldwork at Simbo may have overwhelmed him (see Bayliss-Smith, this volume).

As a result, Rivers never saw that kinship in Vella Lavella may have represented one of those 'surviving' types of 'mother right' societies that he was looking for, particularly so in the context of the island's non-Austronesian language, which he certainly would have known was connected to more 'ancient' Pacific populations. He did note that the language of Vella Lavella, like that of Savo in the central Solomons, formed part of a much older family than that of some (Austronesian) neighbours (Rivers 1914a: 241, 252). Curiously enough, he noted for Savo the importance of the relationship between mother's brother and sister's son, but he missed it for Vella Lavella. As for the enigmatic island name of 'Vella Lavella' itself, Rivers did not manage to ascertain its origins, as Haddon (1937: 107) later noted. Thus, in his search for mother right and the existence of two different systems throughout Melanesia, it is safe to say that Rivers overlooked the potential significance of the island in his puzzle. It may be unfair, though, to criticise Rivers on this specific point, given that much more recent research in linguistics and archaeology has also been unsuccessful in untangling the complex patterns of relationship between Austronesian and non-Austronesian languages and populations in Island Melanesia.[4] It is fairly certain that this region was populated by non-Austronesian groups from around 28,000 BP, with migrations over Bougainville through the Shortland Islands and Choiseul (Wickler and Spriggs 1988; Wickler 1991).

Vexatious and unresolved questions of origins apart, the materials that Rivers collected in Vella Lavella did become a backbone of some of his later work that fuelled debates of the day. In his edited volume on the depopulation of Melanesia, Rivers combined the Vella Lavella materials with genealogies from Simbo for his chapter on the 'psychological factor' (Rivers 1922). This slim volume is interesting for the ways in which Rivers, and other authors who were prominent colonial administrators and missionaries, offered explanations for the perceived accelerating 'extinction' of Melanesian peoples.[5] The reason for this, Rivers argued, was (apart from introduced diseases) an apparent 'lack of will' to live in the rapidly changing circumstances of the new colonies and protectorates of the region (Bennett, this volume). Rivers used Simbo material to strengthen this hypothesis, reinforced with demographic and genealogical materials from Vella Lavella.

Vella Lavella through Multiple Looking Glasses

Although to our knowledge, most of Rivers's material from the Percy Sladen Trust Expedition is now lost, perhaps intentionally destroyed by Grafton

Elliot-Smith when he acted as executor for Rivers's estate (Langham 1981), bits and pieces remain. They have not been systematised, however, and remain in the Haddon Papers in the Rare Books and Manuscript Collection of Cambridge University Library. To my knowledge, the genealogies themselves were rediscovered by Tim Bayliss-Smith in 2004 when he was reassessing the demographic data for Rivers's hypothesis on Melanesian depopulation. In the Haddon Papers, genealogies recorded by Rivers on Vella Lavella were placed with his genealogies from Simbo, which constitute a much larger corpus. Until now it was not widely known that Rivers's original genealogies from Vella Lavella had survived the tooth of time, and that they exist in both rewritten and computed versions produced by Rivers himself.[6] To provide for an even broader picture, the genealogies can be compared to the data sheets Rivers used for physical anthropology measurements, and to the photographs he took during fieldwork.

Below I shall make use of a multi-layered composite of materials from Vella Lavella, in which Rivers's originals as well as his later revised genealogies are compared. The latter were used to compile the materials for his depopulation thesis, which can be seen from the calculations found in the Rivers manuscripts.[7] The former are the original, yellowed, frail sheets he used in Vella Lavella in 1908. Some further comments on my 'experiment' are needed. I have also used Rivers's material on physical anthropology, particularly to ascertain age classes in terms of the people he encountered and who are to some degree present in the genealogies. I have then compared Rivers's photographs of people and places with genealogies and 'physical anthropological measurements', not only to ascertain the exact localities at which these materials were collected in 1908, but also to retrace the route Rivers and Hocart took around Vella Lavella. The materials have been further contextualised in terms of my own fieldwork materials from 1996, 2001/2 and 2009 in order to trace relationships and places. Together, the combined materials, which span a century, convey a striking close-up picture of Vella Lavella in 1908, and provide in-depth demographic insights concerning people living in the villages visited at the time.

I wish to propose some general thoughts on the potential uses of this composite model. Breaking the genealogical sets down to show village composition raises an interesting question in terms of the materials left by Rivers and Hocart. They both seem to have internalised certain local concepts concerning demography and leadership to some degree. For instance, Hocart referred to four 'districts' in Roviana in his notes on leadership,[8] and he also described the social and geographical spheres of influence of certain named chiefs. It appears that power and leadership were not simply centralised but dependent on their potentials for wider reach. This raises questions beyond the scope of this chapter, but social organisation in pre-colonial New Georgia was notable for the ways in which alliances and other dimensions of sociality reached far beyond the mere boundaries of village and island (Hviding, this volume), a pattern that was all too easily misinterpreted by casual European onlookers, who perhaps tended to retranslate what they saw in terms of their own concepts of village, town and country.

For Vella Lavella, the materials in the Rivers manuscripts indicate how Rivers operated with eleven data sets.[9] Having confronted his methodology and the materials it generated against localities from Vella Lavella with which I am familiar, I believe that the data sets emerged from what one might call eleven hamlets, or residential compounds within villages. They represent some three to four generations, thus extending back to the early nineteenth century. From various references in Hocart's published and unpublished materials, I believe it is safe to assume that the units dealt with are indeed hamlets. However, it is important to note the frequent practice, past and present, of co-residence in hamlets or villages as a result of intermarriage among, or even hostility between, clans – implying a trans-localised character of some clans, even in an inter-island fashion (see also McDougall 2000). In actual fact, Rivers and Hocart had some prior knowledge of Vella Lavella before they went there: some of their important informants in Simbo were from the island, which illustrates the New Georgian pattern of inter-island travel and social relationships, and the bearings this had on their fieldwork (see Hviding, this volume).

The composite generative model I worked with reveals data regarding marriage and residence patterns that are much more detailed than what has so far been thought possible from the published works of Rivers. Initially, approaching the work of Rivers in this synthesised form may seem somewhat problematic, not least since Hocart's descriptions are much more in line with contemporary ethnography, with detailed personal information and case materials. It takes some effort when going through the remnants of Rivers's materials to see that he was not only an acute observer but also a very detailed recorder, whose observations shed light even on localised, highly detailed patterns of demography in relation to death and fertility. The potential of this material can be seen in the work of Bayliss-Smith (2006), who argues that infertility on Simbo was mainly a result of an escalation in sexually transmitted diseases. I will not speculate further on this issue, but it is notable that there is a remarkable lack of children in what both Rivers (1922) and Bayliss-Smith (2006) termed 'generation three' as seen from the time of the fieldwork.

The opportunity rarely arises to compare materials collected at a time when genealogical information was relatively uncontested and detailed case studies from almost 100 years later when this kind of information is highly contested. But the availability of such a range of ethnographic and demographic information with a 1908 baseline makes for fascinating long-term comparison, not only of the different ethnographic materials but more importantly of what they portray. I have found it particularly revealing to compare my own genealogical and ethnographic materials from Vella Lavella with those collected by Rivers and Hocart a hundred years earlier. Their materials provide inspiring challenges for other research in the area in terms of both historical and contemporary fieldwork, and the results of the Percy Sladen Trust Expedition cry out for a more contemporary, theoretically refined mode of grasping inter-island networks of marriage, warfare, exchange, migration, leadership and so on (see Hviding, this volume). Breaking down Rivers's own generative models of fertility and death is also the key to understanding the material contained in Hocart's unpublished manuscripts and fieldnotes. Attempts to bring Hocart's largely overlooked material into dialogue with more recent research in the Western Solomons have mostly resulted from initiatives by individual scholars, including McKinnon (1972, 1975), Hviding (1996), Dureau (1998, 1999), Scales (2004), Bayliss-Smith (2006) and Berg (2008). The potential for pan-New Georgian comparison has been particularly recognised by Hviding (this volume). But rarely is such an opportunity of comparison in time and space offered as in the present case of Vella Lavella.

In approaching the original materials left by Rivers, two different types of information were of interest to me, which are also the ones Rivers himself would probably have classified as 'vital' and 'social' statistics (Rivers 1900: 77). I had already assessed my own data on kinship terminology against the terminology with which Rivers was occupied in 1908. For me, the initial obstacle was finding a key to how Rivers organised his materials. The remaining materials are raw data in terms of single sheets and exclude his notes and written-up analysis, except some revised data sheets containing written-up versions of the originals, and some sheets containing codes and numbers. I thus had to start from scratch in finding out not how he had used the materials, which was relatively easy in terms of the publication history for Vella Lavella, since there are very few anthropological publications directly about that island subsequent to Rivers's own contributions (Rivers 1914a, 1922).

And so the main materials I began working with were the genealogies, mostly the faded and original manuscripts, containing multiple deletions and corrections, probably used by River himself in the field.[10] In addition, there are data sheets containing physical measurements of head length, head breadth, cephalic index, nose length, nose breadth and nasal index, all typical of early twentieth-century physical anthropology. Regarding the photographic collection, I concluded that a number of Rivers's photographs held at Cambridge University's Museum of Archaeology and Anthropology are identifiable by name and village name, and show frontal and side views of what seems to be a typical sample of the very same people. At first I struggled to identify Rivers's system for underlining names in genealogies and for assigning information in the Physical Anthropology Manuscripts (PAM), to persons listed as V1 up to V8. The photographs, some used by Haddon in lectures on anthropology, had been mislabelled 'Eddystone'. On the back of each photograph was recorded a name and place in Rivers's own unmistakeable handwriting, and having ascertained that the places and people in question were actually from Vella Lavella I went back to the data sheets in the Haddon Papers.

A person would be entered by Rivers – for example, under 'V6 Morumora 70' – with physical measurements added. The listings are in terms of age; Morumora is the eldest, and the person ending the ordinary list is 'V5 Mbotai 6'. The age span covers three generations, in some cases four. In addition, there are a number of sheets where Rivers obviously had some classification problems, since he had information on persons either living on other islands or of mixed parentage, a puzzle to which I will return. Regarding genealogies, Rivers used the convention of recording male names in capital letters, some underlined twice, and others once. This was another puzzle, but I found that people whose names were underlined once were those living when Rivers was there. Based on the PAM sheets, I found that people underlined twice were also registered with physical measurements. By comparing listings in the genealogies and cross-referencing them with PAM sheets, I found that eight Vella Lavella villages could be reconstructed in terms of Rivers's data. The first he visited, based on the chronological recording of data, was Jurio, misspelled as 'Torio'. The second was 'Mudimudi', the original village site for present day Irigila. That settlement was moved just prior to 1910 because of its unhealthy location among mangroves, a result of the initial move of the population down to the coastal plantation and mission house built in 1904.

It is the village of 'Mudimudi' or Irigila I shall concentrate on here. Rivers recorded genealogical and physical data there for eighteen men. In addition, he recorded those who lived there but who had genealogies from elsewhere, such as a boy from Rauru (Lauru, now Choiseul) named Lesu (which means 'head' in the language of Vella Lavella), and Bio from Bugotu in Isabel. Astonishingly, Rivers also managed to record offspring of inter-island marriages such as 'Lirambule' (age 13) also called Ghasimata, designated as half Rubiana (Roviana), one-quarter Zhava (or Java in Vella) and one-quarter Sabana (western Isabel). Another individual recorded was Narasu or Lolorho (age 55 to 60), designated half Rubiana and half

Bilua (south Vella). All in all, this shows the clarity and depth of Rivers's genealogical work as exemplified by this specific village. Even today, people remember such complex genealogical links generated by inter-island marriages, both concerning themselves and others, a fact which was of great assistance to me when tracing certain relationships through a combination of the materials collected by Rivers and myself.

One question that arose early in my work with Rivers's genealogies and terminological relationships was that the version presented for Vella Lavella in *The History of Melanesian Society* was simplified in terms of affinal terminology. Rivers's data was far more detailed and more complex in its unpublished form than in its brief published outline. What led him to omit and simplify the terminological system in the time between fieldwork, writing up his notes and publishing? I found no clues in the notes apart from several sheets written out in computed form that showed the various versions he had worked on in relation to the 1914 book. But he left several clues in the form of short commentaries on the terminology in the book, which I will look at in greater detail below.

In *The History of Melanesian Society*, Vella Lavella initially received the same status as other islands in New Georgia and elsewhere, amounting only to a short paragraph. Rivers did little to ponder over the materials gathered on that island, and appears to have been more interested in a grander comparative sweep. In no way was this different from other reports on Vella Lavella at that time and in later scholarly and popular publications (Salisbury 1922; Waterhouse 1931; Lanyon-Orgill 1953). Rivers did note that Vella Lavella did not quite fit into the scheme he had devised for the Western Solomons overall, and commented that the island, like Savo, was 'a place where the language departs from the usual Melanesian type' (Rivers 1914a: 252). It may be unjustified to overly criticise his analysis and compilation of the materials from Vella Lavella given that he stayed only for a month or so, but there are some puzzling omissions in his description.

First, Rivers did not describe nor comment on the concept of *toutou* – just as he also omitted, perhaps more spectacularly, the highly prevalent concept of *butubutu* (cognatic descent group) for Simbo and other parts of New Georgia (Scheffler 1962; Hviding 2003 and this volume). Instead, he denied the presence of larger social groupings such as those he had identified in, say, Guadalcanal and Savo by stating that: 'There are no social groups corresponding to clans' (Rivers 1914a: 251). Thus, surprisingly, he entirely missed the importance of matrilineal descent groups called *toutou* in Vella Lavella. *Toutou* are still of paramount importance for social organisation on the island, and even the missionary Nicholson acknowledged their importance just fourteen years after the fieldwork by Hocart and Rivers:

Women were of very great importance – and still are – in that all land belongs to a clan of matriarchal descent called a toutou. There is no individual ownership; in every case the land belongs to this toutou. As a matter of fact the toutou is the strongest term of relationship on the island, and represents the most important factor in the social life of the people. Children always belong to the clan of the mother and never to that of the father. It is because of the tremendous significance of the toutou in land matters that marriage was the cause of much intertribal fighting. (Nicholson 1922: 21)

It thus seems reasonable beyond doubt that *toutou* was in fact a definite social form and force when Rivers and Hocart visited Vella Lavella. But Rivers's neglect of *toutou* may be explained as it has been for the *butubutu* (Scheffler 1962; Hviding 2003): he was much more preoccupied with extracting information on the terminological systems, which he ultimately believed concealed an original element, and proof of, dual organisation. Rivers did not overlook the importance of clan-type group formation elsewhere in the Solomons, for instance in Savo, which was also different from the 'Melanesian type' (Rivers 1914a: 252). But in the Western Solomons, where he (and Hocart) carried out their only long-term fieldwork, he completely missed this analytical level in his own data, and today we may only speculate as to how this came about. Was there something inherent in the very device that he himself had designed – the genealogical method – that prevented him from seeing society at a level higher than that of the individual? Rivers clearly saw 'society', although not using the term, as a collection of individuals bound by certain relationships – those relationships outlined in the genealogies he collected. It is perhaps here that the greatest flaw of the genealogical method can be identified, as he sought the meanings of relationships in the very terms of address used locally to denote them. He thus tried to define relationships not in the wider social settings in which they occurred, but rather in the dyadic sets themselves as defined by kinship terminology. In the case of Vella Lavella, he did not see why certain terms were singled out.

This brings us one step further to the 'system of Vella Lavella'. How did Rivers fare in collecting and analysing the terms he encountered in 1908? He was undoubtedly somewhat puzzled, particularly so regarding the terms for in-laws:

Here, as in Eddystone, there was some doubt about the proper terms for the husband's brother and the wife's sister and their reciprocals. It is probable that the wives of both elder and younger brother are called *niania* while a woman calls both elder and younger brother of her husband *menggora*, but it may be that the use of *niania* should be limited to the wife of the elder brother and *menggora* to the younger brother of the husband. Similarly, was some question whether the elder sister of the wife should not be *niania* and her younger sister *menggora*, but it was almost certain that a man called all the sisters of the wife *niania* and that reciprocally a woman called all the husbands of all her sisters *menggora* whether they were older or younger than herself. (Rivers 1914a: 254)

I have elsewhere described what I believe are the foundational notions of kinship in Vella Lavella (Berg 2008), and will only give a brief description here. The themes of hierarchy, in terms of male and female and of precedence (Bellwood 1996), are seen in the kin terms, and particularly so in those that apply to relations between brothers and sisters. *Kaka* ('elder', also 'higher') and *visi* ('younger', also 'lower') are the only terms used, which points to the importance of age and/or rank regarding genealogical seniority. This is also seen in the excerpt from Rivers just quoted, where he was unsure regarding terms for in-laws. Had he only added the importance of the matrilineal system, it would have become much clearer. The clues were there in his own material, briefly outlined in *The History of Melanesian Society*: '*Sanggi*. A term used in some districts for the brother–sister relationship; probably the correct term for it, though those of different sex usually now address another as *anggaka* or *avisi* according to age' (Rivers 1914a: 254). Had Rivers only pondered why the brother–sister relationship was singled out terminologically with that of the sister's son and mother's brother, he might have realised that what he was dealing with on Vella Lavella was a matrilineal kinship system. In this system, the sister is the custodian of land and is treated with deference by her brothers. Likewise, mother's brothers are the protectors of their sister's sons and will eventually transfer their titles to them in terms of leadership. The brother–sister relationship calls for particular attention within a *toutou*, and that is why the terms of higher and lower (*kaka* and *visi*) should be circumvented in direct address. The term *sanggi* does not in any way connote any sense of hierarchy, and is thus used instead of *kaka* and *visi* between brothers and sisters.

Rivers thus did not see the importance of the relationship between mother's brother and sister's son, which is all the more puzzling since it is singled out terminologically. The *papa–pakora* relationship is the foundation of chieftainship in the island, and depends also on relationships within the matrilineal *toutou*. The mother's brother (or brothers) will transfer the chieftainship (or in small groups, forms of less institutionalised leadership) to their eldest sister's son (or sons).

But we must also take into account the situation in which Rivers and Hocart worked in 1908, one characterised by, if not great turmoil, then definitely rapid and wide-ranging social change. Being a cornerstone in the inter-island raiding and headhunting complex in New Georgia, and one of the last islands to come under the sway of the protectorate, Vella Lavella attracted more than its share of 'pacification attempts' by Resident Commissioner Woodford and the new colonial administrative presence on nearby Gizo. The notorious police officer Mahaffy, Woodford's resident representative on Gizo, had been given the task of curbing headhunting raids in New Georgia (Bennett 1987: 107). With his police force composed of specially trained men from Isabel, Malaita and other overseas locations, Mahaffy undertook several raids on Vella Lavella, destroying war canoes and seizing firearms used in recent headhunting raids. Some Vella Lavella warriors proved resilient to these strategies, however. The very last raids from Vella Lavella took place as late as the time of Rivers's fieldwork, and during 1908 at least one European trader was killed for his head elsewhere in New Georgia, in Marovo. This was only a year before the 'Binskin affair', in which a Vella warrior named Sito killed the family of a resident trader, causing a massacre by a gathering of traders, Malaitan labourers and other islanders who, it appeared, had scores to settle with people in Vella Lavella (Bennett 1987: 107–8).

But an even stronger social force on the island than that of the expanding British Empire was that of the Methodist mission. The Revd R.C. Nicholson had arrived in Vella Lavella as resident Methodist missionary in 1906, and most certainly interacted with Rivers and Hocart during their travels around the island, given that Nicholson later expressed great admiration for Rivers in his book on the converted 'savage' Danny Bula (Nicholson 1922: 15–16). Nicholson's somewhat peculiar invocation of 'the theory of Dr Rivers' shows that he was himself dedicated to a diffusionist interpretation of the island, going into local customs and beliefs in a rather shallow way, but unashamedly drawing comparisons between rituals on Vella Lavella and those of ancient Egypt.

Rediscovering Rivers in Vella Lavella

Having processed the information from another Cambridge visit in January 2009, I returned later that year for more fieldwork in Vella Lavella. Knowing well the risks posed by genealogical knowledge in the context of contested logging rights and disputed knowledge of intangible cultural property in the form of genealogical links, I was very careful as to how I asked and utilised the information I had acquired from the remaining materials of the Percy Sladen Trust Expedition.[11] I had no high hopes in terms of what could actually be made of the information I had obtained from my analysis of Rivers's materials, as the time span of a century is quite substantial in terms of genealogical memory, certainly in a situation where relations of descent often slide into biased clannish memory. For me, a main point of contention was matters that had remained unclear for me since my doctoral fieldwork in 2001/2, mainly concerning the status of one of the ancestors of the *toutou* named Ulukue Susu Sauro, more specifically their apical female ancestor from whom all members of the *toutou* saw themselves as connected to primary land rights in the area.

Given the situation I had been following in 2001/2 of on-going court cases, some dating back to 1992, in which fierce conflict was enmeshed in genealogical relations and land ownership, there were reasons to act carefully in terms of information management. Going about with some caution I followed some clues contained in Rivers's original genealogies, and cross-checked them against people's statements and against court affidavits accessed in Gizo and Honiara. Several of my main informants of the eldest generation in the Mudimudi area bear the names of the very same people Rivers originally questioned, being, as they are, named after famous warrior-chief ancestors. As far as the people involved could tell me (and I cross-checked this in several cases against affidavits), the relationship system recorded by Rivers was correct, and moreover he had managed to identify both adopted and filial kin rights, at least for the *toutou* I am familiar with. There was greater disagreement among the elderly members of the village over some of the terminology that Rivers had omitted from *The History of Melanesian Society*. These were terms that were largely absent in terms of present-day relationships, having been grounded in forms of etiquette encoded in language and relationship dyads that had been abandoned with the arrival of churches and the departure from bush settlements. Some of the more respected bearers of tradition even disagreed amongst themselves, leading me to think that Rivers was right in being somewhat confused about these aspects of kinship terminology. The confusion in Rivers's notes concerned the manner in which gender and hierarchy, the core concepts of Vella Lavella kinship, are extended towards affines. This again is founded on principles of *toutou* hierarchy, which leads relatives to be classed as either higher or lower than oneself. And so, as both in the field and afterwards I reflected on Rivers's confusion regarding the terminological systems for affines, I was led to conclude that this may have been where he got it wrong. All the other terms he recorded were correct, and people use the very same terms today.

Unlike the heady, conflict-laden times of 2001–2, I found that it was a bit easier to question people about land rights and kinship in 2009. The logging of the forest had taken place, and the money from royalties had largely been spent. Another possible influence was the earthquake and tsunami that hit the Western Solomons in April 2007. The village at Irigila had been shattered, which had led to relocation further inland, with just a few people still living at the old village site. In 2009, people in fact lived closer to the areas where their ancestors had lived in 1908. The relocation had not led to the social realignment of houses, however, since people had built new houses according to *toutou* membership. The *toutou* of Ulukue Susu Sauro still resided in a carefully chosen area, closest to their defined ancestral lands. Over the course of a month I had repeated conversations with the two eldest members of the *toutou* on origins and kinship, largely based on Rivers's notes. They were a bit puzzled by the existence of these notes, which gave a slightly different version of their *toutou* history than their own recorded version, which I had also examined in affidavits. It was also a bit embarrassing to ask about information that I had supposedly obtained seven years earlier, and that I should claim that certain relations were omitted in the version I had been given.

One of the contentious issues was the status in local cosmology of adoption.[12] This points back to one of the preoccupations Rivers had in the course of his fieldwork in Vella Lavella. Although the issue of depopulation was explained by the islanders as 'a time of big death' because of the abandonment of ancestor worship, local history clearly pointed to the fact that there were indeed very few births on the island at the time. When the oldest living woman of the *toutou* outlined to me her ancestry back to about 1900, it became clear that quite a few of the *toutou* in the area had experienced severe problems in reproducing themselves. One woman had been adopted from a neighbouring district into the *toutou*, and was in fact reckoned to be the closest apical ancestor by young people, who tend to have a much more shallow genealogical memory than elders do. The issue of adoption had in fact emerged in the notorious court case that lasted from 1992 to 2002, and had ultimately led to the defeat of the *toutou*. When I outlined some abbreviated versions of the genealogies collected by Rivers, the elders were even able to point out an issue of methodology that I had missed when examining Rivers's materials. They recognised names and even knew the locations of certain people at the time of the 1908 fieldwork, and significantly commented that the person who recorded the genealogical information back then – that is, Rivers – must have cross-checked the relationships in several villages, and thus recorded several versions at the same time. Rivers may have done this unknowingly, as he was more intent on checking terms of relationships than on compiling a master genealogy for the entire island.

This also led to the topic of *toutou* as descent groups, and to the lack of any such organisational level in Rivers's original analysis. Given the time span of more than a century, I knew that the task of finding information on the issue would be nearly impossible. But some light was thrown on it anyway in conversations with elders, who pointed to a fact I had already surmised: in the chaotic situation of 1908, with the forced abandonment of the entire ritual complex and local organisation attached to *toutou lekasa* ('descent group chiefs') in relation to headhunting, *toutou* organisation had for a while lost its significance. People did not become attached to the new powers of the colonial state and Christian churches through *toutou* but on a more personal basis. This is indicated in several of the recorded histories of the first converts in the region. As Harwood (1971), Jackson (1978), Bennett (1987) and especially Carter (1981) have shown, quite a few of the early Christians were in fact of chiefly status, like Silas Lezutuni from Veala south of Irigila. This eased the new mission teachers' work among the prospective converts. The organisational importance of *toutou* had, it appears, diminished for some time, which may have led Rivers astray. But we should not overlook another potential source of error, one that is not really a flaw in the genealogical method's approach of modelling social relationships around ideas of kinship, but rather the very manner in which Rivers analysed his materials.

One of the most interesting things to emerge from my queries in 2009 about Rivers's genealogies and about certain individuals in them was that people pointed out how several new *toutou* had emerged in Irigila centred on some of the individuals that Rivers had recorded. This sheds some additional light on the concept of *toutou* itself. Although *tou* (from which *toutou* is a reduplication) means nothing more than 'branch' or 'line' in the local language, it is usually defined as what we would call 'matrilineal descent corporations' (Holy 1996) or, conversely, groups formed from successive links of 'cumulative matrifiliation' (Hviding 2003). It now became clear to me that *toutou* formation could just as well be said to be a process of cumulative matrifiliation, from the manner it was now explained by the elders to the anthropologist.

Given the sensitive nature of these records, I did not follow through with a complete journey around the island to all the villages Rivers had visited, but had to be content to work with a few of the *toutou* with which I was most familiar. Given the background of the logging conflict that had also affected *toutou* in other places on the island (as well as *butubutu* in other islands of New Georgia), I had to move carefully in my research. This situation was perhaps not so different from Rivers's original work, since people must have been puzzled by his and Hocart's travels and the questions they posed as they moved around the island, not least since this was at a rather early stage of colonial history. That two white men, closely connected to a local trader (Fred Green) and also known to be acquainted with the newly arrived missionary (Revd Nicholson) travelled around and asked questions about kinship relations, and even took physical measurements, must have caused local suspicion. This suspicion may, however, have been eased by their rather long-term residence in, and familiarity with the people of, the neighbouring island of Simbo, where not a few inhabitants (and some of the ethnographers' informants) actually originated from Vella Lavella.

Failures and Findings

What Rivers found in Vella Lavella in 1908 was what he was originally looking for but unfortunately did not see: societies with a longer cultural history – that is, that were 'older' – than their surrounding neighbours, organised by 'mother right'. But he failed to see this, and ultimately gave other parts of Melanesia more weight in his comparative, evolutionary analysis in *The History of Melanesian Society*. How he made his error of course remains almost unanswerable today, although I have made some tentative attempts here. In any event, it is possible that the task of completing the massive amount of comparative work needed for his book may have drained Rivers's intellectual powers regarding the finer details of the ethnographic materials he worked with. Then again, I feel it is important to recognise Rivers's and Hocart's abilities as fieldworkers, so as to appreciate what was in my mind their real achievement. This was their ability to follow closely the statements and clues obtained from their informants. Rivers, and to an even greater degree Hocart (see Hviding, this volume), obviously gave both credit and weight to their informants, and it is tempting to ask how radically different the people of Vella Lavella actually appeared to be at the time in that vast sea of relations that spanned the whole of the New Georgia group. We should bear in mind that several of the main informants mentioned by Hocart (1922, 1925, 1931) came from Vella Lavella. Given this, we can see that Rivers's materials really did capture the nature of actual social relations among people, as seen in the genealogies I compared for Irigila. He really did get an overview of the terminology of the Vella Lavella kinship system, although he obviously struggled with affinal relations and missed the all-important relationship between sister's sons and mother's brothers, which in Vella Lavella is the cornerstone of chiefly rights, if not for the entire structural longevity of the *toutou*.

In more generous terms, we may say that Rivers did what he could to record and analyse what may in fact be one of the first modern moments in New Georgia. *Toutou* organisation may have been of secondary importance in the days immediately after the end of headhunting, with the advent of the British Solomon Islands Protectorate and Christianity. Rivers systematically recorded relationships and the relational meanings of kinship terms, while giving less attention to the structural importance of those terms in relation to their incorporation at higher levels in terms of *toutou* structure and membership. In that sense Rivers appears to be a poststructuralist before the fact – although he would probably not have liked that designation. In his quest for the origins of society, he may have given more weight to linguistic evidence than to the social explanation of variance. But aspects of his approach are uncannily similar to linguistic and anthropological debates still going on today (e.g. Fox 1996; Blust 1997), debates Rivers would have felt entirely at home in.

On a final note, returning to matters of kinship and their enduring importance in anthropology, we need to take into account that although the field of kinship studies may have lost its overall importance and even salience for new generations of anthropologists (but see Patterson 2005: 1–17), kinship still plays a crucial role in organising human lives throughout the world. People in north-western Vella Lavella use the same kinship categories today as they did when Rivers visited their island in 1908. The categories may have taken up new meanings through their politicised contestation in the context of large-scale logging and other forces of globalisation, but people are still organised through social frameworks of reference within social hierarchies and *toutou* membership.

Notes

1. Rivers clearly experienced theoretical difficulties in framing several of his most important works. He changed the framework for *The History of Melanesian Society* (see his own introduction), and later on also the introduction to *Medicine, Magic and Religion* (1924).
2. See J.F. Goldie, 'Correspondence, Joint Board for Overseas Mission, Wellington Street, Auckland', Microfilm, Pacific Manuscripts Bureau, Australian National University, Canberra, PMB 925.
3. For more on Nicholson's views, see A.W. Silvester, 'Correspondence, Joint Board for Overseas Mission, Wellington Street, Auckland', Microfilm, Pacific Manuscripts Bureau, Australian National University, Canberra, PMB 934.
4. See Bellwood, Fox and Tryon (1995) for general perspectives, and Sheppard (2004, 2005, 2006) for Vella Lavella.
5. Not least among the other contributors was Charles M. Woodford, the British Solomon Islands Protectorate's first resident commissioner (see Woodford 1922).
6. See Rivers MSS, Haddon Papers, Cambridge University Library, Cambridge (hereafter C/HP), env. 12084.
7. See Rivers MSS, C/HP, env. 12084.
8. See A.M. Hocart, 'Chieftainship', unpublished manuscript, Arthur M. Hocart Papers, MS-Papers-0060-14. Alexander Turnbull Library, National Library of New Zealand, Wellington.

9. See Rivers MSS, C/HP, env. 12009, 12084.
10. See Rivers MSS, C/HP, env. 12084.
11. See Schneider (1996) for a similar story from Roviana, Bennett (2000) and Hviding and Bayliss-Smith (2000) on the relationships between genealogies and land rights in the context of logging operations, and Jaarsma (2002) on ethnographic materials in general.
12. See the contributions to Aswani (2000), particularly McDougall (2000) on adoption in the headhunting era.

References

Allan, C.H. 1957. *Customary Land Tenure in the British Solomon Island Protectorate*, Report of the Special Lands Commission. Honiara: Western Pacific High Commission.

Aswani, S. (ed.) 2000. 'Essays on Head-hunting in the Western Solomon Islands', *Journal of the Polynesian Society* (special issue), 109(1).

Bamford, S., and J. Leach (eds) 2009. *Kinship and Beyond: The Genealogical Method Reconsidered*. Oxford: Berghahn.

Bayliss-Smith, T. 2006. 'Fertility and Depopulation: Childlessness, Abortion and Introduced Disease in Simbo and Ontong Java, Solomon Islands', in Population, Reproduction and Fertility in Melanesia, S. Ulijaszek (ed.), 13–52. Oxford: Berghahn.

Bellwood, P. 1996. 'Hierarchy, Founder Ideology and Austronesian Expansion', in *Origins, Ancestry and Alliance*, J.J. Fox and C. Sather (eds), 19–41. Canberra: Department of Anthropology, Research School of Pacific Studies, Australian National University.

Bellwood, P., J.J. Fox and D. Tryon (eds). 1995. *The Austronesians: Historical and Comparative Perspectives*. Canberra: Department of Anthropology, Research School of Pacific Studies, Australian National University.

Bennett, J.A. 1987. *Wealth of the Solomons: A History of a Pacific Archipelago, 1800–1978*. Honolulu: University of Hawaii Press.

———— 2000. *Pacific Forest: A History of Resource Control and Contest in the Solomon Islands, c. 1800–1997*. Leiden: Brill.

Berg, A.C. 2008. '"A Chief is a Chief Wherever He Goes": Land and Lines of Power in Vella Lavella, Solomon Islands', PhD diss. Bergen: University of Bergen.

Blust, R. 1997. Review of J.J. Fox and C. Sather (eds), *Origins, Ancestry and Alliance*, (1996), *Journal of Southeast Asian Studies* 28(2): 413–15.

Bouquet, M. 1993. *Reclaiming English Kinship: Portuguese Refractions of English Kinship Theory*. Manchester: Manchester University Press.

Carsten, J. 2004. *After Kinship*. Cambridge: Cambridge University Press.

Carter, G.G. 1981. *Tie Varane: Stories about People of Courage from Solomon Islands*. Rabaul: Unichurch Publishing.

Deacon, B. 1927. 'The Regulation of Marriage on Ambrym', *Journal of the Royal Anthropological Institute* 57: 325–42.

Dureau, C. 1998. 'From Sisters to Wives: Changing Contexts of Maternity on Simbo, Western Solomon Islands', in *Maternities and Modernities: Colonial and Postcolonial Experiences in Asia and the Pacific*, K. Ram and M. Jolly (eds), 239–74. Cambridge: Cambridge University Press.

——— 1999. 'Decreed Affinities: Nationhood in the Western Solomon Islands', *Journal of Pacific History* 33: 197–220.

Fox, J.J. 1996. 'Introduction', in *Origin Ancestry and Alliance*, J.J. Fox and C. Sather (eds), 1–17. Canberra: Department of Anthropology, Research School of Pacific Studies, Australian National University.

Godelier, M. 1988. *The Mental and the Material: Thought, Economy, Society.* London: Verso.

Haddon, A.C. 1937. *The Canoes of Melanesia, Queensland, and New Guinea.* Honolulu: Bernice Bishop Museum.

Harwood, F.H. 1971. 'The Christian Fellowship Church: A Revitalization Movement in Melanesia', PhD diss. Chicago: Department of Anthropology, University of Chicago.

Hocart, A.M. 1915. Review of W.H.R. Rivers, *The History of Melanesian Society* (1914), *Man* 15: 89–93.

——— 1922. 'The Cult of the Dead in Eddystone of the Solomons', *Journal of the Royal Anthropological Institute* 52: 71–112, 259–305.

——— 1925. 'Medicine and Witchcraft in Eddystone of the Solomons', *Journal of the Royal Anthropological Institute* 55: 229–70.

——— 1931. 'Warfare in Eddystone of the Solomon Islands', *Journal of the Royal Anthropological Institute* 61: 301–24.

Holy, L. 1996. *Anthropological Perspectives of Kinship.* London: Pluto Press.

Hviding, E. 1996. *Guardians of Marovo Lagoon: Practice, Place, and Politics in Maritime Melanesia.* Honolulu: University of Hawaii Press.

——— 2003. 'Disentangling the *Butubutu* of New Georgia: Cognatic Kinship in Thought and Action', in *Oceanic Socialities and Cultural Forms: Ethnographies of Experience*, I. Hoëm and S. Roalkvam (eds), 71–113. Oxford: Berghahn.

Hviding, E., and T. Bayliss-Smith. 2000. *Islands of Rainforest: Agroforestry, Logging and Ecotourism in the Solomon Islands.* Aldershot: Ashgate.

Jaarsma, S.R. (ed.). 2002. *Handle with Care: Ownership and Control of Ethnographic Materials.* Pittsburgh: University of Pittsburgh Press.

Jackson, K.B. 1978. '*Tie Hokara, Tie Vaka* – Black Man, White Man: A Study of the New Georgia Group to 1925', PhD diss. Canberra: Australian National University.

Langham, I. 1981. *The Building of British Social Anthropology: W.H.R. Rivers and His Cambridge Disciples in the Development of Kinship Studies, 1898–1931.* Dordrecht: Reidel.

Lanyon-Orgill, P.A. 1953. 'The Papuan Languages of the New Georgian Archipelago, Solomon Islands', *Journal of Austronesian Studies* (1): 122–38.

Leenhardt, M. 1979 [1947]. *Do Kamo: Person and Myth in the Melanesian World*. Chicago: University of Chicago Press.

McDougall, D. 2000. 'Paths of Pinauzu: Captivity and Social Reproduction in Ranongga', *Journal of the Polynesian Society* 109(1): 99–113.

McKinnon, J. 1972. 'Bilua Changes: Culture Contact and its Consequences – A Study of the Bilua of Vella Lavella in the British Solomon Islands', PhD diss. Wellington: Department of Geography, Victoria University.

———— 1975. 'Tomahawks, Turtles and Traders: A Reconstruction in the Circular Causation of Warfare in the New Georgia Group', *Oceania* 35(4): 290–307.

Nicholson, R.C. 1922. *The Son of a Savage: The Story of Daniel Bula*. London: Epworth.

Patterson, M. 2005. 'Reclaiming Paradigms Lost', *Australian Journal of Anthropology* 16(1): 1–17.

Radcliffe-Brown, A.R. 1952. *Structure and Function in Primitive Society*. London: Cohen and West.

Rivers, W.H.R. 1900. 'A Genealogical Method of Collecting Social and Vital Statistics', *Journal of the Royal Anthropological Institute* 30: 74–82.

———— 1906. *The Todas*. London: Macmillan.

———— 1914a. *The History of Melanesian Society*, 2 vols. Cambridge: Cambridge University Press.

———— 1914b. *Kinship and Social Organisation*. London: Constable.

———— 1922. 'The Psychological Factor', in *Essays on the Depopulation of Melanesia*, W.H.R. Rivers (ed.), 84–113. Cambridge: Cambridge University Press.

———— 1924. *Medicine, Magic and Religion*. London: Kegan Paul, Trench and Trübner.

Salisbury, E.A. 1922. 'A Napoleon of the Solomons'. *Asia: The American Magazine on the Orient* 22: 9.

Scales, I. 2004. 'The Social Forest: Landowners, Development Conflict, and the State in Solomon Islands', PhD diss. Canberra: Australian National University.

Scheffler, H.W. 1962. 'Kindred and Kin Groups in Simbo Island Social Structure', *Ethnology* 1(2): 135–57.

———— 1985. 'Filiation and Affiliation', *Man* 20: 1–21.

———— 2000. *Filiation and Affiliation*. Boulder, CO: Westview Press.

Schneider, G. 1996. 'Land Dispute and Tradition in Munda, Roviana Lagoon, New Georgia Island, Solomon Islands: From Headhunting to the Quest for the Control of Land', PhD diss. Cambridge: University of Cambridge.

Sheppard, P.J. 2004. 'Bilua Bifoa: Vella Lavella Archaeological Survey Year 1', report to the Royal Society of New Zealand. Auckland: Department of Anthropology, University of Auckland.

_____ 2005. '*Bilua Bifoa*: Vella Lavella Archaeological Survey Year 2', report to the Royal Society of New Zealand. Auckland: Department of Anthropology, University of Auckland.

_____ 2006. '*Bilua Bifoa*: Vella Lavella Archaeological Survey Report 3', report to the Royal Society of New Zealand. Auckland: Department of Anthropology, University of Auckland.

Waterhouse, J.H.L. 1931. 'The Kazukuru Language of New Georgia', *Man* 31: 123–26.

Wickler, S. 1991. 'Prehistoric Melanesian Exchange and Interaction: Recent Evidence from the Northern Solomon Islands', *Asian Perspectives* 29: 135–54.

Wickler, S., and M. Spriggs. 1988. 'Pleistocene Human Occupation of the Solomon Islands, Melanesia', *Antiquity* 62: 703–6.

Woodford, C.M. 1922. 'The Solomon Islands', in *Essays on the Depopulation of Melanesia*, W.H.R. Rivers (ed.), 69–77. Cambridge: Cambridge University Press.

4

Rivers and the Study of Kinship on Ambrym

Mother Right and Father Right Revisited

———————— ◆●◆ ————————

Knut M. Rio and Annelin Eriksen

Puzzles of Melanesian Kinship

The paradigm of kinship studies founded by W.H.R. Rivers, with the genealogical method at its methodological centre, has over the last century served as a model example for ethnographic fieldwork, since asking about relationships is a good way to get to know people everywhere. However, it has also been a major impediment because of its Eurocentrism. More precisely, the method has ontological assumptions built into it concerning the nature/culture divide and the universality of kinship (see Bamford and Leach 2009). A question raised in this chapter, with reference to the great puzzle of kinship on the island of Ambrym, is to what extent Rivers's short visit to the islands of the New Hebrides (present-day Vanuatu; see Figure 4.1) provided valid observations about social life, despite his world-view being enmeshed in durable Western assumptions. Our chapter is organised around the wider cultural implications of what Rivers saw as an entanglement of matrilineal and patrilineal principles. We extend the discussion by looking at questions of group formation. We also address the issue that has intrigued anthropology ever since Rivers: how we should connect affinal and agnatic relations in our models.

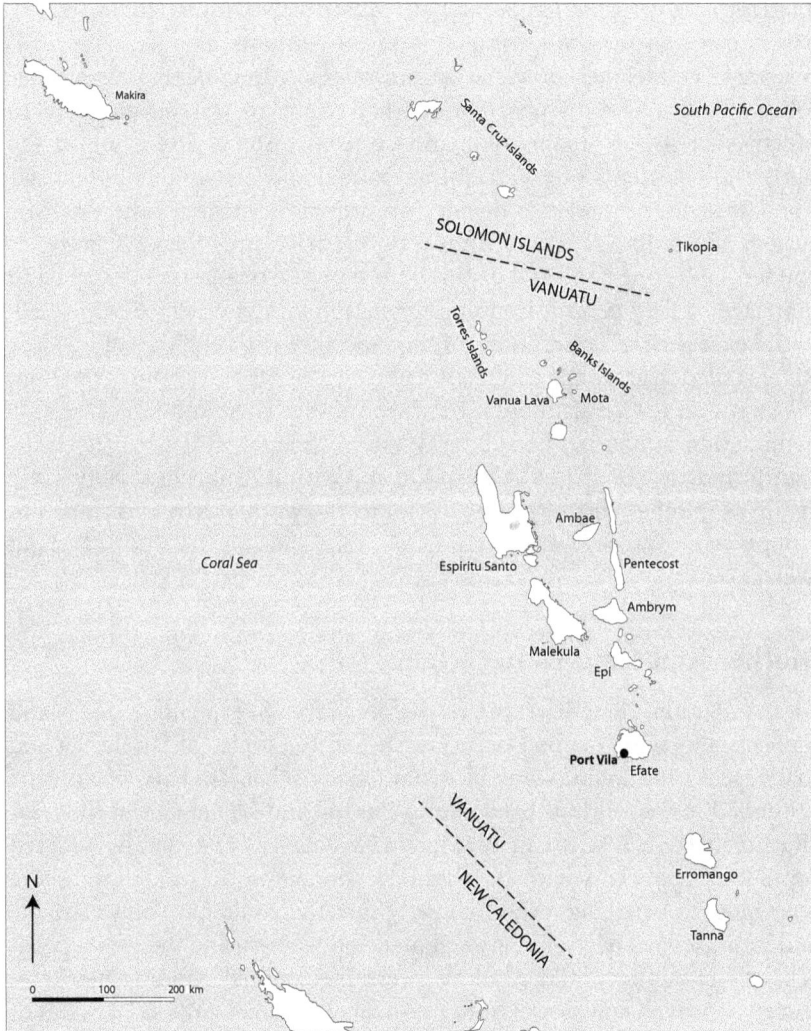

Figure 4.1: Vanuatu (map by K.H. Sjøstrøm, University of Bergen).

The foundational aim of the Percy Sladen Trust Expedition in 1908 was 'to study mother-right communities in the Solomon Islands and to trace the details of the transition from mother-right to father-right' (Haddon 1908: 393), and the expedition took Rivers through Island Melanesia, from the western islands of the Solomons and all the way south through the New Hebrides. He worked mostly on board the Anglican mission ship *Southern Cross,* and the interviews made on board through missionary interpreters enabled him to compile the impressive materials presented in

The History of Melanesian Society (1914; see also Kolshus, this volume). Rivers came to see the kinship system on Ambrym as an early, primitive form of Melanesian social organisation. A long-lasting debate has followed from Rivers's observation that Ambrym was an anomaly in Melanesian social organisation and cultural history, displaying at the same time elements of a patrilineage model and matrimoiety organisation.[1] Moving beyond this debate, we provide a focus on the dualistic system of matrilineal and patrilineal rights, privileging the perspective of gender on the one hand and distinctions between relations of descent and marriage as they pertain to group formation on the other. We thus seek to uncover general conceptions of how sociality works in Vanuatu. While Rivers failed to grasp the connection between rights and group formation, his attention to the distinction between mother right and father right, a formulation influenced heavily by Western thought, still aligns itself insightfully with the dichotomies of kinship within Ambrym society. Here again, as in other chapters of this volume, the work of Rivers is shown to still possess contemporary meaning and relevance for the study of Island Melanesia.

Mother Right and Father Right

In the decades that had passed before Rivers's expedition to Island Melanesia, great effort had been invested in the topics of family life and marriage as the foundations of evolutionary schemes. This was mostly grounded in the work of Bachofen in Europe and McLennan in the USA (Bachofen 1861; McLennan 1865), and was also more generally adopted by all leading social scientists, from L.H. Morgan to E. Durkheim. A core concept of this paradigm was that early societies could have only unstable and promiscuous relations between men and women, and therefore motherhood, or mother–child relations, were the original building blocks of society. Through analyses of both pre-historic sources and the societies of Australia and North America, theorists of social evolution had built a theoretical foundation on the idea that mother right had everywhere preceded father right. Concepts of fatherhood and father rights were presumed to be absent among the most primitive of peoples. This idea could be used as a basis for testing every society regarding its advancement on the evolutionary ladder. As ethnographic records of indigenous peoples around the world were collected and ordered, this type of circular argument prevailed in analyses and comparisons. One established that this or that tribe had matrilineal elements, and so concluded that it was primitive, or even vice versa; that since it was primitive it had to feature matrilineal elements. The paradigm was built on the confusion of imprecise concepts like mother right, mother rule, matriarchy and matrilineal organisation.

Around the turn of the century, this idea became more and more ridiculed as new ethnographic understanding demonstrated, first, that matrilineal descent was not synonymous with mother rule or matriarchy, second, that in matrilineal societies there was often kinship between father and child, and third, that it was hard to create a theory of family life using an evolutionary scale that ran from primitive, matrilineal societies to more advanced, patrilineal societies. As Rivers emerged in the field of social science, the paradigm of mother right was on the verge of collapsing, but he still focused his research and innovations in fieldwork methods on issues relating to this paradigm. His foundational idea was that matrilineal society historically preceded patrilineal society, and this in turn provided the reason for looking at historical change within a part of the world that was regarded as among the most primitive and untouched: Melanesia. *The History of Melanesian Society* (Rivers 1914) was a work solidly within the above-sketched paradigm, and even though he developed the genealogical method and added ethnographic fieldwork to the set of methods used for producing more realistic data, Rivers's work remained surprisingly true to conventional understandings. One could argue that the limitations of the paradigm became the main obstacle to Rivers really discovering what kinship systems were all about (see also Langham 1981).

In the winter of 1914, Rivers returned to the New Hebrides in order to follow up on his findings from the initial trip. His two-volume book was by then in print, and had already met with criticisms that he wished to counter with new evidence. He returned from his research trip with a lot of material from Ambrym island – some of which was published shortly after (Rivers 1915a, 1915b, 1915c). Rivers never visited Ambrym and the material was collected on the small island of Tangoa, off the south coast of Espiritu Santo, where he worked closely with Reverend Fred Bowie, head of the Tangoa Presbyterian mission school. Bowie had been a missionary on Ambrym for two years, and spoke the local language. There were also two Ambrym men on Tangoa working as school teachers – William Temar and Lan from villages in west Ambrym – and they provided Bowie and Rivers with his material, such as genealogies, kinship terms and marriage regulations (Barnard 1986: 134). The evidence was later corrected and re-viewed by Bowie, who communicated with Rivers by letter while the latter was in Cambridge writing up his material.

In Rivers's early effort to map the cultural history of, and cultural diffusion between, different parts of the Pacific, certain topics are kept in the forefront: notably 'dual organisation' (referring mostly to matrilineal moiety organisation as the original state of Melanesian society), the prominent roles of mother's brother and father's sister (Rivers 1901, 1902, 1910, 1914, ii: 556–72), and clan organisation and totemism as principles introduced later in history (1908, 1909, 1914, ii: 337–74). Ambrym turned out to be central to the ethnographic puzzle that involved the transformation from 'mother right' to 'father right' – that is, from matrilineal moiety organisation to patrilineal clans. In the historical model developed by Rivers, dual organisation with matrilineal descent, as well as gerontocracy (or the monopoly over young women by old men), came to be seen as the 'original' Melanesian culture, whereas colonisation by 'kava people' – practising totemism, patrilineal elements, ranking rituals, sitting burials and penis incision – came later.

In this spirit, River (1915b) claimed that his project in Melanesia had been to try to map the region's history of institutional encounters and transformations – tied to the distinction between 'father right' and 'mother right' as indicative of different cultural elements and cross-cultural exchanges. Whereas he had found that Pentecost Island in the New Hebrides practised what he saw as the original state of Melanesian society – dual organisation with matrilineal descent ('mother right') – he had been surprised to find on neighbouring Ambrym a clear patrilineal bias. He found Ambrym villages to be exogamous, and, complementary to the hamlet as an agnatic social set, he however found the sibling set (*vantinbul*) to be a cross-section of the hamlet group. This was an important observation, since it juxtaposed one generation of the hamlet and the next, enabling a view of the hamlet group as in fact divided into two halves by alternating generations – similar to matrilineal moiety organisation but not explicitly so.

To get to the bottom of these anomalies, Rivers turned to ceremonial life. He observed that in ceremonies introduced from other islands, such as the *mage* ritual hierarchy, there was no expression of kinship, whereas in other Ambrym ceremonies – such as status-acquiring pig killings, circumcision and girl's puberty rites – the mother's brother and father's sister featured as absolutely central in the ritual polity. This distinction was later confirmed in the materials collected by Mary Patterson in the 1960s (Patterson 1981). The tendency was equally reflected in mortuary ceremonies, in which heirs of the deceased presented pigs to the mother's brother of the deceased, while the mother's relatives killed pigs in return for these. It also seemed that the spirit of the deceased returned to their mother's place after death. These facts led Rivers to state that '[t]he social ties with the mother's brother show themselves only in ceremonial and not in the transactions of everyday life' (Rivers 1915b: 232). He saw this as a strong indicator of a cultural survival of dual organisation from an earlier stage.

From this we can read a general claim that carried some weight: that historical and cultural change was articulated in changing models for structuring kinship and ritual, and further, that old kinship and marriage organisation still provided Melanesian society with its basic infrastructure by continuing as a cultural foundation for ceremonial life and beliefs.

'The Unlucky Affair Involving the Ambrym Kinship System'

In his paper on 'Melanesian gerontocracy', Rivers (1915a) searched for a historical explanation for three types of prescribed marriage: with brother's daughter's daughter, with mother's brother's widow, and with father's father's widow. Having obtained new evidence, he was determined to strengthen his theory. All three marriage types seemed unlikely, but he could now report that on Ambrym there were marriages with father's father's widow. His views about gerontocracy had also been confirmed by the observation, and supported by Felix Speiser (1913: 234), that: 'it is difficult for a young man to obtain a young wife but has to content himself with an old widow, the young women capable of work being all bought by the old men' (Rivers 1915a: 147). Hence, Rivers deduced a form of social organisation and model for leadership based on the control of young women. In *The History of Melanesian Society* he formulated the hypothesis that the types of marriage mentioned above were also the remains of an original matri-moiety system in which old men held a monopoly over women:

> We have no record of any dominance of elders in Melanesia such as it seems to exist in Australia, but the most natural way of explaining the granddaughter marriage is by the supposition that at one time such dominance not only existed in Melanesia, but reached a pitch far surpassing anything which has been recorded in Australia, a dominance so great that the elders were able to monopolise all the young women of the community, the young women of each moiety becoming as a matter of course the wives of the elders of the other moiety. (Rivers 1914, ii: 59)

An immediate reaction to this assertion came the following year in a review of *The History of Melanesian Society* by Rivers's former fieldwork colleague A.M. Hocart. Hocart, himself now having spent three years in Fiji as a schoolteacher, from his experience of the Solomon Islands and Fiji did not recognise the type of monopoly over women proposed by Rivers (Hocart 1915). In a gentle way Hocart was dismissing Rivers's proposal as a complete misreading of the kinship materials, or at least as a biased historical explanation of the features of kinship terms.

This critique of Rivers indicated a new turn in the development of the discipline: away from historical explanations to synchronic interpretations. Features of kinship terminology were no longer attributed the same kind of historical significance, but were used instead to explain sociological features. In other words, marriage with a granddaughter or grandmother turned out to be terminological features and artefacts of systemic ways of classifying kin. The mistakes made by Rivers had been caused by over-zealous translations between European kinship terms and Melanesian ones, or at the very least by exaggerated belief in the historical origins of kinship and marriage terms.

Just after his death in 1922, a young student of Rivers, T.T. Barnard, took it upon himself to work more closely with the Ambrym marriage system. He did not succeed in getting to Ambrym to do fieldwork, but he had the opportunity to take into account all the manuscripts left by Rivers, as well as responses in letters from Revd Bowie and from Ambrym islanders William Temar and Lan. In his review of Rivers's research process, Barnard noted that he had found the materials from Ambrym 'more than usually unsatisfactory', and that he 'could not see that [Rivers's] deductions [were] in any way justified' (Barnard 1986: 5). What Rivers had understood as gerontocracy on account of marriages between men and their granddaughters or grandmothers was instead a system of classificatory relationships and marriage classes. Barnard's suspicion that Rivers had been quite mistaken in the case of Ambrym was confirmed by Revd Bowie's letters. In one of them Bowie wrote about the concept of *vantinbul* ('group of brothers') – which had been a crucial concept for Rivers – pointing out that *vantinbul* actually constituted a group formation alternative to the patrilineally structured hamlet:

> Lan and the others here differ entirely from William [Rivers] about the *vantinbul*. For more than one reason I am certain that William's statements are wrong. The *vantinbul* are those who call one another brother and sister, including the father's father and his brothers and sisters and the son's children. There are only two *vantinbul* in Lonwolwol composed of members of alternate generations. (Bowie, cited in Barnard 1986: 135)

This, then, is a very accurate description, and one obvious to all those who later came to revisit Ambrym kinship through actual fieldwork. It placed Ambrym alongside other class-based marriage systems, with three patrilineally defined places – my place, my mother's place, and my mother's mother's place – cross-cut by alternate generations of matrilineal descent like the *vantinbul*. A few years later, Bernard Deacon, a student of Radcliffe-Brown, made the breakthrough in an article where he confirmed, after a short visit to Ambrym, that Ambrym was not an anomaly but a regular marriage class system with relational terms falling into six categories (Deacon 1927). What Rivers had confounded with inter-generational marriages between old men and young women were in fact same-generation marriages between alternate generations classed together. And so, if the ethnographer's question was 'can you marry your father's father's widow?' – the reply would have to be 'yes, she is my wife', since she would be classified together with the father's father's wife. This confusion was an outcome of Rivers's unwillingness to recognise the problematic dichotomy between biological and social relations in his own Western ontology (see Astuti 2009: 216). The historical issues that concerned Rivers, of whether the present system had developed from a moiety system, were completely abandoned.

After the publication of Deacon's article, he received praise from within a new paradigm of kinship studies with Radcliffe-Brown at the forefront (see Radcliffe-Brown 1927). Ambrym thus became a test case from which the new paradigm could demolish the old (see Langham 1981). The fact that Rivers never actually visited Ambrym gave him a particular disadvantage in relation to later followers. T.T. Barnard revisited Rivers's notes shortly after his death in 1922, and Bernard Deacon spent some weeks in Ambrym in 1926. They both understood that the Ambrym system was not an exotic survival of a pre-historic era, but a case that fell nicely into the fold of other Australian and Melanesian class systems in the new comparative science of anthropology. It was from within this particular new regime of kinship studies that Rivers was proven wrong, just as Deacon and Barnard and other advocates of the theory of marriage classes were proven wrong when the new order of emic ethnographic representation took over from the 1970s (Scheffler 1970; Patterson 1976). As noted by Langham (1981), Ambrym provided a test case for Rivers's mother-right paradigm, but also in itself forced the shift towards a new paradigm, since it actually proved so ill-fitted to support Rivers's ideas. This was what Langham called '[a]n unlucky affair involving the Ambrym kinship system' (Langham 1981: 199; see also Rio 2007a: 35–63).

The details of the Ambrym kinship system went back and forth for many decades in discussions in anthropological journals, some authors claiming it had a patrilineal character, others claiming it was matrilineal, others again that it was cognatic. In some ways the debate was also implicitly about whether Ambrym had a kinship system or a marriage system: whether kinship determined marriage, or whether marriage determined kinship. In the end, talk of a marriage-class system was even cancelled completely through the work of Scheffler, who stated that the debate had been borrowing from a marriage-class system idea that 'never had any basis in ethnographic fact' (Scheffler 1970: 56), and that all the 'odd' qualities of marriage and kinship were merely artefacts of a system of classification revolving around alternating generations. Needham then noted that 'Scheffler's re-examination of the Ambrym case seemed to have demolished the accepted idea that a six-section system existed there and thus to have relieved anthropology of an incomprehensible arrangement which was impossible to relate to other section systems and tended increasingly to become a theoretical embarrassment' (Needham 1971: civ). The dismissive responses by Scheffler and Needham came at a point when anthropology was beginning to deconstruct the idea of 'group' altogether. Hence, the matrilineally constructed sibling set (River's *vantinbul* or Deacon's *bataton*), the totemic groups, and even mother right or father right, could no longer be seen as having to do with group formation, but appeared merely as misrepresentations generated from shallow ethnographic work.

But whereas these shifts in paradigms have taken place under the logic of both moral and political 'othering' (see Dureau, this volume), we would like to explore further Rivers's ideas on their own terms. After all, the direction that kinship studies took after Rivers, dominated by Radcliffe-Brown and his students, was a very specific and narrow way of dealing with synchronic social organisation. The break with Rivers was not only made on the basis of the shortcomings of his ethnography, but more implicitly constituted a new turn towards calculations of relationships in the form of 'algebra' (see Malinowski 1930), and a marked departure from any interest in cultural history. When looking into Rivers's ethnographic materials from the Percy Sladen Trust Expedition and his subsequent visits to Melanesia, it is tempting to speculate about other possible directions that the study of kinship could have taken. After all, most of the later publications on Ambrym kinship have provided few clues as to understanding what was actually going on in Ambrym social life and cultural history. And so in the rest of this chapter we wish to hint at some directions the study of social relations on Ambrym could have taken if guided by the spirit of Rivers.

While it has been documented how Rivers was wrong in some of his most stubborn ideas about cultural history and diffusion (see Allen 1981a), his ethnographic observations from the early colonial era about social regulations still have validity. This is demonstrated in more recent studies of kinship in Vanuatu, quite simply by the fact that much has continued to revolve around the entanglements of 'mother right' and 'father right' and the various cultural implications these have in different parts of the archipelago (see Rodman 1973; Poewe and Lovell 1980; Allen 1981b; Patterson 1981; Facey 1989). We propose two different angles for relating mother right and father right to contemporary Vanuatu ethnography. The first angle is to look at the dualism of 'mother right' and 'father right' from the point of view of what we call gendered social forms; the second is from the point of view of a distinction between relations of descent and marriage and the question of group formation. Both these angles can be representative of general conceptions of how sociality unfolds across Vanuatu, even though we attribute it specifically to Ambrym, with which we are most familiar through our own fieldwork.

Why Rivers Was Not So Wrong After All: Recognising Gendered Social Forms

In *The History of Melanesian Society*, Rivers attempted to empirically ground the hypothesis that all human societies develop from 'mother right' to 'father right'. As we have outlined above, from the accounts he heard of Ambrym he understood that Ambrym ceremonial could be taken as a test case for his general theory. What interested Rivers in these accounts was the focus on 'mother right' in ceremonies in a context that he perceived to be a 'father right' dominated social organisation. We suggest a return to the insistence by Rivers that these principles formed the basic mechanism of social organisation. If, for the present purpose, we ignore his diffusionist bias, a claim can be made that Rivers's main hypothesis remains helpful for an understanding of Ambrym social life in general.

In our writings on Ambrym, based on fieldwork in 1995/96, 1999/2000 and 2006, we have argued that two principles of social organisation work simultaneously. Eriksen (2008) has called these principles the female and the male 'social form', drawing on Rivers's basic distinction between mother right and father right. However, instead of focusing solely on the transmission of rights from parent to child, it may be argued that these two principles can be found in every aspect of social life on Ambrym: in the relation to place and landscape, in village composition, in ceremonial life – and, of course, in institutions of inheritance and marriage. From this perspective, two different ways of organising social relations in Ambrym social ontology appear: the lineal (and to some extent also hierarchical) way, what may also be called the male mode of sociality; and the lateral way, or what may be called the female mode of sociality (see also Bamford 2004: 295). A focus on inheritance follows the male focus on descent, creating a hierarchy of men who have access to land and other resources. Patrilineal genealogies traced back to origin places are the primary assets for gaining access to these resources. In principle, only men inherit and pass on land on Ambrym, and the system is based on a form of competition where the person with the most access to knowledge often gains the upper hand. This has been especially obvious in recent trials involving land claims; during which knowledge of ancestral movements and land tenure often open the door to future land claims. In this system of land transferral, women are at the mercy of their fathers, brothers and husbands, and cannot claim land in their own right. Inheritance, then, is an example of what Rivers called 'father right', and what we call a male social form. A man is said to represent his place on Ambrym, and to a certain extent a man stands in a metonymic relationship to his place. Old men are often seen seated on the ground outside their dwelling house, talking to passers-by, smoking or surveying the activities of their household. Visitors come by and stop for a chat. Men, young as well as old, generally move only in certain areas and follow only certain paths between villages. They never trespass onto other peoples' paths, and they stand in a strict avoidance relationship with a number of in-laws, which makes their movement in the landscape extremely restricted. The immobile man can be seen as a representation of the genealogical relationships that link him to the ground.

Women, on the other hand, are not restricted by this immobility. Women are constantly on the move and are not submitted to the same avoidance relationships. The term for sister, *metehal*, literally means 'end-point of the path' (like an arrowhead, *mete*) and hints at the importance of women's movement. Women connect people and places. They move at marriage and connect their husbands' families to their own natal families in a circle of reciprocity that lasts throughout their lives. This reciprocity is linked to what Rivers called 'mother right'. Although land and inheritance follow 'father right', blood as the source of life is transmitted through the mother. Throughout their life, a person must continuously give compensation for the gift of life given by the mother's side (see also Rio 2007b, 2007c). This is based on what Mary Patterson calls 'ontological debt'. A cycle of reciprocity is particularly visible in ceremonial life, where mother right is the central focus. Rivers himself mentioned different ceremonies in which mother right is displayed: *pakvi wor* and *yengfah* (Rivers 1915b: 231; see also Patterson 2001). During our fieldwork in 1996 and 1999, we found that many of the features of ceremonial life described by Rivers and documented later by Patterson (1981) remained the same.

These ceremonies hide from view the place of birth, the genealogical link to the land and origin places, and the seniority of men. It is the movement of women and the flow of blood between places that is revealed. In the *yengfah* ceremony, which Rivers mentions and Patterson (1976, 1981) later explores, girls compensate the mother's brother for the loss of his sister (the girls' mother) through different forms of payment. *Yengfah* remains today a ceremony in which girls pay for the symbolic gifts they receive during the ceremony from their mother's brother or mother's brother's wife. The ceremony is performed at the time when a girl has her first period, and is also a payment for the right to spill the blood she has received from her mother's place. A key component of the ceremony is the decoration of the young woman by her mother's brother's wife.[2] The aunt (*ina*) puts a bangle made from trochus shell around the girl's wrist and a band of beads around her neck. She then paints the left side of the girl's face and hair red. The red colour is usually pointed out as referring to the blood on which the ceremony centres. The girl pays back her blood to her mother's hamlet, represented in person by her mother's brother and his wife. The mother's side is seen to be on a person's left side, and the painting of only the left side of the head is an overt expression of where the blood comes from. The mother's brother's wife then fastens pandanus rings around the girl's legs, and finally places colourful feathers in her hair. When the decoration is finished they give the girl a mirror. For every item fastened on her, the girl pays money to her mother's relatives. In the past, it was yams and pigs that were given to the mother's side, but today it is almost exclusively money that is used. In a ceremony that took place just after our first arrival on Ambrym in 1995, the mother's side had been paid 1,000 vatu (approximately $10) for each item fastened on the girls, as well as for the mirror. Finally a pig was killed by the girl's father on behalf of his daughters and given to the mother's brother.

A number of different ceremonies take this form. The *maljel* ritual, a circumcision ceremony for boys, is very similar to the *yengfah* in that boys pay their mother's brother and receive small presents in return. The general focus in these ceremonies is on lateral connections to other kin groups and other hamlets. These lateral connections might be described in terms of a female social form, the opposite of the focus on genealogy, linearity, hierarchy and immobility – all characteristic of the male social form, expressed in inheritance practices and the relationship of men to the landscape. 'Mother right' thus describes a lateral mode of relation making while 'father right' establishes another, and the two articulate complementary spaces of interaction.

On Ambrym, as on several other islands in north-central Vanuatu, there was in pre-colonial and early colonial times a dominant ceremonial institution called the *mage* (or *namange* in Bislama). It has been referred to as a 'male graded society' (see Guiart 1951; Allen 1981b; Bonnemaison 1996). This institution was usually exclusively for men, and consisted of thirteen to fifteen named grades into which men became initiated after having paid for the rights to wooden or stone emblems and the names that accompanied them (see Rio 2009). Every grade-taking involved two parties: men of a sibling set who wanted to achieve the rights to a grade in the ritual hierarchy, and the person or sibling set who already had such rights and who received payment from the buyer. Through the act of approaching the grade, the grade-taker would display his ability to acquire pigs from his relatives. One might say that the male version of expressing the value of relationships in the graded society implied making oneself the representation of relationships through the achievement of grades. No women or uninitiated men were allowed to witness preparations for the ceremonies, and this form of ceremonial work was exclusively male. There was no parallel institution for women. On the rare occasions when a woman was initiated into the graded society, it only happened in old age, and when these women took on male qualities. Women in the graded society thus became associated with magical potency and were generally perceived as dangerous (see Eriksen 2009: 99–100).

As noted by both Rivers and Patterson, it seems as if the historical popularity of this ritual order almost managed to make invisible the uterine bias in previous ceremonial life. However, although the values of a male social form might have dominated social life at the time when Rivers visited the area, we should keep in mind that they never existed in isolation. For analytical purposes our point is that the values of male and female social forms complement each other, and at various times have stood in relations of tension. Hence, we also argue that the values expressed in mother-right institutions – that is, in the lateral connections between places and the spiral of reciprocity and marriages – gained a new and institutional expression with Christianity. Whereas the *mage* institution had been male dominant, exclusive and competitive, and creating ritual hierarchies, the Church displayed contrasting values. Christianity as a value system became tightly associated with women and the female mode of sociality; in many ways it took the place of kinship ceremonies with uterine horizons of 'mother right' (see Eriksen 2008).

The first missionary on Ambrym, a Presbyterian missionary from Scotland, Charles Murray, declared in 1887 that the Church, now translated as *imkon* (or, the sacred house of a high-ranking man of the *mage* institution), was open to everyone: men, women and children. Thus the Church challenged a patriarchal structure and promoted inclusiveness and egalitarian values at the expense of the exclusiveness and focus on stratified relations that had been so prominent in the ritual polity (see Rio and Eriksen 2013) and the male social form. Men associated with the *mage* were therefore not interested in the Church as a new ceremonial institution in the early years of its establishment, as they realised that it was not based on the concept of exclusive male membership and on the rules associated with the established ceremonial order. For instance, when Murray tried to recruit women and children to the Church, one of the highest-graded men of the *mage* cult, who was also a village chief at the time, declared the church forbidden territory and asked people to stop giving food to the missionary. He wanted to get rid of Murray, and in the end he managed to make missionary life so difficult for him that leaving Ambrym became the only option. After some weeks in solitude, Murray left (see Eriksen 2008: 88–90).

However, after a couple of decades, when the mission schooner again visited Ambrym, some women and uninitiated men had taken over the mission station with the help of a couple of returned labourers, who had come to know the Bible while working on sugar plantations in Queensland. This is described by later missionaries (Lamb 1905; Frater 1922). Lamb visited the mission station in Ranon a decade after Murray's departure and writes: 'the teacher had beat the school drum; and, in response, some twenty to thirty ill-looking, limping specimens, of all sizes and both sexes, gathered on the veranda' (Lamb 1905: 43). In other words, as a result of the turn away from the Church by the high-graded men, the Church seems from early on to have been a movement for outcasts and those who did not succeed in the *mage* society: men of low esteem, and women. And so it was those who were excluded from the existing male ritual hierarchy who became the first converts. Furthermore, women from the mission areas on Ambrym worked almost as native missionaries as they married into far-away villages, and to a certain extent movements of women implied movement and growth of the Church. In this sense, Church denomination followed the mother-right institution as women married and brought the Church to their new villages.

To sum up so far: the focus on mother right and father right, and the idea of a tension between social relations focussed on descent and inheritance on the one hand (what we have called the male social form) and a focus on lateral connections on the other (what we have called the female social form), may still be a useful perspective for understanding Ambrym social organisation. Another important issue that also hinges on this dichotomy is the question of group formation. Keeping in mind Rivers's materials on Ambrym, we move further into the ethnography of contemporary Vanuatu.

Alternating Group Constitution

A question that has long been underlying the debate about the Ambrym system is whether it should be seen to be a kinship system or a marriage system. Are relatives classed together for the purpose of marriage, or are marriages prescribed on the basis of kinship? As Dumont commented with regard to Rivers's 'dual organisation' and Dravidian kinship terminology, it is problematic that we can only think about alliance relations though a language of kinship, such as for instance the concept of 'cross-cousin marriage' (Dumont 1953). His point is that alliance relationships are as much 'natural' to the native mind as descent, since they are as much seen as inherited relations. For example, my relation to my cross-cousins is 'inherited' from my father's relation to my mother's brother. As seen from the point of view of the Kamea of Papua New Guinea, Bamford phrases this as follows: 'parents produce siblings, who produce cousins, who produce spouses' (Bamford 2004: 295). This would also be closer to both the Dravidian terminology documented by Dumont (1953) in India and the Vanuatu terminology for tracing marriage partners (see Rio 2005). As also noted by Bamford, seen from a different angle, 'cross-cousin spouses' may be seen as 'affinal siblings' if affinity is given priority over genealogy (Bamford 2004: 299).

Similarly, it has by now become obvious that the suggested prescribed marriage with father's sister's daughter's daughter on Ambrym was an awkward way of framing the prescription. It was awkward because marriage was not traced through kin in the way indicated by the term: one did not trace a marriage partner through the generational aspects of kin but instead as a path between hamlets where one found one's terminological 'wife' in a specific hamlet. It has now been established for Vanuatu that this has to do with place or hamlet as a primordial principle of origin, and that prescriptions for marriage work like a system of traffic control between hamlets. If we look at kinship terminologies, the tendency of conflating different kin under the same term (such as grandfather with grandson, or father's sister's son with mother's brother's son) only indicates that they should be resident in the same hamlet and share position with regard to marriage. They are the 'same' with regard to alliance and Ambrym ways of classification, but 'different' with regard to kinship and generation, and our anthropological way of classification (see also Yoshioka 1985: 35). We suggest that the generations of anthropologists coming after Rivers and his genealogical approach got themselves into massive problems with the Ambrym system because they considered marriage to be secondary to descent, and therefore constructed marriage-class or section systems based on groups of genealogical kin. This is on the whole alien to the logic of practice.

Above, we have instead described lateral connections (that is, marriage relations) as a female social form, and descent relations as based on a male social form. Further, we conclude that people on Ambrym continuously have their relational attention divided between those people who are in their mother's hamlet, and the hamlets of those with whom they can marry. We have also described how ceremonial life revolves around paying back the 'ontological debt' to the mother's hamlet, with whom one shares blood and to whom one returns after death. But people also take care to give tribute to the 'other side' – that of their in-laws. Whereas ceremonies for the mother's relatives are symbolised by the left hand, ceremonies for in-laws have to do with the right hand. No ceremonial attention is given to patrilineal relations, as Rivers pointed out. As men and women are expected to continually contribute to people of their mother's hamlet or the classificatory equivalents – that is, to their left side – they are equally required to contribute to their in-laws on their right side. Whether this is recognition of affinal relations as 'non-kinship' or, on the contrary, that it is another way of recognising kinship, is an open question – but it is nevertheless an under-debated issue in the discussion of the Ambrym social system.

As has been described in a very clear-cut manner by Patterson (2001), Ambrym social relations are always seen from a particular person's point of view. The group of relatives who are traced through the mother are termed *wuruen*, in the sense that they provide a harbour and a passage (*wur*). Patterson calls them 'harbourers' since they provide favours of nurture, clothing, mats and care throughout a person's life and at life-cycle ceremonies. They bring you 'the gift of life' (see Rio 2007c) and provide the gendered dynamics of what we have above called the female social form. On the other side there are the people in whose hamlets a person and their siblings can find a potential spouse: that of affines and in-laws. They are termed *mukuen*, which literally means 'you are chased among them'. Patterson calls this side 'harriers'. There is a strong sense of taboo involved in this relation. A person has to stay away from their hamlet, cannot swear or eat in the presence of a father-in-law or mother-in-law, and should not get in a position where they are above them on a path or in a tree.

But we begin to realise that this system does not form the basis of a stable group, or a description on the level of a stable model, since the people who are 'harbourers' to oneself will be 'harriers' to one's father and son, the alternate generations of the hamlet. And, furthermore, one's father-in-law (*wunjong*), who must be avoided and respected as a 'harrier', will reciprocally relate to one as part of their class of 'mother's brothers' (*mesong*). Hence, if you are my in-law or 'harrier', I am your mother's relative or 'harbourer'. We therefore have to realise that affinity is here the flip-coin of kinship, and that relations alternate between drawing out, respectively, blood in one instance and marriage in another. This pattern has also been confirmed for other parts of the Vanuatu. For the case of Nguna in central Vanuatu, Ellen Facey (1989) describes a system that focuses on patrilineal 'lines', but where matrilineal 'blood' equally gives direction to these lines, pointing them in the direction of marriage. Likewise, for Ambae, an intriguing composition of brothers and sisters and their children has been described. Whereas sisters contribute to their brother's bridewealth, the return from the brother to the sister comes when the brother's sons later give pig meat to their father's sisters in ceremonies of rank (Rodman 1973; Poewe and Lovell 1980). Poewe and Lovell write: 'Making a child the intermediary ritually underpins the simultaneous recognition of two sets of ties and two sets of principles; sibling ties because sister shares the substance with her brother, and marital ties because the brother's son is the combined substance of brother and brother's wife. Consanguineous and affinal principles are given equal status' (Poewe and Lovell 1980: 86).

A similar point has been argued by Rio (2007a), describing how two aspects of relationships are potently articulated simultaneously in all ceremonies of Ambrym kinship. On the ceremonial ground on which the exchange for a marriage is carried out, one can thus observe several flows of prestations simultaneously. The father of the groom hands over the bride-wealth (money) to the bride's brother. As the bride is the groom's father's 'mother' (classed together with his father's wife after the logic of alternating generations), this is by definition a payment to his 'harbourers'. The bride wealth is merely one payment of this kind to his 'harbourers' in a series of life-long obligations. But another payment that can easily be thought to be just the same is in effect drawing out the other side of the relation between the two hamlets. The groom and his brothers simultaneously give live pigs to sons of the bride's brothers. These young boys are classed as 'harriers', and they will be the future in-laws for the groom's grandsons (Rio 2007a: 142–43). This gives an interesting nuance to the question of group consti-tution. One could easily make the mistake of thinking that the ceremony is an exchange between a group of patrilineally related men on the one hand and their affines on the other. But what actually takes place is that father and son look to the wife-giving hamlet from different perspectives: the father sees the bride as another 'gift of life' from his 'harbourers', whereas the groom receives her as a payment from his future 'harriers'. The unity of the patrilineal hamlet is broken into two parts: one sibling set goes here, and the other goes there.

This was why Rivers's *vantinbul* and Deacon's *bataton* became so im-portant, as the sibling set, not the patrilineal clan, seemed to be the basic unit of group formation. As observed by Rivers, the Ambrym idioms of mother right and father right cross-cut to the degree that group formation and belonging is continually alternating. The hamlet is a stable unit, with the sibling sets of father and son alternating in leadership and authority. But whereas the sons look to one side for support, the father looks to another. However, whereas this seems to suggest that the sibling set is a matrilineally created group, to a certain degree that remains a theoreti-cal construction. The group of siblings, including siblings separated by a generation, theoretically forms a group because they all share the set of terms for relatives, and thus share the same perspective on the social world. Therefore they also join hands in ceremonial work, and they are interchangeable when it comes to representing the sibling set at ceremo-nies. But through marriage with spouses from different hamlets, and in different church locations, thus invariably taking up the perspectives of their spouses, they are always a dispersed form of unity.

Further, a remaining question is where to place affinal relatives within the dualism of father right and mother right. This is another interesting aspect of the model of alternation between generations. In the minds of our informants in north Ambrym, the question of which relatives to marry has always been simple: as a man you will find a spouse through your father. It is your father who will go to the hamlet of your future wife to ask if his 'mother' is available for marriage (remember: son's wife is classed together with father's wife). In other words, the father is the key to addressing affines, and it is his 'mother right' that will secure you a wife. In an important sense, father right combines with mother right for pointing the totality of the system to marriage. Therefore the concept of sister is *metehal* (*meteselav* in Rivers's material, see Barnard 1986: 19), a construct that gives the sister a sense of being an arrow (*mete* is arrowhead, *hal* is path), a vector that escapes and flies from the father right *qua* mother right constitution and becomes the point of its release and fulfilment. 'Blood' from the mother and 'bone' from the father combines in this process to situate and eject the person as a marriageable entity towards the outer world. From one perspective, it is all about consanguinity, but from another it is all about marriage. The girl prepared for a *yengfah* ceremony is likewise constructed as a person, and half of that person is painted red, symbolising blood and denoting obligations towards the mother's relatives. But at the height of the ceremony she is for the first time given a mirror so that she can look at herself and her dual constitution. In the mirror, left turns into right, so to speak, and it is at this moment that she becomes an arrow point and a vector heading for marriage.

Viveiros de Castro (2009) points out that for the purpose of anthropological openness we have to consider that cultural comparison can serve both ways: it can create similarities as well as differences. In other words, the fundamental difference in Western culture between nature and society, or kinship as consanguinity and kinship as marriage, can be both different and similar to what we find elsewhere, and the interesting question is how to compare that difference across cultures. He questions the success of anthropology in ever being able to escape the consanguineous bias in our thinking, despite new emic models. For instance, we are unable to think of a sibling set or the term 'brother' without implying a sense of natural correspondences in blood. For the Amazonian world, Viveiros de Castro (2009: 252) has to consider that brother-in-law can be attributed with a solid form of relational substance that does not hold for a brother. In his view, this possibility should be regarded as the greatest achievement of Lévi-Strauss, though he doubts the ability of Lévi-Strauss to think affinity without thinking consanguinity first.

In this context, the Ambrym lesson lies in the complementary relation between the female form of laterality and the male form of lineality. But as we have seen, this is also more concretely foreshadowed in the relation between a man and his father-in-law. From the nephew's perspective, it is an affinal relation; from the father-in-law's perspective, it is a consanguineous relation. Marriage thus becomes the site for the exchange of kinship perspectives, as pointed out by Marilyn Strathern (1988: 230), in a system where consanguinity and affinity are two parts of the same whole. In this regard, an important point has been raised by Poewe and Lovell in their comparison of African and Oceanic systems:

> The most serious flaw in Scheffler's formal analysis is his claim that systems of affinal or in-law classification are logically dependent on systems of kin classification, but that systems of kin classification are *not* logically dependent on systems of affines. The Longana material effectively disproves this claim, for only if all marriages in the parental, offspring, and grandchild generations are known can the classification of the children of grandchildren be predicted. (Poewe and Lovell 1980: 89, original emphasis)

The contribution of Vanuatu's systems of kinship and marriage to this debate is to reinvigorate a discussion of what we mean when we say 'kinship-based societies'. This discussion conveys many interesting aspects of contemporary Melanesia, among them the ways that kinship and marriage continue to articulate important social changes.

A case in point here is an aspect of everyday life in Vanuatu that has always intrigued us during our fieldwork: the importance of never addressing a person by their name. On Ambrym, and generally in much of Melanesia, one addresses someone by their kinship term, and if they do not have one a person will invent one. Even nowadays in the capital of Port Vila, people take care to call bus drivers or shop workers 'uncle', 'auntie', 'grandfather' or 'sibling', either to show respect or levelling with them. People say that to use a person's name shows lack of respect, that it doesn't feel right, and that if people call you by your name you do not feel well. Parents tend to smack their children if they use a person's name as a term of address. The only exception to this rule is relatives who are in-laws, in which case you can complement coarse language and joking with their names when addressing them. In this sense, the name is seen as an intimate part of a person, alongside the genitals that are also part of joking and implicated in the laughable marriage-relation – the name and the genitals are equally 'private', but more importantly, they only feature inside affinal relations.

This all amounts to two interesting facts of Melanesian life: that people in Vanuatu remain interested in a complementary relation between kinship and marriage as two parts of a whole, but also that affinal relations are the proto-relations that other kinship relations revolve around. They are kinship's 'private parts'. From the point of view of Ambrym, the dull relation with mother's brother (*mesong*) is only a step in the direction of the much more interesting relation with mother's brother's son/father (*tubiung*), a joking relationship and which ultimately leads towards marriage in the next generation.

Conclusion

In the century of anthropological studies of kinship after Rivers's study of Melanesian society, the most durable problem has circled around the dichotomies of descent and affinity, of lineality and laterality, and nature and culture. The problem has hinged on whether we can universally claim a givenness of descent, biological or social, or if descent and affinity are equally constructed. Viveiros de Castro (2009: 253) has recently pointed out that the century or more that has passed since Rivers and Morgan has not really substantiated our understandings of specific cultural worlds. Instead, paradigm shifts in kinship studies have paralleled changes in Western attitudes, rather than really grasping indigenous worlds. As pointed out by Hviding and Berg (this volume), from a certain perspective the Percy Sladen Trust Expedition became notable for its members' inability to grasp the connection between 'rights' and actual social group formation. In this chapter we have tried to point to different aspects and possibilities of Rivers's distinction between mother right and father right. Even though it is very clear that the dichotomy was conceived within Rivers's own British culture of kinship and its evolutionary machinery, it nevertheless resonates with dichotomies within the Ambrym culture of kinship. Mother right and father right, as mirrored in Ambrym concepts like *wur* ('harbour', passage or access to mother's place) and *buluim* ('doorway', passage and point of entry in father's place) work well as descriptions of both a way of thinking about gender as the different forms that action takes, and of a way of re-solving issues of consanguinity and affinity.

Acknowledgements

We would like to thank the contributors to this volume for their inspiring dialogue in the making of this chapter, the two anonymous reviewers for their useful comments, and Edvard Hviding and Cato Berg for their comments on previous versions.

Notes

1. See Deacon (1927), Radcliffe-Brown (1927), Guiart (1956), Lane and Lane (1956, 1958), Löffler (1960), Josselin de Jong (1966), Guilbaud and Levi-Strauss (1970), Scheffler (1970), Needham (1971), Patterson (1976), Langham (1981), Barnard (1986), Jorion (1986), Yoshioka (1993), Rio (2005, 2007a) and Eriksen (2008).
2. This can also be carried out by father's sister, as she stands by necessity in the same relation to the girl.

References

Allen, M.R. 1981a. 'Rethinking Old Problems: Matriliny, Secret Societies and Political Evolution', in *Vanuatu: Politics, Economics and Ritual in Island Melanesia*, M.R. Allen (ed.), 9–34. Sydney: Academic Press.

———— (ed.) 1981b. *Vanuatu: Politics, Economics and Ritual in Island Melanesia.* Sydney: Academic Press.

Astuti, R. 2009. 'Revealing and Obscuring Rivers's Pedigrees: Biological Inheritance and Kinship in Madagascar', in *Kinship and Beyond. The Genealogical Model Reconsidered*, S. Bamford and J. Leach (eds), 214–37. Oxford: Berghahn.

Bachofen, J.J. 1861. *Das Mutterrecht: eine Untersuchung über die Gynaikokratie der alten Welt nach ihrer religiösen und rechtlichen Natur.* Stuttgart: Verlag von Krais und Hoffmann.

Bamford, S. 2004. 'Conceiving Relatedness: Non-substantial Relations among the Kamea of Papua New Guinea', *Journal of the Royal Anthropological Institute* 10: 287–306.

Bamford, S., and J. Leach (eds). 2009. *Kinship and Beyond: The Genealogical Model Reconsidered.* Oxford: Berghahn.

Barnard, T.T. 1986 [1924]. 'The Regulation of Marriage in Ambrym and Paama', in *New Trends in Mathematical Anthropology*, G. De Meur (ed.), 3–55. London: Routledge and Kegan Paul.

Bonnemaison, J. 1996. 'Graded Societies and Societies Based On Title: Forms and Rites of Traditional Political Power in Vanuatu', in *Arts of Vanuatu*, J. Bonnemaison, C. Kaufman, K. Huffman and D. Tryon (eds), 200–17. Bathurst: Crawford House Publishing.

Deacon, B. 1927. 'The Regulation of Marriage on Ambrym', *Journal of the Royal Anthropological Institute* 57: 325–42.

Dumont, L. 1953 'The Dravidian Kinship Terminology as an Expression of Marriage', *Man* 53: 34–39.

Eriksen, A. 2008. *Gender, Christianity and Change in Vanuatu: An Analysis of Social Movements in North Ambrym.* Aldershot: Ashgate.

———— 2009. 'Healing the Nation: In Search of Unity through the Holy Spirit in Vanuatu', *Social Analysis* 53: 67–81.

Facey, E.E. 1989. 'Blood and Line: Exploring Kinship Idioms of Nguna, Vanuatu', *Culture* 9(2): 77–87.

Frater, M. 1922. *Midst Volcanic fires.* London: James Clarke & Co.

Guiart, J. 1951. 'Société, rituels, et mythes du nord Ambrym', *Journal de la Société des Océanistes* 7: 5–103.

———— 1956. 'Systeme de parenté et organisation matrimoniale à Ambrym', *Journal de la Société des Océanistes* 12: 301–26.

Guilbaud, G.T., and C. Lévi-Strauss. 1970. 'Systeme parental et matrimonial au nord Ambrym', *Journal de la Société des Océanistes* 26: 9–32.

Haddon, A.C. 1908. 'The Percy Sladen Trust Expedition to Melanesia', *Nature* 78(2026): 393–94.

Hocart, A.M. 1915. Review of *The History of Melanesian Society* by W.H.R. Rivers, *Man* 15: 89–93.

Jorion, P. 1986. 'Alternative Approaches to the Ambrym Kinship Terminology: A Critique of Scheffler', in *New Trends in Mathematical Anthropology*, G. De Meur (ed.), 167–98. London: Routledge and Keegan Paul.

Josselin de Jong, P.E. de 1966. 'Ambrym and Other Class Systems', *Bijdragen tot de taal-, Land- en Volkenkunde* 122: 64–81.

Lamb, R. 1905. *Saints and Savages: The Story of Five Years in the New Hebrides*. Sydney: William Blackwood and Sons.

Lane, B., and R. Lane. 1956. 'A Re-interpretation of the "Anomalous" Six-section Marriage System of Ambrym, New Hebrides', *Southwestern Journal of Anthropology* 12: 406–14.

————— 1958. 'The Evolution of Ambrym Kinship', *Southwestern Journal of Anthropology* 14: 107–35.

Langham, I. 1981. *The Building of British Social Anthropology: W.H.R. Rivers and his Cambridge Disciples in the Development of Kinship Studies, 1898–1931*. Dordrecht: Reidel.

Löffler, L.G. 1960. 'The Development of the Ambrym and Pentecost Kinship Systems', *Southwestern Journal of Anthropology* 16: 442–62.

McLennan, J.F. 1865. *Primitive Marriage*. Chicago: University of Chicago Press.

Malinowski, B. 1930. 'Kinship', *Man* 30: 19–29.

Needham, R. 1971. 'Remarks on the analysis of kinship and marriage', in *Rethinking Kinship and Marriage*, R. Needham (ed.), 1–33. London: Tavistock.

Patterson, M. 1976. 'Kinship, Marriage and Ritual in North Ambrym', PhD diss. Sydney: University of Sydney.

————— 1981. 'Slings and Arrows: Rituals of Status Acquisition in North Ambrym', in *Vanuatu: Politics, Economics, and Ritual in Island Melanesia*, M. Allen (ed.), 189–237. Sydney: Academic Press.

————— 2001. 'Breaking the Stones: Ritual, Gender and Modernity in North Ambrym, Vanuatu', *Anthropological Forum* 11(1): 39–54.

Poewe, K.O., and P.R. Lovell. 1980. 'Marriage, Descent and Kinship: On the Differential Primacy of Institutions in Luapula (Zambia) and Longana (New Hebrides)', *Africa* 50(1): 73–92.

Radcliffe-Brown, A. 1927. 'The Regulation of Marriage in Ambrym', *Journal of the Royal Anthropological Institute* 57: 343–48.

Rio, K. 2005. 'Discussions Around a Sand-drawing: Creations of Agency and Society in Melanesia', *Journal of the Royal Anthropological Institute* 11(3): 401–25.

————— 2007a. *The Power of Perspective: Social Ontology and Agency on Ambrym, Vanuatu*. Oxford: Berghahn.

———— 2007b. 'Exposer la vie après la mort: les effets sociaux des prestations mortuaires au Vanuatu', *Journal de la Société des Océanistes* 123/4: 67–81.

———— 2007c. 'Denying the Gift: Aspects of the Gift and Its Counter-prestation in a Vanuatu Society', *Anthropological Theory* 7(4): 449–70.

———— 2009. 'Subject and Object in a Vanuatu Social Ontology. A Local Vision of Dialectics', *Journal of Material Culture* 14(3): 283–308.

Rio, K., and A. Eriksen. 2013. 'Missionaries, Healing and Sorcery in Melanesia: A Scottish Evangelist in Ambrym Island, Vanuatu', *History and Anthropology*, 24(3): 398–418.

Rivers, W.H.R. 1901. 'On the Function of the Maternal Uncle in Torres Strait', *Man* 1: 171–72.

———— 1902. 'The Sister's Son in Samoa', *Folklore* 13(2): 199–201.

———— 1908. 'Totemism in Fiji', *Man* 8: 133–36.

———— 1909. 'Totemism in Polynesia and Melanesia', *Journal of the Royal Anthropological Institute* 39: 156–80.

———— 1910. 'The Father's Sister in Oceania', *Folklore* 21(1): 42–59.

———— 1914. *The History of Melanesian Society*, 2 vols. Cambridge: Cambridge University Press.

———— 1915a. 'Melanesian Gerontocracy', *Man* 15: 145–47.

———— 1915b. 'Descent and Ceremonial in Ambrim', *Journal of the Royal Anthropological Institute* 45: 229–33.

———— 1915c. 'Mother-Right', *Hastings' Encyclopaedia of Religion and Ethics*, 8: 851–59.

Rodman, W. 1973. 'Men of Influence, Men of Rank: Leadership and Graded Society in Longana, East Aoba', PhD diss. Chicago: University of Chicago.

Scheffler, H.W. 1970. 'Ambrym Revisited: A Preliminary Report', *Southwestern Journal of Anthropology* 26: 52–66.

Speiser, F. 1913. *Two Years with the Natives of the Western Pacific*. London: Mills and Boon.

Strathern, M. 1988. *The Gender of the Gift*. Berkeley: California University Press.

Viveiros de Castro, E. 2009. 'The Gift and the Given: Three Nano-essays on Kinship and Magic', in *Kinship and Beyond: The Genealogical Model Reconsidered*, S. Bamford and J. Leach (eds), 237–69. Oxford: Berghahn.

Yoshioka, M. 1985. 'The Marriage System of North Raga, Vanuatu', *Man and Culture in Oceania* 1: 27–54.

———— 1993. 'The Six-section System as a Model', *Man and Culture in Oceania* 9: 45–68.

5

A House upon Pacific Sand

W.H.R. Rivers and His 1908 Ethnographic Survey Work

◆●◆

Thorgeir S. Kolshus

Polyphonic Reality and Scientific Realism

In 1912, Charles Seligman, member of the 1898 Torres Strait Expedition, wrote in a letter to his student Bronislaw Malinowski: 'field research in anthropology is what the blood of martyrs is to the Church' (in Stocking 1995: 115). In this book, Arthur Maurice Hocart and William Halse Rivers Rivers are credited for their significant share in this generative sacrifice that brought about the discipline's distinguishing traits. This should be regarded as a modification of the established opinion that Malinowski was the first to both carry out and codify what is still to a large extent regarded as proper anthropological fieldwork. Rivers's concise description of the 'intensive work' in ethnology in the fourth edition of *Notes and Queries* (Rivers 1912; see also Rivers 1913: 6–7) anticipates all the key methodological points in the famous opening chapter of Malinowski's *Argonauts of the Western Pacific* (1922: 1–26), and consequently contributed to anthropology's character as grounded theory.[1]

Similarly, on a practical fieldwork level, the incoherencies in Hocart's published accounts from Simbo reflect the actualities of the social distribution of knowledge, and are obviously the outcome of 'a constant process of checking, validating, comparing, and qualifying' (Hviding, this volume).

The slightly chaotic impression betrays a highly structured search for the polyphonic rather than the monolithic qualities of ethnographic data. In his writings on method, Rivers provides a general framework for Hocart's multifaceted strategy for data collection, and particularly encourages the search for contradictory remarks. In other words, the two appear in tandem and seem to complement each other. The recurring contradictions in Hocart's ethnography represent an almost insurmountable obstacle to generalisation, but express a desire to give ethnography the right of way at the expense of scientism. The rapport that Hocart obviously established with people on Simbo also reflects upon Rivers, who consequently has been regarded as an equally mindful fieldworker.[2] But there is reason to suspect that the fieldwork talents of Hocart and Rivers differ almost as widely as their scientific ambitions – or at least that Rivers, when decoupled from Hocart, seems less inclined to expose himself to information that contradicts his hypothesising. This becomes particularly visible in what, in terms of publication, was the main outcome of the Percy Sladen Trust Expedition, Rivers's two-volume *The History of Melanesian Society* (1914), which he also intended to be his ethnological masterwork (Stocking 1995: 204).[3]

Presentism or Essential Critique?

Rivers's methodological outline expands the ethnographer's tool set by drawing a distinction between 'intensive work' and 'survey work' in ethnology (Rivers 1912; see also Rivers 1914, i: 1–2). This establishes a two-tier discipline, partly connected by the genealogical or 'concrete' method which is attributable to both approaches, but otherwise with little by way of methodological common ground. The ethnographic research that constitutes the basis for *HMS* belongs to the 'survey' variety, and the present article provides some of the missing or subdued context for the two most comprehensive ethnographic portraits in the book, namely those of Mota, in the Banks Islands of what today is Vanuatu, and Tikopia, the southernmost of the Solomon Islands. Rivers unequivocally declares how his overall argument rests on the accuracy of these two accounts: 'No one who studies the part taken in my theoretical scheme by the facts collected from the Banks Islands and Tikopia can fail to recognise how this scheme would have suffered if this part of my work had not been done, or had been done less fully' (Rivers 1914, i: viii). I base my discussion on a close reading of *HMS*, juxtaposed with archival resources and published missionary and ethnographic literature that provide historical and methodological background for Rivers's survey work. These will at times be contextualised by empirical details from my own two years of fieldwork on Mota.[4] I also draw on Raymond Firth's extensive writings from Tikopia, including the crushing critique he directs at Rivers's material and interpretations.

To some, a critical reappraisal of a century-old work might appear as undue presentism (see Dureau, this volume). This view is also to some extent anticipated in Rivers's numerous reminders to the readers of *HMS* that mention the insufficient empirical foundations for his theorising. Throughout the two volumes, his message seems to read: judge me by the overall analysis and not by the details (see e.g. Rivers 1914, i: vi, 2–5; Rivers 1914, ii: 588–91). But while Rivers admits that *HMS* has its limitations due to the doubtful quality of the data, he insists that 'there has only been included such material as I believe to be correct in essentials, though doubtless often incomplete or even inaccurate in detail' (Rivers 1914, i: 2). Coming from the man who advised anyone who aspired to ethnographic accuracy to get the corroboration of two or more witnesses and embrace contradictory statements, this comment commands reliability. The level of empirical detail in *HMS* also bestows academic legitimacy upon Rivers's theoretical project, since it gives an appearance of strictly inductive reasoning for 'a working hypothetical scheme t[hat] form[s] a framework into which the facts are fitted, and the scheme is regarded as satisfactory only if the facts can thus be fitted so as to form a coherent whole' (Rivers 1914, ii: 586). However, for the hypothesis to work, initial qualifying adjectives erode as the argument proceeds. The creation of these 'linked sausages of supposition' (Stocking 1995: 207), by which early hypotheses reappear later in the argument as established fact, holds a methodological lesson that still has relevance.

One last point that warrants a critical assessment of Rivers's survey work is related to the accuracy of the history of anthropology. Since Langham's (1981) revaluation of the British anthropology of the first three decades of the twentieth century, where he holds that the functionalist winners of the 'war' produced a biased history that distorted Rivers's work, Rivers's reputation as a creative and original thinker has grown. As many of the contributions to this volume reveal, this restoration is justified with regard to his intensive work and to his role in placing social relations at the core of our study. But Langham also mentions a particular conceptual tool of Cambridge institutional memory: in order to rescue Rivers's seminal ideas from his more idiosyncratic contributions and increasingly speculative theorising, one must separate the 'earlier' from the 'later' Rivers (1981: 311–14). According to this scheme, the 'earlier' Rivers was an unadulterated free spirit and academic all-rounder who paved the way for what was to come, but who was cruelly erased by Radcliffe-Brown and his compatriots from the annals of anthropology, while the 'later' Rivers was corrupted and derailed by his association with Grafton Elliot Smith and William Perry's

Egyptological hyper-diffusionism. Although critical of Elliot Smith, Langham expresses some reluctance against accepting this mythological device. But he also holds that Rivers's survey work is an important anthropological heirloom that should be restored. *HMS* is consequently nominated for the academic equivalent of beatification, being labelled 'a classic', usually defined as a work that is widely referred to but rarely read. I do share Firth's admiration for 'the industry with which [Rivers] ... amassed so much of his data' (Firth 1963: xviii), but I also suspect that some of the scholarly admiration of *HMS* is due to secondary enthusiasm, based on approval of an imagined or taken-for-granted ethnographic accuracy. Against this background, taking Rivers seriously by providing additional background information for a critical assessment of his research seems justified.

Rivers and the Melanesian Mission

In 1909, Rivers addressed the annual meeting of the Anglican Melanesian Mission (MM), 'with which I spent a very pleasant time last year', where he acknowledged the value of the mission's work for the discipline of anthropology.[5] Rivers's gratitude towards the MM as an organisation and a number of its individual members is more than reasonable. In fact, his survey work was fully dependent on the mission's unmitigated support and goodwill. He was a passenger on board the Mission's ship, the *Southern Cross*, and occasionally lodged in the limited number of mission stations; and several missionaries acted as consultants on local customs both during the ship's journeys and subsequent letter exchanges, in addition to introducing Rivers to key informants and translating questions and answers between Mota, the MM's lingua franca, and English. For such crucial assistance, Rivers was duly thankful.

In his address, he gives special credit to the MM's culturally sensitive mission policies.[6] These had been outlined by mission founder George Augustus Selwyn, the first Bishop of New Zealand, and codified and expanded upon by John Coleridge Patteson, the first Bishop of Melanesia and head of the MM from 1861 until his martyrdom on the islet of Nukapu ten years later (Kolshus and Hovdhaugen 2010). Patteson's missionary philosophy was based on the principle of 'accommodation': a universalistic religion could not be associated with a specific socio-cultural mode, but should be generally adaptable to the local styles of thought and social requirements of different peoples – a principle that was fashionable within prominent circles of Anglican mission ideologists in the Victorian age but which was institutionalised by the MM to a degree exceeding that of all other foreign missions (Darch 2009). This also led to Patteson's attitude of non-interference with customs that were not directly contradictory to vital Christian dogmas or outright offensive in the eye of an imagined general public. To the latter belonged infanticide and headhunting, while Patteson advised against Melanesians adopting English clothing, arguing that a clean body was more appealing to God's eye than shabby whitish shirts.

Accordingly, until the early 1900s, the MM left it to the proselytes themselves to decide which practices they could not reconcile with their newly embraced teaching, and consequently should abandon (see Montgomery 1904). Added to this acclaimed awareness of the value of cultural continuity were the facts that the MM lacked the staff for successful large-scale evangelisation and their ideological insistence on building the Melanesian Church bottom-up, consequently becoming less an agent of change than might be expected.[7] These points are vital to Rivers's project and subsequent theory building, because they bestow an air of uncorrupted authenticity on the lives and world-views he describes. Consequently, he emphasises the culturally sensitive approach of the MM in the introduction to *HMS* (Rivers 1914, i: 2–3), apparently in anticipation of criticism for his reliance on indigenous informants that were almost exclusively Christian converts, while mercifully leaving out the MM's evangelical shortcomings. Rivers insists that this should not affect the trustworthiness of the data, since 'I am perfectly confident … that their new religion has had little or no influence on most of the facts I have recorded. I deal chiefly with the details of social organisation which suffer little if any change as the result of mission influence and least of all in the field of the Melanesian Mission' (Rivers 1914, i: 2).

Rivers's Key Informants

It is indeed likely that the work of the MM had had little effect on the social organisation on the various islands he incorporates in his study. But Rivers seems to overstate the importance of the genealogical work to the theory building in *HMS* while downplaying its reliance on other key factors that were much more likely to have undergone considerable change due to the mission influence. So, while his explicit purpose for the survey was to obtain systems of relationships and factors that were required for their interpretation, he 'did not neglect any opportunities of acquiring knowledge on other topics', and 'two such subjects seemed to me so important that I devoted much time to their study, even in some cases at the expense of my primary object' (Rivers 1914, i: 5). These were the ethnography of Tikopia, provided by John Maresere of Uvea (Wallis Island), who had lived among his fellow Polynesians for an estimated twenty years; and the *Suqe* graded male society and the *Tamate* secret male societies of Mota (Banks

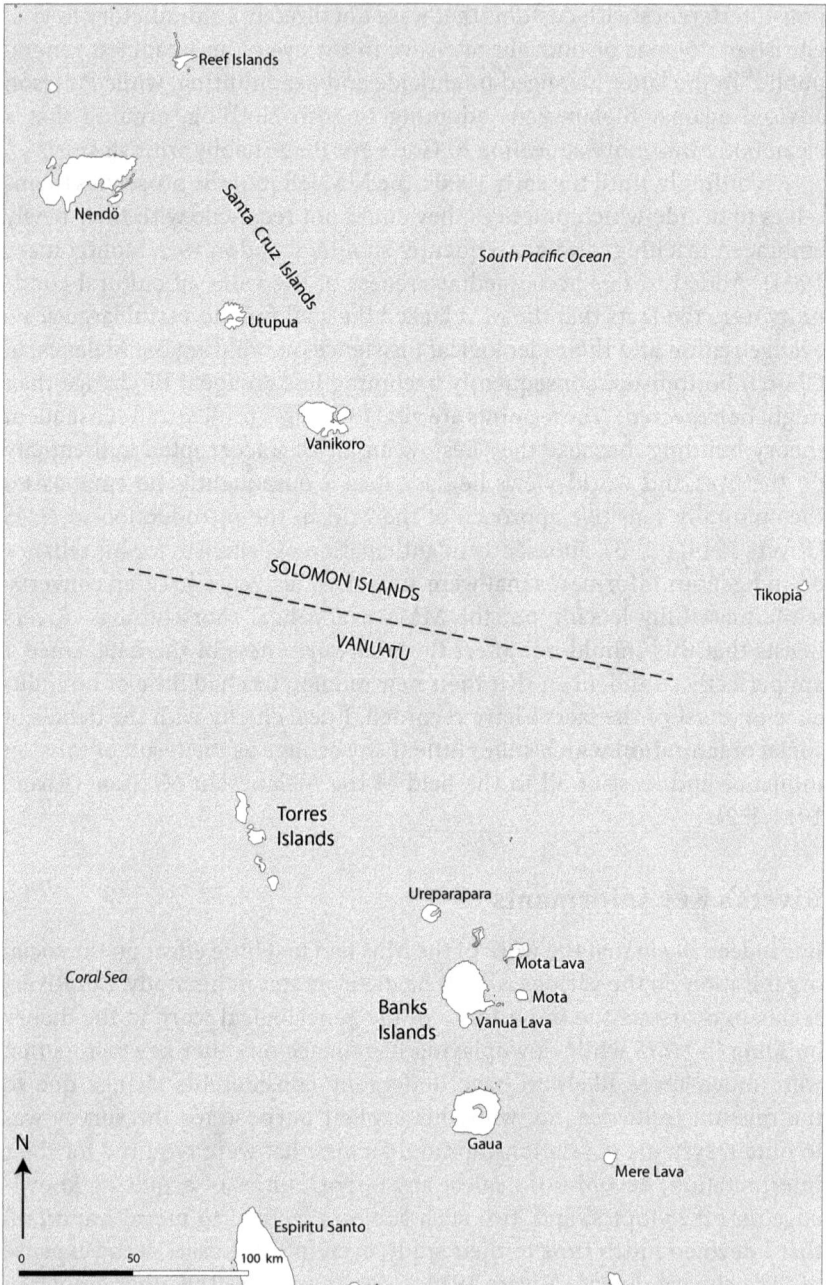

Figure 5.1: The southern part of the Island See [*sic*] of the Melanesian Mission (map by K.H. Sjøstrøm, University of Bergen).

Islands), of which the Mota man John Pantutun was more than willing to talk (Rivers 1914, i: 5–6). The two were not merely passive respondents but 'entered heartily into the work of trying to make me understand the customs and beliefs with which they are familiar' (Rivers 1914, i: viii). Rivers found that their intelligence gave hope for the future of Melanesia and Polynesia, although 'the two were doubtless above the average of their fellows' (Rivers 1914, i: viii).

As anyone with ethnographic fieldwork experience will know, there is nothing out of the ordinary with letting research interests follow the availability and expertise of able informants. But the information provided by Maresere and Pantutun does not only make up much of the ethnography of *HMS* – it is also a sine qua non to Rivers's grand theorising on the peopling of the Pacific, to which his concluding remarks bear testimony: 'There are certain features of my scheme which are so essential that if they are proved to be wrong, the whole will have to go. Such are the substitution of patrilineal for matrilineal institutions, the immigrant character of the secret cults, and the relative lateness of chieftainship' (Rivers 1914, ii: 589).[8] These three axioms evolved from talks with Maresere and Pantutun, and were substantiated by ethnography from Tikopia and Banks Islands. There is reason to question whether this is a case of serendipitous fortune rather than mere convenience. Either way, the choice of these two can hardly be regarded as a deliberate strategic selection of informants. They were both associated with the MM, and the opportunity to spend time with an inquisitive and appreciative Englishman must have been a welcome change from the monotony of uneventful journeys on board the MM's legendary ship *Southern Cross V*, under the command of the equally legendary, and patently misnamed, Captain Sinker. By giving explicit credit to Maresere and Pantutun, Rivers showed less of a colonial attitude towards his informants than had been common.[9] But apart from the favourable assessment of their intellectual capacities, which has the side effect of stressing the quality of his material, Rivers provides little information on Pantutun's background while being selective in his introduction of Maresere. Considering the time of publication, this is hardly remarkable. But there exist sources that mention these two key informants in different contexts, and provide additional background to assess the interview situation and the accuracy of the empirical foundation of *HMS*.

John Pantutun

The Mota man Pantutun worked as a teacher and catechist in the MM's elaborate system of village schools, and had been associated with the MM's headquarters on Norfolk Island. Rivers does not only commend Pantutun for his intellectual capacities but, even more importantly, for his readiness to admit the limits of his knowledge (Rivers 1914, i: 4), which makes him particularly trustworthy as an informant. He was Rivers's main source not only on Mota and the other Banks Islands, but also on Pentecost Island, where Pantutun had spent some time as a teacher. Since Rivers considered Pentecost to be the most archaic of all the societies included in his survey (Rivers 1914, ii: 87), this information formed a crucial piece in his historical conjectures about migration patterns in the Pacific and the course and dynamics of change. And even though he at one point critically assesses Pantutun's version of Pentecost social organisation (Rivers 1914, ii: 74), seemingly because it did not adhere to his overall design, Pantutun is elsewhere regarded as a fully reliable provider of data on the island. He is even credited for a snide comment on how Pentecost 'was a place where they married their granddaughters' (Rivers 1914, i: 199), which serendipitously provided Rivers with the key to coming to terms with what to him was utter chaos.[10]

In fact, Rivers seems so reassured by Pantutun's reliability that he frequently abandons his own methodological principle of securing alternate accounts. This is, of course, understandable given the circumstances under which the research was conducted – but it also makes a considerable

Figure 5.2: 'Life on deck of the S/Y *Southern Cross V*' (photograph by J.W. Beattie, 1906 – by permission of the General Secretary of the Anglican Church of Melanesia).

share of the research outcome rest uneasily on the capacities of this one informant. Even in the published version certain passages indicate that this reliance is unwarranted, and some of the factoids Rivers obviously obtained from Pantutun appear unambiguously incorrect even to the most casual reader. Rivers's description of how some of the matrilineages of the Mota moiety to which Pantutun does not belong are called *veve qaqae*, 'the foolish' (compassionately translated to Rivers as 'eccentric') lineages, who eat their meals in reverse order and imprudently hack off the outrigger of their canoes when finding it difficult to land their canoes on the reef (Rivers 1914, i: 23),[11] is so blatantly distorted that it virtually screams out for further examination. But since it suited Rivers's theory on the nature of the 'dual organisation' of kinship, which according to him originated from the influx of two distinct peoples, he admits this information without further ado. Some historical materials also mention traits in John Pantutun's personal character that, while circumstantial when seen in isolation, when put together should modify his status as a super-informant. During an 1892 visitation to the MM, Bishop Montgomery of Tasmania (Montgomery 1904: chap. 2, 2–3) describes John Pantutun playing the organ in St Barnabas chapel at the MM headquarters with 'vigour and much feeling'. He was also a 'very good cricketer', and one of two who according to the Bishop 'could be trained up to good English county eleven standard'. There is of course nothing inherently incompatible with being well-versed in several cultural complexes and still being a valuable informant. Indeed, it could be argued that precisely this multicultural background made him an even more acute and reflexive observer, and consequently better positioned to act as a cultural translator. Neither should it disqualify him that he was the eldest son of one of the first Melanesian clergymen, Robert Pantutun, and therefore was raised under quite different conditions from those of his peers. But some of the dispositions that are pointed out in Pantutun's obituary in the *Southern Cross Log* nevertheless call forth questions concerning Rivers's reliance on him. In addition to mentioning his musical talents as an organ player and composer of several hymns, the obituary states that he was one of the most gifted Melanesians ever to come to Norfolk Island. But his 'gifts were not altogether to his advantage. He became more the white man's friend and understudy than was desirable, and perhaps vanity helped his undoing; but we could not help it – we all loved John, and turned to him in every emergency'.[12] The obituary does not mention the cause of his death, but the contemporary version on Mota claims that he was killed on board the *Southern Cross* by a falling crate – which had been deliberately cut loose by a person who for some reason was jealous with him.[13]

   In short, there were a number of aspects related to the interview situation that, when added together, makes it reasonable to suspect that the interaction between Rivers and Pantutun acquired a certain reinforcing dynamic, which made Rivers pose questions favourable to his evolving hypothesis while Pantutun responded in a way that further stimulated Rivers's attention. For Pantutun, being questioned for days on end must have been an agreeable break from the dullness of a sea journey he had made regularly since he was a child. Also, the encouragement of the keen attention and possibly favourable comments of an English scholar admired by the MM staff, and the presence of either Revd Charles Fox or Revd Walter Durrad to translate the questions and answers, would invigorate traits in Pantutun's character that made him particularly eager to please his European associates.[14] Rivers's deviation from his own research principle of seeking contradictory sources contributes to an echo-chamber effect, by which what initially were explicit conjectures and assumptions return without further substantiation at a later point in Rivers's extended argument as established axioms for yet new conjectures and assumptions. In addition, the *Suqe* graded male society and the *Tamate* secret male cults[15] that were of particular interest to Rivers and for which Pantutun was virtually the sole source, were at the time of Rivers's journey topics of great concern and much discussion within the MM, as will be seen below. Pantutun was aware that these were highly delicate matters, and having to work through an MM translator might have made him modify his answers.

John Maresere

While Pantutun was a Mota man providing information on life and beliefs of the island where he grew up, Maresere was an outsider on Tikopia. He was one of three young men who had landed there almost two decades earlier, after their canoe had been driven off course on their way between their home island of Uvea and Samoa. And even though Uvea shares the western Polynesian cultural core with Tikopia, Maresere's status would not primarily be that of a fellow Polynesian. Rather, as a Christian convert he represented a cultural force which to Tikopians by the turn of the century had become much more demanding and increasingly invasive. In the early MM literature, Tikopia, 'The Isle of Giants' (Armstrong 1900: 67), consistently figures as a difficult case and a thorn in the flesh of successive episcopacies (Firth 1959: 38–39).[16] The Tikopians engaged with the MM in barter, even though the MM's unwillingness to deal in alcohol, muskets and tobacco made them less popular partners than the more unscrupulous traders (Armstrong 1900: 37). And for several decades, the four Tikopia *ariki* (paramount chiefs) unilaterally decided the range of interaction – an attitude that exacted the missionaries' respect, among other things because they realised that in the wake of the MM's ship *Southern Cross*, frequently disease and misery followed, confirming the good sense of the chiefs' decision (see Wilson 1932: 105–6; Firth 1959: 40; 1970: 306). As long as the *ariki* fulfilled their ritual duties, Tikopia seemed resistant to the new teaching. But the effects of the trade in indentured labour and the impact of the colonial government added to the less tolerant approach of the MM from around 1900, and slowly chiefly authority was eroded, opening a space for the MM's evangelical breakthrough.

By 1909, the MM had two good schools attended by two hundred Tikopians, many of whom could speak and write Mota (Firth 1970: 306), while the MM reports that in 1915, there were 'a good many' who spoke Mota and/or English.[17] As a Christian, Maresere was a controversial figure among the Tikopian traditionalists that Rivers so desired to describe, since the authentic state of Tikopia was crucial to his argument. Consequently, Rivers departs from his otherwise preferred genre of dry scientism and describes the approach to Tikopia where he would spend one day: 'The scene was one which I had no idea might still be witnessed in the Pacific. The evidence of outside influence was of the slightest; very few of the people wore anything but the native dress, a loin-cloth of tapa stained with turmeric' (Rivers 1914, i: 298).

After thus establishing Tikopia as an uncorrupted cultural environment, Rivers moves on to give a short biography of Maresere and a four page scrutinous assessment of his qualities, painfully aware that the analysis rests on 'his veracity and trustworthiness' (Rivers 1914, i: 299). He regrets Maresere's lack of interest in, and even contempt for, folktales, but, as with Pantutun, gives him credit for his readiness to acknowledge the limits of his knowledge. According to Rivers, both he and Revd Durrad double-checked the stories obtained from Maresere while they were ashore, and during a two-months stay in 1910 Durrad, assisted by the Maori man Poata (Firth 1959: 40), could not find any serious flaws in the information he provided (Rivers 1914, i: 300–1). Still, it is obviously with some consternation that Rivers first presents Maresere's narrative (Rivers 1914, i: 303–33) and then compares his version with Durrad's and those of castaway seamen and other more accidental observers (Rivers 1914, i: 350–55). This is not only because Rivers was aware of his doubly problematic status as an outsider and a Christian, but also because Maresere had been ostracised from Tikopia a few years earlier, the reasons for which Rivers does not provide. Their visit was Maresere's first trip to Tikopia after what must have been a prolonged exile in the Banks Islands, during which he also learnt to speak Mota.[18] And when Rivers and the *Southern Cross* called at Tikopia six months later, Maresere left the island, apparently for good.

In his elaborate evaluation of Maresere as informant, Rivers pauses to make a point of a more general nature:

> One great task of the future anthropologist will be the valuation of evidence, and it is partly in the hope that John's account may be useful in this respect that I give it untouched, for it is probable that we may yet obtain a full and accurate account of Tikopian culture which will enable the value of this story to be fully gauged. (Rivers 1914, i: 302)

This remark deserves praise for its transparency. It would also prove to be prophetic, as anyone with even the slightest acquaintance with anthropological history will know. Raymond Firth's fieldworks on Tikopia originated with reference to Rivers's work, as part of an attempt to understand the relation between Melanesian and Polynesian cultures that was such a crucial question to Rivers (Firth 1967a: 15).[19] Twenty years after Rivers, Firth too was a passenger on the *Southern Cross*, travelling almost the exact same route. But during the seven weeks on board, Firth's confidence in Rivers's work was shattered: 'while I admired the industry with which he had amassed so much of his data, from brief calls at villages and sessions with natives on the deck of the vessel I became increasingly convinced of the arid quality of this material, its superficiality and lack of perspective' (Firth 1963: xviii). Throughout his voluminous work on Tikopia, Firth makes impatient remarks on the numerous errors, misunderstandings and confusions in Rivers's account, and on his reliance on information from one man to which Rivers 'attached an exaggerated value' (Firth 1963: xviii). Characterisations like 'purely gratuitous' (Firth 1963: 468), 'quite incorrect' (Firth 1963: 262) and one 'need not take seriously' (Firth 1967a: 59) abound. He also underlines Rivers's not living as he taught, being 'content to reproduce the material of a single informant, a foreigner, collected in a *lingua franca*, without the possibility of check by direct observation' (Firth 1963: xviii). This becomes particularly problematic given the context in which the interviews were conducted. Firth indicates that their presence on a mission ship made Maresere deny the continued existence of polygamy, which was common even at the time of Firth's first fieldwork. More idiosyncratic, yet illustrative of the single-source problem, was Maresere's insistence that adultery was rare, and that it would absolutely never occur between a married man and an unmarried woman. Firth provides the significant piece of information regarding Maresere's exile that had been left out by Rivers: 'One can perhaps understand the vigour of this when it is realized that it was precisely for this offence, committed with the sister of his "father" and protector the Ariki Tafua ... that he had been banished from Tikopia' (Firth 1963: xviii).

Firth seems to be aware that his assessment of Maresere as an informant and his opinion on Rivers's work on Tikopia might appear uncustomarily harsh. He also anticipates the concern of Oceanic scholars for not engaging *HMS* in a more comprehensive fashion, since at the time of his research it was the most systematic ethnographic source on the island (Firth 1963: xviii). But he nonetheless insists that the poor quality of the Tikopia material in particular, and his general impression that Rivers's work during the many short calls of the *Southern Cross* was substandard – mentioning the 'utter worthlessness of casual observation derived from the stay of a day or so' (Firth 1963: 367) – made it impossible for him to use data from *HMS* to check against his own findings. This could of course be due to Firth's dependence on Radcliffe-Brown during his early career, and his consequent sense of commitment to his tutor's rivalry with Rivers, his former supervisor (see Radcliffe-Brown 1964). But not even in his earliest works does Firth subscribe to Radcliffe-Brown's structural-functionalist approach, and he soon developed an original analytical position that overcame several of the impediments of structural-functionalism. Consequently, Firth appears to be a highly independent scholar of great integrity. His unfavourable judgment of Rivers's work could of course also be seen as a young academic's strategy to rise from the shoulders of a renowned predecessor. However, it seems odd that he would continue criticising Rivers in his main publications on Tikopia over a full four decades, long after Rivers's intellectual heritage had been ostracised and Firth had assumed his seat in the anthropological pantheon.

Walter J. Durrad

While Firth had reservations concerning Rivers's work with Maresere, he is much more appreciative of his other main source and interpreter, Revd Walter Durrad, an ordained priest and Cambridge graduate who worked as a field missionary from 1905 to 1919. This may be due to Firth's considerable personal debt to Durrad, who lent Firth all his notes and photographs from his 1910 stay prior to Firth's departure for the field, and who had also co-published a book of Tikopian vocabulary which Firth had found very useful when acquiring the language. But he is as consistent in his appreciation of Durrad's talents as an observer as he is in his questioning of Maresere's, and uses the paragraph before the denunciation of Rivers to acknowledge the accuracy of Durrad's account: 'comparison of my work with [his] will show that I was able to substantiate most of his conclusions' (Firth 1963: xvii–xviii). This, of course, intensifies the impact of his negative assessment of Rivers – who, for his part, is in full agreement with Firth's appreciation for Durrad, as well as expressing an even more substantial debt (Rivers 1914, i: viii). The expressed gratitude of these two prominent anthropologists must have been heartening to Durrad, who throughout his many years in the field found himself in a quandary. On the one hand, he obviously had a great desire to understand and document the customs and world-views of the people he was living with and cared so much for – influenced by the greatest of missionary ethnographers, Robert Henry Codrington, under whom he studied and worked in Chichester, and who with all probability was instrumental in Durrad's choice to join the MM and leave for the Pacific.[20] Durrad also desired being an advocate for the interests of his Melanesian friends and fellow Christians, turning European attention to their plight – as is visible in his contribution to Rivers's edited volume on the depopulation of Melanesia (Durrad 1922).[21]

On the other hand, he was instrumental in arresting the MM's wavering attitude towards the *Suqe* graded male society, by making an ethnography-based and academic argument for why the MM should actively discourage the organisation and its related practices (Durrad 1920). Durrad's ambivalence also materialises in *HMS*, since he evidently is the source behind this statement from an anonymous missionary:

> I could not help feeling that the existence of the *Suqe* does much to foster the virtues which go to make up the successful citizen and man of business and so maintain the vigour of the community ... [A] man must have unlimited patience, indomitable perseverance, excellent health, and a strong physique to enable him to recover from the perpetual succession of losses of which he runs the risk. (Rivers 1914, i: 143)

Durrad's ambivalence is caused by his realisation that abandoning the MM's principle of 'accommodation' would mean a radical change in mission policy, which in its turn could aggravate the negative effects of acculturation that he points to as a factor in the depopulation effect: 'There is no doubt that social life as a whole is a more drab affair now than it used to be' (Durrad 1922: 12). And even though he holds that the stimulus of a truly vibrant Christian life outweighs the consequences of culture loss, he sees the tepidness of much Melanesian Christianity, mainly due to the half-hearted efforts of the local catechists, as the greatest challenge to people's *joie de vivre*. He also criticises the unequivocal condemnation apparent in Bishop Cecil Wilson's characterisation of the *Suqe* as '*nalinan Satan*', the voice of Satan, or Satan's call (Durrad 1920: 21). But he nevertheless realised that the *Suqe* proved an obstacle to evangelical success after the initial millenarian enthusiasm of the new converts had faded and the first generation of legendary Melanesian clergy had passed away.

The *Suqe* and the *Tamate* around 1908

Durrad's hesitant but eventually determined confrontation with the organisations that were so crucial to Rivers's theory epitomised the MM's attitude. In an 1883 letter to Codrington, the first Melanesian priest George Sarawia of Mota wrote about the *Suqe* and the *Tamate* in a way that shows that the organisations had been of concern to the MM for decades prior to Rivers's research:

> And regarding the thing you wrote, that some of the news from us here is still not good and in the same way as you always hear from us, it is true that something maybe is true while other things are only accusations, [Revd John] Palmer will examine and then speak on the matter, whereas regarding the tamate they do not pray to the tamate that they pay for, no, they are not allowed to pray, this is true but they nevertheless continue to pay, while regarding the suqe it is not on their minds as it was before, only the ideas of a few which rarely go far, I go and see them to establish whether there are any unsound ideas behind it, in order for them to change.[22]

The prayers Sarawia refers to were incantations used during the ceremonials of the *Tamate* cults, either in preparations for the dances of the various cults or when ritually clearing an area as a *salagōrō* – practices that remain strong on Mota today, which suggests that the members either revived practices the Church had discouraged, or that Sarawia's report was not entirely accurate when he holds that they no longer used the prayers. He also seemed confident that the importance of the *Suqe* was in decline.

Even if this were true at the time of the letter, the development was no doubt reversed. When recollecting his episcopacy from 1894 to 1911, Bishop Wilson writes of Mota, the MM's stronghold since 1861:

> Every time I stayed there I felt the island was to all intents and purposes heathen and the Mission's work a ghastly failure, and I have no doubt whatsoever that the cause of the failure was the *Sukwe* [sic]. This little island of Mota was, in fact, for one half of the year nominally Christian and for the other half heathen, and all because of this native freemasonry – truly described by some of our most trusted native teachers as 'partly good and partly bad'. (Wilson 1932: 76–77)

Church attendance of the second generation of Christians was low compared to the enthusiasm with which people celebrated the ceremonies following *Suqe* grade-taking. Two letters from the Melanesian catechist Dudley Virsal to the repatriated Codrington, written eight years apart, illustrate the resilient nature of the *Suqe* in Vureas on Vanua Lava (where Durrad served from 1911 to 1919). In 1901, Virsal writes:

> The suqe is over, save for two villages on Mota and Mota Lava, where they might abandon it or not. Really, my brother, these two villages first received the word of God, but they stubbornly stick to the teachings of old. Truly sorry for them if they don't forsake their manners, because the suqe is not good for them. If only they had followed the word of God, like some islands where they threw away [the old practices] only to realise that the way of the suqe was not good, while the word of God burns and only becomes stronger than before.[23]

By 1909, the tone has changed:

> As long as the Father stayed in this village the school was solid, and the people came for meetings and for daily prayers, and Sundays they numbered 200 or 100. But now, there are only ten and some days five or two or eight for the daily prayers, and Sundays ten or twenty while a mere thirty are counted as a good turn-out. Really, my brother, already this place merely glows; it does not burn, but glows tepidly, like the power has come to nothing in this place. The reason is that the message of the suqe and the salagoro [Tamate cults] keeps them under control and prevents them from seeking the word of God. And in addition, the teachers in this village are careless; they don't encourage the people to go to prayers.[24]

A compromise in 1904 reduced the celebrations associated with a man's advance within the *Suqe* to a single day, but the regulations proved futile. Also, in order to produce the pigs and money required for advancement in the societies, sacrifices and prayers to spirits were necessary. This meant that the beliefs in non-Christian ethereal beings endured. Codrington's view had been that these beliefs were a resource that facilitated the under-standing of the Christian pantheon, but this position was being questioned by the new leadership. From the mission's point of view, another disquieting element of the *Suqe* was the eating taboos that prohibited members of different ranks from eating together and men from eating with women, thus effectively obstructing people from partaking in the Holy Communion, the ritual hallmark of Christian unity (Montgomery 1904: chap 12, 2; Fox 1958: 147). Leonard Robin, who in 1890 established himself as a mission-ary in the Torres Islands to the northwest of the Banks Islands, made the resignation of positions within the *Suqe* (in Torres called *Hukwe*) a con-dition for baptism. When the great chief of Tegua, Teqalqal, deliberately ate his way down the grades and emerged as a 'free' man, many others followed his example (Armstrong 1900: 326). This success was stimulating to those who advocated a less accommodating tactic towards the *Suqe*. In

1910, deacon Robert Pantutun, John's father, revealed during his deathbed confessions that George Sarawia owed his public esteem not only to his position in the Church but from reaching one of the highest grades of the *Suqe*. Sarawia was also a member of the exclusive *Tamate* cult *Oviov*.[25] In the same year, towards the end of his long service, Bishop Wilson made up his mind: 'Forty years have now passed since these islanders accepted Christianity; we find that all our efforts to curb or Christianize the cere-monies of this Society have failed, and that we must either forbid them altogether to the Church, or else see the Church go under' (quoted in Fox 1958: 46).

In other words, the *Suqe* graded male society and the *Tamate* secret male cults of the Banks Islands, which were of such interest and importance to Rivers that almost one quarter of the descriptive first volume is dedicated to these institutions alone, and which form the linchpin of Rivers's general argument, were at the time of the first collection of data and the subse-quent despatches from Durrad to Rivers a highly contentious issue to his informants and hosts, as indeed they had been for decades. Rivers's claim that the institutions had not been substantially changed due to the MM's principle of non-interference seems questionable. And coming from the man behind the dystopian hypothesis on how pacification and missionisa-tion as obstacles to cultural reproduction had made Melanesians lose their ability to reproduce physically (Rivers 1922a), it sounds more like wishful thinking in order to shield an important piece of ethnography from critical remarks.

The Anatomy of an Undeserved Exoneration?

I have presented a number of points that contextualise Rivers's research and challenge the quality of his material, and subsequently his conclu-sions. His admirably clear methodological programme is echoed in the very first and some of the last sentences of HMS. But when the siren of generalisation beckons, he abandons these convictions in his quest for the one unifying hypothesis. The pre-emptive remark from the introduction to HMS mirrors his predicament: 'The methods I have used have led to the formulation of a scheme of Melanesian history so complicated that it may seem at first sight to go far beyond the conclusions warranted by the facts now at our disposal' (Rivers 1914, i: vi). In a certain sense, generali-sations seem to be the privilege of those who are too far from the nuances to be enamoured, and can consequently let them go without agony – or, in Stocking's biting prose: 'when Rivers took the bit of an hypothesis in his teeth, he was sometimes willing to ride roughshod over empirical dif-ficulties that got in the way' (Stocking 1995: 188; see also Kroeber, quoted in Désveaux 2002: 124). His references to Codrington's work, remarkably limited in number, also frequently reveal a sloppiness in reading that seems almost wilful.[26] But Rivers's survey work facilitated him pointing out some very interesting connections, including one particularly fascinating ethnographic conundrum: the absence of secret male societies in the Solomon Islands while they were present to the north and south – visible for instance in the *Dukduk* societies of New Ireland and the *Tamate* of the Banks Islands, which clearly resemble each other both visually and structurally (Rivers 1914, ii: 510–15). This lesson on the value of a translocal perspective inherent in Rivers's 'multi-sited research strategy' explains why *HMS* has been mentioned in connection with the increasing number of challenges to the so-called classical anthropological fieldwork tradition from allegedly more regionally and globally minded scholars during the past two decades.

Rivers's distinction between intensive work and survey work also mirrors a current predicament in anthropology regarding the breaking point between complexity and applicability. It can be argued that the proof of the anthropological pudding no longer lies in the quality of the ethnography. There is a tendency to embrace high-flying theoretical ambition while leaving ethnographic accuracy as an un-hugged wallflower. The synthesisers with generalising ambitions attract attention while ethnographic rigour seems to be taken for granted. This flouts the intentional distinction between 'fieldwork' and 'field trip' that sets anthropology apart from our neighbouring disciplines. There is of course a significant element of chance whether crucial empirical cases are played out during the course of fieldwork, but it is nevertheless systematic and patient work and stubborn presence that put the ethnographer in the right situations and locations in the first place, and which enable them to recognise the substance of momentary action and inaction. The subjectivity of the fieldworker is a highly disciplined one (Scheper-Hughes 2000). In this volume, Rivers and Hocart are credited for their fieldwork talents, while Rivers is also rightfully praised for his role in carving out the anthropological method and for placing the social at the core of anthropology. This chapter by no means reduces the virtues of these achievements. But it might adjust an image of Rivers as someone who as a matter of principle kept a keen eye on the necessity of empirical grounding in his inductive reasoning. Alone on the *Southern Cross*, Rivers seems complacent and less inclined to examine counterfactuals, while back in his study these shortcomings cause cumulative errors that diminish the potential impact of *HMS*. The lesson might then after all be that the quality of ethnography has the right of way, since the higher storeys of theory will not last when resting on shoddy craftsmanship – or, as in this case, upon Pacific sand.

Notes

1. This makes it all the more puzzling that Rivers refused to discuss matters relating to method when he accompanied John Layard to his fieldwork on Atchin in 1914. While on board, Rivers spent all his time correcting the proofs of his forthcoming book (Rivers 1914), and since the Atchinese were not as welcoming as he had anticipated, Rivers abandoned Layard for a passing ship ten days after their arrival (MacClancy 1986: 51–52).

2. Stocking also seems to suggest this difference between them regarding fieldwork skills by underlining Hocart's ability to listen rather than asking detailed questions, without mentioning Rivers in this regard (Stocking 1995: 221). Rivers's fieldwork among the Toda in the Nilgiri Hills of South India and his subsequent monograph (Rivers 1906) have received much praise for inaugurating the era of the 'new anthropology', both in methodological terms and in the way the work put the social at the core of anthropology. Stocking emphasises his dependence on an interpreter who for ten years had been trying to convert the Toda to Christianity – a fact that Rivers himself mentions but to which he attributes little significance – and that the interviews were conducted in Tamil, the third language of Toda men and known by but few women, a methodological limitation Rivers does not reveal (Stocking 1995: 189).

3. Hereafter I refer to *The History of Melanesian Society* as *HMS*; volume numbers in references to this source are indicated by lower case Roman numerals.

4. My fieldwork in 1996–7 and 2002–3, with a five-week trip in 2012, bespeaks Rivers's impact on my academic life. His mention of no less than seventy-seven secret male cults among only 400 people on the island of Mota in the Banks Islands of north Vanuatu so intrigued me that I chose Mota as the site for my research. Rivers followed me there too. A photocopy of *HMS* endured leaking roofs and cellulose-starved rats, before being strategically mislaid by one of the parties in a land dispute that had been triggered by the return of Rivers's genealogical charts (see Kolshus 2011). And on the evening of my arrival, dropping the name of John Pantutun, Rivers's key informant from Mota, was the fieldwork equivalent of 'open sesame': a number of people present turned out to be the grandchildren or great-grandchildren of Pantutun. And since he had chosen to work closely with someone whose background and quest were similar to mine, Pantutun's descendants extended to me the courtesy he had shown towards Rivers.

5. W.H.R. Rivers, *Southern Cross Log* (quotation from p.140). In this address, Rivers anticipates several of the main points in his hypothesis on the causes of depopulation in Melanesia (Rivers 1922a). He also provides those attending with practical advice, and voices the concerns of MM personnel, emphasising the need for more missionaries as well as medical staff. It is therefore

not surprising that Rivers is consistently referred to in the *Southern Cross Log* (MM's periodical) as a friend of the Mission (see e.g. *Southern Cross Log* 1912, p.325). Rivers's father was himself an Anglican clergyman (Stocking 1995: 184).

6. One former missionary is singled out: 'I do not know how many of you are aware that one of the greatest of living anthropologists is a member of this Mission. Wherever anthropologists are to be found, whether in this country, on the Continent, or in America, one of the most honoured names is that of Dr. Codrington' (Rivers, in *Southern Cross Log* 1910, p. 143). As far as I can tell, Codrington's work on kinship and social organisation covers all the essentials of Rivers's much acclaimed 'genealogical method'. Rivers makes no explicit note of this connection, but his expansion upon one of Codrington's genealogical charts (Codrington 1891: 38; Rivers 1914, i: 26–27) shows the relatedness between their approaches (see also Kolshus 2008). I have argued elsewhere (Kolshus 2010) that the quality of Codrington's work was crucial in placing Melanesian ethnography at the heart of general anthropology – a position that it still holds to a considerable degree.

7. When, around the time of Rivers's visit, the MM leadership realised these impediments to the Christianisation of Melanesia, they changed their policies and based their organisation on European and Antipodean missionaries rather than Melanesian clergy. Accordingly, the attitude towards local customs changed.

8. For Rivers, the cults pointed to the settlement on an already populated island of a small group of men from a superior cultural background, who continued to practise their old religion in secret. Therefore, he could track the size of colonising groups and whether they settled among the indigenous population or established new and independent settlements – which according to him accounts for the absence of male cults in the Solomon Islands while they are found both to the north and the immediate south (Rivers 1914, ii: 205–7, 574).

9. By providing the names of his research collaborators, Rivers also shows a dedication to transparency that facilitated the critical assessment in this chapter.

10. Later assessments of Rivers's Pentecost material show its generally vague or even erroneous character (see Taylor 2008 for a summary). Even after the eureka moment caused by Pantutun's joking remark, Rivers found the Pentecost system inexplicable (Langham 1981) – which is quite understandable, since there are a number of different systems on the island (Taylor 2008: 203–4).

11. These points are further exaggerated in Rivers (1914, ii: 558) in anticipation of the conclusions.

12. *Southern Cross Log* (Auckland and Sydney), 1 May 1914, p.327.

13. Pantutun is also credited with having brought *nōōta*, pandanus used for roof-making, from the Solomons to Mota. However, since it already has an entry in Codrington and Palmer's dictionary, featured as the subspecies *ōta man* (Codrington and Palmer 1896: 110), this is probably historically incorrect.

14. Counter to claims concerning Pantutun's vanity is the fact that he does not mention their conversations in a letter he wrote to Codrington less than a year later; see letter from Pantutun to Codrington, 18 July 1909, Codrington Papers, Rhodes House Library, Oxford (hereafter RH/CP), MSS Pac s7. He mentions that his son Henry, named after Codrington, recently had a child who was baptised Robert.

15. Rivers uses 'secret male cults' and 'secret societies' interchangeably.

16. Mission founder George A. Selwyn and his successor John Coleridge Patteson were both fluent in Maori, and were able to communicate with Tikopians already during their first brief call, which took place either in 1857 or 1858 (Firth 1959: 37).

17. *Southern Cross Log* 1915, p. 494. In 1916, three Tikopian missionaries went to neighbouring Anuta, where they were allowed to stay and teach the new doctrine. This proved immensely successful, since a major cyclone that hit Anuta later that year convinced the whole island to convert (Feinberg 2004: 31). In 1923, the Ariki Tafua, second in ritual importance, converted, and all the people in his district followed him (Firth 1970: 308). Thus, at the time Firth arrived in 1928, approximately half the population was baptised. When he returned in 1952, 90 per cent of the Tikopians were Christians (see Firth 1970: 317–20 for a qualitative contextualisation of these figures), among them two out of four paramount chiefs. Four years later, every Tikopian was baptised, and when Firth returned in 1966, he found the melancholy sight of neglected temples and sacra in decay (Firth 1967b: 473–75; 1970).

18. In other words, Maresere answered highly specific ethnographic questions translated from English into a language he had only recently learnt but which did not share the basic Polynesian vocabulary in which many of the concepts and practices are represented. The semantic pitfalls in this endeavour must have also been obvious to Rivers.

19. According to Stocking, Firth had wanted to work on Rennell but was sent to Tikopia by Radcliffe-Brown at the expense of Reo Fortune, whose proposed project on Tikopia was too 'psychological' for Radcliffe-Brown's taste (Stocking 1995: 340–41).

20. Durrad's ethnographic interests eventually resulted in the publication of several articles in *Oceania*, based on his notes. Walter Ivens and Charles E. Fox were two other prominent and academically productive missionaries-cum-ethnographers who served with the MM. During the 1908 expedition, the latter was smitten by Rivers's enthusiasm for ethnology and

remained dedicated to ethnographic descriptions for the following decades, serving as a correspondent for the Royal Anthropological Institute (RAI) from 1913 to 1938, publishing an interesting monograph (Fox 1925) as well as a score of articles. During a sabbatical in 1915, Fox stayed with Rivers at St John's College, Cambridge, while following his lectures. Rivers became ever more intrigued by Fox's work and its Egyptological implications, drawing heavily upon them in what would be his final presidential address to the RAI (Rivers 1922b: 15–18), and according to Grafton Elliot Smith, Rivers found Fox's work to be 'one of the most important, if not *the* most important, piece of field-work that has ever been done in social anthropology' (Elliot Smith 1925: viii). Fox, for his part, is the likely author of an unenthusiastic review of *HMS* in the *Southern Cross Log* 1917, pp.19–23, emphasising the numerous inaccuracies and misunderstandings in the ethnographic accounts.

21. In this respect Durrad also follows in the footsteps of Codrington (see Kolshus 2010).

22. Letter from Sarawia to Codrington, 22 June 1883, RH/CP, MSS Pac s5, my translation from Mota, punctuation unedited.

23. Letter from Virsal to Codrington, 12 October 1901, RH/CP, MSS Pac s7, my translation from Mota.

24. Letter from Virsal to Codrington, 7 November 1909, RH/CP, MSS Pac s7, my translation from Mota.

25. R.H. Codrington, 'Journal of Voyage 1870', entry for 8 September, MelM 1/2, Special Collections, School of Oriental and African Studies Library, London.

26. See e.g. the internal inconsistencies in Rivers (1914, i: 138–39) and Rivers (1914, ii: 86, 100, 324–25); cf. Codrington's descriptions (Codrington 1891: 45–46, 54).

References

Armstrong, E.S. 1900. *The Melanesian Mission*. London: Isbiter and Co.

Codrington, R.H. 1891. *The Melanesians*. Oxford: Clarendon Press.

Codrington, R.H. and J. Palmer. 1896. *A Dictionary of the Language of Mota*. London: Society for Promoting Christian Knowledge.

Darch, J.H. 2009. *Missionary Imperalists? Missionaries, Governments and the Growth of the British Empire in the Tropics, 1860–1885*. Eugene, OR: Wipf and Stock.

Désveaux, E. 2002. 'Some Current Kinship Paradigms in the Light of True Crow Indian Ethnography', in *Anthropology, by Comparison*, R. Fox and A. Gingrich (eds), 124–42. London: Routledge.

Durrad, W.J. 1920. *The Attitude of the Church to the Suqe*. Norfolk Island: Melanesian Mission Press.

_____ 1922. 'The Depopulation of Melanesia', in *Essays on the Depopulation of Melanesia*, W.H.R. Rivers (ed.), 3–24. Cambridge: Cambridge University Press.

Elliot Smith, G. 1925. 'Preface', in *The Threshold of the Pacific*, C.E. Fox (ed.), v–ix. New York: Knopf.

Feinberg, R. 2004. Anuta: *Polynesian Lifeways for the Twenty-first Century*. Long Grove, IL: Waveland Press.

Firth, R. 1959. *Social Change on Tikopia*. London: Allen and Unwin.

_____ 1963 [1936]. *We, the Tikopia*. Boston: Beacon Press.

_____ 1967a. *Tikopia Ritual and Belief*. Boston: Beacon Press.

_____ 1967b. *The Work of the Gods in Tikopia*. London: Athlone Press.

_____ 1970. *Rank and Religion in Tikopia*. Boston: Beacon Press.

Fox, C.E. 1925. *The Threshold of the Pacific*. New York: Knopf.

_____ 1958. *Lord of the Southern Isles*. London: Mowbray and Co.

Kolshus, T.S. 2008. 'Adopting Change: Relational Flexibility as Vice and Virtue on Mota, Vanuatu', *Pacific Studies* 31(3/4): 58–86.

_____ 2010. 'Relativisme, Intervensjonisme og Aktivisme: Robert Henry Codrington og Den Anglikanske Melanesian Mission i Imperialismens Tidsalder [Relativism, Interventionism and Activism: Robert Henry Codrington and the Anglican Melanesian Mission in the Age of Imperialism]', *DIN: Tidsskrift for Religion og Kultur* 16(1/2): 95–120.

_____ 2011. 'The Technology of Ethnography: An Empirical Argument against the Repatriation of Historical Accounts', *Journal de la Société des Océanistes* 133: 299–309.

Kolshus, T.S., and E. Hovdhaugen. 2010. 'Reassessing the Death of Bishop John Coleridge Patteson', *Journal of Pacific History* 45(3): 331–55.

Langham, I. 1981. *The Building of British Social Anthropology: W.H.R. Rivers and his Cambridge Disciples in the Development of Kinship Studies, 1898–1931*. Dordrecht: Reidel.

MacClancy, J. 1986. 'Unconventional Character and Disciplinary Convention: John Layard, Jungian and Anthropologist', in *Malinowski, Rivers, Benedict and Others*, G.W. Stocking (ed.), 50–71. Madison: University of Wisconsin Press.

Malinowski, B. 1922. *Argonauts of the Western Pacific*. London: Kegan Paul.

Montgomery, H. 1904. *The Light of Melanesia*. London: Society for the Promotion of Christian Knowledge.

Radcliffe-Brown, A.R. 1964 [1922]. *The Andaman Islanders*. New York: Free Press.

Rivers, W.H.R. 1906. The Todas. London: Macmillan.

_____ 1912. 'A General Account of Method', in *Notes and Queries on Anthropology*, 4th ed., British Association for the Advancement of Science (ed.), 108–27. London: Royal Anthropological Institute.

_____ 1913. 'Report on Anthropological Research Outside America', in *The Present Condition and Future Needs of the Science of Anthropology*, W.H.R. Rivers (ed.), 5–28. Washington, DC: Carnegie Institute.

_____ 1914. *The History of Melanesian Society*, 2 vols. Cambridge: Cambridge University Press.

_____ 1922a. 'The Psychological Factor', in *Essays on the Depopulation of Melanesia*, W.H.R. Rivers (ed.), 84–113. Cambridge: Cambridge University Press.

_____ 1922b. 'The Unity of Anthropology', *Journal of the Royal Anthropological Institute* 52: 12–25.

_____ (ed.) 1922b. *Essays on the Depopulation of Melanesia*. Cambridge: Cambridge University Press.

Scheper-Hughes, N. 2000. 'Ire in Ireland', *Ethnography* 1(1): 117–40.

Stocking, G.W. 1995. *After Tylor: British Social Anthropology 1888–1951*. Madison: University of Wisconsin Press

Taylor, J.P. 2008. *The Other Side: Ways of Being and Place in Vanuatu*. Honolulu: University of Hawaii Press.

Wilson, C. 1932. *The Wake of the Southern Cross*. London: John Murray.

6

Colonialism as Shell Shock

W.H.R. Rivers's Explanations for Depopulation in Melanesia

◆●◆

Tim Bayliss-Smith

After the Great War

On 12 March 1920, William Rivers reached his fifty-sixth birthday and, despite some persistent health concerns, he was arguably in the prime of life. Transformed by his experiences in the Great War, Rivers was no longer the diffident and reclusive young scientist whose stammer and shyness had once made lecturing at Cambridge University something of an ordeal. After a five-year absence, his colleagues and friends welcomed back to St John's College a more confident and much happier man (Myers 1923; Bartlett 1937, 1968; Slobodin 1978; Langham 1981; Whittle 2000). Since his return from Melanesia in 1915, Rivers had developed an overriding interest in theories of the unconscious, dreams and psychoanalysis. Meanwhile, Cambridge had become the centre in England for research into 'abnormal psychology', and a centre in the movement for reform of the lunacy laws that constrained the treatment of mild forms of mental illness through psychoanalysis (Forrester 2008: 38). In short, the university provided for him an ideal base (Figure 6.1).

The outbreak of the Great War in August 1914 had found Rivers in Australia on his way to Melanesia to carry out fieldwork, but after returning to England he joined the Royal Army Medical Corps in July 1915. From then until 1919 Rivers worked as an army psychotherapist, treating soldiers and airmen for neuroses that came under the popular heading of 'shell shock'. His pioneering methods of psychotherapy were widely discussed and in many cases were successful. His reputation in experimental psychology and neuro-physiology was already established – the work he carried out before 1908 had made him a Fellow of the Royal Society and gained the award of a Royal Society Gold Medal in 1915.

His reputation in the new discipline of social anthropology was also high. In 1920 he was elected president of the Folklore Society, and in 1920–21 he became president of the Royal Anthropological Institute. Having resumed his fellowship of St John's College in 1919, he took up with enthusiasm a new teaching role in Cambridge, and renewed his interactions with colleagues in the natural sciences, ethnology and the humanities. At the summit of his powers and with every opportunity to climb new peaks, in what direction would Rivers turn next?

It is perhaps not surprising, given his restless intellect and polymathic tendencies, that during the four post-war years before his sudden death on 4 June 1922, Rivers continued to research across a bewildering range of disciplines and topics, and he also became much more widely known. He invited to St John's College several visitors, including missionaries, politicians, novelists and poets, some of them his former patients. He gave numerous public lectures, was active in learned societies and on government committees, visited the USA, became involved in Labour Party politics, and of course published extensively, including articles and book reviews in journals ranging from the *Lancet* to the *British Journal of Psychology* and *Psycho-analytic Review*, and from the *Church Missionary Review* to *American Anthropologist, Man in India, Folklore* and *History*. His curriculum vitae shows the appearance of twenty-five substantive articles in these four years, of which two relate to neuro-physiology, eleven are on topics in psychology and psychiatry, and the remaining twelve are primarily on anthropology.

There was also the book *Instinct and the Unconscious*, which Rivers published in 1920 (with a second edition appearing in 1922), in which he combines the insights of Sigmund Freud with his own observations from a lifetime spent observing individuals and analysing societies, and based especially on his years of wartime clinical practice. The underlying aim of this book was to present an integrated view of the various forms of psycho-neurosis, and to provide a biological explanation that was consistent with evolutionary theories of the sensory nervous system that he had followed throughout his career (Myers 1923; Young 1999; Loughran 2007; Pearce 2008).

Rivers's continuing interest in Melanesian anthropology has been regarded as quite separate from his work in psychology (Bartlett 1920: 207;

Costall 1999), but I shall argue that there was in fact a substantial overlap. In this chapter I focus on a small part of his late anthropological writings, the four papers that relate to the impacts of colonialism on Melanesian society, and in particular its effects on population (Rivers 1917a, 1920a, 1920b, 1922b). These writings culminate in Rivers's last important paper (Rivers 1922b), which formed one chapter in a book of essays on the depopulation of Melanesia. In this paper he repeated the detailed arguments he had already presented regarding the psychological factors affecting Melanesians (Rivers 1920a), and he provided in addition a quantitative analysis of the historical demography of Simbo and Vella Lavella in the western Solomon Islands.

We should not forget that these writings on colonialism reflect only one strand of his research, and were written alongside many papers in other fields. Rivers's wartime experiences had strengthened his belief that 'suggestibility' was an important means whereby patients could be cured of anxiety neuroses. He had witnessed indigenous healers in the Solomon Islands produce cures through faith and suggestion, and he 'now believed that these mechanisms, properly adjusted to local conditions, produced similar effects in England' (Young 1999: 375). According to his literary executor Grafton Elliot Smith (1924: v), Rivers continued working on the relationships between medicine, magic and religion during the last six years of his life, amassing 'a vast collection of bibliographic references' and evidence from other fieldworkers, but he did not write anything new on this topic. His posthumous book *Medicine, Magic and Religion* (Rivers 1924) was a reprint of his 1915–16 FitzPatrick lectures.

After the war, Rivers's Melanesian interests focused mainly on colonialism and cultural diffusion. By the 1920s his passion for kinship systems, which had culminated in the two-volume *History of Melanesian Society* (Rivers 1914), seems to have abated. Between 1919 and 1922 he published just two papers on kinship, both relating to India, whereas cultural diffusion was the subject of at least six papers. His work in this field developed with encouragement from his friend Elliot Smith and his former student William Perry, but even at the time this work was judged by most anthropologists to be weak, lacking in empirical support and excessively speculative. The work on cultural diffusion took Rivers far from his academic roots in medical science, neuro-physiology and psychology, and we might hope that his late work on the psychological basis for population change in Melanesia would be more firmly rooted.

I shall argue in this chapter that the quality of Rivers's work on depopulation in Melanesia is just as uneven as his other late work in anthropology. From genealogies he generated some remarkable historical data, but his interpretations of these data are generally unconvincing. I review first of

Figure 6.1: Portrait of William Rivers by the Scottish artist Douglas Gordon Shields (by permission of St John's College, Cambridge).

This picture was bequeathed by Rivers to St John's College, Cambridge, in his will, and it was subsequently hung in the college's Senior Combination Room (Bartlett 1923). Rivers probably sat for the portrait in 1917, during his period of Royal Army Medical Corps service at Craiglockhart War Hospital for Officers in Edinburgh. Lieutenant Douglas Gordon Shields (The Royal Scots, Lothian Regiment) was 'honourably discharged due to wounds or sickness' in 1917, and he may have been one of the shell-shock patients treated by Rivers at Craiglockhart.

all the information that he produced and which enabled him to reconstruct the historical demography of Simbo and Vella Lavella. Using these data, he was able to show that low fertility rather than high mortality was the proximate cause of rapid population decline, and he recognised that probably the same process was happening all across Island Melanesia. The vital statistics that he used were based on a careful analysis of the genealogies from Simbo and Vella Lavella that he had collected with Arthur Maurice Hocart in 1908, and since the raw materials for this analysis survive in the Haddon Papers at Cambridge University Library, the calculations can be checked.

Secondly, I consider Rivers's interpretations of these data, and the 'psychological factors' that he invoked in order to explain the scale and timing of the catastrophic decline in the numbers of children born and surviving in Simbo and Vella Lavella. I conclude that these psychological factors are not convincing, verging as they do on 'conjectural anthropology' (Miller 1972: 76). However, I suggest that Rivers's explanation makes sense in the context of his advocacy of neo-Freudian theories of psychology and his views about the disturbing effects of war and the post-war tensions in his own society.

Rivers was unwilling to erect sharp boundaries between the psycho-neuroses of the people he had once called 'savages' and those of so-called civilised mankind. However, he recognised that in the colonised world of Melanesia, psychological 'disturbance' probably had arisen in different ways. In his various articles on depopulation, Rivers is not explicit about the processes of 'disturbance' to the unconscious mind that resulted from colonialism, but in *Instinct and the Unconscious* (Rivers 1920c) he had already outlined a general model of disturbance and the role of suggestion in the spread of psycho-neurosis.

From these writings we can infer that, in the aftermath of enforced pacification, indentured labour and missionary intervention, Rivers believed that the psychic equilibrium of Melanesians had become unbalanced. In their own way, Simbo islanders were victims of a form of 'post-traumatic stress disorder', or 'shell shock' in the jargon of the time. Their case was somewhat parallel to the British soldiers and airmen who survived the mass slaughter of the First World War, only to become victims of shell shock, conditions diagnosed at the time as 'hysteria' and 'neurasthenia', or 'anxiety-neurosis' as Rivers preferred to call it (Loughran 2008). Broken soldiers suffered symptoms of amnesia, motor disorders (tremor and paralysis), anxiety, delusion, depression and suicidal tendencies. As in the case of Solomon Islanders, some of the primary instincts had become unbalanced and their self-preservation was at risk.

Did Rivers really see colonialism as a form of shell shock? In his own writings there are no direct comparisons between the two forms of 'disturbance'. Had he lived beyond his fifty-eighth year, he might have provided us with a more explicit account of the links between the two sources of traumatic experience. What follows is my attempt to interpret the colonised world of the Solomon Islands in 1908 through the lens of Rivers's own writings about instinct, the unconscious, the power of suggestion to cause the 'suppression' of psychic contradictions, and the negative effects that resulted both for the individual and for society.

Vital Statistics for Simbo and Vella Lavella

It was his work on Melanesian genealogies that provided Rivers with the factual basis for his concerns about depopulation in the Western Solomons. He had proposed at the outset of his career in social anthropology that genealogies not only revealed aspects of social organisation, they also had the potential to generate 'vital statistics' (Rivers 1900). Population decline was something that Rivers had already encountered in Torres Strait in 1898, and again in the Nilgiri Hills of south India in 1902. Although Rivers says little about historical demography in *The Todas* (Rivers 1906), a Cambridge colleague made creative use of the Toda genealogies that he had collected and demonstrated the value of this approach for historical demography (Punnett 1904; Rivers 1904).

Rivers's intention during the Solomon Islands expedition of 1908 was therefore to collect genealogies that were both accurate and complete. This aspiration was spurred by a discovery that he had made in 1898 when working in the Torres Strait Islands:

> I discovered that people preserved in their memories with great fidelity a complete and accurate record of their descent and relationships. It was possible to collect pedigrees so ample in all collateral lines they could serve as a source of statistical enquiry into such features as the average size of family, infant mortality, and other subjects that furnish the basis for conclusions concerning the fluctuations of population. (Rivers 1922b: 96–97)

For these reasons, collecting genealogies became one of the first tasks that Rivers, Hocart and Wheeler set themselves when they arrived in the Solomon Islands. After just one month of preliminary fieldwork on Simbo, Rivers reported to his sponsors in London that '[t]he social organisation has been worked out to a great extent, though there is still much detail to fill in'.[1] The 'genealogical method' provided the main basis for this statement, and Rivers and Hocart later carried out similar work on Vella Lavella, generating insights that Rivers summarised in his expedition report a year later.[2] It was a summary of the sociology of the western Solomon Islands that far from reflected the complex realities of social organisation in the region (see Hviding and Berg; Hviding, this volume).

It is significant that Rivers made almost no mention of demography in this 1909 report, nor in the big book that followed (Rivers 1914). It would seem that Rivers's interest in the connections between psychology and demography did not fully emerge until his FitzPatrick lectures in 1915/16, at a time when he was engaged in full-time war work. Rivers may have analysed the genealogies from the Solomons soon after the 1908 fieldwork so as to generate 'vital statistics', but it seems more likely that he left this task until after the Great War. It was then that Rivers needed ethnographic material to support his argument about the links between psycho-neurosis, reproductive instincts and population change. It was only in the early 1920s that Rivers managed to use the information gained from the Simbo and Vella Lavella genealogies for what became his last publication on the depopulation of Melanesia (Rivers 1922b: 98).

I have discussed elsewhere Rivers's methodology and the validity of his interpretations (Bayliss-Smith 2006). The genealogies for the two sample populations in the Western Solomons provided Rivers with aggregate data for the number of 'marriages', how many children were born per marriage, and the mortality rate of these children. These data he calculated for three reconstructed generations, called I, II and III (Rivers 1922b: 98). Rivers did not put these generations into a chronology, but from the ages of sample individuals we can estimate that marriages in generation I involved women who were born from about 1830 to 1850, in generation II from about 1850 to 1870, and in generation III from about 1870 to 1890. Unlike the women in generations I and II, the women in generation III were still in their reproductive years at the time of the 1908 fieldwork (see Table 6.1). I have checked the allocation of individuals to generations and the numbers of children born by analysing the original genealogies, all of which are preserved in the Haddon Papers, and found that Rivers's figures are accurate apart from a few trivial errors and minor repetitions.

Rivers claimed for Simbo that his genealogies included almost the entire living population of around 400 as well as their ancestors, in a population that numbered about two thousand individuals during the past three generations. Summary tables that he produced show that the women in generation I gave birth to 267 sons but only 180 daughters,[3] an apparent imbalance in the sex ratio at birth that cannot be real. It could result from a process of selective infanticide or neglect of female infants, or – Rivers's preferred explanation – it may have arisen because many girls who died young and without issue had been forgotten – at least by male informants – and so are left out from the genealogies, whereas dead boys tend to be remembered.

Table 6.1: Fertility on Simbo for three generations: women born approximately 1830s and 1840s (generation I, married and fertile *c.* 1850–1870); those born approximately 1850s and 1860s (generation II, married and fertile *c.* 1870–1890); and those born approximately 1870s and 1880s (generation III, married and fertile *c.* 1890 to 1908). Sources: Rivers (1922b: 98), Rivers (Genealogies from Simbo and Vella Lavella, Haddon Papers) and Bayliss-Smith (2006: 29), with corrections.

Rivers's 'Generation' (1)	Estimated period of the Generation women's fertility (2)	No. of marriages of women in their child-bearing years during the period of (3)						No. of children born	
		Total no. of marriages	Childless	1–2 children	3–5 children	6 or more children	No. of children unknown (4)	Total number of children born (5)	Average number of children per marriage (5)
I	*circa* 1850– *circa* 1870	207	40	90	68	9	0	447	2.2
II	*circa* 1870– *circa* 1890	295	136	85	56	10	8	379	1.3
III	*circa* 1890–1908	110	58	36	6	0	10	72	0.7

Notes

(1) Rivers divided his genealogies into three successive generations numbered I, II and III, Generation III being families recently completed or nearing completion in 1908. He stated that 'the division into generations was necessarily rough, but was effected before any attempt was made to estimate fertility' (Rivers 1922b:198).

(2) Based on an estimated 20 years between generations apart from the 18 years of the incomplete Generation III.

(3) Numbers are calculated from the statistics provided by Rivers (1922b:98) for the percentage of marriages in each category.

(4) Rivers (1922b:95) admits that the apparent changes in birth rate between Generation II and III 'may be illusory owing to certain families [10 in the Simbo case] being still incomplete'. In contrast the 8 families in Generation II where the number of children is 'doubtful' apparently reflect some gaps in the data.

(5) Rivers admits that these figures are likely to underestimate fertility: 'There is the possibility that male children who died young would be remembered better and that some female children who died in infancy may have been forgotten and therefore omitted' (Rivers 1922b:100).

The 180 daughters of generation I parents constitute the female part of generation II. According to Rivers's data, some of them died young (8 persons) or died before the age of marriage (16 persons), and 8 women were recorded as 'unmarried', a term not explained by Rivers but perhaps meaning 'women never in a socially sanctioned permanent relationship'. The remaining 148 females in generation II became married, the great majority (134 women, 91 per cent) having only one marriage, 13 women (9 per cent) marrying twice, and one with three marriages. The sex ratio of the children born to these 180 women in generation II is almost balanced (195 sons, 184 daughters, total 379), which suggests that the genealogical data for this time period are more complete than those for generation I. By 1908, the generation II women had finished child bearing but were mostly still alive, so that they, or more likely their husbands, were in a good position to provide Rivers and Hocart with complete and accurate information.

Rivers (1922b) calculated an average of 1.3 children 'per marriage' in generation II (see Table 6.1), but a more revealing statistic is the average fertility per woman. The 180 women in generation II gave birth to 2.1 children per woman, which is below the replacement rate in a society where at least 13 per cent 'died young' or before the age of marriage, and there was further mortality among infants and others whose births and deaths had been forgotten. By comparison, the women of Lesu, a declining population in New Ireland studied by Powdermaker (1931: 357) using the same genealogical method, had an average fertility of 2.1 for the generation born between about 1855 and 1880, and 2.6 for the generation born about 1880 to 1905.

As well demonstrating low fertility, Rivers also showed that childlessness was remarkably common on Simbo, although his data refer to the proportion of childless marriages, not childless women. From his data it appears that in generation II almost half of all marriages had no children (Figure 6.2), and the proportion on Vella Lavella was almost as high (Rivers 1922b). Childlessness could therefore explain some of the population decline on Simbo – the fertility rate was simply too low for population replacement.

What about mortality rates? Among adults, deaths during epidemics may have left many widows and widowers who failed to remarry, but the scale of adult mortality cannot be estimated from the genealogies. For non-adult mortality, Rivers suggests that his figures may be underestimates for the earliest generations. In the genealogies he included information about the deceased, with the phrase 'died young' attached to many names on the handwritten charts, but he admitted that, '[t]here is the possibility that male children who died young would be remembered better and that some female children who died in infancy may have been forgotten and therefore omitted' (ibid.: 100). The data indicate that this is mainly a problem in generation I, where Rivers recorded 267 male issue but only 180 females. If we assume a normal 1.05 male:female birth ratio, the 267 males reported should have been accompanied by about 254 females, implying that about 74 female infants or children died and were 'forgotten'. If we add these 74 forgotten births to the mortality that Rivers was able to record ('died young' plus 'died unmarried'), then total mortality before marriage for generation I amounts to 168 persons or 32 per cent of all births. This represents a high death rate but not an impossible one for mothers to replace by new births.

For generation II, although the data may also under-estimate the death rate somewhat, again we do not find that infant and child mortality rates were dramatically high (Table 6.2). Women in generation II were giving

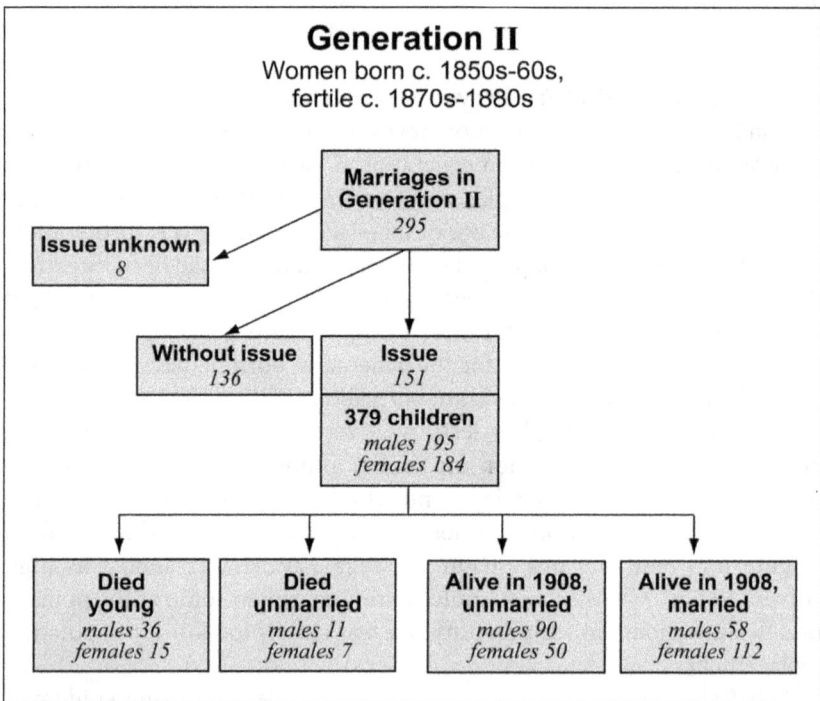

Generation II
Women born c. 1850s-60s,
fertile c. 1870s-1880s

Marriages in Generation II
295

Issue unknown
8

Without issue
136

Issue
151

379 children
males 195
females 184

Died young	**Died unmarried**	**Alive in 1908, unmarried**	**Alive in 1908, married**
males 36	*males 11*	*males 90*	*males 58*
females 15	*females 7*	*females 50*	*females 112*

Figure 6.2: Rivers's 'vital statistics' for generation II on Simbo, based on the genealogies collected by Rivers, Hocart and Wheeler in 1908. While generation I may have been too far back in time for accurate recall of all details, and generation III had not yet completed their child-bearing years, generation II may represent a tolerably complete reproductive cohort. The women in these marriages were born in about the 1850s and 1860s, and were in their child-bearing years from about the 1870s to 1880s. Sources: Rivers (1922b: 98) and Bayliss-Smith (2006: 29).

birth mainly in the 1870s and 1880s, and Rivers reported that 69 out of 379 children born had died before the age of marriage,[4] a death rate of 18 per cent (see Table 6.2). The equivalent rate for generation III, its reproduction still incomplete but with the best record of births and deaths, was higher at 26 per cent, reflecting perhaps the impact of recent epidemics. We can conclude that in all three generations deaths could easily have been compensated by more prolific births, but these births were lacking. With this lethal combination of moderate or high mortality and low fertility, the Simbo population was clearly heading for extinction.

Explaining Depopulation: The 'Psychological Factor'

It would be easy to dismiss the demographic information that Rivers derived from the genealogies as unreliable because it derived from fieldwork methods that were inaccurate. For example, apart from some young men in generation III who provided precise ages, the information on age that Rivers and Hocart recorded was based on estimates (such as '45–50'). No doubt some estimates were misleading or ages had been forgotten by Simbo informants, and in the process of translation there were many opportunities for misunderstanding.

There seems no reason, however, to doubt the general picture that this analysis reveals, as it merely represents in statistics for two particular islands what was, by 1908, widely recognised as a general pattern throughout Island Melanesia. Populations in the region were generally in rapid decline, and most contemporary observers believed that the decline resulted from the introduction of new diseases (Bennett 1987: 151; this volume). Charles Woodford, a long-term resident of the Solomons and head of the British administration, spoke in his public writings only about his fear of labour shortages in the future (e.g. BSIP 1911: 47). However, in 1910 Woodford wrote in a confidential report that 'nothing in the way of the most paternal legislation or fostering care, carried out at any expense whatever, can prevent the eventual extinction of the Melanesian race from the Pacific' (cited by Hilliard 1978: 157).

For Simbo it seems likely that a rapid decline of its population began in the 1860s and 1870s, following the rise in trade and labour recruitment (Bayliss-Smith 2006). We may be able to see an impact on mortality at this time in the genealogies, where there are estimates of the ages of 154 people (127 men and boys, 27 women and girls). The age cohorts of those under 30 and those over 40 years old are well represented, but people in their 30s (born about 1858 to 1869) are few in number, with only five men and one woman in the age category 35 to 39 years. What had happened to deplete this cohort?

Table 6.2: Mortality on Simbo for three generations, showing children of parents in generations I, II and III respectively, who either 'died unmarried' or 'died young'. There is male bias in the reported mortality in generation I (see text), and mortality in generation III was still incomplete in 1908. Source: Rivers (Genealogies from Simbo and Vella Lavella, Haddon Papers).

Rivers's 'Generation'	Approximate chronology	A BIRTHS No. of children born to parents in GI, GII and GIII M + F = total [no. per marriage] (1, 2)	B INFANT DEATHS No. of children who 'died young', M + F = total [% of births] (1)	C OTHER DEATHS No. of children who 'died unmarried', M + F = total [% of births] (1)	D TOTAL DEATHS B + C = All children dying 'young' or 'unmarried' [% of births]
I	People born circa 1830s–40s; women fertile circa 1850–1870	267 + 180 = 447 [2.2]	17 + 8 = 25 [6%]	53 + 16 = 69 [15%]	94 [21%]
II	People born circa 1850s–60s; women fertile circa 1870–1890	195 + 184 = 379 [1.3]	36 + 15 = 51 [13%]	11 + 7 = 18 [5%]	69 [18%]
III	People born circa 1870s–80s; women fertile circa 1890–1908	45 + 27 = 72 [0.7]	14 + 4 = 18 [25%]	1 + 0 = 1 [1%]	19 [26%]

Notes

(1) Rivers admits that some of these figures are likely to be underestimates: 'There is the possibility that male children who died young would be remembered better and that some female children who died in infancy may have been forgotten and therefore omitted' (Rivers 1922b:100).

(2) These figures comprise the two categories established by Rivers (1922b:98), 'children [who] died young' and 'children [who] died unmarried'; and they represent mainly deaths before the normal age of marriage. His other categories are 'children [alive in 1908 but] unmarried', 'sons [who] married', some of them alive in 1908 and some dead, and 'daughters [who] married', again some alive and some dead.

The evidence suggests that around 1870 foreign ships began to visit Simbo more frequently, and 'blackbird' labour was recruited for Queensland. The growing stream of foreigners and returning plantation labourers interacted with a population no longer living inland in scattered hamlets but now clustered in a few coastal villages, and thus vulnerable to more effective disease transmission. A number of direct shipping connections with Sydney can be documented involving cargoes of sulphur that almost certainly were derived from the Simbo volcano (Bennett 1987: 365–67; Bayliss-Smith 2006: 34–35). There are also several records of labour recruitment, for example in 1884 (Rannie 1912: 22–29). White men were visiting more regularly, and traders became resident on Simbo after 1896 (Bennett 1987: 386).

More trade meant more contact, which in turn increased risks of infection. In Roviana, the Methodist leader George Brown noticed in 1899 'a great apparent decrease in the population from that which I had seen twenty years before', an impression which traders like Wickham confirmed (Brown 1908: 516). The district commissioner reported in 1906: 'There has been a tremendous amount of sickness among the natives, both in Simbo and Rubiana [Roviana]. They have been dying every day and are still doing so. It is carrying off all the old men and women' (Edge-Partington 1907: 22).

Despite all this evidence, by 1922 Rivers had convinced himself that there was no clear evidence of epidemics of introduced diseases in the Western Solomons: 'There is no record of any very severe epidemics. Tubercle and dysentery, the two most deadly diseases in Melanesia, do not appear to be, or to have been, especially active; and though both the chief forms of venereal disease exist on the island, they do not seem to have done any great amount of mischief' (Rivers 1922b: 101). Furthermore, he believed that several of the other factors commonly cited in Melanesia, including changes in clothing, house type, alcohol use and firearms, were also absent on Simbo or negligible in their effects. Because of this diagnosis, and confronted by the data on low birth rates that he generated from his genealogies, Rivers decided to invoke what he called 'the psychological factor'. Suggested effects were the reluctance of women to conceive, their eagerness to secure abortions and their neglect of babies. By the 1870s these practices were seen as having a severe effect on population replacement, as shown by reduced family size and high infant mortality rates. His overall conclusion has often been cited:

> We have here only another effect of the loss of interest in life which I have held to be so potent in enhancing mortality. The people say to themselves: 'Why should we bring children into the world only to work for the white man?' Measures which, before the coming of the European, were used chiefly to prevent illegitimacy have become the instrument of racial suicide. (ibid.: 104)

Beyond one dubious anecdote ('The people say to themselves...'), what evidence could Rivers find to support this thesis? He and Hocart had invested much effort in documenting the perceived causes of disease and death on Simbo. Rivers was clearly impressed by 'about a hundred examples of ... conjoined processes of taboo and medicine' that they had recorded (Rivers 1924: 32–48). They documented sixty such cases in detail, including magical spells and ritual practices connected to conditions like insanity and epilepsy, as well as remedies for introduced infections like pneumonia and dysentery. Epidemics were attributed to a spiritual power called Ave, whose coming was indicated by broken rainbows, shooting stars, red clouds, raindrops falling during sunshine, and also by the presence of fever, headache and cough (ibid.: 47). These accounts convey an impression of a community in which much psychic and ritual effort was expended in gaining protection from the many sources of morbidity and mortality.

However, what this ethnography cannot provide is any real support for the 'colonialism as shell shock' thesis. Rivers and Hocart had as their main object the documentation of pre-contact medical beliefs and practices rather than the study of new challenges to that world view. Most of their information about medicine and magic reflects a strong male bias, and it tells us little about women's knowledge of conception, pregnancy, birth and child care. Did Rivers investigate how far women were complicit in his hypothetical process of 'racial suicide', through their supposed practices of contraception, induced abortion and bad mothering? Did Rivers and Hocart actually talk to the women of Simbo at all?

The impression is conveyed in Rivers's and Hocart's writings that the Solomons in 1908 was a man's world of chiefs, headhunters and sorcerers. It was certainly a world in which European men would normally not approach Melanesian women except to ask for sexual favours. Rivers was far from being that kind of man, being shy and unused to heterosexual contacts in his own English world of all-male schools, societies and colleges. Despite a brave attempt at intensive fieldwork, Rivers's knowledge of Simbo women's beliefs and practices was not adequate to support his thesis about the psychology of depopulation. By the 1920s, Rivers's ideas about psycho-neurosis and reproductive instincts had expanded well beyond his 1908 fieldwork agenda, and he developed an explanation for depopulation that he struggled to support with ethnographic data.

Sexually Transmitted Infections

As an alternative explanation, the demographic impact of sexually transmitted infections (STIs) was hardly mentioned by Rivers (1922b: 101), even though he reported their presence on Simbo ('both the chief forms'). The symptoms were published in clinical detail by Hocart (1925: 237), with graphic descriptions which demonstrate a close knowledge by Simbo men of the effects of both gonorrhoea and syphilis.[5] However, given the widespread prevalence among Solomon Islands children of yaws, a disease spread by *Treponema pallidum* subspecies *pertenue*, the impact of syphilis (*T. pallidum* subspecies *pallidum*) may have been diminished by acquired immunity (Pirie 1972: 188–89). Gonorrhoea was probably the more important STI, as was the case in New Ireland (Hamlin 1932; Scragg 1954). After her many months of intensive fieldwork in Lesu, New Ireland, Powdermaker asserted that '[i]f three or four boys leave their village to work in the white man's capital or on some large plantation and return with [STIs], it would not take long for the disease to spread, in view of their rather promiscuous sexual life' (Powdermaker 1931: 374). Rivers's (1926) own account of Simbo sexual beliefs and practices before and after marriage indicate that STIs, if present, would have quickly infected most of the unmarried population. He considered it 'exceptional and almost certainly unknown in the past' that a woman remained a virgin before marriage, and having multiple sexual partners was an accepted and integral part of a young woman's puberty rituals.

It seems unlikely that white men in the nineteenth century were in any way excluded from sexual relations with unmarried women, and the likely outcome was widespread STI infection of both women and men. Rivers alludes to contraceptive and abortion practices, but his evidence consists of hearsay about rituals, spells and the ingestion of plants with unknown pharmacological properties, with no evidence at all for their efficacy. Instead, STI infection itself can account for many of the cases observed by Rivers of childlessness, as suggested for other populations in the region (Hermant and Cilento 1929; Powdermaker 1931; Hamlin 1932; Scragg 1954). From studies in West Africa it is well known that gonorrhoea leads to sterility among both men and women. Syphilis also increases the rate of miscarriage, and many of the women who suffer a spontaneous abortion become permanently sterile. In one rural area of Upper Volta (Burkina Faso) 31.5 per cent of women had syphilis, 28 per cent of women aged 50 and over were childless, and 24 per cent of their pregnancies ended in miscarriages or stillbirths (Retel-Laurentin and Benoit 1976: 280, 291). In this case the proportion of women who were childless appears very comparable to Simbo and Vella Lavella in the late nineteenth century, but whereas Rivers was inclined to blame women for securing their childlessness through induced abortion or contraception, STIs could easily have achieved the same result.

We can conclude that in the Western Solomons the effects of STIs on spontaneous abortion (miscarriage) and sterility were combined with the effects of epidemic disease on mortality rates. Among adults such deaths resulted in many marriages being terminated by the loss of one spouse, so fewer children were born and inevitably there was some neglect of orphans. Moreover, the high infant mortality rate among the small number of children born further reduced the population's capacity for replacement. The result was a decline that probably started before 1850, and accelerated in the last two decades of the nineteenth century.

The demographic data derived from the Simbo and Vella Lavella genealogies are wholly consistent with this model, but it contrasts starkly with Rivers's own preference for an explanation based upon the psychological state of Melanesians. Both men and women, he believed, were suffering from a kind of 'shell shock' as a result of colonial traumas. In the remainder of this paper I explore the reasons for this insistence by Rivers on the primacy of 'the psychological factor' in the depopulation of Melanesia.

Instincts and Suggestion

In his *Instinct and the Unconscious*, Rivers (1920c) provides the key to understanding the highly original if somewhat perverse line of argument that he pursued in his explanations for the depopulation of Melanesia. The book is based on a series of lectures that he gave in Cambridge in the summer term of 1919, and delivered again at the Johns Hopkins Medical School in Baltimore in the spring of 1920. Added to the main argument of the book are six appendices based on articles on war neurosis and Freud's psychology that Rivers had already published between 1917 and 1920.

In the book, Rivers makes some use of anecdotal evidence for 'suggestion' among Solomon Islanders, but most of his empirical material derives from his clinical experience of shell-shock cases, plus some analysis of his own repressed childhood memories. Basic to his argument is the distinction that Rivers and Henry Head made between 'protopathic' (emotional, instinctive) and 'epicritic' (rational, refined) sensibility, based on the nerve regeneration experiments they carried out from 1903 to 1907. The book begins with a discussion of instinctive behaviour, within a framework that closely follows the model developed by his former colleague on the Torres Strait Expedition, William McDougall (1908).

Both Rivers and McDougall thought instincts were innate rather than acquired, and they saw each primary instinct as having an associated emotion – for example, the instinct of flight from danger is associated with fear as an emotion (Table 6.3). McDougall had been a student of experimental psychology under Rivers in the 1890s, and he had spent five months on the Torres Strait Expedition before undertaking his own anthropological fieldwork in Borneo. While following McDougall, Rivers places more emphasis on the so-called 'herd instincts' and, as usual, he pursues an evolutionary explanation for instinctive behaviour. He proposed that all instincts derived ultimately from the 'protopathic' sensibility that he and Henry Head had proposed was linked to an early stage in mankind's evolution, being attributable to the primitive thalamus of the brain's physiology (Rivers and Head 1908).

Table 6.3: Rivers's classification of the instincts (from Rivers 1920c: 5, 52–60).

Instincts	Conscious states (reactions)
1. SELF-PRESERVATION (a) Appetitive instincts – the satisfaction of nutritional needs, hunger and thirst. (b) Danger-instincts – protection from danger (flight, aggression, manipulative activity, immobility), or collapse if the danger seems overwhelming.	Attraction to the useful (eating, drinking). Repulsion from the harmful (avoidance). Acquisition (hunting, collecting). Fear (flight). Anger (aggression). Absence of affect (manipulative activity). Suppression (immobility). Terror (collapse).
2. CONTINUING THE SPECIES (a) Sexual instinct. (b) Parental instinct.	Attraction (sexual interactions). Tender emotions (caring for children and the elderly).
3. MAINTAINING THE HARMONY OF SOCIETY Gregarious instincts.	Imitation, Sympathy, Suggestion, Intuition (both cognitive and unwitting ways through which group norms are communicated, especially in groups with leaders).

Note
Rivers believed that 'as in most branches of psychology, there are no sharp lines between the three branches of instinct' (Rivers 1920c: 53).

Jonathan Miller (1972) has shown how the basis for this model was originally developed by John Hughlings Jackson, a consultant neurologist working at the National Hospital for the Paralysed and Epileptic, where Rivers first met him in 1891. However, the ideas can be traced back even further to Herbert Spencer: 'Spencer ... had developed a fairly elaborate notion of the nervous system in which he saw, as it were, a double animal in each living creature. There was the higher, well-integrated, organised animal at the summit of its own evolutionary branch, and within it an older, more incoherent animal which represented its ancient incapable ancestry' (ibid.: 74). Rivers and Head equated the more highly evolved nervous system with the epicritic and the more primitive one with the protopathic.

The 'double animal' or split personality was not an idea restricted to neurology. It was also a trope within the Romantic imagination, and it inspired the gothic novel *Dr Jekyll and Mr Hyde* by Robert Louis Stevenson, which first appeared in 1886, the same year that Rivers qualified in medicine from St Bartholomew's Hospital. During the 1890s Rivers discussed these ideas with Henry Head, who worked with him at the National Hospital for the Paralysed and Epileptic (Langham 1981; Young 1999; Pearce 2008). In the Rivers–Head model of human psychology it was the task of epicritic sensibility to regulate protopathic forms of perception. To adopt Miller's (1972) metaphor, 'the dog beneath the skin' needed to be kept in check. When Rivers came to study Freud's writings at Maghull Military Hospital while working there on shell-shock cases (Costall 1999: 350), he decided that 'neurosis' in the Freudian sense was the outcome of an unbalanced relationship between protopathic and epicritic sensibilities. If we use the Jekyll–Hyde metaphor, Rivers saw psycho-neurosis as a state of mind that developed when 'the dog' of protopathic instinct (Mr Hyde) tried to escape from the epicritic control exerted by his master (Dr Jekyll).

For Rivers, all instincts are rooted in this protopathic realm, with instinct being defined as 'a set of dispositions to behaviour determined by innate conditions' (Rivers 1921: 101). At the same time, he recognised that only rarely is human behaviour purely instinctive because every instinct undergoes modification through experience. He divided human instincts into three main types (Rivers 1920c: 5, 52–60).

First, instincts associated with the self-preservation of the individual, including those satisfying the appetites of hunger and thirst, and also those that are instinctive reactions to danger and serve to protect the individual by provoking flight, aggression, manipulative activity, or immobility. In his book Rivers pays particular attention to these various reactions to danger, which he suggests are very neglected in the Freudian interpretation of neurosis, with its exclusive focus on sexual instincts.

Second, individual instincts associated with the continuing of the species, which Rivers divides into sexual and parental instincts. In both cases emotions of attraction and tenderness are generated, with positive outcomes for the reproductive success of the group.

Third, so-called gregarious or 'herd instincts' maintaining the harmony of the group, which were analysed by Rivers under the headings of mimesis (unwitting imitation), sympathy, intuition and suggestion. Taken together these represent 'the process which makes every member of the group aware of what is passing in the minds of the other members of the group' (ibid.: 91). Communication and imitation are regarded as cognitive aspects of the gregarious instinct, and leadership magnifies their effect. To a large extent, however, herd instincts act unwittingly, Rivers suggests, and processes like suggestion are part of the unconscious mind.

It is important to note that Rivers was proposing a classification of instincts that would apply to humanity as a whole, although he allowed for the possibility that in certain societies some instincts might be more strongly experienced than others:

> There is reason to believe that [the] superiority of the unwitting process of sugges-tion over intellectual process remains good among the different varieties of Man. [However,] existing families of Mankind differ greatly in their degree of gregarious-ness and with this there seems to be different degrees in the potency of suggestion as a means of producing uniformity of social action. Thus the Melanesian is distinctly more gregarious than the average European. His whole society is on a communistic basis, and communistic principles work throughout the whole of his society with a harmony which is only present in certain aspects of the activity of our own society, and even there the harmony is less complete. (ibid.: 94)

This statement appears to be the main exception that Rivers allows to the universality of his scheme. However he qualifies the exception at once, suggesting that 'a speculative Melanesian who watched the traffic in the streets of a great English town would be greatly struck by the harmony of the passage of people on the pavements, in which the rarity of jostling is to be explained by an immediate intuition of the movements of others which takes place unwittingly with all the signs of instinctive behaviour' (ibid.: 96). In other words, Melanesians and Europeans basically share the same psychology, and in both cases the processes of mimesis, sympathy, intuition and suggestion help to promote group welfare.

In *Instinct and the Unconscious*, Rivers examines the ways in which an unbalanced relationship emerges between instinct and consciousness, focusing mainly on modern warfare as the source of disturbance to the instincts of self-preservation. His four years of clinical practice among shell-shock patients uniquely qualified him to mount a formidable critique of the Freudian emphasis on repressed sexuality as the key to psychic dis-turbance, and to suggest instead a more comprehensive understanding of psycho-neurosis (Table 6.4). Disturbance to parental instincts are not dis-cussed in the book, but in other writings from this period Rivers implies (rather than states) that the parental instinct had become deficient among islanders in those colonised parts of Melanesia that were experiencing rapid population decline (Rivers 1920a, 1920b, 1922b).

Table 6.4: Summary of the main processes in Rivers's (1920c) model of psycho-neurosis, showing the various disequilibria that stem from traumatic disturbances of the sexual instinct and the instincts of self-preservation. In the third row the model is extended to disturbance of the parental instinct under the traumatic impact of colonialism, which is implicit rather than explicit in Rivers's various papers on depopulation (Rivers 1920a, 1920b, 1922b).

Instinct	Normal controls (the equilibrium that is maintained by suggestion, repression and conformity to social forces)	Disturbances to the normal controls	Symptoms of disequilibrium
Sexual	Social taboos, prohibitions and kinship rules. Repression by individuals in conformity with social norms.	Puberty, incest, illicit love, etc.	Psycho-neurosis (*sensu* Sigmund Freud).
Self-preservation	Education that discourages the expression of emotions especially fear. Army training that promotes notions of discipline, honour, shame and *esprit de corps* through suggestion, repression and sublimation.	War	'Shell-shock', i.e. warfare-induced hysteria, anxiety-neurosis and psychosis.
Parental (especially Maternal)	Social rules and practices that balance the instinctive desire to maximise fecundity and longevity with other goals.	Colonialism	Distortions of the parental instinct, leading to increased practices of contra-ception, abortion and infanticide.

In the case of 'shell-shock' among soldiers, Rivers identified normal controls on the instincts of self-preservation as processes that were amplified in young men by education and training. For most army officers, their previous education had typically discouraged the expression of emotions, especially fear, or sublimated it through sport. In the army these controls were reinforced in training by means of suggestion, repression and sub-limation, in order to promote notions of discipline, honour, shame and *esprit de corps*. Under the trauma of modern warfare, which most men experienced after only brief and inadequate training, up to 10 per cent of soldiers proved unable to reconcile instinct with experience, and consequently suffered from breakdowns (Rivers 1918). Some of them were assisted towards recovery by psychotherapy, dream analysis and hypnotism, all of which Rivers used in his clinical practice.

The Maternal Instincts

Breakdown of the parental instinct under the traumatic impact of colonialism is also included in Table 6.4, but here the analysis of Rivers's position has to be reconstructed because on this subject his writings, or perhaps what he was able to put on paper before his sudden death in June 1922, are not so explicit. It is clear, however, from his diagnosis of the causes of Simbo's depopulation that he envisaged a traumatic disturbance to maternal instincts in particular.

Rivers considered that the normal and instinctive desire of women was to conceive, to sustain and protect their infants and young children, and to maintain the family, including the elderly. These innate and instinctive feelings, which to some extent were shared by men, had somehow become distorted in the western Solomon Islands. In pre-colonial times the instinct towards maximum fecundity was regarded by Solomon Islanders as almost a threat, given their limited means for increasing island resources (Rivers 1920a: 44). In normal times this instinct therefore needed some regulation by social controls on promiscuity, the age of marriage and sexual practices within marriage. With colonial contact the situation had changed, cultural norms had been overturned and new diseases had been introduced.

As usual, Rivers and Hocart view the process of colonial impact through men's eyes. Hocart quotes their main Simbo informant Njiruviru as saying: 'No one is mighty now: they are all alike, they have no money; they cannot go headhunting; they all "stop nothing" [Melanesian Pidgin: 'live lives without action or purpose']' (Hocart 1922: 79). Inevitably the women were also caught up in these changes, but their views do not emerge from the ethnographies. Yet it was the neglect of maternal care that Rivers invoked as the main factor to explain the observed patterns of low fertility, a high incidence of childlessness and alleged practices of contraception, abortion and infanticide.

Bringing 'the savage mind' of the men and women of the Solomons into an integrated biological explanation for psycho-neurosis was a project that appealed to Rivers. Throughout his life he drew attention to minor differences yet basic similarities in the perceptions of people in all the places that he visited. Psychology, ethnology and medicine should, he believed, be combined, 'working with a common purpose, and with common principles, towards the better understanding of that which makes man what he is, which makes human society what it is – the mind' (Rivers 1919: 892). My version of his universal model of psycho-neurosis, in which the traumas of colonialism, sexuality and warfare are included within one integrated scheme, is shown in Figure 6.3. Its logic is based on the power of the epicritic mind to maintain a balance over more primitive protopathic instincts through processes of 'suppression', which is the underlying argument of *Instinct and the Unconscious*. Individuals or groups experience a loss of normal equilibrium when experiences normally suppressed begin to overwhelm the capacity of the unconscious mind to cope with them.

Almost all of Rivers's late work in psychology and anthropology is therefore an expansion of the two sentences with which Rivers and Head concluded their account of the famous experiment on severed nerves in

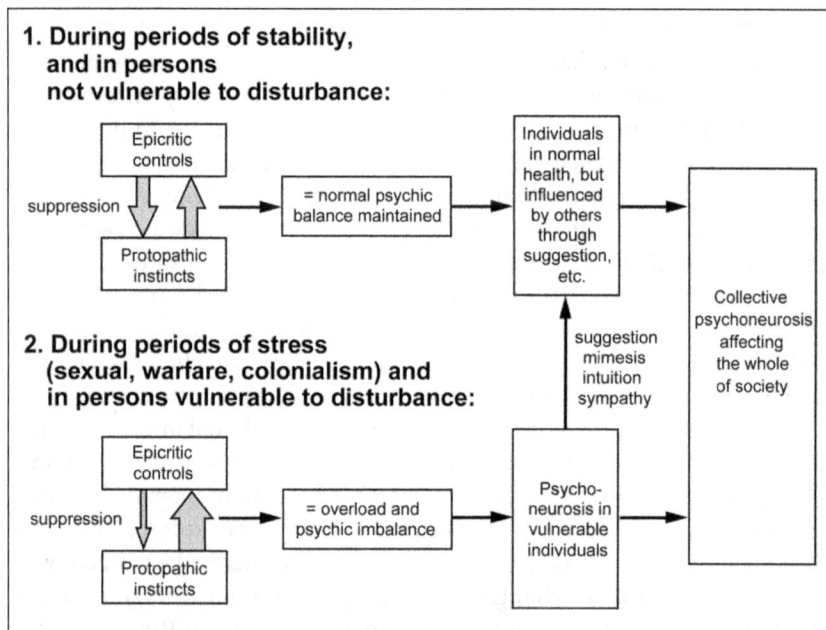

Figure 6.3: Rivers's model of psycho-neurosis reconstructed in diagrammatic form. In traumatic circumstances (sexual conflicts, warfare, colonialism), and in the minds of vulnerable individuals, there is a breakdown in the normal balance between conscious epicritic controls and unconscious protopathic impulses. As a result, certain persons individually experience various forms of psycho-neurosis. If the disturbance that caused this condition is sufficiently severe and prolonged, then through the operation of the gregarious instincts (suggestion, imitation/ mimesis, intuition and sympathy) all members of society begin to share a state of collective psycho-neurosis.

Head's left forearm: 'We believe that the essential elements exposed by our analysis owe their origin to the developmental history of the nervous system. They reveal the means by which an imperfect organism has struggled towards improved functions and psychical unity' (Rivers and Head 1908: 449). Twelve years later, Rivers felt able to extrapolate these interpretations far beyond the recovery of sensation in Head's left forearm to encompass the whole human psyche. He now considered that damage to 'psychical unity' was what Sigmund Freud had been observing among the Viennese bourgeoisie, whose symptoms of neurosis were the outcome of repressed sexual instincts. Rivers believed that his own wartime patients had experienced severe psycho-neurosis because of extreme battlefield experiences that awakened their instincts for self-preservation. When these memories were suppressed they caused hysteria, anxiety neuroses or more extreme symptoms of disturbance.

I believe that in Rivers's view the islanders of Simbo and Vella Lavella fell into a third category, but in their case it was the traumatic experience of colonialism and a consequent disturbance to the parental instincts. In former times these maternal and paternal emotions were in balance with social norms that maintained the balance of populations, or 'the continuance of the race' as Rivers termed it, but in the late nineteenth century epidemic mortality, the suppression of warfare, the labour trade and an overturning of cultural norms resulted in a pathological disequilibrium. Women in particular began to behave in ways that threatened Melanesian populations with imminent extinction.

From Individual to Universal Psycho-neurosis

For Rivers to be able to extrapolate a model of psycho-neurosis derived from his clinical insights into the minds of particular soldiers to whole societies, he needed to invoke the gregarious instincts. He believed that unwitting 'suggestion' was the principal means through which psychic processes could spread among groups rather than just reside in the minds of individuals. He needed attitudes and beliefs to be transmitted collectively, even among groups that lacked overt forms of leadership.

Rivers recognised that leadership was an efficient way for groups to acquire a common world-view and sense of purpose, but in the case of Melanesia he could not invoke this form of social organisation. Mankind had inherited from its evolutionary history both individualistic and 'communistic' tendencies, and he considered the latter tendency to be more prominent among 'lowly' peoples like Melanesians. Rivers travelled to Melanesia in 1908 via the islands of Hawaii, Samoa and Fiji, where he observed the continuing power of chiefdoms. In contrast to Polynesia he saw relatively weak forms of leadership prevailing in most of Melanesia. For example, he wrote that 'when studying the warfare of the people of the Western Solomons I was unable to discover any evidence of definite leadership' (Rivers 1920c: 95).

Leadership in Melanesia was a topic that Rivers and Hocart had been discussing in correspondence during the First World War. In one letter to Rivers, Hocart had written:

> Going through the account of chieftainship makes me wish more than ever that there was a decent account of that subject in print. It is a fundamental thing in a large part of the South Seas and where it is not fundamental socially it is of great historical importance on account of its survivals. Chieftainship in Eddystone [Simbo] was mostly in a state of survival; there were many things we should have understood much more readily and many clues we might have followed if we had before us an account of the real thing as it exists in Fiji and elsewhere.[6]

With chiefdoms in the Solomon Islands being weak and lingering in this 'state of survival', Rivers needed an alternative process to create and maintain the complex mosaic of cultures in the region. He was interested in both the mosaic of traditional cultures and the new patterns being produced by colonialism. This problem may have pushed Rivers towards his conclusion that the gregarious instincts, although common to all mankind, flourished most strongly in places like the Solomons (Rivers 1920c: 94). Here the processes of suggestion, intuition, sympathy and mimesis (unconscious imitation) were particularly effective, enabling groups to share psychic norms and pursue common cultural practices. In this respect Melanesians, it seems, were different.

On the other hand, in a prestigious public lecture that he gave in 1919, and later published, Rivers presented some powerful arguments in support of a universal model of gregariousness. The occasion was his presidential address to the British Association for the Advancement of Science, Section on Physiology, Sub-section Psychology. In the lecture Rivers suggested that people in England had seen their whole society threatened with destruction during the Great War and its aftermath. In some cases, for example children subjected to air raids, the 'danger instincts in their cruder form' had been activated, but for most people it was the 'danger instincts as modified by gregarious influences' that had been aroused:

> For the last five years we have all been living under the shadow of a great danger … It was the danger of the destruction of the social framework, in which each one of us has his appointed place, which acted as the stimulus to reawaken tendencies connected with the instinct of self-preservation … [T]he alteration in the internal

[British] social order which is evidently approaching is keeping danger instincts in a state of tension, while the fatigue and strain which few have escaped during the war is at the same time giving these aroused instinctive tendencies a wider scope than would otherwise be open to them. Since this reawakening of the danger-instincts affects nearly every member of the population of the world, it is producing a state which may be regarded as a universal neuro-psychosis which explains much that is now happening in human society. Owing to the different conditions under which the danger-instincts have been aroused in different nations, the social disorder is taking different forms in different countries. We should hardly expect that a disorder of the national life should follow exactly the lines taken by the psycho-neurosis of the individual, but we should expect to find analogues of the chief forms of solution adopted by the individual organism.[7]

In other words, the 'social disorder' prevailing in Simbo in 1908 was somewhat different from the disorder in, say, Ireland or Germany or Russia in 1920, because its external causes were different. However, the outcome was the same: a state of 'universal neuro-psychosis' provoked by perceived threats to self-preservation and maintained by the instincts of gregariousness. In the published version of his lecture, Rivers changed 'universal neuro-psychosis' to 'universal psycho-neurosis', and it is a state he would restrict to 'the more civilised populations of the world' (Rivers 1922a: 256), but his global intentions are still clear. The development of the individual is mirrored in the development of society, both follow the same evolutionary path, and any theory of mind is also a theory of society.

Evidence for 'Racial Suicide'

In his speculations about a 'universal psycho-neurosis' in post-war western society, Rivers makes no mention of colonised peoples. However, his separate writings on depopulation are based upon an argument that Rivers twice reiterates: that Melanesians were particularly susceptible to colonialism because of 'the enormous influence of the mind upon the body amongst the Melanesians and other lowly peoples' (Rivers 1920a: 109; 1922b: 95). This racial explanation was consistent with the prevailing beliefs in British psychiatry, that hysteria and neurasthenia were illnesses that lacked any identifiable pathology but were certainly linked in the individual to their 'neurotic temperament', while temperament itself had a national or even a racial aspect:

[Before the First World War] hysteria and neurasthenia were both viewed as evidence of the biologically determined neurotic or neuropathic temperament ... The construction of neurasthenia as a malady fostered by the conditions of modern life was undoubtedly present in the pre-war literature … but commentators were equally likely to refer more generally to the increase of all nervous disorders as a concomitant of the 'rise in the general level of culture and civilisation in a race' … Hysteria and neurasthenia were therefore framed as indicators of national and political health. (Loughran 2008: 39–40)

One commentator, writing in 1910 in the *Lancet*, took the racial argument one step further by arguing against the view that emotional shock was the main causal factor in the development of hysteria. Instead this anonymous author argued that both as individuals and collectively 'the Latin races' were less emotionally stable than the 'Teutonic' ones, and the prevalence of both hysteria and social upheaval in France, for example the volatile character of the Parisian mob, could all be linked to this fact. Other authors suggested that Jews were also emotional and more liable to hysteria, whereas neurotic behaviour was essentially un-English (ibid.: 40).

Rivers aspired to a universal model of the psyche, yet by identifying colonised Melanesians as especially vulnerable to psycho-neurosis he was echoing (but inverting) some of the explicitly racial explanations prevalent in psychiatry at the time.[8] However, the main emphasis of *Instinct and the Unconscious* is to subsume national or racial differences within a general scheme, and the underlying explanation is always the evolutionary theory that Rivers developed in the early 1900s with Henry Head. Even some of Rivers's contemporaries had doubts about his research method. Near the end of his life, Frederic Bartlett, a former student of Rivers and also a fellow of St John's College, wrote an appreciation of his mentor in which he points out that, although Rivers began and ended his life as a psychologist, he preferred to work by logical deduction rather than through induction from experiments or observations. Rivers would adopt some general principle, then search for illustrative material, and finally by scrutinising this material 'with complete fairness' he would reach a conclusion:

In this manner it is quite extraordinary how practically everything of length that [Rivers] wrote followed closely the scheme of the general [epicritic/protopathic] theory worked out by Head and himself in their experimental study of cutaneous sensibility. There is a basic primitive organisation, little differentiated and subject to an 'all or none' type of expression. Then bit by bit this is invaded by incoming elements or influences which are 'integrated' with the primitive organisation, and may appear to transform it or even supplant it. But the foundation organisation is still there, and may be revealed by shock, disease, long continued stress, experiment or analytical study. This theme appears over and over again in Rivers's writings, whether sociological, anthropological, or psychological. (Bartlett 1968: 156)

Even after the Great War 'the method of his lectures remained the same: from general principle, through specific illustration, and back to general principle' (ibid.:158).

Mary Douglas has pointed out the difficulties intrinsic in this method, especially when the individual is regarded as a valid analogue for society at large:

> Evading any tough technical analysis, Rivers was able to float around. He was successful in his generation because instead of an analytical tool he had a magic wand that he used to vanquish his opponents and to develop fashionably acceptable metaphors of mind and society. His favourite metaphor, which recurs in everything he wrote, is a model of control in the nervous system extended to control of the mind and extended to social control. (Douglas 1987: 85)

In the Rivers model, logical thinking by the epicritic mind exerts control over the unconscious, which is the 'lower level' where both dreams and myths are formed (Rivers 1917b). If we extrapolate by analogy, then according to this model civil society becomes 'a structure dominated from the top by a refined elite, holding in restraint an incoherent, raucous mob of savages' (Miller 1972: 76). And perhaps in the societies of Simbo and Vella Lavella, with their institutions in a state of collapse following the suppression of headhunting, chiefs had become weak, men could no longer exert control over women, and women's disturbed maternal instincts and reckless behaviour were leading to rapid population decline. In all Rivers's writings on depopulation in Melanesia this model is implicit rather than explicit, but nonetheless his line of argument is perfectly clear.

Unfortunately it was not possible for Rivers to support this argument with hard evidence. As Forrester suggests, by 1919 'Rivers's ethnology was deeply entangled with his preoccupation with psychoanalysis' (Forrester 2008: 56). However, in contrast to what he knew about other forms of psycho-neurosis, no clinical evidence was available to Rivers regarding the psycho-neurosis of Melanesians. One could even say that the evidence available to him in support of his psychological explanation for depopulation was verging on the impressionistic (Table 6.5). His travels in colonised parts of the world had been extensive, including Australia, Egypt, India, Hawaii and Melanesia, but his 'intensive' fieldwork was restricted to a few weeks on a few islands in the western Solomon Islands and northern New Hebrides. In the absence of his own diaries or those of Hocart, we cannot reconstruct in detail Rivers's four and a half months on Simbo island.[9] However, it is clear that for Rivers the work of recording Simbo genealogies, investigating sorcery and magic spells, and physical anthropological measurements occupied most of his time.

Table 6.5: The scientific basis for River's models of psycho-neurosis.

Origins of trauma	Rivers's first-hand experience	Other sources available to Rivers
Sexuality	Probably limited; his own sexuality seems to have been strongly repressed. During the Great War he commented on 'those sexual repressions which are so frequent… among the more leisured classes of the community', in contrast to the sexual lives of ordinary soldiers which he described as 'wholly normal and commonplace' (Rivers 1917c: 913–914).	Wide reading, especially Sigmund Freud (e.g., 1912, 1913, 1914) and others (e.g., Prince 1914; Jelliffe and White 1915; Holt 1915; Ferenczi 1916).
Warfare	1915–19: psychotherapeutic treatment of male soldiers and airmen at Maghull and Craiglockhart Military Hospitals, Royal Flying Corps Central Hospital, and Empire Hospital for Officers.	Discussions of case histories with colleagues at military hospitals, and wider reading (e.g., MacCurdy 1918).
Colonialism	Observations during anthropological fieldwork in Torres Straits (1898), Egypt (1900), south India (1902), Hawaii, Fiji, New Hebrides and Solomon Islands (1908), and New Hebrides (1914–15). However his only prolonged period of 'intensive' fieldwork was with Hocart on Simbo island, western Solomons, for five months in 1908.	Interviews with indigenes, mostly men, in English or pidgin English; discussions and correspondence with ethnologists, missionaries and administrators; reading the anthropological literature in English, German and French.

Hocart's investigations in the western Solomons in 1908 had been more wide-ranging, but ten years later the two men may not have found collaboration easy. For example, both attended the British Association for the Advancement of Science meeting in Bournemouth in September 1919, but by that stage their projects had diverged considerably. On 9 September, Rivers gave his presidential address to the Psychology Sub-Section on psychology and the war (Rivers 1922a), while on 11 September Hocart spoke to the Anthropology Section on death ritual on Simbo (Hocart 1922). While Hocart's interests remained rooted in ethnography, the anthropology of Rivers was becoming more and more conjectural.

One of Rivers's problems in discussing women's role in depopulation was a lack of first-hand information. In the Western Solomons it is clear that male informants had been his prime source of information, while Rivers's shyness and his avoidance of heterosexual relationships may have inhibited him from interviewing women.[10] As a result he simply lacked any reliable knowledge of topics like abortion and contraception. All of his work was done in pidgin English, which few women spoke, or by using male interpreters.

Rivers struggled to overcome these difficulties, and he was assiduous in collecting information in the local language, particularly kinship terms, magic spells and the names of spirits, but inevitably his investigations were biased towards men's knowledge. In the manuscript genealogies that survive in the Haddon Papers there are some estimates by Rivers and Hocart of the age of people living on Simbo in 1908. It is striking that out of the total population of about 400 there are 127 males for whom an age estimate was assigned, but only 27 females, and only nine women who were aged over 30. For women's knowledge of abortion and contraception Rivers partly relied on anecdotes sent to him in letters by Fred Green, an English trader resident on Simbo and married to a local woman.[11] Rivers was therefore in a weak position to provide evidence for the supposed deficiency in the Melanesian maternal instinct.

In published accounts, Rivers does not reflect upon his position in the Solomons, and he does not discuss the difficulties that he faced in field-work: as a white man, as a non-native speaker, and as a representative of the colonising force in Melanesia. However, in a letter to his sponsors the Percy Sladen Trust, he admits frankly that Simbo in 1908 was initially a difficult place for the type of 'intensive' fieldwork that he wanted to achieve. Sitting in his tent in Narovo Bay on 14 June 1908, and using his portable typewriter, Rivers made the following rather gloomy report:

> Circumstances have not been very favourable so far: the south-east season has been very late in setting in and in consequence we have had a great deal of rain; the people are very reticent and were at first very suspicious; the whole district is very unsettled, and all three members of the expedition [Rivers, Hocart and Wheeler] have had fever, but in spite of this we have done very well.[12]

Rivers reported that his team had largely 'worked out' the social or-ganisation of Simbo 'though there is still much detail to fill in'. A start had also been made in physical anthropological measurements, and the investigation of technology, magic and religion. This was indeed a brave attempt to go beyond 'survey methods' and achieve a more 'intensive' type of fieldwork, and Hocart and Rivers continued this work on Simbo for a further three months.

One hundred years later it seems churlish to criticise this pioneer fieldwork and to expect different kinds of information (see Dureau, this volume). What Rivers, Hocart and Wheeler achieved in the Western Solomons is very impressive, but it was a programme of fieldwork that offered only limited opportunities for the participant observation of everyday lives, especially women's lives. It was certainly the first professional project of social anthropology in Melanesia, but it did not provide a credible basis for Rivers to make bold statements fourteen years later about the impacts of colonialism on the psycho-neuroses of Simbo islanders, especially not those of women. None of Rivers's interviews in Melanesia were the equivalent of his repeated psycho-therapy sessions with soldiers in army hospitals, generating the insights that became the basis for his tentative ideas about a 'universal psycho-neurosis' emerging in British society. Despite his openness to the views of missionaries long-resident in the islands, such as Charles Fox in the Solomons and Walter Durrad in New Hebrides, Rivers simply did not have enough information to make a soundly based diagnosis of psycho-neurosis in Melanesia. Invoking 'suggestion' as the process through which the thoughts of individuals could be shared by others, indeed by whole populations, is another assertion that Rivers could not support from convincing ethnographic evidence.

From Intensive Fieldwork to Wild Speculation

We can contrast Rivers's bold, one could say wild, speculations about the causes of depopulation on Simbo and Vella Lavella with his extreme care in compiling genealogies and calculating vital statistics, or indeed his meticulous early work on colour perception, fatigue, the effect of alcohol and other drugs on muscular function, and protopathic/epicritic sensibilities in the nervous system. For example, we can cite the celebrated experiments in Rivers's rooms in St John's College that were carried out between April 1903 and December 1907. Rivers measured the gradual recovery of 'epicritic' feeling in Head's left forearm after a surgeon had severed the nerves, and they involved thousands of precise readings during 167 different days of measurement. Unable to measure with any precision the impact on the Melanesian psyche of colonialism, Rivers seems to have gone to the opposite extreme of imaginative reconstruction, as also happened in some of his late writings on cultural diffusion (Langham 1981: 160–99).

Rivers must have realised that his evidence for the breakdown of the parental instinct among Solomon Islanders was inadequate. This realisation may account for his failure to make explicit in any published papers his model of Melanesian psycho-neurosis. In the context of the general neglect in England of Freudian psychology, Rivers commented that 'few will find it worthwhile to study the details of a structure resting on foundations they reject' (Rivers 1920c: 4). In the case of Freudian psychology, the shaky foundations stemmed from Freud's insistence on repressed sexuality as the principal basis for psycho-neurosis. Might Rivers have feared that anthropologists and colonial policy-makers would reject his interpretation of the 'psychological factor' in Melanesian depopulation if they realised how shaky were its foundations? In what he published, Rivers was cautious, and he did not make explicit his model of how colonial impacts in places like Simbo had induced 'universal psycho-neurosis' through suggestion, with consequent disturbance to maternal instincts. If Rivers had been more explicit it would have demonstrated to his readers that his model was largely deductive, intuitive and speculative, and therefore it would have revealed how inadequate was the fieldwork upon which his assertions were based.

Because academic caution and a strong respect for evidence had characterised so much of River's professional work, it is slightly shocking to discover this other side to his academic personality. Yet Rivers in his later years was still capable of common sense and caution. For example, in relation to the merits of psychotherapy, he suggested in 1917 that 'Freud's psychology provides a consistent working hypothesis to aid us in our attempts to discover the role of unconscious experience in the production of disease' (Rivers 1917a: 914).

Unfortunately the psychological factor in the depopulation of Melanesia was not presented by Rivers (1920a, 1922b) as 'a consistent working hypothesis', but rather as fact. In relation to all of his post-war work in anthropology, there is significance in some remarks that Rivers made at this time, and which were twice recalled in later years by Bartlett:

> [Rivers] would dash in at all sorts of times with new ideas ... He abounded in schemes. He said to me often that his real work was finished, and that he would just 'let out' ideas and leave them to live or to die. (Bartlett 1937: 106)

> He was back with a bang to psychology and [public] affairs. He said to me 'I have finished my serious work (he meant the Melanesian studies) and I shall just let myself go'. This he emphatically did. (Bartlett 1968: 158)

Charles Myers, a colleague and friend from the Torres Strait Expedition and Cambridge experimental psychology, wrote about the 'distinct change in his personality and writings' that occurred in Rivers during the war:

> [H]e became another and a far happier man. Diffidence gave way to confidence, hesitation to certainty, reticence to outspokenness, a rather laboured literary style to one remarkable for its ease and charm ... It was a period in which his genius

was released from its former shackles, in which intuition was less controlled by intellectual doubt, in which inspiration brought with it the usual accompaniment of emotional conviction. (Myers 1923: 167–68)

We must conclude that in the case of depopulation in Melanesia Rivers's 'intuition' and 'inspiration' exceeded the bounds of careful science and sensible scholarship. While his reconstructions of nineteenth-century demographic change on Simbo and Vella Lavella have lasting value as a unique record of the impact of European disease in the colonised islands of Melanesia, Rivers's speculations about the psychological causes of depopulation cannot now be afforded the same respect. Undoubtedly, European contact had some devastating impacts on Melanesian society, but Rivers's model of 'colonialism as shell shock' should now be viewed as a speculative hypothesis that when tested later by others was found to be implausible (see Bennett, this volume). This type of 'conjectural anthropology' was a throw-back to nineteenth-century ways of thinking, and despite its impact on contemporaries it is not surprising that Rivers's 'psychological factors' have been largely ignored by later scholars.

Notes

1. Letter from Rivers to A.W. Kappel, secretary to the trustees, Percy Sladen Memorial Trust, from Simbo, 14 June 1908 (3 pp.), Linnean Society Archives, London (hereafter LSA). Reproduced as Appendix 1.1 (this volume).
2. Rivers, 'The Western Solomons', typewritten report sent from St John's College, Cambridge, to A.W. Kappel, 'Clerk to the Trustees' of the Percy Sladen Memorial Trust, 4 May 1909, LSA. Reproduced as Appendix 1.3 (this volume).
3. Information in this and the following paragraph come from Rivers, 'Genealogies from Simbo and Vella Lavella', Haddon Papers, Envelope 12084, Cambridge University Library, Cambridge (hereafter C/HP).
4. Rivers, Genealogies from Simbo and Vella Lavella, C/HP Envelope 12084.
5. S. Ulijaszek, Oxford University (personal communication).
6. Letter from Hocart to Rivers, 17 March [year unspecified] sent from c/o Chief Censor, Army Post Office 4, C/HP, env. 12018.
7. W.H.R. Rivers, 'Psychology and the War', typescript corrected in Rivers's hand of lecture delivered as presidential address to the British Association, Sub-Section Psychology, British Association for the Advancement of Science, Bournemouth, September 1919, C/HP, env. 12004 (quotation from pp. 17–18). This text, with some changes of wording, was included as a new appendix in the second edition of *Instinct and the Unconscious* (Rivers 1922a).
8. See Dureau (this volume) for other examples of Rivers's racial thinking.

9. However, see Berg (this volume) for a tentative reconstruction of the Vella Lavella fieldwork.
10. See Berg (this volume) regarding the absence of women from the physical anthropology data sets.
11. See F. Green, six letters to Rivers from Narovo, Simbo, 1908–1910, C/HP, env. 12018.
12. Rivers to Kappel, 14 June 1908, LSA.

References

Bartlett, F.C. 1920 'Lectures on Folk-lore: Review of R.R. Marett, *Psychology and Folklore*', *Nature* 106: 207–8.

———— 1923. 'Obituary: W.H.R. Rivers', *The Eagle, St John's College, Cambridge* 43: 2–14.

———— 1937. 'Cambridge, England, 1887–1937', *American Journal of Psychology* 50: 97–110.

———— 1968. 'W.H.R. Rivers', *The Eagle, St John's College, Cambridge* 62: 156–60.

Bayliss-Smith, T. 2006. 'Fertility and Depopulation: Childlessness, Abortion and Introduced Disease in Simbo and Ontong Java, Solomon Islands', in *Population, Reproduction and Fertility in Melanesia*, S. Ulijaszek (ed.), 13–52. Oxford: Berghahn.

Bennett, J.A. 1987. *Wealth of the Solomons: A History of a Pacific Archipelago, 1800–1978*. Honolulu: University of Hawaii Press.

Brown, G. 1908. *George Brown, D.D., Pioneer-Missionary and Explorer: An Autobiography*. London: Hodder and Stoughton.

BSIP 1911. 'Handbook of the British Solomon Islands Protectorate'. Tulagi: Government of the British Solomon Islands Protectorate.

Costall, A. 1999. 'Dire Straits: The Divisive Legacy of the 1898 Cambridge Anthropological Expedition', *Journal of the History of the Behavioural Sciences* 35: 345–58.

Douglas, M. 1987. *How Institutions Think*. London: Routledge and Kegan Paul.

Edge-Partington, T.W. 1907. 'Ingava, Chief of Rubiana, Solomon Islands: died 1906. Extract from a letter', *Man* 7: 22–23.

Elliot Smith, G. 1924. 'Preface', in W.H.R. Rivers, *Medicine, Magic and Religion*, v–viii. London: Kegan Paul Trench Trubner.

Ferenczi, S. 1916. *Contributions to Psycho-analysis*. Boston: Badger.

Forrester, J. 2008. '1919: Psychology and Psychoanalysis, Cambridge and London – Myers, Jones and MacCurdy', *Psychoanalysis and History* 10(1): 37–94.

Freud, S. 1912. *Selected Papers on Hysteria and other Psychoneuroses*. New York: Journal of Nervous and Mental Disease Publishing Co.

———— 1913. *Totem und Tabu: einige Übereinstimmungen im Seelen leben der Wilden und der Neurotiker*. Leipzig and Vienna: Hugo Haller.

_____ 1914 [1901]. *The Psychopathology of Everyday Life*, trans. A.A. Brill. London: Fisher.

Hamlin, H. 1932. 'The Problem of Depopulation in Melanesia', *Yale Journal of Biology and Medicine* 4(3): 301–21.

Hermant, P., and R.W. Cilento. 1929. *Report of a Mission Entrusted with a Survey on Health Conditions in the Pacific Islands*. Geneva: League of Nations.

Hilliard, D. 1978. *God's Gentlemen: A History of the Melanesian Mission, 1849–1942*. St Lucia: University of Queensland Press.

Hocart, A.M. 1922. 'The Cult of the Dead in Eddystone of the Solomons', *Journal of the Royal Anthropological Institute* 52: 71–112, 259–305.

_____ 1925. 'Medicine and Witchcraft in Eddystone of the Solomons', *Journal of the Royal Anthropological Institute* 55: 229–70.

Holt, E.B. 1915. *The Freudian Wish and its Place in Ethics*. London: Methuen.

Jelliffe, S.E., and W.A. White 1915. *Diseases of the Nervous System: A Textbook of Neurology and Psychiatry*. Philadelphia: Lea and Febinger.

Langham, I. 1981. *The Building of British Social Anthropology: W.H.R. Rivers and his Cambridge Disciples in the Development of Kinship Studies, 1898–1931*. Dordrecht: Reidel.

Loughran, T. 2007. 'Evolution, Regression, and Shell-Shock: Emotion and Instinct in Theories of the War Neuroses, c. 1914–1918', *Manchester Papers in Economic and Social History* 58: 1–24.

_____ 2008. 'Hysteria and Neurasthenia in Pre-1914 British Medical Discourse and in Histories of Shell-shock', *History of Psychiatry* 19(1): 25–46.

MacCurdy, J.T. 1918. *War Neuroses*. Cambridge: Cambridge University Press.

McDougall, W. 1908. *An Introduction to Social Psychology*. London: Methuen.

Miller, J. 1972. 'The Dog beneath the Skin', *The Listener*, 20 July, pp.74–76.

Myers, C.S. 1923. 'The Influence of the Late W.H.R. Rivers', in W.H.R. Rivers, *Psychology and Politics and Other Essays*, ed. G. Elliot Smith, 147–81. London: Kegan Paul Trench Trubner.

Pearce, J.M.S. 2008. 'William Halse Rivers Rivers (1864–1922) and the Sensory Nervous System', *European Neurology* 60: 208–11.

Pirie, P. 1972. 'The Effects of Treponematosis and Gonorrhoea on the Populations of the Pacific Islands', *Human Biology in Oceania* 1(3): 187–206.

Powdermaker, H. 1931. 'Vital Statistics of New Ireland (Bismarck Archipelago) as Revealed in Genealogies', *Human Biology* 3(3): 351–75.

Prince, M. 1914. *The Unconscious*. New York: Macmillan.

Punnett, R.C. 1904. 'On the Proportion of the Sexes among the Todas', *Proceedings of the Cambridge Philosophical Society* 12: 481–88.

Rannie, D. 1912. *My Adventures among South Sera Cannibals: An Account of the Experiences and Adventures of a Government Official among Natives of Oceania*. London: Seeley Service.

Retel-Laurentin, A., and D. Benoit 1976. 'Infant Mortality and Birth Intervals', *Population Studies* 30: 279–93.

Rivers, W.H.R. 1900. 'A Genealogical Method of Collecting Social and Vital Statistics', *Journal of the Royal Anthropological Institute* 2: 80–81.

_____ 1904. 'Note to "On the Proportion of the Sexes among the Todas" by R.C. Punnett', *Proceedings of the Cambridge Philosophical Society* 12: 487–88.

_____ 1906. *The Todas*. London: Macmillan.

_____ 1914. *The History of Melanesian Society*, 2 vols. Cambridge: Cambridge University Press.

_____ 1917a. 'The Government of Subject Peoples', in *Science and the Nation*, A.C. Seward (ed.), 302–28. Cambridge: Cambridge University Press.

_____ 1917b. 'Dreams and Primitive Culture', *Bulletin of the John Rylands Library, Manchester* 4: 287–410.

_____ 1917c. 'Freud's Psychology of the Unconscious', *Lancet* 95: 912–14.

_____ 1918. 'War-neurosis and Military Training', *Mental Hygiene* 2(4): 513–33.

_____ 1919. 'Psychology and Medicine', *Lancet* 97: 889–92.

_____ 1920a. 'The Dying Out of Native Races', *Lancet* 98: 42–44, 109–11.

_____ 1920b. 'Anthropology and the Missionary', *Church Missionary Review* 71(831): 208–15.

_____ 1920c. *Instinct and the Unconscious: A Contribution to a Biological Theory of the Psycho-neuroses*. Cambridge: Cambridge University Press.

_____ 1921. 'The Instinct of Acquisition', *Psyche* 2: 100–9.

_____ 1922a. 'Appendix VII: Psychology and the War', in *Instinct and the Unconscious: A Contribution to a Biological Theory of the Psycho-Neuroses*, 2nd edn., 248–59. Cambridge: Cambridge University Press.

_____ 1922b. 'The Psychological Factor', in *Essays on the Depopulation of Melanesia*, W.H.R. Rivers (ed.), 84–113. Cambridge: Cambridge University Press.

_____ 1924. *Medicine, Magic and Religion*. London: Kegan Paul, Trench and Trübner.

_____ 1926. 'Sexual Relations and Marriage in Eddystone Island of the Solomons', in *Psychology and Ethnology*, ed. G.E. Smith, 71–94. London: Kegan Paul, Trench, Trubner.

Rivers, W.H.R., and H. Head 1908. 'A Human Experiment in Nerve Division', *Brain* 31: 323–450.

Scragg, R.F.R. 1954. 'Depopulation in New Ireland: A Study of Demography and Fertility', MD diss. Port Moresby: Administration of Papua and New Guinea.

Slobodin, R. 1978. *W.H.R. Rivers, Part 1: Life*. New York: Columbia University Press.

Whittle, P. 2000 [1997]. 'W.H.R. Rivers and the Early History of Psychology at Cambridge', in *Bartlett, Culture and Cognition*, A. Saito (ed.), 21–35. London: Psychology Press.

Young, A. 1999. 'W.H.R. Rivers and the War Neuroses', *Journal of the History of the Behavioural Sciences* 35(4): 359–78.

7

A Vanishing People or a
Vanishing Discourse?

W.H.R. Rivers's 'Psychological Factor' and Depopulation in the Solomon Islands and the New Hebrides

◆●◆

Judith A. Bennett

A psychologist visits a depopulated area and pronounces depopulation to be due to psychological causes; a missionary points to polygamy, an atheist to the dying out of polygamy, a malaria-expert to mosquitoes and an anthropologist to the loss of power by chiefs: yet guess work, powerfully aided by preconception, would be a more fitting name than Science for their investigations.

—John R. Baker, 1929

Depopulation in the Colonial Pacific

With eighteenth-century European explorers and their train of whalers, traders, missionaries and settlers to the Pacific Islands came their continental diseases in epidemics, which quickly found out vulnerable insular populations.[1] By the early nineteenth century, rapid population decline in some Polynesian archipelagos, especially the Hawaiian Islands, the Marquesas and Tahiti, was apparent.

Not all islands suffered to the same extent. It is Stephen Kunitz's thesis that those people who retained their lands and thus their subsistence base and kinship links, though as liable to be infected by epidemics as those whose lands were alienated, had more resources for successful recovery (Kunitz 1994: 43–81). This seems true for the extremes such as the Hawaiian group, with a high rate of land loss, and Samoa, where land remained largely in indigenous hands. Several other factors, however, also may have operated as, for example, the Marquesans who held their lands still suffered horrific decline until the 1930s, while the Tahitians had stabilised in numbers by the 1880s, a change Rallu suggests was assisted by Western medicine (Rallu and Ahlburg 1999). At the time, Western medicine had its limitations with treatments such as bleeding, but vaccination by missionaries against smallpox for example, in the 1840s and 1860s probably saved thousands of lives in Tahiti (Gunson 1962) and Tonga (Shineberg 1978), as did the emphasis on basic nursing, such as keeping people fed, sheltered and calm.

Western medicine, however, was captive to prevailing scientific paradigms, and those were simultaneously determinants and products of certain mentalities. Until the late nineteenth century, medical opinion held that most contagion came from the environment. This Hippocratic view of contaminating airs, especially 'miasmas', waters and places, dominated until research by scientists such as Louis Pasteur and Joseph Lister began to elucidate the action of microbes, and Robert Koch's discovery of the tuberculosis bacillus challenged the older paradigm. Germ theory or 'contagionism' gradually replaced the earlier view (Harrison 2004: 98–100, 118–38). Along with it, 'medicine was becoming a science based on testable theories' (Denoon 1999: 332). Another potent paradigm, prefigured by older mentalities of racial hierarchies and reinvigorated by Charles Darwin's *Origin of Species* in 1859, derived from Herbert Spencer's articulation of social Darwinism in his idea of the 'survival of the fittest'. This attributed the decline of native peoples to their inability to adjust to contact with a supposedly superior 'white' race.

While this paradigm seemed a good fit for much of the central and eastern Pacific, it was less so for western Melanesia, given that there, and on the coast of northern Australia, settler Europeans succumbed to various fevers and diseases, an outcome that sowed seeds of doubt in Australian colonists regarding their fitness to live and work in the humid tropics, but provided a rationale for using 'coloured' labour.[2]

Although some Polynesian societies had begun to stabilise in numbers in the late nineteenth century, observers, unaware of the epidemiology of continental diseases among previously isolated 'virgin soil' populations, lamented the losses and posited causes. Like the islanders, environmental, social, mental, racial and even spiritual explanations appealed to Westerners. In 1874, Litton Forbes, former medical officer in Fiji, believed population decline was due largely to 'that great unsettling of the native mind, which almost eludes all accurate analysis' (Roberts 1927: 65). Ignoring introduced diseases, Robert Louis Stevenson, himself infected with tuberculosis, when writing about 'depopulation' in the 1880s, attributed Pacific decline to 'melancholy' due to significant cultural changes. He claimed, however, that many Polynesian peoples by then had 'become inured to the new conditions'. He believed that Samoans had never suffered depopulation because they retained their old ways, including regular 'hedge warfare' that kept them from depression (Stevenson 1908: 41).

Taking an overview of the Pacific islands, the gradually receding waves of depopulation in Polynesia continued westwards along the shores of Melanesia as contact with Europeans became more regular. In Fiji, one of the few island groups where more than localised ideas of population numbers existed, the Fijians declined probably by a conservative 25 per cent, starting to recover in about 1910, with the exception of the Spanish pandemic influenza losses of 1918 (McArthur 1966: 1–67). New Caledonia was exposed to continental diseases almost as early as Fiji, but unlike Fiji the French alienated its arable land and herded the indigenous people into reserves where their numbers declined sharply until 1922, when they stabilised and began to slowly recover. In sharp contrast to British Fiji, the French colonial government did little during this time to assist indigenous people with Western biomedicine (Connell 1987: 84–87).

In the more westward groups, outsiders increasingly noted depopulation by the 1870s and 1880s. At this time too, the new imperialism, intent on acquiring colonies as symbols of national greatness, incorporated a massive discourse on the ways 'civilised' powers ought to behave towards the colonised. The 'civilising mission', along with intertwined humanitarian and Christian values, became an appealing rationale for imperial control, though its beneficial outcomes in the colonies were limited (Lattas 1996; Cooper and Stoler 1997: 31). Since the survival of colonised peoples was an imperial responsibility, evidence of depopulation created concern. From this time until, in some cases, the outbreak of the Second World War, outsiders as well as some Melanesians themselves voiced a range of perceptions of this process. While outsiders could promulgate their views through trans-imperial networks, the Melanesians' scant written discourse in a foreign language, reported appeals to colonial representatives and observed behaviour provided only vestigial evidence of their concerns and mentalities. Professional outsiders – missionaries, various natural scientists, administrators, imperial governments, medical practitioners, ethnographers, anthropologists and planters – almost universally believed depopulation to be a reality, and tried to explain and combat it. Over more than fifty years, changing perspectives in home societies informed mentalities concerning the Pacific and, more particularly, Melanesia. Such outsider mentalities, and thus the discourses they produced, were also shaped by religious, economic, political and professional projects enacted and experienced in Melanesia itself.

Missionary Misgivings: 'Now as Good as Gone'

The earliest to stay any length of time in Melanesia were the Christian missionaries. To read their writings regarding the Solomons and the New Hebrides is to confront an extended obituary for the Melanesians, the doleful recital relieved occasionally by increases in births and marriages. Missionaries' records reveal a litany of concerns about the impact of diseases such as measles, which carried off many in the New Hebrides in 1875, and successive waves of influenza, dysentery and whooping cough.[3] Seeing the effects of disease, they condemned the labour trade to Fiji and Queensland and, after 1904 when Queensland closed, commonly to other islands in the New Hebrides and New Caledonia, for taking young men, women and children away. Such depleted numbers reduced the likelihood of successful families and the subsistence and social viability of communities.[4] Missionaries criticised the New Hebrides Condominium government for allowing such scandals in a part-British dependency after 1906 when the vague Joint Naval Commission with France ceased and an administration became established at Port Vila, Efate (Shineberg 1999: 122, 189–90).

As early as 1870, the Anglican Melanesian Mission ethnographer R.H. Codrington wrote that, as Christianity infiltrated, fighting had ceased, but: 'The question is what is to be the next step and supposing them all to be Christianised what in the world are they to find to do. The Queensland and other people try to solve the problem prematurely by introducing them to the slave [labour] trade. We are in great alarm about it, it has depopulated already some regions'.[5] By 1920 and back in England, he summarised the losses in the Banks Islands (Mota): 'The depopulation of the islands is so great that the making of new dioceses seems to me in vain. Bishop Selwyn [1850s] said there were 20,000 people in Mota. Palmer [in the Banks Islands from 1863 to 1891] said there were 700, and now as good as gone'.[6] The labour trade did not simply relocate New Hebrideans from the village, however.[7] While some did settle elsewhere, between 4.5 and 15 per cent of recruits died yearly from about 1865 until 1929, with averages close to 8 per cent. These people, under thirty years of age, died most commonly from tuberculosis or dysentery, as well as from epidemic diseases such as measles (Shineberg 1999: 185–98).

Here and there in the Solomon Islands – on Ulawa for a few years, on Florida for a time and likewise on north Malaita – the live birth rate would flourish, usually to be set back by a fresh epidemic. Missionaries by the early 1900s in the Solomons complained less about labour mobility than in the New Hebrides, where French recruiting was especially destructive under the harsh conditions in plantations and the New Caledonia mines.[8] From 1909, the Solomons administration limited the recruiting of women unless married to a fellow recruit (Bennett 1993: 147). Yet in the New Hebrides, young men and some women went willingly, were sent to gain money or status, or fled from some disaster, though fewer went when they could get local employment or could sell their own copra (Shineberg 1999: 75–89, 125–202, 225). Such interactions with Western commerce via Christianity, the labour trade and the trade in tropical products inevitably induced social correlates.

Anthropological Calculations

These social and demographic changes in Melanesia were a spur to the early British ethnographers and aspiring anthropologists. The Cambridge Torres Strait Expedition of 1898, led by Alfred C. Haddon, was an attempt to collect as much knowledge about the people before their 'low culture' passed away (Langham 1981: 69). W.H.R. Rivers, then a medical doctor and lecturer in experimental psychology at Cambridge, was a member of the expedition, during which he developed the 'genealogical method', assembling kinship data over several generations from informants. Almost an unintended outcome of Rivers's interests in sensory psychology and its possible link with biology, this method emerged as an effective tool to give anthropology some statistical and thus objective measurement, which could assist its legitimisation as a scientific discipline. Rivers's main concern became the efficacy of this method to elucidate social organisation. Many of his disciples adopted and refined it, notably in the New Hebrides (Langham 1981: 64–93).

Along with his contribution to the analysis of social organisation, Rivers found other uses for the genealogical method (Langham 1981: 118–99). During the Percy Sladen Trust Expedition in 1908, Rivers worked for about four months with A.M. Hocart on Simbo (Eddystone) and briefly on Vella Lavella and Kolobangara. After that Rivers went on to the New Hebrides for more 'survey work', while Hocart stayed on in the Western Solomons until the end of the year. The 'intensive' fieldwork carried out on Simbo provided a range of insights beyond immediate anthropological concerns. As Tim Bayliss-Smith (2006; this volume) has shown, Rivers proved via the genealogical method that depopulation was a fact on Simbo. In 1922, years after his work in Melanesia, Rivers, along with others, offered an explanation of the causes and possible policy solutions in a small edited volume of essays on the depopulation of Melanesia (Rivers 1922b).

In this book, three missionaries of the Melanesian Mission (MM), a Swiss anthropologist, two former administrators – C.M. Woodford, resident commissioner of the Solomons, and W. MacGregor, medical officer in Fiji and governor of Papua – as well as Rivers himself discussed the several factors they believed caused or exacerbated depopulation. Rivers is given credit for enunciating the 'psychological factor' as a cause. He argued that the advent of the colonial administration and changes wrought in indigenous society resulted in a 'loss of interest in life', a reluctance to bring children into the world and a fatality of mind in the face of sickness or setback (Rivers 1922a: 94, 96, 101, 107).

Given his training as a psychologist, Rivers's emphasis is not surprising. He had already discussed 'apathy' as a cause of depopulation in 1917, and refined his thesis in the *Lancet* in 1920 (Rivers 1917: 313; 1920). Moreover, his experiences with treating sufferers of 'shell shock' or war neuroses in the Great War provided a basis for emphasising the power of the mind in determining individual physical health and well-being, the link 'between psychology and ethnology' (Langham 1981: 51–54; Slobodin 1978: 55–68; Stocking 1996: 242; Bayliss-Smith, this volume). He even went so far as to declare that on Simbo at least, the 'psychological factor' was paramount to all other possible causes, especially infectious diseases. He quotes what one man said to him: 'Why should we bring children into the world only to work for the white man?' (Rivers 1920: 110; 1922a: 104). Yet with Rivers's ignorance of the vernacular language (he relied on the Melanesian Pidgin English of the day), it is difficult to know the context of this remark. Given that the Simbo people had little reason to trust white men because the government had carried out several violent 'pacification' raids as recently as 1900, was this question ironic, desperate or even a sign of passive aggression to a white man's inquiry into domestic life that might not have been welcome?[9] Although not coy about sexual matters (Rivers and Head 1908; Rivers 1926: 71–94), Rivers discounted venereal diseases and consequent infertility, yet seems not to have examined possible sufferers, despite his medical training. Hocart described what was likely to have been a case of either gonorrhoea or granuloma inguinale (Hocart 1925: 237), both of which can cause sterility. Syphilis was uncommon in Melanesia because universal infection by a closely related organism that caused yaws usually induced immunity (Buxton 1926: 438–39; Lambert 1928: 368; see also Bayliss-Smith, this volume).[10]

Contrary to popular belief, Rivers did not discount other factors said to have caused population decline, such as introduced diseases and the labour trade, but rather he gave emphasis to the psychological aspect, suggesting substitutions for activities outlawed by the government that had formerly stimulated interest in life, such as headhunting. Here, Rivers thought a pig's head might suffice. More generally, he supported 'the ordinary [Western]

principles of hygiene' but also recommended administrative action on economic development to engage Melanesians. A friend of the MM, he urged
the missions to undertake 'industrial development' as well as evangelism
in sympathetic and syncretic Christianity for indigenous peoples.[11]

Although there was an air of fatalism about the decline of native peoples
in other influential publications – including G.H. Pitt-Rivers's book *The
Clash of Cultures and the Contact of Races* and Stephen H. Roberts's
Population Problems of the Pacific, both published in 1927 – some administrators did not think the situation irredeemable. Sir Everard im Thurn,
former governor of Fiji, wrote the preface to Rivers's edited collection on
depopulation, urging study 'of the habits, customs and ideas natural to the
Melanesians' to obviate unwise decisions by those in authority over them
(im Thurn 1922: xvii).

Rivers's concept of 'loss of interest in life' found a wide audience. His
personal network linked him not only to the Anglican Church but also
to the political and literary establishment. Before his sudden death in
June1922 he was elected President of the Royal Anthropological Institute,
and was about to run for Parliament as a Labour candidate in London.
During the Great War, using new knowledge from psychology, he had
treated the poet Siegfried Sassoon for battle neurosis, and was esteemed
by Sassoon's associates, Robert Graves and Wilfred Owen, as well as his
other soldier patients (Kuklick 1991: 179–80). Rivers's remarks about
'loss of interest in life' soon attained more general circulation in contemporary writing via a clever conceit in a commentary on the death of
entertainer Marie Lloyd, written in December 1922 by T.S. Eliot for a
literary magazine:

> In a most interesting essay in the recent volume of *Essays on the Depopulation of
> Melanesia* the great psychologist W.H.R. Rivers adduces evidence which has led
> him to believe that the natives of that unfortunate archipelago are dying out prin-
> cipally for the reason that the 'Civilization' forced upon them has deprived them
> of all interest in life. They are dying from pure boredom. When every theatre has
> been replaced by 100 cinemas, when every musical instrument has been replaced
> by 100 gramaphones [*sic*], when every horse has been replaced by 100 cheap cars,
> when electrical ingenuity has made it possible for every child to hear its bed-time
> stories through a wireless receiver attached to both ears, when applied science has
> done everything possible with the materials of this earth to make life as interest-
> ing as possible, it will not be surprising if the population of the entire civilized
> world follows the fate of the Melanesians. You will see that the death of Marie
> Lloyd had a depressing effect, and that I am quite incapable of taking any interest
> in any literary events in England in the last two months, if any have taken place.
> (Eliot 1922: 659–63)

Colonial Pragmatics and Planters' Pleas

More seriously, officials at the Colonial Office began to consider Pacific policy through Rivers's prism. In many ways, the British Empire was a 'ramshackle conglomerate' (Mackenzie 1997: 222), with the Colonial Office often offering ad hoc policies to its far-flung dependencies. Although the secretary of state allowed policy in each colony to evolve within certain parameters and valued the opinions of governors, he used the veto in financial matters, common amid a bureaucracy that insisted colonies be self-funding. When, in 1923, the draft Native Regulations for the Solomon Islands Protectorate were sent for consideration, a percipient official, J.M. Greene, warned that no officer in the Protectorate had any special knowledge of native affairs and that 'there was no organ of native opinion'. Thus the introduction of regulations that interfered with the natives' private lives, such as regards adultery, was:

> likely to have serious results, especially in islands such as Guadalcanal and Malaita, where the natives are still practically independent in the interior; and may aggravate that lack of interest in life which the late Dr Rivers (who knew more about natives than any other man, with the possible exception of Mr Woodford) regarded as the chief cause of their decay.[12]

Colonial administrators shared this opinion. In the New Hebrides, where the cumbersome arrangement of the Anglo–French condominium meant minimal administration of islanders except in areas of European settlement, British Resident Commissioner Smith-Rewse had a similar view in 1923 of Rivers, 'than whom none was more competent to speak' regarding the 'psychological factor'. He decried the weakening of customary ways by 'the would-be civilizers in their actions towards natives and native institutions'.[13]

The Colonial Office, however, saw Rivers's theory within a wider economic and political context. Another discourse on depopulation soon was offered by those economically affected: the planting community of resident Europeans. Little interested in recouping the indigenous population, they petitioned the Colonial Office for help.[14] To remedy the shortage of workers, the planters wanted more draconian labour regulations and the importation of Asian indentured labour because thousands of acres of potential plantation land were still to be 'developed'.[15] The Colonial Office was against imported labour because of concerns about Australia's opposition to 'coolies', since there were suggestions Australia might relieve Britain of administering the Solomons. Since federation in 1901, Australia had adopted a 'White Australia' policy, a consequence of racism and fear of the Asian 'yellow peril' to its vulnerable north. In the Condominium, Britain disallowed 'coolies' for its British planter subjects despite the more numerous French enjoying the advantage of cheap Asian labour. Both the Colonial Office and the Australian government were concerned also about the social and political implications of the growing migrant Indian population in Fiji. However:

> the problem of the British Solomons from an industrial as well as from a humani-tarian point of view, is essentially one of the preservation and development of the native. The political importance of prompt measures for this purpose has been enhanced by the grant of a mandate for the ex-German Solomon Islands [north-east New Guinea] which the League [of Nations] is giving close attention to native welfare, and by the success which is believed to have attended Mr Murray's methods in Papua.[16]

Caught in the contradiction of the dual mandate to develop islanders and assist white settlers, as well as appeasing 'White Australia', there was no easy remedy for the Solomon Islands. Already in April 1924, the secretary of state for the colonies had disallowed estimated expenditure on public works and new appointments in the face of 'population decreasing', and thus declining revenue.[17] Because Asian labourers were unlikely to be in-troduced, the only way to satisfy the planters and ensure the economic via-bility of the British Solomon Islands Protectorate was to arrest population decline. But the problem was enormous because of uncertainty over its extent and causation, and thus a remedy. Greene listed the many possible causes and the centrality of Rivers's theory: 'Firearms, drink, European diseases, clothing, intermarriage, etc., the first place being held, by a con-sensus of opinion, in the loss of interest in life due to contact with a higher civilization, leading to apathy, neglect of sanitary observances, decay of native industry and art, abortion and infanticide'.[18]

In spite of increased spending on administrative staff since the pioneer-ing days when the first resident commissioner, C.M. Woodford, took up his position in 1896, nothing had been done 'to educate or interest the native', whom Woodford in 1909 believed to be bound for extinction. Yet after 1921/23, Solomon Islander men were paying a head tax, and so deserved more than being simply 'administered'.[19] Government medical work was concentrated on expatriates and their labourers, the foundation of the plantation economy (Bennett 1987: 176–77). In Greene's view, it was 'doubtful whether the post-war policy of extending administration, while largely ignoring the social and sanitary needs of the natives has been a success'. Keeping in mind the League of Nations mandate adjacent to the Solomons, he believed it was incumbent on Britain to act in the

Protectorate because 'the native population is decreasing in a manner which is not creditable to the British administration'. Greene thought that 'anthropological and medical research seems urgent'.[20] The secretary of state was so concerned that he sent the Western Pacific high commissioner Sir Eyre Hutson from Fiji to inspect the Solomons in late 1925.

Yet Hutson's report did not address the causes of population decline. Despite a lack of data on population, he considered there had been underestimation in the past and was sanguine of increase in the future, if there were more medical facilities available. Yet three government doctors, one government hospital in the capital, Tulagi, small ones at Gizo, Western Solomons, and at Su'u, Malaita, and one about to be set up on Vanikoro to service a logging operation, plus the training of illiterate native dressers, seemed limited in the face of an estimated population of 100,000 to 150,000 scattered over 28,450 square kilometres, even adding to this the three mission hospitals (Bennett 1987: 210).[21] Moreover, a few weeks before Hutson wrote his report to the secretary of state, planters had petitioned him for imported labour, quoting the Catholic Marist priests' predictions of native extinction on Guadalcanal and imprecise figures for the Lord Howe group (Ontong Java), the Shortland Islands and Makira (San Cristobal), indicating significant population decrease.[22]

Anthropology Ascendant?

Such depopulation provided a cause for the emerging British anthropology establishment. Anthropologists who wanted to work in Oceania represented depopulation as problematic for the colonial enterprise for their own reasons: The 'loss of valuable scientific material', and to further their own profession and employment. The former was important to them but too esoteric to appeal to most administrators. In 1923, riding on the currency of Rivers's book, resolutions at the second Pan-Pacific Science Congress in Melbourne had urged that colonial officials be trained in the basics of anthropology, with the subject to be taught in Australian universities in the hope this might assist policies to arrest depopulation by educating potential administrators. Aware of the discourse of planters and administrators, the anthropologists reinforced their case by emphasising the practical outcome of increasing the labour supply (Lightfoot 1924: 35–36, 40–43).[23]

In many respects this second congress was both microcosm and catalyst of current academic mentalities across the sciences broadly defined 'to think in Pacific terms' (Gregory 1921: 936–37). Unlike the first Congress in 1920, for anthropologists Melanesia was a focus, along with Polynesian New Zealand and Aboriginal Australia. No American anthropologists attended, the main participants being Australians, New Zealanders and British (Haddon 1924: 12). Australia was conscious that its national standing, in need of redemption after its bloody record with Aborigines before federation in 1901, was at stake, and so had to demonstrate its capacity to govern Pacific 'subject peoples'. The congress confirmed that aspiration (Lattas 1996: 141–43, 157; MacLeod and Rehbock 2000: 222–23).

Australia's first colony was Papua (south-east New Guinea), and its administrator from 1909 to 1940 was J.H.P. Murray. As lieutenant governor, Murray had expounded a similar idea to im Thurn's, and he was conversant with Rivers's article on the government of subject peoples (Rivers 1917) and the edited volume on depopulation (Rivers 1922b). Citing this collection several times when addressing the 1923 congress, Murray believed that 'disturbance' of the native people by outsiders, including disease as a factor, resulted in a 'loss of interest in life'. As Rivers recommended, the administration and the missions needed to marshal the means to minimise harm, including using anthropology to reconcile 'the old and new' ways (Murray 1924: 231–40; Stocking 1996: 385).

Murray's interest in anthropology was much older, however.[24] He had been impressed with the practical ethnography of C.G. Seligman, with the Cambridge expedition to the Torres Strait of 1898, and among the Massim peoples of south-east Papua in 1904. In 1914, Murray had met with the Torres Strait Expedition's leader A.C. Haddon in Cambridge, an academic milieu familiar to him since he was an Oxford graduate and his brother, Gilbert, lectured in Classics there. Haddon was a major publicist for the utility of anthropology to the colonial project and lobbied accordingly at the 1923 congress. He hoped the Colonial Office would work with professional bodies he directed. From these discussions, Murray decided that the administration of indigenous people required knowledge of their cultures, not simply for the gratification of anthropological and scientific curiosity, but more importantly to assist the government to proceed with policies of advancement that would give the least offence to cultural sensitivities (Haddon 1924: 12–16; Kuklick 1991: 48–50; Campbell 1998: 69–90, 70–73). He would pacify Papuans 'through culture rather than through violence' (Lattas 1996: 141). He justified this as applying 'systematic and formulated [Western] knowledge', a keystone of scientific colonial administration (Murray 1932: 2). Murray employed F.E. Williams as government anthropologist in 1921 in Papua, as did the Australian administration with E.W.P. Chinnery in the mandate of New Guinea in 1924, partly on the grounds of preserving the population. In the event, however, these two pursued a narrow functionalism that rarely addressed depopulation (Denoon 1999: 345–46).

A respected thinker on native administration, Murray fought successfully for the establishment of a chair of Anthropology at the University
of Sydney. It gave administration cadets destined for Papua and New
Guinea from the late 1920s onwards an understanding of indigenous
social processes (Campbell 1998: 81–90). Despite his support of anthropology as a key to the preservation and the governing of the Papuans,
Murray did not believe these people to be declining numerically, a view
that 'infuriated a number of his anthropological critics' (O'Brien 2009:
110).

Nonetheless, anthropologists had limited influence on the British
Pacific dependencies, though the New Hebrides was of major interest
to them. A.B. Deacon, a student of Haddon and an associate of Rivers in
the New Hebrides, echoed their concerns of the early 1920s about loss of
valuable data on human societies in 1926, a year before his death in the
field from blackwater fever:

> At the present rate of depopulation here, it is not beyond possibility that say in 10
> years there will be no people at all in Malekula ... One died in my village (where
> I am stationed) of dysentery yesterday, another last week. And so many, so terri-
> bly many are the old men, the last men who 'know' ... What with depopulation,
> recruiting or the gravitation of the native to the big French settlement in Santo,
> to Vila, some to New Caledonia, intensive work is impossible. Most of the 'home'
> population are only between jobs, or are returned Queenslanders [from the labour
> trade], everything is broken up. Everything has been led away by the glitter of
> civilization.[25]

In relation to the Solomon Islands, the Colonial Office accepted the 'psychological factor' as an explanation of depopulation, but saw it as one of
several, including diseases. Australian historian Stephen Roberts clearly
favoured Rivers's 'psychological factor', though gave Rivers credit only for
its final enunciation. Roberts too mentioned epidemic disease as being
important, but since he believed, unlike Rivers, that the Melanesians had
been 'enfeebled' and were on the way to extinction before the Europeans
came, he was less inclined to emphasise amelioration by Western biomedicine. Changed administrative practices ranked more highly. And he
allocated no specific role for anthropology, seeing any change in practice
originating from colonial authorities and, presumably, their common
sense (Roberts 1927: 59–65, 252–57).

Despite the professional lobbying of governments and at the 1923
congress, the anthropologists in the British Western Pacific dependencies were not to be a full partner with the medical profession to remedy
depopulation. None of these dependencies was profitable, though Fiji's

economic base was the strongest, which explains in part why its more protectionist administration from the 1880s, under the medical leadership of W. Macgregor, could set aside funds for medical work that expanded along with sugar-based revenue in the early twentieth century. Since Fiji's native population was in recovery mode by the 1920s and it had a reasonable medical service with native paramedics, the administration clearly had done something right (Joyce 1971: 31–32; Guthrie 1979: 15–19; Scarr 1984: 118–23), so there was no need for anthropological expertise.

For the rest, the poor Western Pacific cousins – the Solomon Islands Protectorate, the Condominium of the New Hebrides and, in Micronesia, the Gilbert and Ellice Colony – which sold inferior copra at falling prices from the late 1920s until the Second World War, any specialist technical people were a rarity. Administrative officers were expected to be practical and solve problems locally (Kuklick 1991: 48).

A dominant issue at the 1923 congress, the preservation of native populations, certainly remained a concern (MacLeod and Rehbock 2000: 222), but statistics were needed for 'scientific' government. During the 1920s in the Solomons, administrators made localised population counts, which revealed conflicting data: increase in some areas, stability in some but decrease in several. Some district officers, including William Bell on fractious Malaita, urged their superiors to spend money on health, but although this was received sympathetically action was slow to come.[26] Bell also urged that Malaita, the source of about 65 per cent of plantation labour, not be over-recruited, especially regarding married men without their wives – because this could affect population numbers even further.[27] On Malaita, where the population was reckoned at about 70,000, mostly living inland, there was resistance to the new male head tax of 1921–23.[28] In 1925, Resident Commissioner Kane brought the government medical officer over from Tulagi to address native leaders, assuring them that their tax ensured them 'a hospital and medical officer at Su'u, payment of headmen, the supply of medicines to the District Officer for natives and to such missionaries and traders as were willing to issue them' and unpaid and illiterate 'trained dressers'.[29] This was a very small return, and Bell often ran out of these basic medicines.[30]

If more money were to be allocated, it had to be to a professional or technical field that not only returned results but could also be seen as having done so. Arguably, biomedicine's impact would be easier to gauge and thus justify than that of anthropology. In the Colonial Office's view, at least as regards the Western Pacific, anthropologists would be a luxury, not an essential to administration.

Strategic Medical Messiahs

Voices as pragmatic but more powerful began to dominate the discourse on depopulation. The powers found that the League of Nations now required more specifics about and accountability of the 'civilising mission'. With increased international scrutiny in the Pacific, the Colonial Office as well as the Australian government throughout the 1920s began to seek ways to reduce depopulation (MacLeod and Rehbock 2000: 222), with the medical profession offering promise. Though Rivers was always a supporter of applying Western medical practice, especially sanitation and surgery,[31] its practitioners soon began to challenge his views.

By the early 1900s medical opinion held that most diseases originated from some bacterium or parasite (e.g. Manson 1898). This powerful paradigm became the foundation for the discourse on depopulation in the Pacific. Sylvester M. Lambert, a medical doctor, of the International Health Board (IHB) of the philanthropic Rockefeller Foundation of America, by persistence and a dash of showmanship, had been the impetus behind a hookworm control campaign designed to improve the efficiency of native labour in the Solomons in 1921 and Papua and New Guinea in 1921/22, after which he went on to Fiji. Such a specific project was appealing to colonial officials and the commercial communities that wanted a healthy work force. Lambert had also worked with effect in north Queensland in 1918. Annie Stuart believes that when in the Solomons in 1921, Lambert, assisted by government medical officer N. Crichlow, had 'discerned clear evidence for his theory that the decline of indigenous populations had a single cause: lack of immunity to introduced diseases', and there was nothing 'inevitable about the demise of Pacific Island races' (Stuart 2003: 108). Nonetheless, he was not yet prepared to assert publicly that other alleged causative factors may not have been operative, a position shared by the Solomons' resident commissioner.[32] Ever the scientist, he needed more data.

By 1922, when the Rivers collection on depopulation appeared, Lambert's reputation was established. Based in Suva, from where the Western Pacific territories were governed, Lambert had plans to persuade the IHB to assist the rationalisation of the skeletal medical services in the dependencies of the five colonial powers: Britain, the United States (American Samoa), New Zealand, Australia and even the difficult French. Initially, the IHB were unconvinced, mainly because they favoured big projects that could show significant results, unlikely to be achieved in the scattered and under-populated islands (Stuart 2003: 110–40).

In the early 1920s other medical men also had plans, but tended to leave factors other than the medical solution in the mix. In Australia, the director-general of the federal government's Department of Health was J.H.L. Cumpston. At the Pan-Pacific Congress in 1923 he acknowledged Rivers's recent volume, not mentioning the 'psychological factor' as such, but rather 'a state of helplessness and hopelessness'. Cumpston did not comment on 'the social phases' of the depopulation question, but asserted the 'the disease problems, however, are open to direct attack, and present no difficulties which money and trained men cannot remove' (Cumpston 1924: 1390). Accordingly, he developed an elaborate, costly scheme to be based in Sydney for all the colonial powers to fund laboratories and shipping to improve the health of the islanders.

Cumpston's rationale, however, was as political as humanitarian. He foresaw that the continuing decline of Pacific native peoples was leaving a gap already being filled by Asian labour, for example in Fiji, New Caledonia and the New Hebrides, a view reinforced by the historian Roberts, who believed 'Asiatic hybridisation' would produce more vigorous peoples (Cumpston 1924: 1393; Roberts 1927: 279–91; Stuart 2003: 132–34). Though in 1923 Cumpston did not mention Micronesia, its status as a Japanese mandate was a forerunner of increasing Japanese migration there and a great concern to the Australian government, which had wanted these islands (Thompson 1980: 207–11).[33] With shrewd perspicacity, Cumpston predicted, '[t]he next phase will be the introduction of the higher types of the same races, and the final phase, not over-distant, will be serious international conflict, diplomatic or military' (Cumpston 1924: 1380). So, for strategic reasons and to protect 'White' Australia, he advocated thriving Pacific islanders, just as Hubert Murray did with the Papuans (Murray 1925: ix). Like Murray with his penchant for anthropology, Cumpston sought support at the 1923 Pan-Pacific Congress for an extended medical service attending to the full range of diseases afflicting the islanders.

At the same congress, the director of the Australian Institute of Tropical Medicine, R.W. Cilento also emphasised disease but acknowledged economic, social and psychological factors at work in depopulation. He too supported an enlarged, systematic medical service for the South Pacific. In addition, he made recommendations for the greater participation of native people in economic activity, and for tighter control of recruiting of labour to protect village and family life (Cilento 1924: 1395–99). Despite such professional support in Australia,[34] its high cost and the lack of colonial cooperation saw Cumpston's grand Pacific Medical Service fail, unassisted by the limited vision of the IHB, which did not plan to work on more than a few target complaints, such as hookworm. Whatever Cumpston's motives were, however, he and his medical colleagues believed the main cause of depopulation to be introduced diseases and poor sanitation.[35]

Lambert doggedly lobbied the IHB for a greater commitment to medical work in the islands, involving training local men to be medical practitioners. For decades Fiji successfully had trained such men for their own needs, and Lambert wanted this extended in scope and a medical education of four years instead of three. The idea was taken to the Colonial Office, but they wanted more data on the feasibility of his plans in 1924. During 1924/25, Lambert conducted health surveys in several island groups. The IHB saw the setting up of a Central Medical School (CMS) in Fiji to serve the region as merely producing mainly public-health aides or paramedics trained for only three years. The goal of the IHB was to produce fully trained, professional medical doctors who would need more education than three years. Unlike many tropical medicine specialists and the IHB, Lambert believed the public-health approach was essential and local men best able to communicate with their native communities. This along with basic biomedicine would solve the worst problems in a relatively inexpensive and culturally acceptable manner.

Failing to win initial IHB support, he took matters into his own hands in 1925 and found Tonga's Queen Sālote supportive of a modified scheme, whereby contributing territories financed the CMS. The idea gained momentum, supported by Sir Maui Pomare, the first fully trained Māori medical practitioner and Minister in the New Zealand government for the Cook Islands. Fiji and the Western Pacific territories came on board, and New Zealand took its mandate, Western Samoa, into the scheme. In 1928, the French in the New Hebrides and New Caledonia agreed too, but only to the extent of having Fijian native medical practitioners (NMP) work in the New Hebrides, as they refused to help fund the CMS. By then the IHB was persuaded and assisted with finance. The CMS opened in 1928 with forty islander students to study medicine for three years, soon extended to four. In spite of the dearth of young men suitably educated for entry, in the 1930s the first graduates took up medical work at home and in other territories. Lambert's struggle to obtain a unified medical service based in Fiji continued, and although not fully realised by the Second World War, the energetic American, building on the Fijian example, had laid the foundation for the dominance of a medical model of defeating depopulation (Stuart 2003: 221–53).

Competing Discourses

Older discourses can coexist with newer ones. In 1925, Lambert, working with British entomologist and medical doctor Patrick A. Buxton and the Fijian NMP Malakai Veisamasama, had carried out a health survey of the New Hebrides. In his report, Lambert briefly canvassed the various postulated causes of depopulation, not mentioning Rivers's 'psychological factor', but he did include 'the decay of native customs under the pressure of civilization with nothing adequate to replace them' while elevating the 'greatest lack of all, no attention to preventive, and little to curative medicine' as causing depopulation.[36] A year later, Buxton published an essay on the depopulation of the New Hebrides and other parts of Melanesia. With the best set of population statistics gathered to that time, he questioned Rivers's analysis: 'the depopulation of the New Hebrides is an extremely complex problem, and ... it results from the interaction of many factors. The late Dr Rivers studied the question as a psychologist, and though he held a medical qualification, he gave slight heed to the simple ills of the flesh' (Buxton 1926: 449).

Running parallel to Lambert's medical discourse, John Baker, a zoologist, scrutinised Rivers's theory along with several others in 1927. He debunked Rivers with the argument that villages with minimal decay of old customs were declining in numbers more than mission villages in the Sakau district, Santo, where he carried out a field census. To many, the small islands of the Pacific offered human laboratories. Baker's novel suggestion was a politically impractical solution to depopulation: isolate an island, leave the people quarantined for twenty years except for a visiting medical team. If the population increased this method should be applied throughout the Condominium. So in Baker's view at least, this was Western medicine's role in what was an ethnic isolation ward to cure Western-introduced diseases (Baker 1929: 39–80). In the Solomon Islands, the administration had legislated for a modified form of this, making closed districts of the small islands of the Shortlands and the Polynesian outliers of Ontong Java, Sikaiana, Tikopia, Rennell and Bellona, so protecting their declining populations from exposure to diseases on plantations (Bennett 1987: 177, 272).

Theories of melancholy, apathy, despair and a lack of interest in life received a major jolt in the Solomons. In late 1927, a Kwaio clan leader named Basiana, living inland from Sinalanggu, Malaita, led a war party which murdered two government officers, Bell and cadet Lillies, and thirteen policemen, because, as part of their loss of power to the colonial administration, they objected to the male head tax which returned them nothing (Keesing and Corris 1980). A few months earlier, a police party had also been attacked in inland Guadalcanal. Maybe this resistance was the work of desperate men, but hardly apathetic ones.

Sir H.C. Moorhouse's inquiry into these killings indicated that the Protectorate government was not fully aware of native society and systems of leadership, yet it was tinkering with them, as Greene had opined earlier. This and the first government census in 1931 induced the new resident commissioner, F.N. Ashley, to emphasise to its district officers that they needed to study local customs and government. Their annual reports began to reflect this (Bennett 1987: 211–13, 266, 282). More formally, the Colonial Office came out in support with specific instructions in 1936/37 about what customs and material culture needed study.[37] As Murray of Papua understood, culture was an easier path than violence. Unlike the Australians who employed anthropologists in their territories, however, the British in the midst of the Great Depression preferred practical administrative ethnographic observation as a much less expensive alternative.

By the 1930s there was no shortage of opinion against Rivers's 'psychological factor'. Amateur ethnographer Tom Harrisson came to the New Hebrides as an ornithologist in 1933, and stayed on in 1935 as acting district agent for the British on Malekula, whose societies he had observed.[38] As with Baker in 1927, Harrisson provided another logical riposte to the significance of the 'psychological factor'. He reported that the inland people, well away from Europeans and not under the administration's sway, were following their old customs, including what Rivers would have thought gave them an interest in life: fighting. Even so, they too were rapidly dying out, but 'a small amount of medical work would probably stabilise them' along with the cessation of local wars.[39] Evidence was accumulating. Mission doctors in the New Hebrides considered disease to be the cause of depopulation.[40] Administrators there agreed, with 'apathy' coming in as a fourth contributing factor, preceded by 'malnutrition' and 'lack of industry'.[41]

Shifting Blame

Yet, in the wake of the 1927 killings in the Solomons, the Protectorate government's discourse on depopulation took an interesting stance on alleged causation. Even with the official caveat of mistaken reading of indigenous leadership, Ashley used Rivers's concept to blame missionaries for the decline of indigenous numbers. He seemed unaware that the site of Rivers's research in 1908 – Simbo – was not evangelised at the time, and that several old customs that the administration would have disapproved of, such as taking slaves, persisted (Hocart 1925: 262). Prior to the first census of 1931, Ashley informed the high commissioner in Fiji that Rivers had been mistaken in claiming there was no significant decline in population before Europeans came. Before 1840, so Ashley claimed, 'European influence had nothing to do one way or the other with the increase or decrease of population', and that the 'depopulation of the Protectorate cannot be attributed directly to the introduction of disease'. He went on to assert:

There can be little doubt that the advent of the Missions who at once set to work to destroy all old forms of culture which closely associated with native religion and the spirit worship of their forefathers destroyed all self-assertion, and complete apathy and depression set in, this last perhaps being largely responsible for the sterility of the native. There was in the early days no Administration to respect and maintain the good native customs, nor anyone in authority who was tolerant of their beliefs. The islands which still today maintain their native customs still carry their former population.[42]

Ashley's motives for his condemnation of the missions sprung from his resentment of their critique of the Solomons' administration and their popular support (Bennett 1987: 107–8, 246–7). He overlooked the several government punitive raids from the late 1890s which had taken place throughout the New Georgia Islands, including Simbo, which sought to destroy war canoes and canoe houses associated with headhunting, capture traditional warriors such as Sito on Vella Lavella, and liberate people taken as slaves. Colonial violence or government 'pacification' had had a more profound effect on customary practices than the peaceful missionaries (Bennett 1987: 108).[43] Although Ashley did not deny the current need for medical help, his casuistry regarding the cause of population loss was slanted to shift any blame from the British administration, so even in 1930 Rivers's discourse was employed selectively to this end.

A 'Virile Race' for Planters

When the results of the 1931 Solomon Islands census were known, the planting community was shocked to find that the overall population was only around 94,000. Earlier estimates ranged from 100,000 to a more sanguine 150,000. Selectively addressing the higher estimate, F.R. Hewitt of Lever's Plantations thus deduced a massive decline; whether it had 'reached its ebb' was 'debatable', though the resident commissioner and the senior medical officer believed so. Hewitt opined the evidence was scant, and went on to point to Rivers's 'psychological factor', but in such a way as not to exclude the effects of introduced diseases: 'The cause of any decline cannot be advanced dogmatically but most will agree that the primary cause is psychological. The interference with or the forcible suppression of time honoured customs, superstitions and traditions, has robbed them of their interests and beliefs and left them an easy prey to alien diseases, etc.'. He stated that more or less continual warfare in the past had kept communities apart from each other, so lessening the likelihood of the spread of disease. Warfare had kept men potent enough to father large families whereas, more recently, they married late and had small families. Harking back to the perennial shortage of plantation labour, Hewitt thought the situation could be remedied by the importation and intermarriage of a more 'virile race such as the Chinese', echoing Stephen Roberts' conclusions.[44]

The requests for foreign workers intensified when in the mid-1930s a gold mine opened on Guadalcanal and the planters feared diversion of labour from them. The resident commissioner appealed to the Colonial Office to allow companies to introduce free Chinese labour at least, as he believed that 'the country cannot develop without it'.[45] The Colonial Office, however, was not encouraging and was again to seek the views of Australia and New Zealand before any Chinese could be introduced under civil contracts.[46] War clouds were gathering in China, and the matter was not settled before the Second World War began.

Medical Discourse Triumphant

In 1928, S.M. Lambert had added another nail to the coffin of Rivers's 'psychological factor' – by ignoring it. As the newly appointed deputy medical authority of the Western Pacific high commissioner, Lambert wrote a review of medical conditions in the Pacific. He argued that the Fiji case had shown medicine with a public-health approach had assisted in the recovery of the Fijian population, in spite of the losses to the pandemic of Spanish influenza. He referred to Rivers only in terms of the supposed settlement patterns of ancient Melanesia, but made no mention at all of his 'psychological factor' relating to depopulation (Lambert 1928: 365). The Australian R.W. Cilento was just as critical. He conducted medical research in New Guinea as the director of public health, studying the causes of depopulation and reporting to the League of Nations in 1926/27 (Cilento 1926). In 1928, he and his French colleague, P. Hermant, surveyed health conditions across the South Pacific and produced a report for the League, concluding that in many areas the population was now in a second phase after initial losses, a state of 'unstable equilibrium' to which Western medicine could bring positive stability and increase when the third stage would be achieved. The report mentioned the various factors that earlier observers had considered important, such as the 'psychological factor', but this was merely the background to its assertions of the importance of Western medical and public health practices in controlling diseases (Hermant and Cilento 1929). Even more strongly, in 1932 Cilento repudiated Rivers's central premise:

> Until 1923 I had accepted, with some reservation the psychological factor suggested by W.H.R. Rivers as a primary cause of native depopulation. The actual investigation [in the 1926/1927 Annual Report to the League of Nations of the Territory of New

Guinea] ... led me to relegate it to the ranks of effects and complications rather than primary causes. It became only too apparent that the attitude of 'hopelessness' upon which such stress had been laid, was itself directly proportional to the degree of local disease prevalence. It arises as a direct sequel of disease, and is not a primary condition resulting from mere disruption of native customs.

Population was found to be declining in places where native institutions flourished with all their original vigour, as well as where they had been destroyed so long as foodstuffs were scanty and disease rife, and people found thriving in places where white men had entirely disrupted their social organization (as, indeed, they must inevitably disrupt it everywhere in the course of time), but only where disease was controlled and food abundant. (Cilento 1932: 481)

Two year later, Lambert too reinforced this and, in an indirect criticism of Rivers, declared that such alleged causes as lessened fertility, frequent miscarriage and deliberate abortion or infanticide, 'ought to have statistics to support them. That was the line of argument in Fiji 50 years ago'. Lambert believed that, in terms of population and ill health, much of the rest of Melanesia was like Fiji sixty years before (Lambert 1934: 37).

In spite of the advocacy of Cumpston, Cilento, Lambert and, in the Western Pacific, a growing band of Fiji-trained NMPs, immediate coverage of all the islands' populations with the sparse resources available was impossible, with medical officers struggling to administer areas 'as large as medieval kingdoms' (Cilento 1932: 483). In the Solomons in 1935, when District Officer Bengough did a field census in the 'Are 'Are district on Malaita that indicated population decline, he rehearsed all the possible causes that Rivers had covered, including 'apathy'. The Colonial Office sent his data to P. Glanville Edge of the London School of Tropical Medicine. Glanville Edge did not discount any of Bengough's possible causes of depopulation, but urged 'systematic enquiry' of all of them, along with some refinements in the data collected in future.[47] While medical men such as Lambert and Cilento did what they could to persuade governments to act, cautious territorial administrators concentrated more on surveys and data collection in the 1920s and early 1930s than on major efforts to extend medical coverage, particularly as the Depression years decimated revenue in copra-dependent economies.

Melanesian Voices

Melanesian views regarding depopulation were more cryptic in the records than outsiders'. In the early 1900s, a Fijian who worked for the administration attributed population decline to his people's abandonment of the 'natives' deities' (*vu*) who looked after earthly matters, such as the body, in favour of Jehovah, who was concerned only with 'matters spiritual'. He disparaged Westerners' bottles of medicine, claiming the forest pharmaco-poeia of Fiji more potent when the *vu* were honoured (Hocart 1967: 166). Conversion, not depression, caused depopulation.

Yet where Western medicine had a beneficial effect it was increasingly sought. Following the success of the Rockefeller-sponsored campaign against endemic yaws in the 1930s and the worth of Western medical treat-ment when Melanesians could get it, Melanesians themselves, the subjects of all these studies, began to join the discourse. In 1932, the people of Aoba, Pentecost and Maewo in the New Hebrides wanted the MM to open a hospital on Aoba for their sick.[48] In 1934, the second Fijian NMP to be assigned to the New Hebrides, Mesulame Taveta, had his own professional views on the value of Western medicine: 'depopulation only takes place in Christian villages far away from missionaries or hospitals where they can be treated and looked after regularly and depopulation takes place more rapidly amongst the bush-people and natives in villages close to [the] seas which are not yet touched by modern civilization'.[49] The New Hebrides people responded well to the work of the two NMPs even in areas rarely 'penetrated' by government, such as inland south Santo.[50]

The first NMPs to the Solomons, the Fijian Eroni Leauli who began work in 1936, followed by Solomon Islanders George Bogese, Hughie and Kitchener Wheatley, Henry Kuper and Guso Rato Piko, had a positive impact on health. In 1939, the people of the central Solomons, assisted by the English priest Richard Fellowes of the MM, petitioned the ad-ministration for 'dispensaries in every big district with a native medical practitioner in charge'.[51] On Malaita, the 'Are 'Are people voiced their fears of depopulation in 1939 to the touring high commissioner, Harry Luke. In consultation with District Officer Bengough, Luke suggested to the secre-tary of state for the colonies the establishment of an NMP in the area and a road to assist access to the medical base, all of which the secretary agreed to, but the Second World War supervened.[52]

Tentative Recovery

There were signs of population decline slowing and numbers even begin-ning to recover in parts of the Western Solomons by the late 1920s, a trend which continued into the 1930s.[53] By the later date, even in the poorly ad-ministered New Hebrides, some islands showed increasing numbers while declines elsewhere had slowed, this despite epidemics that still occurred periodically in islands where population loss since the late nineteenth century had been catastrophic.[54] The New Hebrides annual report of 1939 attributed the increases on Tanna, Tangoa and Paama to 'prolonged close contact with the missions and medical facilities'. Hermant and Cilento's stage of 'unstable equilibrium' of population seemed to be approaching.

No one factor brought about this change. In the Solomons, after Roman Catholic priest L.M. Raucaz had visited all the Catholic missions in the mid-1920s, he attributed the population decline largely to disease and upset caused by the money economy, but he opined that the people 'may in time learn the use of the safeguards of civilised life and then the decline in the population may cease and the curve of natality take an upward turn' (Raucaz 1928: 65–68). Certainly, government regulations in the Solomon Islands at least from 1922 began to see more sanitary arrangements in village settlements that appear to have created conditions where the people were less susceptible to introduced and some endemic diseases (Bennett 1987: 149–54). Several missions reinforced these sanitary trends in village life, especially the Methodists and the Seventh-Day Adventists, both denominations running hospitals in the western Solomon Islands (Bennett 1987: 112, 210; Stuart 2003: 108). Many inland people relocated to the coast, encouraged by missionaries and the government, as well as by easier access to trade. Mission influence too seems to have lessened the impact of pre-contact patterns on the limitation of children.

The new rule of law itself meant people were not forced to retreat to bush hideouts or avoid gardens for fear of attack, living in unhealthy situations, suffering from exposure and malnutrition (Bennett 1974: 121–55). The introduction and spread of the sweet potato (*Ipomoea batatas*) from the mid to late nineteenth century may have made the raising of bigger families easier because less labour is needed for cultivation (Bennett 2000: 38; Allen 2005). Sweet potato is more nutritious than the potato (*Solanum tuberosum*) of temperate areas, and on a par with taro (*Colocasia esculenta*) as a staple (Salaman 1949; Langer 1997).[55] Moreover, by the 1930s in many areas, more inland people were living in coastal settlements, where sweet potato grows well in sandy soils. Generally, diet in coastal areas was much better than among the bush people, being more varied and richer in oils and protein from fish and shellfish.

Similar patterns were beginning to emerge in the New Hebrides. Without sanitary precautions, forms of dysentery were common. Living conditions in small, poorly aired leaf houses contributed to the widespread prevalence of tuberculosis as well as forms of influenza, two diseases rarely addressed until after the Second World War. By 1938 there were two NMPs in the islands and, for Port Vila only, a sanitary inspector to enforce public-health regulations. The French funded hospitals at Vila on Santo and Malekula, as well as two aid posts. The Presbyterian mission had one hospital each at Vila and Tanna, and the MM had one at Aoba and an aid post on Pentecost. The Seventh-Day Adventists also ran an aid post on Aore. The main sanitation work, which aimed at disease prevention rather than cure, however, came from missionary exhortation and example dating back decades.[56]

Exogenous factors, however, were probably of the greatest significance, and have been largely overlooked by demographers and historians (e.g. Howe 2000: 64–68). In both the New Hebrides and the Solomons, government quarantine of incoming vessels assisted public health. Quarantine efforts, for example, seem to have prevented the importation of the worst strains of Spanish influenza to these territories, as well as to Papua, New Guinea and American Samoa. Its disastrous effects in Fiji and Western Samoa had awakened many administrations to the need for more stringent border checks of vessels.[57] Organised by the League of Nations in 1921, the development of detailed 'epidemiological intelligence', transmitted by radio and cable, linked the Western Pacific, Southeast Asia and the Middle East to weekly bulletins that warned of the advent of new waves of infections, rapidly alerting officials enforcing the surveillance of borders (Bashford 2004: 115–36).[58]

The decline of infectious disease microbes in incoming people was significant in reducing epidemics. The overseas labour trade ceased in 1911 in the Solomon Islands, and tapered off dramatically in the New Hebrides in the late 1920s in the face of the Great Depression in New Caledonia, so by the 1930s there were far fewer regular returnees, perhaps a dozen or so a year. These returnees probably had been the most effective carriers of diseases from overseas, as they often lived inland where Europeans did not go.[59] Foreign visitors were less likely to be carrying disease pathogens because of the steady reduction of pools of infection for several diseases in their homelands. From the late nineteenth century on, as in many parts of the Western world, quarantine, public health and sanitation measures in Australia and New Zealand had reduced the occurrence of many diseases, such as typhoid and diphtheria. In Australia and New Zealand, in addition to quarantine, vaccination against smallpox was commonplace and its incidence rare, while in the 1920s and 1930s vaccines to protect against diphtheria were becoming established and administered widely. Overall though, it was the rising living standards of the metropolitan population and public sanitation that dramatically reduced disease prevalence (Feery 1981; Rosen 1993: 312–19; Dow 1995: 108–11; Day 2008: 27–58).[60]

It is possible that successive infections of introduced diseases gradually made Melanesian survivors less susceptible and gave children some immunity to some complaints, but this declined once they were about a year old. It is also possible that a certain degree of natural selection was going on with only the strongest producing offspring. Whatever the nexus of changed epidemiology, overall, in the New Hebrides in the late 1930s, 'severe epidemics [were] seldom now seen'.[61]

Anthropological Revisions

Between the tentative recovery of populations in some districts, along with the promise of Western medicine on the one hand and the consolidation of the anthropological profession, now with usually extensive fieldwork, on the other, anthropologists were disinclined to push the 'psychological factor' in depopulation discourse in Melanesia. Less obsessed with cultural obituary writing, they still had something to offer. Even Cilento, having experience of working with Chinnery, the government anthropologist in New Guinea, saw a role for these professionals to assist Melanesians' 'adaptation' to a changing world (Cilento 1932: 483). Adapting introduced structures to Melanesian armature seemed a more positive approach to the colonial project, with medicine to cure or prevent introduced diseases, as least as far as anthropologist Ian Hogbin was concerned (Hogbin 1934). In 1939, Hogbin attributed depopulation in the Solomon Islands to introduced diseases and criticised Rivers's argument, stating that in his experience he had never seen 'a native die of despair' (Hogbin 1939: 136). His views neatly encapsulate his Melanesian field experience as well as over half a century of striving by the new sciences of psychology and anthropology for disciplinary recognition. Along with his own research, Hogbin had garnered observations from district officers and missionaries. Most, even though they might add other exacerbating factors, pointed towards disease, not despair, as the reason people died in such large numbers (Hogbin 1934).

Not that anthropologists had much cachet in the territories of the Western Pacific High Commission. Following the lead of Rivers, who valued fieldwork, his students and associates – J. Layard, C.B. Humphrey, T.T. Barnard and A. B. Deacon – all did research in the New Hebrides on social organisation, but their findings had little direct influence on the practices of colonial administration. In the Solomons, the ethnographies and dictionaries of MM clerics Walter Ivens and Charles Fox became highly regarded (e.g. Fox 1924; Ivens 1927). The Colonial Office in 1927 listened to Ivens's views on depopulation due to disease and the need for people, especially on Malaita, to receive medical treatment in return for their taxes.[62] But by the 1930s, few anthropologists had the same moral authority and understanding of the Solomon Islanders as these. Although Austrian anthropologist Hugo Bernatzik came to the Solomons with an endorsement from Downing Street, Ashley deported him for carnal knowledge of underage girls on Santa Ana in 1932.[63] Certainly interested in the state of the population, Ashley was unimpressed with Hogbin on Malaita and the professionals he represented, stating that their 'main object is to go to some place about which very few people know and a still smaller number of those that do are interested enough to read anthropological notes and of those again only a few able to write well enough to tell the truth or criticize'.[64] A year later, in 1934, a sometime district officer, R.H. Garvey, when commenting on Methodist missionary J.F. Goldie's letter about native grievances against the rate of the head tax voiced at a large meeting at Roviana, New Georgia, noted perhaps ironically that, 'it indicates that the "psychological despair" which is talked about so glibly by anthropologists can be set aside if sufficient stimulus is given'.[65] By this time Rivers's 'psychological factor' had almost vanished from administrative discourse or had become a gibe.

Certainly, medical opinion on the eve of the Second World War dismissed apathy and fatalism as causes of depopulation among Melanesians and favoured the less subjective disease factor (cf. Anderson 2009: 148 n.25): 'For us, diseases are the true cause of the depopulation: the fact seems to us to be self-evident'.[66] What was to reinforce the power of the medical model as a remedy for depopulation was the war itself. Not only did the powerful 'sulfa' drugs of the occupying Americans reduce suffering among peoples near bases in the New Hebrides and the Solomon Islands, but in addition hundreds of villagers and labourers were treated with atebrin for malaria, though less for their benefit than to reduce their 'seedbed of infection' for the military (Bennett 2006). The people flocked to such treatments because they were used to the efficacy of some of the white man's medicine. Its pragmatic promulgators, using a modicum of anthropological insight, couched its action and effects, not in Western science, but in alternative rationalities accessible to the mentalities of Melanesians.[67] Pre-war, the injections to combat yaws, the 'nila' of Solomons and the 'stick medicine' of the New Hebrides, had won believers. Wartime research saw the advent of the antibiotic penicillin in 1944, which soon came into common use in peacetime. As part of post-war decolonisation, the gradual but successful post-war reduction of diseases through basic public health measures, vaccination and drug therapy induced rapid population expansion. The worry now is how public health services can cope with this and newer diseases such as HIV/AIDS and the increasing occurrence of non-communicable diseases related to poor diet and lack of exercise, concerns W.H.R. Rivers could never have envisaged.

Rivers's theory on the 'psychological factor' in depopulation was influential on colonial thought and accessible to most readers. He boldly applied new insights from his experience as a clinical psychologist during the Great War to a major social problem (see Bayliss-Smith, this volume). But this application of what was an individual mentality of depression to entire populations was an uneasy fit, as accumulating evidence from the islands revealed. Nonetheless, the apparent clarity of the 'psychological factor' found resonance in the mentalities of many outsiders. It challenged administrators, several of whom developed a certain fatalism of their own when they could not get funding for anything more that the most basic structures of administration. Missionaries saw in it a weapon against the social evils of the labour trade, but soon those with medical training and island experience attributed depopulation to disease. For anthropologists, it cemented their rationale for heading to the region to collect what, in their view, was about to become the archaeology of a people, rather than its anthropology.[68] They soon realised that this knowledge harvesting was of little appeal to any but the most erudite administrators, and so linked it with practical application. Some administrators saw that with this cultural knowledge the natives could be persuaded to comply rather than be pushed to rebellion, could be controlled with a gentle hand rather than the whip, and could be medicated and preserved, and thus make good workers.

Planters were focused on economic survival and the need for workers. Given past imperial habits, Asia seemed the best source. Likewise, even for the most humanitarian of medical professionals, spending could be best coaxed out of administrations if the threat of the demise of native labour and of Asians getting a grip on the Pacific of the 'Westerners' could be brought to bear (e.g., Lambert 1942: 408–10). The economic stringency of imperial rulers hindered their plans. Even so, conscious of the ethos of the League of Nations and their earlier 'civilising mission', governments at least funded the preliminary work of data gathering and a successful, if embryonic, regional medical service. Moreover, this gave them a clearer assessment of their subjects and potentially greater control of their lives, so strengthening the imperial state via several applications of 'the scientific method'. Just as, in 1898, Haddon and Rivers had turned to Western scientific methodology to validate their anthropology and Rivers his psychology, the medical profession and administrators did the same. Their health surveys, empirical observations and data on disease in the islands, along with the potential uses of censuses, provided increasing evidence for the case against the explanation of depopulation in terms of the 'psychological factor' alone. Objective sociological and epidemiological methods would underpin the biomedical model, it seemed.

Yet both Lambert and Hogbin, as representatives of their professions, were capable of ignoring evidence to the contrary regarding the power of the mind on physical health. Both had experience of how belief in sorcery – *ndraunikau* ('magic of leaves') in Fiji, and *veiveisi'ovi* and *vele* on Guadalcanal – induced death in believers, independent of any physical infection or injury (Lambert 1942: 157–72; Hogbin 1964: 55–57). Bio-immunological research since the 1970s suggests that psychological stressors, whatever their origin, can make individuals depressed, anxious, hostile and sad, and thus more susceptible to both bacterial and viral infections, cardiac malfunction and some varieties of cancer. Mind and body are not separate domains. The bio-psychosocial connection that the prescient Rivers posited, but struggled to substantiate, is now being proven (Cohen 1997; Engel 1997; Glaser 2005; Vedhara and Irwin 2005; Antoni et al. 2006; Irwin et al. 2011).

Rivers, of course, had not discounted the factors of disease, alcohol and other culture-challenging effects of Western contact. In his view, however, changed social structures and customs induced hopelessness and apathy, made Melanesians disinclined to reproduce and left them susceptible to diseases, while the medical experts believed it was the ravages of disease first and foremost that induced such mental states. Rivers, however, also suggested remedies for depopulation more far-reaching and holistic – and more costly – than simply the much-quoted example: substituting hunting a pig's head for a human one. His critics as well as some of his supporters set up a straw man when they took the novel aspect of his seminal essay, the 'psychological factor', and isolated it from the complexity of social and medical aspects of depopulation, long before this distorted version of it entered into anthropological text books (see Goldenweiser 1937: 429). By then, portrayed as an unsubtle single-factor explanation, it had been debunked and largely abandoned. From 1922 onwards, others – whether missionary, anthropologist, scientist, planter, administrator or medical doctor – had used it, as well as caricatures and rejections of it, to defend their position or to advance their cause. Meanwhile, Melanesians, it seems, simply wanted to live healthier lives.

Acknowledgements

My thanks go to Barbara Brookes, Ian Campbell, Murray Chapman and Charlotte Paul, as well as two anonymous readers for their comments and advice.

Notes

1. While the consequences were patently visible, until the 1950s and 1960s no Western scientific research on the size of populations needed to keep viable a disease organism, such as the measles virus, fully addressed this. These numbers (the critical community size) were in the hundred thousands, and few South Pacific islands before the late twentieth century had such populations in regular contact with one another, so leaving them susceptible to epidemic forms (Cliff, Haggett and Smallman-Raynor 2000: 85–117).

2. In the 1870s, the Marquis de Ray's band of 800 French and other European colonists on New Ireland succumbed to malaria (and their own ignorance of what crops would grow) (Niau 1936). Similarly, in hyper-endemic malaria-infested areas of the New Guinea coast, Germans as well as Chinese died in shocking numbers in the 1880s (Firth 1982: 35–39, 42). Several attempts at European settlement in tropical northern Australia on Melville Island (1824), Fort Wellington on the Cobourg Peninsula (1827) and Port Essington (1838) failed because of disease, including fevers. Even the convict outpost in Moreton Bay (Brisbane) in the 1820s suffered heavily from disease, including malaria, until drainage seems to have lessened the problem (Anderson 2003: 76–77).

3. This was a sequel to the measles infection that Fijian chiefs had brought back from Sydney to Fiji where, from early 1875, it had carried off about 22 per cent of the Fijians. Labourers returning to the New Hebrides carried the disease back to their homes. See Codrington, Journal, 3 May, 1 July 1875, Codrington Papers, Rhodes House, Oxford (hereafter RH/CP), Mss Pac s. 5. 2–33, and McArthur (1966: 8–11).

4. See Eton Association of the Melanesian Mission, *Annual Reports* (London, 1872–1912), Melanesian Mission, *Annual Reports* (Auckland and Sydney, 1852–1920) and the Melanesian Mission periodical *The Island Voyage* (Ludlow, 1874–1890).

5. Codrington to Aunt, 27 October 1870 RH/CP, Mss Pac s. 4, Letters. See also Melanesian Mission, *Annual Report, 1873* (Auckland 1874), pp. 23–24.

6. Codrington to Brooke, 19 Oct 1920, RH/CP, Mss Pac s. 28, Letters.

7. Eton Association of Melanesian Mission, *Annual Report 1910* (London, 1911), pp. 32, 34; Melanesian Mission, *Annual Report* (Auckland 1911): 49; Melanesian Mission, *Southern Cross Log* (Auckland and Sydney 1912), p. 340, (1913), p. 291.

8. Eton Association, *Annual Reports* (1872–1912), Melanesian Mission, *Annual Reports* (1852–1920), and *The Island Voyage* (1874–1890).

9. Freeman to Commander-in-chief, 24 June 1898; Woodford to O'Brien, 3 October 1899, 24 June 1900, 10 September 1900, Western Pacific Archives, University of Auckland, Auckland (hereafter WPA), WPHC 285/1898.

10. N. Crichlow, Annual Report of Medical Dept., Solomon Islands, 1921. The National Archives of the United Kingdom, Kew, London (hereafter TNA), CO225/184. One of Rivers's contributors, Felix Speiser, blamed syphilis for depopulation in the New Hebrides despite his admission of meeting 'few cases' (Speiser 1922: 29). Many observers confused the symptoms of yaws with those of syphilis.

11. Rivers, 'Speech at the Annual General Meeting in England', *Southern Cross Log*, 5 February 1910, pp. 140–44, and Rivers (1922a: 107–13). The evolution of a Melanesian Christianity, however, was more achievable than an

industrial mission for most denominations. The Melanesian Mission was supportive at Maravovo, Guadalcanal, but a boys' school was the best it could achieve in 1925 when it could not get trained instructors. See Rivers papers, Haddon Papers, Cambridge University Library, Cambridge (hereafter C/HP), envelopes 12030, 12039, 12043, 12081. See also Hilliard (1978: 192, 226–27).

12. J.M. G[reene], Minute, 10 September 1923, TNA, CO 225/190/34062. C.M. Woodford was the first Resident Commissioner (hereafter RC) of the Protectorate from 1896 until 1915. Prior to this, Woodford had carried out research on natural history in the islands in the 1880s.

13. Annual Report (hereafter AR), Condominium of the New Hebrides, 1923, WPA, NHBS 1/1, 106/1924.

14. T. Fell to Acting Resident Commissioner (hereafter ARC), 24 April 1924, WPA, WPHC 850/1924.

15. T. Fell to RC, 29 October 1924, WPA, WPHC 1091/1924.

16. J.M. G[reene], Synopsis of the position in the British Solomon Islands, 1 November 1924, TNA, CO 225/201.

17. Sec. of State to Acting High Commissioner (AHC), 3 April 1924, WPA, WPHC 813/24.

18. J.M. [Greene], Synopsis, 1 November 1924, TNA, CO 224/201.

19. J.M. G[reene], Synopsis, 1 November 1924, TNA, CO 225/201; Woodford to im Thurn, 26 December 1909, WPA, WPHC 111/10.

20. G[reene], Synopsis, 1 November 1924, TNA, CO 225/201.

21. Eyre Hutson to Amery, 26 October 1925, TNA, CO 220/205, and WPA, WPHC 2352/1925.

22. Deputation to the HC of Representatives of Residents, 29 September 1925, WPA, WPHC 1184/1925.

23. H.F. Marriott, Report of Representatives of HM Government, 1923, at Pan-Pacific Scientific Congress, TNA, CO 225/202/299226.

24. Murray to Minister for External Affairs, 23 February 1925, Murray to Minister for External Affairs, 4 October 1916, Murray to Minister of State, Home and Territories, 28 May 1918, National Archives of Australia, Canberra, A452 (A452/1) 1959/4708.

25. Deacon to Haddon, October 1926, Deacon file, C/HP, env. 16006. See also Deacon to W.E.A., 1 March 1926, under heading 'Depopulation' in Deacon file, C/HP, env. 16006. Deacon's research was edited by the anthropologist Camilla Wedgewood and published after his death (Deacon 1934).

26. Bell to RC, 9 August 1922, TNA, CO 225/185; Bell to RC, 11 June 1927, and minutes, TNA, CO 225/220.

27. Bell to Kane, 9 August 1926, WPA, WPHC 3343/26.

28. Bell to HC, 11 June 1927, TNA, CO 225/220, and WPA, WPHC 287/17.

29. Kane to HC, 24 June 1927, WPA, WPHC 287/27; see also Kane to HC, 4 April 1925, WPA, WPHC 938/25.

30. Bell to HC, 11 June 1927, WPA, WPHC 287/17.

31. Rivers, 'Speech at Annual General Meeting in England', *Southern Cross Log*, 5 February, pp. 140–44.

32. AR BSIP, WPA, WPHC 2781/22.

33. By the outbreak of the Second World War, over 94,000 migrants from Japan had settled in Micronesia and made up over half of the total population (Peattie1988: 160–61).

34. See the *Medical Journal of Australia*, 22 Sept 1923, pp. 305–6; 5 April 1924, pp. 341–432; 4 Sept 1924, pp. 321–22; and 13 Sept 1924, p. 279.

35. *Medical Journal of Australia*, 22 September 1923, pp.305–6; Stuart (2003: 133, 135).

36. Lambert, Health Survey of the New Hebrides, 1925, WPA, WPHC 2494/25. In his retirement, Lambert still held that disease was the paramount cause of depopulation but was less critical of Rivers (Lambert 1942: 407–8).

37. HC to RC, 24 July 1936, Harrison to Ormsby Gore, 25 June 1937 and enclosures, WPA, NHBS 1/1, 264/1936.

38. Harrisson to RC, September 1933, WPA, NHBS 1/1, 43/1933. See also Harrisson (1937).

39. Harrisson, Quarterly report for Malekula, January–March 1935, WPA, NHBS 1/1, 83/1935.

40. Frater, Medical work in the New Hebrides, Presbyterian Mission, c. 1937, WPA, NHBS 1/1, 381/1936.

41. British Resident, Depopulation, 15 July 1930, WPA, NHBS 1/1, 246/1930.

42. Ashley to HC, 20 June 1930, WPA, WPHC 1160/30.

43. Regarding Simbo, see Freeman to Commander-in-chief, 24 June 1898, Woodford to O'Brien, 3 October 1899, 24 June 1900, 10 September 1900, WPA, WPHC 285/1898.

44. F.R. Hewitt to Levers' Sydney Office, 7 September 1931, WPA, WPHC 83/32. See Roberts (1927).

45. RC to HC, 12 August 1937, WPA, WPHC 1605/37.

46. Ormsby Gore to HC, 3 December 1937, WPA, WPHC 1605/37.

47. Granville Edge, Comments on Bengough's Report, 4 June 1935, and enclosures, TNA, CO 225/291.

48. Godfrey to British RC, 25 October 1932, WPA, NHBS 1/1, 391/1932.

49. Taveta, Report, Medical Work on Malekula, 14 February 1934, WPA, NHBS 1/1, 52/1934.

50. Tuidraki to Chief Medical Officer, Report, 16 December 1944, WPA, NHBS 1/1, 85/40.

51. Natives of Solomon Islands to HC, c. June 1939, enclosure, WPA, WPHC 2811/39.

52. Luke to Sec. of State, 6 February 1940, and enclosures, TNA, CO 225/323/86086.

53. AR Isabel District, 1927, WPA, WPHC 1832/28; AR Gizo District, 1928, AR Isabel District, 1928, WPA, WPHC 1422/29; AR Isabel District, 1931, WPA, WPHC 1214/32; AR Gizo, 1930, WPA, WHPC 2222/31; AR Gizo 1931, WPA, WPHC 1214/32; AR Gizo 1935, WPA, WPHC 1052/36; AR Guadalcanal, 1932, WPA, WPHC 1522/33; AR Guadalcanal, 1935, WPA, WPHC 1052/36. See also Bennett (1974: 149–55).

54. AR New Hebrides Condominium, 1939, notes, WPA, NHBS 1/1, 129/1940; Depopulation, 1930, WPA, NHBS 1/1, 246.

55. See also the nutritional values listed at http://www.elook.org/nutrition/vegetables/3390.htm, retrieved 20 January 2009.

56. Joy, Review of Medical Work and Organisation, New Hebrides, 8 March 1948, WPA, NHBS1/1, 207/1938; Mackenzie to King, 23 December 1910, and enclosures, WPA, NHBS 1/1, 18/1910; Robinson to Joy, 29 May 1930 and enclosures, Dysentery on Tanna, 1930, WPA, NHBS 1/1, 253/1930.

57. AR Medical, BSIP, 1919, TNA, CO 225/169; Crichlow to RC, 16 July 1920, TNA, CO 225/171; Quarantine, New Guinea, 1925, enclosures, TNA, CO 225/206; International Sanitary Convention 1926, Report for BSIP 1929, TNA, CO 225/239; Crombie, Monthly report of Medical officer, June–July 1908, Dubruel and Crombie to British RC, 1 February 1911, WPA, NHBS 1/1, 5/1908; Smith-Rewse to HC, 26 October 1924, WPA, NHBS 1/1, 124/1924; Smith-Rewse to HC, 3 November 1925, WPA, NHBS 1/1, 125/1925. See also Lambert (1928: 372) and McLeod et al. (2008).

58. See e.g. WPA, NHBS 1/1, 6/25 and 7/25.

59. Michelson to Blandy, 18 Sept. 1931, WPA, NHBS 1/1/200/1926.

60. Alison Day (personal communication, 21 April 2009).

61. Frater, Medical report, Presbyterian mission, c. 1937, WPA, NHBS 1/1, 381/1936.

62. Ivens to Stanton 13 January 1927, and enclosures and minutes, TNA, CO225/216.

63. Rather than charging the European perpetrator, this was a common way of dealing with such offences in the Solomons: Turner to HC, 12 September 1932 and enclosures, 12 September 1933, WPA, WPHC 2148/1933.

64. Ashley, Inspection notes, Solomon Islands, 1929–1938, p.94, Rhodes House, Oxford, Mss. Brit. Emp. S422.

65. Garvey, Minute, 15 January 1934, WPA, WPHC 3808/33. Garvey had been district officer of the Santa Cruz district in 1931 and had undertaken a census, so he was aware of the impact of disease as well as early local warfare. Garvey, The Depopulation of Vanikoro, January 1932, WPA, WPHC 83/32.

66. 'Pour nous les maladies sont les vraies causes de la dépopulation; le fait nous paraît une évidence'. Hérivaux, Revue coloniale de médecine et de chirurgie, September 1939, cited in Monfort, Rapport, 18 March 1940, WPA, NHBS 1/1, 85/1940.

67. *Annual Report of Territory of Papua* (Port Moresby: Government Printer, 1919/1920), p.106; Lambert (1942: 96–98); Stuart (2007: 10–11). See also Rivers (1926: 57–61).
68. See Deacon to W.E.A., 1 March 1926, under heading 'Depopulation', Deacon file, C/HP, env. 16006.

References

Allen, M.G. 2005. 'The Evidence for Sweet Potato in Island Melanesia', in *The Sweet Potato in Oceania: A Reappraisal*, C. Ballard, P. Brown, R.M. Bourke and T. Harwood (eds), 99–108. Pittsburgh: University of Pittsburg; Sydney: University of Sydney.

Anderson, W. 2003. *The Cultivation of Whiteness: Science, Health and Racial Destiny in Australia.* New York: Basic Books.

———— 2009. 'Ambiguities of Race: Science on the Reproductive Frontier of Australia and the Pacific between the Wars', *Australian Historical Studies* 40(3): 143–60.

Antoni, M.H., et al. 2006. 'The Influence of Bio-behavioural Factors on Tumour Biology: Pathways and Mechanisms', *Nature Reviews Cancer* 6: 240–48.

Baker, J.R. 1929. *Man and Animals in the New Hebrides.* London: George Routledge and Sons.

Bashford, A. 2004. *Imperial Hygiene: A Critical History of Colonialism, Nationalism and Public Health.* Basingstoke: Palgrave Macmillan.

Bayliss-Smith, T. 2006. 'Fertility and Depopulation: Childlessness, Abortion and Introduced Disease in Simbo and Ontong Java, Solomon Islands', in *Population, Reproduction and Fertility in Melanesia*, S. Ulijaszek (ed.), 13–52. Oxford: Berghahn.

Bennett, J.A. 1974. 'Cross-cultural Influences on Village Relocation on the Weather Coast of Guadalcanal, Solomon Islands, c. 1870–1953', MA diss. Honolulu: University of Hawaii.

———— 1987. *Wealth of the Solomons. A History of a Pacific Archipelago, 1800–1978.* Honolulu: University of Hawaii Press.

———— 1993. '"We Do Not Come Here to Be Beaten": Resistance and the Plantation System in the Solomon Islands to World War II', in *Plantation Workers: Resistance and Accommodation*, B.V. Lal, D. Munro and E.D. Beechert (eds), 129–85. Honolulu: University of Hawaii Press.

———— 2000. *Pacific Forest: A History of Resource Control and Contest in Solomon Islands, c. 1800–1997.* Leiden: Brill; Cambridge: White Horse Press.

———— 2006. 'Malaria, Medicine, and Melanesians: Contested Hybrid Spaces in World War II', *Health and History* 8(1): 27–55.

Buxton, P.A. 1926. 'The Depopulation of the New Hebrides and Other Parts of Melanesia', *Transactions of the Royal Society of Tropical Medicine and Hygiene* 19(8): 420–58.

Campbell, I.C. 1998. 'Anthropology and the Professionalisation of Colonial Administration in Papua and New Guinea', *Journal of Pacific History* 33(1): 69–90.

Cilento, R.W. 1924. 'The Depopulation of the Pacific', in *Proceedings of the Pan-Pacific Science Congress, Australia, 1923,* G. Lightfoot (ed.), 1395–99. Melbourne: Australian Government Printer.

———— 1926. *The Causes of Depopulation in Western Islands of New Guinea.* Melbourne: Australian Government Printer.

———— 1932. 'The Value of Medical Services in Relation to Problems of Depopulation', *Medical Journal of Australia* 2: 480–83.

Cliff A.D., P. Haggett and M. Smallman-Raynor 2000. *Island Epidemics.* Oxford: Oxford University Press.

Cohen, S. 1997. 'Social Ties and Susceptibility to the Common Cold', *Journal of the American Medical Association* 277(24): 1940–44.

Connell, J. 1987. *New Caledonia or Kanaky? The Political History of a French Colony.* Canberra: Australian National University.

Cooper, F., and A.L. Stoler (eds) 1997. *Tensions of Empire: Colonial Cultures in a Bourgeois World.* Berkeley: University of California Press.

Cumpston, J.H.L. 1924. 'The Depopulation of the Pacific', in *Proceedings of the Pan-Pacific Science Congress, Australia, 1923,* G. Lightfoot (ed.), 1389–94. Melbourne: Australian Government Printer.

Day, A. 2008. 'Child Immunisation: Reactions and Responses to New Zealand Government Policy 1920–1990', PhD diss. Auckland: University of Auckland.

Deacon, A.B. 1934. *Malekula: A Vanishing People of the New Hebrides,* ed. C.H. Wedgwood. London: Routledge.

Denoon, D. 1999. 'An Untimely Divorce: Western Medicine and Anthropology in Melanesia', *History and Anthropology* 11(2/3): 329–50.

Dow, D.A. 1995. *Safeguarding the Public Health: A History of the New Zealand Department of Health.* Wellington: Victoria University Press.

Eliot, T.S. 1922. 'London Letter', *The Dial* (New York) 73(6): 659–63.

Engel, G.L. 1997. 'From Biomedical to Biopsychosocial: Being Scientific in the Human Domain', *Psychosomatics* 38(6): 521–28.

Feery, B. 1981. 'Impact of Immunization on Disease Patterns in Australia', *Medical Journal of Australia* 2: 172–76.

Firth, S. 1982. *New Guinea under the Germans.* Melbourne: Melbourne University Press.

Fox, C.E. 1924. *The Threshold of the Pacific: An Account of the Social Organization, Magic and Religion of the People of San Cristoval in the Solomon Islands.* London: Kegan Paul.

Glaser, R. 2005. 'Stress-associated Immune Disregulation and Its Importance in Human Health: A Personal History of Psychoneuroimmunology', *Brain, Behaviour, and Immunity* 19: 3–11.

Goldenweiser, A. 1937. *Anthropology: An Introduction to Primitive Culture.* New York: Crofts & Co.

Gregory, H.E. 1921. 'Remarks', *Proceedings of the First Pan-Pacific Science Conference* (Bernice P. Bishop Museum Special Publication 7), 936–37.

Gunson, N. 1962. 'An Account of the Mamai'a or Visionary Heresy of Tahiti', *Journal of the Polynesian Society* 71: 209–53.

Guthrie, M. 1979. *Misi Utu: Dr D.W. Hoodless and the Development of Medical Education in the South Pacific.* Suva, Fiji: Institute of Pacific Studies.

Haddon, A.C. 1924. 'Proceedings of Societies: Anthropology at the Second Pan-Pacific Science Congress', *Man* 24: 12–16.

Harrisson, M. 2004. *Disease and the Modern World: 1500 to the Present Day.* Cambridge: Polity Press.

Harrisson, T. 1937. *Savage Civilization.* New York: Knopf.

Hermant, P., and R.W. Cilento 1929. *Report of a Mission Entrusted with a Survey on Health Conditions in the Pacific Islands.* Geneva: League of Nations.

Hilliard, D. 1978. *God's Gentlemen: A History of the Melanesian Mission, 1849–1942.* St Lucia: University of Queensland Press.

Hocart, A.M. 1925. 'Medicine and Witchcraft in Eddystone of the Solomon Islands', *Journal of the Royal Anthropological Institute* 55: 229–70.

———— 1967. 'A Native Fijian on the Decline of his Race', in *Beyond the Frontier: Social Progress and Cultural Change*, P. Bohannan and F. Plog (eds), 165–80. Garden City, NY: Natural History Press.

Hogbin, H.I. 1934. 'Culture Change in Solomon Islands: Report on Fieldwork in Guadalcanal and Malaita', *Oceania* 4(2): 264–65.

———— 1939. *Experiments in Civilization: The Effects of Cultural Change on a Native Community of the Solomon Islands.* London: Routledge and Kegan Paul.

———— 1964. *A Guadalcanal Society: The Kaoka Speakers.* New York: Holt, Rinehart and Winston.

Howe, K.R. 2000. *Nature, Culture, and History.* Honolulu: University of Hawaii Press.

im Thurn, E. 1922. 'Preface', in *Essays on the Depopulation of Melanesia*, W.H.R. Rivers (ed.), v–xviii. Cambridge: Cambridge University Press.

Irwin M.R., et al. 2011. 'Major Depressive Disorder and Immunity to Varicella-Zoster Virus in the Elderly', *Brain, Behaviour, and Immunity* 25: 759–66.

Ivens, W.E. 1927. *The Island Builders of the Pacific.* Philadelphia: Lippincott.

Joyce, R.B. 1971. *Sir William MacGregor.* Melbourne: Oxford University Press.

Keesing, R.M., and P. Corris 1980. *Lightning Meets the West Wind: The Malaita Massacre.* Melbourne: Oxford University Press.

Kuklick, H. 1991. *The Savage Within: The Social History of British Anthropology, 1885–1945.* Cambridge: Cambridge University Press.

Kunitz, S. 1994. *Disease and Social Diversity: The European Impact on the Health of Non-Europeans.* Oxford: Oxford University Press.

Lambert, S.M. 1928. 'Medical Conditions in the South Pacific', *Medical Journal of Australia*, 22 September, 362–78.

———— 1934. *Depopulation of Pacific Races*. Honolulu: Bernice Bishop Museum.

———— 1942. *A Doctor in Paradise*. London: Dent; Melbourne: George Jaboor.

Langer, W.L. 1997. 'Europe's Initial Population Explosion', in *Biological Consequences of the European Expansion, 1450–1800*, K.F. Kiple and S.V. Beck (eds), 344–59. Aldershot: Ashgate.

Langham, I. 1981. *The Building of British Social Anthropology: W.H.R. Rivers and his Cambridge Disciples in the Development of Kinship Studies, 1898–1931*. Dordrecht: Reidel.

Lattas, A. 1996. 'Humanitarianism and Australian Nationalism in Colonial Papua: Hubert Murray and the Project of Caring for the Self of the Coloniser and Colonised', *Australian Journal of Anthropology* 7(2): 141–64.

Lightfoot, G. (ed.). 1924. *Proceedings of the Pan-Pacific Science Congress, Australia, 1923*. Melbourne: Australian Government Printer.

McArthur, N. 1966. *Island Populations of the Pacific*. Canberra: Australian National University Press.

Mackenzie, J. 1997. 'Empire and the Apocalypse: The Historiography of the Imperial Environment', in *Ecology and Empire: Environmental History of Settler Societies*, T. Griffiths and L. Robin (eds), 215–28. Edinburgh: Keele University Press.

McLeod, M.A., M. Baker, N. Wilson, H. Kelly, T. Kiedrzynski and J.L. Kool 2008. 'Protective Effect of Maritime Quarantine in South Pacific Jurisdictions, 1918–19 Influenza Pandemic', *Emerg Infect Dis*. Retrieved 1 April 2009 from: http://www.cdc.gov/EID/content/14/3/468.htm.

MacLeod, R., and P.F. Rehbock 2000. 'Developing a Sense of the Pacific: The 1923 Pan-Pacific Science Congress in Australia', *Pacific Science* 54(3): 209–25.

Manson, P. 1898. *Tropical Diseases: A Manual of the Diseases of Warm Climates*. London: Cassell and Co.

Murray, J.H.P. 1924. 'The Population Problem in Papua – Lack of Direct Evidence: A Priori Considerations', in *Proceedings of the Pan-Pacific Science Congress, Australia, 1923*, G. Lightfoot (ed.), 231–40. Melbourne: Australian Government Printer.

———— 1925. *Papua of To-day or, An Australian Colony in the Making*. London: King and Son.

———— 1932. *The Scientific Aspect of the Pacification of Papua*. Port Moresby: Government Printer.

Niau, J.H. 1936. *The Phantom Paradise: The Story of the Expedition of the Marquis de Rays*. Sydney: Angus and Robertson.

O'Brien, P. 2009. 'Remaking Australia's Colonial Culture? White Australia and its Papuan Frontier 1901–1940', *Australian Historical Studies* 40(1): 96–112.

Peattie, M.R. 1988. *Nanyo: The Rise and Fall of the Japanese in Micronesia, 1885–1945*. Honolulu: University of Hawaii.

Rallu, J-L., and D.A. Ahlburg. 1999. 'Demography', in *The Pacific Islands: Environment and Society*, M. Rapaport (ed.), 258–69. Honolulu: University of Hawaii Press.

Raucaz, L.M. 1928. *In the Savage Solomon Islands: The Story of the Mission*. Lyons: Society for the Propagation of the Faith.

Rivers, W.H.R. 1917. 'The Government of Subject Peoples', in *Science and the Nation*, A.C. Steward (ed.), 302–27. Cambridge: Cambridge University Press.

———— 1920. 'The Dying Out of Native Races', *Lancet* 198: 42–44, 109.

———— 1922a. 'The Psychological Factor', in *Essays on the Depopulation of Melanesia*, W.H.R. Rivers (ed.), 84–113. Cambridge: Cambridge University Press.

———— 1922b. *Essays on the Depopulation of Melanesia*. Cambridge: Cambridge University Press.

———— 1926. *Psychology and Ethnology*. London: Kegan Paul, Trench and Trubner.

Rivers, W.H.R., and H. Head. 1908. 'A Human Experiment in Nerve Division', *Brain* 31: 323–450.

Roberts, S.H. 1927. *Population Problems of the Pacific*. London: Routledge.

Rosen, G. 1993. *A History of Public Health*. Baltimore: Johns Hopkins University Press.

Salaman, R.N. 1949. *The History and Social Influence of the Potato*. Cambridge: Cambridge University Press.

Scarr, D. 1984. *Fiji: A Short History*. Hamel Hempstead: Allen and Unwin.

Shineberg, D. 1978. '"He Can but Die …": Missionary Medicine in Pre-Christian Tonga', in *The Changing Pacific*, N. Gunson (ed.), 285–96. Oxford: Oxford University Press.

———— 1999. *The People Trade: Pacific Island Laborers and New Caledonia, 1865–1930*. Honolulu: University of Hawaii Press.

Slobodin, R. 1978. *W.H.R. Rivers*. New York: Columbia University Press.

Speiser, F. 1922. 'Decadence and Preservation in the New Hebrides', in *Essays on the Depopulation of Melanesia*, W.H.R. Rivers (ed.), 25–61. Cambridge: Cambridge University Press.

Stevenson, R.L. 1908. *In the South Seas*. London: Chatto and Windus.

Stocking, G.W. 1996. *After Tylor: British Social Anthropology 1888–1951*. London: Athlone Press.

Stuart, A. 2003. 'Parasites Lost? The Rockefeller Foundation and the Expansion of Health Services in the Colonial South Pacific, 1916-1939', PhD diss. Christchurch: University of Canterbury.

———— 2007. 'We Are All Hybrid Here: The Rockefeller Foundation, Sylvester Lambert, and Health Work in the Colonial South Pacific', *Health and Hybridity* 8(1): 1–16.

Thompson, R.C. 1980. *Australian Imperialism in the Pacific: The Expansionist Era 1820–1920*. Melbourne: Melbourne University Press.

Vedhara K., and M.R. Irwin (eds) 2005. *Human Psychoneuroimmunology*. Oxford: Oxford University Press.

Objects and Photographs from the Percy Sladen Trust Expedition

◆●◆

Tim Thomas

Neglected Collections

Amongst the many obscure and neglected dimensions of the Solomon Islands fieldwork carried out in 1908 by W.H.R. Rivers and A.M. Hocart is the extent and nature of their photography and artefact collecting. Though it could hardly be said that the published articles and archival manuscripts produced from their endeavour are widely known, they are comparatively well understood and have repeatedly been made use of by regional specialists and others. In contrast, no summary account of the collected artefacts or photographs exists, and barely any have ever appeared in print. Despite the recent resurgence of academic interest in photographic and ethnographic collections made during the early years of anthropological enquiry, and extensive studies of the motives and methods of collectors (e.g. O'Hanlon and Welsch 2000; Gosden and Knowles 2001; Pinney 2011), the collecting practices of Rivers and Hocart have completely escaped notice.

This neglect is largely a residual outcome of the patchy publication of results suffered by the Percy Sladen Trust Expedition. Indeed, if we were to rely on the published texts alone there would only be scattered hints to suggest that such collections were even made. Hocart published a selection of photographs to accompany some of his articles on Simbo (Hocart 1922, 1925, 1931), and occasionally made passing reference to artefact purchasing there (see Hocart 1922: 279, 295 for characteristic asides). Rivers published a brief article on Solomon Islands basketry illustrated with specimens obtained on Simbo (Rivers and Hingston-Quiggin 1910), but there are no ethnographic photographs or illustrations of artefacts deriving from the 1908 expedition in the remainder of his published output. In his primary publication stemming from the expedition, Rivers (1914) relies entirely on photographs taken and objects collected by others. On this evidence it would be easy to assume that photography was a minor element of the fieldwork and that the collection of artefacts was merely incidental to the concentrated gathering of information about social organization, kinship and ritual. But the near absence of objects and images from the available texts is misleading.

The Cambridge University Museum of Anthropology and Archaeology (MAA) holds a substantial assemblage of artefacts, glass plate negatives and prints accessioned as part of its Rivers Collection. These items derive from the places Rivers conducted fieldwork or visited during anthropological surveys, though not all items were collected directly by him – some were purchased at auction, some sent by resident contacts in previous field sites, and many were collected by expedition participants (particularly Hocart; see below). Included are photos and/or artefacts from India, Vanuatu, the Solomon Islands and other parts of Oceania. In the following I restrict my discussion to material that is identifiably related to, or derived from, the activities of Rivers and Hocart in the Western Solomons.[1]

Currently it is possible to identify nearly 400 artefacts that meet these criteria – with the vast majority being from Simbo, Roviana, Ranongga and Vella Lavella, though a few items attributed to Isabel, Choiseul and the Bougainville Straits are also likely to have been acquired in the New Georgia group. To put this in perspective, this number exceeds the size of probably all other museum collections of artefacts from the New Georgia region attributed to a single donor. This includes the large Lt. H.B.T. Somerville collection at the Pitt-Rivers Museum, which comprises approximately 300 items acquired during an eleven-month Royal Naval survey of New Georgia in 1893–95 (Waite 1984, 2000), as well as the results of the avid collecting pursued by resident colonial officers C.M. Woodford (who served in the Solomons from 1896 to 1914) and A.W. Mahaffy (1898 to 1904), who each deposited under 150 objects from the Western Solomons in museums (O'Brien 2011).

The photographic collection, too, is very large. Over 600 glass-plate negatives and prints from Rivers's and Hocart's Western Solomons fieldwork exist in the MAA photographic archive, and whilst many of these are duplicate images the numbering system on the negatives suggests over 320 photographs were taken.

Clearly then, artefact collecting and photography were not incidental or minor activities during the expedition. In fact, the collection Rivers and Hocart produced is amongst the most tightly provenanced and information-rich from the Solomon Islands. A careful examination of the MAA collections enables this material to be tied in quite closely to surviving unpublished manuscripts and fieldnotes, and this has the potential to considerably expand our understanding of those texts. In many respects the collections can be understood as an integral part of the unpublished record of the expedition – the material and visual elements of an aggregate archive. These are not simply subsidiary illustrations of written information, but an important part of the way data and evidence were constructed during ethnographic practice. In the following I give a brief and preliminary overview of these collections, describe some aspects of the motives and contexts of their production, and identify some questions for future research.

Artefacts, Images and Early Social Anthropology

One reason underlying the absence of the New Georgia collection from Rivers's publications is that the 1908 expedition occurred at a turning point in his intellectual trajectory, which saw his primary anthropological focus shift from the careful refinement of appropriate ethnographic methods and data production to the 'ethnological' interpretation of social facts according to a theoretical perspective that had little use for material culture. Rivers went to the Solomon Islands as someone who broadly supported the evolutionary approach of A.C. Haddon and others, which tended to use material culture data as a key line of evidence. But post-fieldwork, Rivers became convinced of the importance of diffusion in determining patterns of variation in culture, and argued it was necessary to sort this out before turning to evolutionary questions. This required a different type of data appropriate to the task, and perhaps not coincidentally Rivers argued that the sort of information on social structure gathered via his own pioneering methods was the key.

The clearest expression of this shift in thinking appears in Rivers's Presidential Address to the Anthropological Section of the British Association for the Advancement of Science (Rivers 1911), where he describes his conversion as being driven by data obtained during the 1908 expedition. As Langham (1981: 125) has noted, the Solomon Islands fieldwork is a recurring focal point at times of personal reflection in Rivers's later writings, with key incidents being called upon to illustrate moments when his thinking dramatically changed. It may be that the particular connectivity of island networks in the Western Solomons (see Hviding, this volume) drew Rivers's attention to culture contact and diffusion-mediated change, and perhaps working with Hocart – who, having had two years education in Germany, was already more influenced by geographical thinking – helped motivate this shift in theoretical perspective. If so, it is ironic that one outcome of the change was that a large subset of data from the expedition, the material culture collection, was rendered suddenly of little analytical value. The 1911 address is explicit: Rivers argues material culture is too easily transmitted by contact rather than the 'true admixture of peoples', and thus essentially inadequate for ethnological analysis: he had seen in Hawaii and Melanesia that people could adopt European ways in all material aspects of life, but still retain traditional social structures (Rivers 1911: 394). Consequently, social structure was reasoned to be resilient and thus the most reliable index of historical relationships – an argument that can be seen, retrospectively, as the birth of a growing disillusionment in twentieth-century British social anthropology with material culture as a legitimate data source (Stocking 1995).

Rivers gradually solidified his perspective, and we see similar points made and expanded upon in subsequent writing (e.g. Rivers 1914, ii: 440), all of which makes the existence of a large museum collection of objects attributed to him somewhat surprising. Resolving the paradox depends, I think, upon recognising that the establishment of the collection mostly predates Rivers adopting diffusionism, and is instead part of his early focus on methodological refinement. Furthermore, the majority of items of material culture in the collection were not collected by Rivers at all. We can address each of these points by reviewing Rivers's experiences and work preceding the 1908 expedition.

The Percy Sladen Trust Expedition followed a model of fieldwork established during the 1898 Cambridge Torres Strait Expedition (Herle and Rouse 1998). Though that expedition was led by A.C. Haddon, Rivers was a prominent member of the team and responsible for key innovations, including his 'genealogical method'. Both expeditions combined broad survey work with periods of intensive study in a set locale, and were framed as a kind of salvage ethnography. In 1898 Haddon, with team members Ray, Seligman and Wilkin, surveyed mainland Papua New Guinea, taking photographs and collecting artefacts to generate comparative material, before turning to the intensive study of Torres Strait communities (Edwards 2000). Rivers participated in the latter, conducting a series of psychological tests, gathering genealogies and recording anthropometric data – but left the photography and collecting to others (officially at least). Ten years later in the Solomon Islands much the same balance of evidence and scales was attempted, broad survey work being combined with intensive study.[2]

There was, however, much more crossover and collaboration in terms of the research activities of expedition members since the Percy Sladen Trust

Expedition team was so much smaller. In the Solomons, Rivers definitely collected artefacts and probably took some of the photographs in the MAA collection. It is difficult to be precise due to the fragmentary nature of the remaining documents from the expedition, and there is no master list of who collected what. Nevertheless, preliminary indications suggest under fifty objects can be attributed to Rivers with certainty. About thirty objects have pencilled annotations written on their surface referring to page numbers in Rivers's fieldnotes, and we know he collected many of the baskets amongst other things. This number is dwarfed by the contributions of Hocart: there are many more items accompanied by captions in his handwriting and references to pages in his fieldwork notebooks. Additionally, almost all of the glass-plate negatives and prints have written annotations, and these are universally in Hocart's hand.

Hocart spent more time in the Western Solomons than Rivers, and although very few of Rivers's fieldnotes or other documents from the expedition survive, it appears the younger man made the more detailed record. Rivers's time was probably greatly occupied by physical anthropology and recording genealogical information, touring Simbo to generate a complete record of every person on the island. He was certainly with Hocart at house-building ceremonies, funerals, trips up the hill, and visits to ritual sites, but the men also spent time apart. Hocart, being the junior member of the team and closer in age to the younger men of Simbo, may have found himself more quickly drawn into local daily life – and Rivers, despite his apparent fondness for his time on Simbo, does seem to have preferred survey work. Whatever the case, the majority of artefacts and photographs were collected, produced and annotated by Hocart.

It is currently unclear when this material was first deposited in the museum – it was possibly sent there during or soon after fieldwork ended. But due to overcrowding and other issues, items were sometimes not catalogued until several years later. The bulk of the objects in the collection, however, have low accession numbers, suggesting that they were among the first 500 artefacts given catalogue numbers by the museum. Correspondence indicates that Rivers continued to add to the collection via the service of a variety of agents post-fieldwork. Letters from Fred Green, a trader on Simbo, suggest that Rivers was trying to fill gaps and oversights made during his brief stay by collecting items associated with practices described in his notes. In one letter Green mentions that he has included 'the shells … you have a note about'.[3] In the same letter it is indicated that sound recordings were also being made to order.[4] In late 1909, Rivers sent Green a list of animals to acquire, with jars and formalin for their preservation, and these specimens were sent back along with various artefacts.

The outcome is that the Western Solomons portion of the MAA Rivers Collection is really a work of supervised assembly – Rivers was the meta-collector of the items it contains. It is possible that his efforts in depositing material in the museum were more to do with helping establish systematic reference collections for the discipline as a whole, rather than personal interest. Unlike the object-oriented Haddon (Herle 1998), Rivers was not overtly interested in material culture in an analytical sense, even at this stage of his career as an anthropologist. He does not seem to have collected a significant number of artefacts during the Torres Strait Expedition, and the MAA collection contains only two objects from his 1901/2 fieldwork in South India (two pieces of cloth). Prior to his turn to diffusionism, Rivers's few writings on material culture are mostly restricted to technical aspects of description and theory. In the Torres Strait, for example, he helped devise a method and terminology for recording string figures (Rivers and Haddon 1902), but whilst actual examples were collected during that expedition, in the Solomons he was content to record only written descriptions utilising the terminology he had devised. Rivers's published account of Solomon Islands basketry similarly consists of a technical description of construction methods. Characteristically, it ends with a point of caution about processes of evolution generalised in a manner that reveals where his true interest lay: 'This affords a good illustration of a principle which in its application is not confined to technology. Because a social or religious institution has a certain effect it does not follow that it was brought into being to produce that effect, though it may have been that effect which has allowed it to survive' (Rivers and Hingston-Quiggin 1910: 163).

Such methodological and interpretive cautions are common in Rivers's writing, and are part of his deep interest in scientific method and procedures for gathering unbiased data (Langham 1981). The Torres Strait Expedition is justly famous for its methodological innovation and the birth of embedded fieldwork. Participants in the expedition quickly established their positions as the most experienced field researchers in British anthropology. An indication of this is that, during 1907, Rivers, Haddon and other Torres Strait team members were appointed to a British Association for the Advancement of Science committee to write a new edition of the fieldworker's guidebook *Notes and Queries in Anthropology*, which finally appeared in 1912.[5] Rivers was tasked with refining a series of technical terms for use in recording kinship and social organisation, and in the published book he wrote a long section stressing the importance of methodology in the collection of material, the need to learn the local language, take notes and make drawings. He continuously emphasised the need to collect 'concrete facts' in an objective way, uncoloured by personal interpretation.

An excellent example of this is his advice (echoing Durkheim) on the need to pay attention to 'primitive classification': 'Often objects which seem to us to differ little have nevertheless different names, while others which seem to us of a wholly different nature are grouped together under the same term' (BAAS 1912: 116). Collecting both the words and things in the raw, without assumption, would allow the proper study of different classificatory schemes. This stress on the concrete was intended to avoid generalist accounts of culture provided in the past by untrained travellers:

> a modern ethnologist is not content, or should not be content, to give a general account of the functions of chiefs, but he gives fully the names of the present chiefs, illustrating their descent by pedigrees; he describes as accurately as possible the districts over which their powers and privileges extend, and his account of these powers and privileges is based on concrete records in which actual persons, actual places, actual objects, and actual incidents are utilized as fully as possible. (Rivers 1912: 460)

This is an almost perfect account of what Rivers and Hocart did, and the approach they took to evidence, during their fieldwork in the Western Solomons. The abstract was approached via the concrete: chiefly societies were composed of the elementary particles of actual people and the material and social facts of their lives.

The inclusion of 'actual objects' in the above quotation is indicative of the role given to material culture collecting in this construction of data: artefacts are conceived as fragments of a social whole, factual elements that are part of the solid form of society. Collecting was thus part of a much broader ethnographic endeavour, designed to show (and produce) facts – it was never an end in itself. Thus while Rivers may have had no great academic interest in material culture per se, he considered its collection an essential part of ethnographic fieldwork.

Hocart's subsequent written output indicates that he totally supported such procedural refinement, and excelled at it. His collecting of material culture during the 1908 expedition exemplifies the desire for exactness and concrete pedantry inherent in Rivers's methodological advice. For example, while discussing the role of supernatural beings in dictating weather conditions, he records the collection of a particular charm:

> Hiro, half Rovianese, half Ysabellan, sold us an object consisting of a stick of *ekolo* with a *mbulau* ring tied on each side with the *lave* creeper; a section of a spiral shell (*rango*) is tied on either side of the tip of this stick. It is a copy of his Rovianese father's charm. It is stuck in the shield when they go abroad, its object is to prevent storms. If a gale comes up, Hiro says: 'Clear up Mburavusu, clear up, Koluka, clear

up in Leoko' … Pa Leoko is in Gizo; Koluka is the skull-house in Simbo. (Hocart 1922: 290)

This account is then followed by a meticulous description of the shrines linked to the charm, their location, form and contents, as well as the men involved in tending them and controlling their use. The account spirals outwards from a single object to a socio-spatial network of persons and places – a kind of topogeny (Thomas 2009).

In another instance Hocart relates a myth featuring the god Magoana's search for a shell ring thrown into the sea, before noting that 'the ring Ango [the Roviana narrator] believed to be still in the possession of Siana, Rembo's wife, but it is really in the Cambridge Museum' (Hocart 1922: 279). Completing the act of collection, Ango was also asked to compose a pencil sketch illustrating his narrative (Hocart 1922: pl. 19, fig. 1). Conversely, when an artefact's association was questionable, acquisition was not pursued: 'A sacred ring (*poata*) was brought for sale. It was made by a marine god (*tamasa pa n'ivere*). After some reflection the name was given as Heleveni; but they seemed so uncertain that it was not bought' (Hocart 1922: 295).

Each case reveals a concern with accuracy and exactness in which synthetic statements are avoided and uncertain claims disregarded. Information is broken down into its constituent elements and itemised. As with 'chiefs', a proper account of a charm consisted of the collection of named, actual persons and relationships, the arrangements of words spoken and actual objects deployed, and the precise geography gathered therein. The interesting rejection of an alleged sacred ring is an emblematic contrast with a prior antiquarianism that regarded the value of artefacts as being inherent – in this instance Hocart has no interest in the ring as a type specimen. It was not enough to simply collect a ring on its own, or even to collect a ring accompanied by a general statement such as 'some rings, like this one, could be considered sacred'. Instead, an actual ring with a known sacred history was required to demonstrate the point.

Photography was an integral element of this approach to evidence. Edwards (2000: 105) supplies a very useful distinction between two broad styles of ethnographic photography that coexisted in early anthropology. One form aspired to a naturalistic, non-interventionist portrayal of ethnographic subjects, and was used as a kind of visual notebook – a neutral record, or memory aid. The other form was interventionist scientific photography designed to establish and show facts – subjects were posed in order to show relevant detail, scenes were altered for clarity and purpose. Edwards argues that the latter approach was eclipsed by the former by the mid twentieth century, but in the early days of ethnographic anthropology, photography still functioned as a fieldwork tool used to produce and collect primary data. It was a form of collecting through visual survey, gathering evidence of otherwise non-transportable things – people, buildings, events. As we will see below, this style dominates the photography of Rivers and Hocart, but amidst such images the more naturalistic form also emerges – often encouraged by local participants.

As with so much of the remaining record of the expedition, though, only brief glimmers of personal involvement and subjectivity appear. There are no direct photographs of Hocart or Rivers in the field, for example – they appear only as shadows and reflections. The same is true of the written record too: we have no diaries and few personal reflections in the field notebooks, no self-conscious introspection in the manner of Malinowski (cf. Pinney 2011: 50–60). Whilst Hocart's letters to Rivers post-fieldwork can be, at times, remarkably emotive and lyrical in their recollection of time spent on Simbo,[6] this was suppressed in the presentation of data. Such absences are not remarkable given the methodological stances related above – subjective positions were purposefully avoided in the conveyance of facts. Similarly, most traces of 'modernity' are missing from the written work, the photographs and the material culture collected. There are hints here and there about European artefacts replacing local ones, about white travellers and so on, but European influence is generally noticeable by its absence. Such was the salvage paradigm, interested mainly in gathering together the fossil traces of a vanishing past.

Photography played an important role with regard to the latter point, in that its realism testifies to authenticity whilst remaining superbly manipulable. Nevertheless, in some of the photographs we see a kind of humanity escaping from its positioning as data – in the faces and expressions of those posed for anthropometric images we see real people with names and lives; their agency shines through. Perhaps this tension is just a sign that method, however rigorous, can never completely turn life into a series of data points – but it is also tempting to see it as a mark of the conviviality and respect characterising the relations struck up with local people by Hocart and Rivers during their fieldwork, their willingness to put themselves in other's shoes. One of my favourite asides in Hocart's fieldnotes illustrates this: 'Poponggu (ta piara): seems specially used by women. Used it e.g. when somebody related something I had done or said which they thought very funny e.g. if carried tomahawk etc, appeared in native dress, etc.'[7]

The fact that we can laugh along with the Simbo women at the (imagined) image of Hocart wearing a loincloth and holding a tomahawk has to be a tribute to the multifaceted nature of the record he left behind. However confined by the strictures of method, the interlocking strands of this record are rich and extensive enough to exceed the limitations of the day.

In the following Appendix, I give a preliminary overview of the objects and photographs in the MAA collection, hopefully bringing to light some of the once-hidden material and visual dimensions of this aggregate archive.

Appendix: The Cambridge Museum of Archaeology and Anthropology Rivers Collection

Objects

Valuables

Perhaps the most common New Georgian artefacts collected in world museums are shell-ring exchange valuables made from sub-fossil *Tridacna gigas* clam shell. Hocart and Rivers collected numerous examples of these, including all of the primary types and a range in different stages of manufacture (and various tools used during manufacturing). Several of these have pencilled references written on the surfaces of the objects – usually to particular page numbers in fieldnotes. Some have numerals indicating the price paid, for example, '1000 sticks' – of tobacco presumably.

Such value equivalences were reported by Hocart along with a description of the various types of ring, the method of manufacture and their variety of uses in exchange.[8] Interestingly, the objects apparently served as partial fieldnotes for Hocart's account – not only were key pieces of information written on the things themselves, but each fact is supported by a collected item. For example, in discussing the manufacture of a class of ring known as *hokata*, Hocart writes that several of these could be sawn from a single blank via latitudinal cuts, and in the MAA collection there are two examples of this from a workshop in Roviana. In another case he notes that, on Simbo, 'rings from Choiseul are occasionally met with: they have a biconvex section with flat tops' – and again several examples are in the collection with pencilled notes such as 'Eddystone Is. Choiseul type'. For the most part the writing on these rings is in Hocart's hand, though there are page-number references to Rivers's fieldnotes in a hand that is slightly different from Hocart's and perhaps too legible to be Rivers's. Only a few small charm rings collected on Vella Lavella have pencil script obviously matching Rivers's barely legible, diminutive script.

As suggested above, some of the shell rings collected by Hocart are accompanied by extensive biographical histories associating particular artefacts with named ancestors and places. A good example of this is shown in Figure 8.1, a *riko* or sacred clam-shell ring. The field note page referenced on the artefact contains the following information:

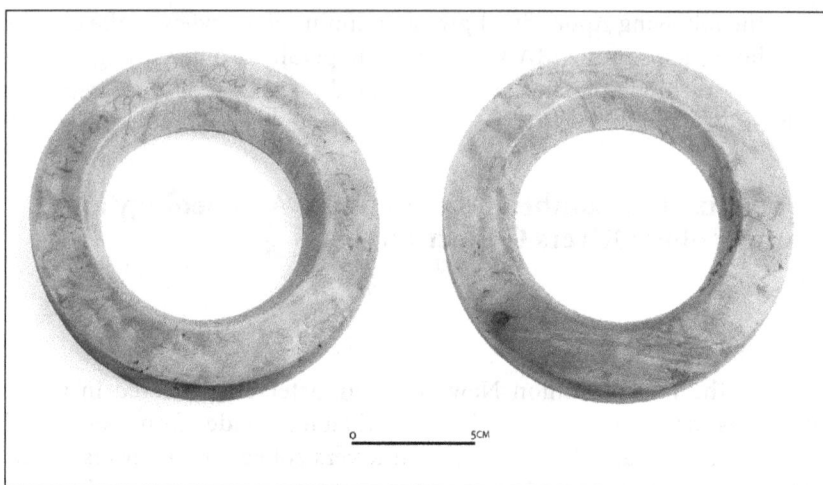

Figure 8.1: A sacred *bakiha* shell ring collected by Hocart on Simbo (MAA z.149). The pencilled writing on the ring reads 'Riko: Tonggo Kela H.1320 fm. Lungga'.

Riko. Ngana, Ale. [two informant's names, given in short form]. Made in Kela big mountain in Lungga [Ranongga]; man of Kela took it & went to Lauru [Choiseul], put into tomoko & went to Lauru: they fought in one place in Lauru; one man in Lauru took it; finish in Lauru went to Vaghena, finish long Vaghena came to Lungga; from Lungga to Nduke [Kolombangara]. Man of Nduke he said he no belong me & gave it back & it returned to Lungga. It came down to Ngana. Name of riko = tonggo kela. Ria Kamerani [people of the old days/tamasa, see Hocart 1922: 296] made it: but then he added tamasa. Ngana's mama [father] (= tamanggu) left it to Ngana. Children say mama, says Ale, can't talk good. Was kept in house. Ngana's father = Rani. There is a tamasa pa Ovana.[9]

Other valuables in the collection include two fragments of large fret-worked clam-shell plaques known as *barava* or *porobatuna*, collected on Vella Lavella and in Munda, New Georgia; and nine sperm whale teeth collected by Hocart on Simbo. A shell ring mounted and embellished with beadwork to be worn on the chest (known as *bakiha rapoto* in Roviana) may have been collected by the Simbo trader Fred Green and sent to Rivers after fieldwork – it was accessioned during 1911, and Green mentions sending one of these in a letter to Rivers dated November 1910.[10]

Charms

Three small charms consisting of a small woven bag holding a relic (usually a tooth or the hair of an ancestor) have variable provenance – two were clearly collected on Simbo, with one noted as having been made by Rembo (a key Simbo informant), whilst the third has a late accession number and may be part of a small collection of Isabel provenanced material sent to Rivers by an unknown donor. Usually referred to in the New Georgia group as *liqomo*, these charms would be tied to a fighting shield and carried into battle, offering various forms of protection and enhanced skill. Better documented is the weather charm sold to Hocart by Hiro, and described at length in the quote above (see Figure 8.2). Formally the artefact belongs to a class of charms common in the New Georgia region, composed of a central stave of wood upon which *Conus* rings, *Terebra* shells, clam-shell plaques and other relics are lashed. The wood serves as a mount for the charm, enabling it to be stood up at a shrine or in a canoe during journeys (see Hocart 1931: 309–10), although in this case the artefact has been miniaturised enabling it to be mounted on a shield.

0   5CM

Figure 8.2: Weather charm from Simbo, sold by Hiro to Hocart (MAA z.338).

Personal Ornament and Dress

Various items of dress or personal ornament were collected during visits to several islands in the New Georgia group, though often the collection location is occluded by the practice of recording the place items were made rather than acquired. Such items include hair combs of several types (some from New Georgia, others of apparently Bougainville Straits style), plaited plant-fibre arm and leg bands, waist belts or girdles, sun visors, pearl-shell pendants and other shell necklaces. Very few of these items have any information recorded detailing who collected them, though a few small shell pendants from Vella Lavella have local names written on them in Rivers's handwriting.

We can include within this class of objects a group of items related to the practice of artificially blackening the teeth. Most of these consist of containers used to hold a mixture of geological material, oil and *Terminalia* leaf. Of particular interest are four dwarf coconut containers (Figure 8.3), decorated with a variety of incised designs, described in Hocart's fieldnotes as being used for this purpose – they have a chalky material and leaves stuffed inside.[11] Known as *nggeva*, these are particularly rare items, with none having been previously documented. Amongst Rivers's surviving papers in Cambridge University Library is a sheet with pen-and-ink

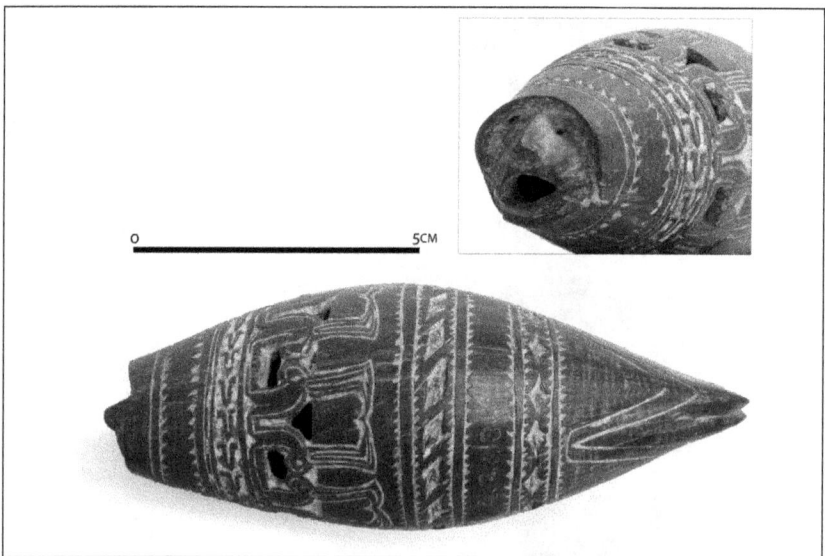

Figure 8.3: Side view, and end detail (inset), of an incised coconut container, *nggeva* (MAA z.243c). This item is described by Hocart in his fieldnotes: it was made by 'Waghru the son of Kundakolo', a Simbo informant, and was acquired in Karivara district.[12]

drawings of these objects, either commissioned by Rivers or drawn by him.[13] One coconut container was collected by Rivers (a reference to page 387 in his fieldnotes is written on a slip of paper stuffed inside the object), but the others are attributable to Hocart, who documents that one was made by the son of Kundakolo, an important Simbo informant.

Rivers sent some of the material inside the coconut containers to a geologist for categorisation, who, apparently bemused at Rivers's ethno-geology, replied that he could not see how the 'basalt and pyroxene-andesite' came to be of use in teeth-blackening, or that 'chemical analysis would throw any more light on the matter'.[14] He obviously missed the point – Rivers's intention was very likely to establish a baseline characterisation so that comparisons could be made with other cultural groups who also practised teeth blackening, thus enabling the tracing of diffusion patterns and so on.

Barkcloth

Twenty-four rolled pieces of barkcloth and one barkcloth beater, from Simbo and Roviana, are present in the collection. Some of these are plain and used in local forms of loincloth covering, but others are extensively decorated with blue/black painted motifs. Hocart's fieldnotes contain descriptions of some of these designs as related by informants, and the names of the women responsible for making them. Some of the MAA photographs of the decorated cloths have appeared in Richards and Roga (2005: 40–43).

Canoe Parts

A single canoe prow figurehead of a type known as *nguzunguzu* (or *muzumuzu, toto isu* in regional languages) is present in the collection. Page number references to Hocart's fieldnotes are associated with the object, but the pages in question are missing from the archives. These are very common artefacts in museum collections and much has been written about them (Waite 1999). The example collected by Hocart is well preserved and finely detailed, with remnants of coloured paint used around the mouth and top of the head easily visible (Figure 8.4).

Rarer are three spirit images carved in wood, made to sit atop the high curved prow of a war canoe (that is, finials). Two of these are anthropomorphic figures in Janus arrangement – one in the conventional prognathic style of spirit images in the New Georgia region, the other rendered more naturalistically. The former is almost identical to an item in the British Museum recorded as being donated by Hocart and provenanced to Roviana.[15] It is likely that this was considered a duplicate and so redistributed during curation. The more naturalistic example (Figure 8.5) is likely a piece carved for sale – an early form of tourist art. It lacks a mode of attachment at its base for affixing it to the canoe prow, and naturalistic depiction is typical of non-ritual imagery during this period (cf. Somerville 1897: 378).

The third canoe prow finial is of a single crouched figure with a prognathic head merging into a frigate bird form – characteristic of images of the spirit *Kesoko*. Hocart describes this item in his fieldnotes, in a sequence of pages written on Vella Lavella in the Njurio region. He describes the artefact as being called *Nggalana* in the local language, and that it is the same as *Kesoko*.[16]

Other canoe parts include a selection of nautilus-shell inlay motifs, nine mounted on a card for display, and eighty strung together for convenience. These were used to decorate war canoes, being set into black *Parinarium* nut paste coating the outer surface of plank-built canoes. The provenance information for these items has been lost during display and subsequent re-boxing for storage.

0   5CM

Figure 8.4: Canoe prow figurehead, *nguzunguzu* (MAA z.224).

Figure 8.5: Canoe prow finial, *beku* (MAA z.226).

Weapons

Several bows, arrows and wooden clubs are attributed to the Rivers Collection, but the curatorial documentation surrounding these objects is currently poor and somewhat contradictory. Several have not yet been located in the collection, and others have conflicting accession numbers. It is likely that this is an effect of objects having been used for displays then returned to storage.

Better documented is a set of wicker shields collected by Hocart on Simbo and in Roviana. Two are recorded as having been collected in Munda but transported from Choiseul, where they were made. Two shields have Hocart's handwriting in pencil on their surface, documenting the place of collection, 'Eddystone', but are completely wrapped in pandanus leaves. This was a form of packaging used to transport trade goods between regions – wicker shields being a specialist product of north New Georgia. Again the practice of recording both place of collection and place of manufacture creates a map of regional relationships. Packaged shields are rare in museum collections, with collectors and curators usually focusing on items as archetypes typifying regional styles rather than modes of transport and trade. The fact that Hocart collected packaged shields and wrote the place of acquisition on the packaging without removing it suggests, again, an attention to ethnographic detail and sensitivity to provenance in terms of how social networks connect.

Trade Items

Hocart's interest in trade networks and regional relationships, as reflected in his collections of shell rings, packaged shields and so on, is also expressed in his collection of items ready to be taken on trade expeditions. The best examples of this are two cylindrical parcels made to contain dried *Canarium* nuts (the collected items are empty). Known as *boboro*, the cylinders are made from *sinu* leaf wrapping, the whole being bound together with vine and attached to a carry handle. Nuts were a crucial part of the economics of Simbo, being the primary export item taken to Roviana and elsewhere, and thus the main means of acquiring shell-ring valuables and other goods. These parcels are described by Hocart, though he notes the form of packaging was 'rare in Eddystone, and the technique appears to belong to Vellalavella, two dummies were made for us by a man of Vellalavella' (Hocart 1922: 302).

Lime Containers and Pestles

Numerous bamboo lime containers from the New Georgia region, Isabel and elsewhere are present in the Rivers Collection. Mostly these have little documentation, but appear to have been primarily collected by Rivers, perhaps as part of a comparative study of the decorative motifs incised upon the exterior surface. One object, collected on Ranongga, has a series

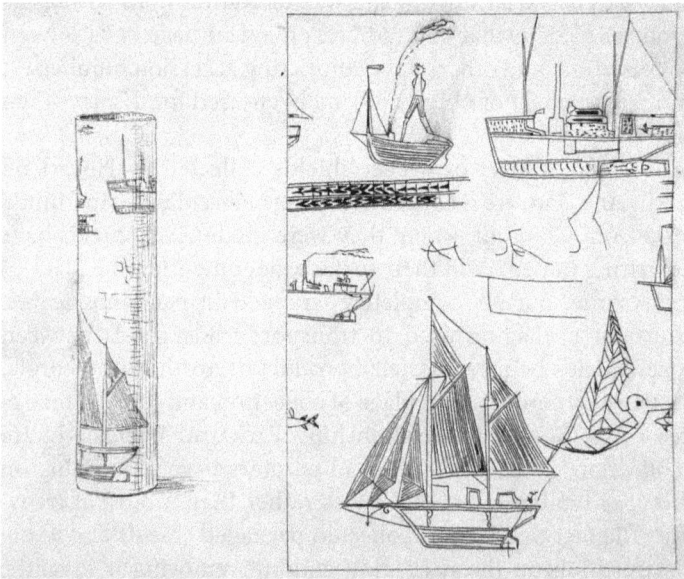

Figure 8.6: Drawing of lime container collected by Rivers; the drawing was either made or commissioned by Rivers (MAA 2010.440.tif).

of depictions of European ships and boats, in a kind of 'x-ray style' (that is, with internal cabins, engines and so forth shown) that apparently captured Rivers's interest – a pen and ink drawing of the designs was made, and this survives in the Cambridge University Library (Figure 8.6). A single lime pestle was also collected by Hocart.

Fishing Equipment

Fishing gear includes numerous nets, wooden floats, traps and hooks of various types. Many of the specific items collected illustrate descriptions provided in Hocart's paper on fishing techniques deployed on Simbo (Hocart 1937), and as such have very detailed contextual information, tying particular objects to species of fish, and methods of capture.

Within this category we can include a group of bamboo water scoops (*pio*), which superficially look similar to lime containers (and have been mixed with these by curators). These are finely incised with common regional motifs focusing on frigate birds and bonito fishing (Figure 8.7).

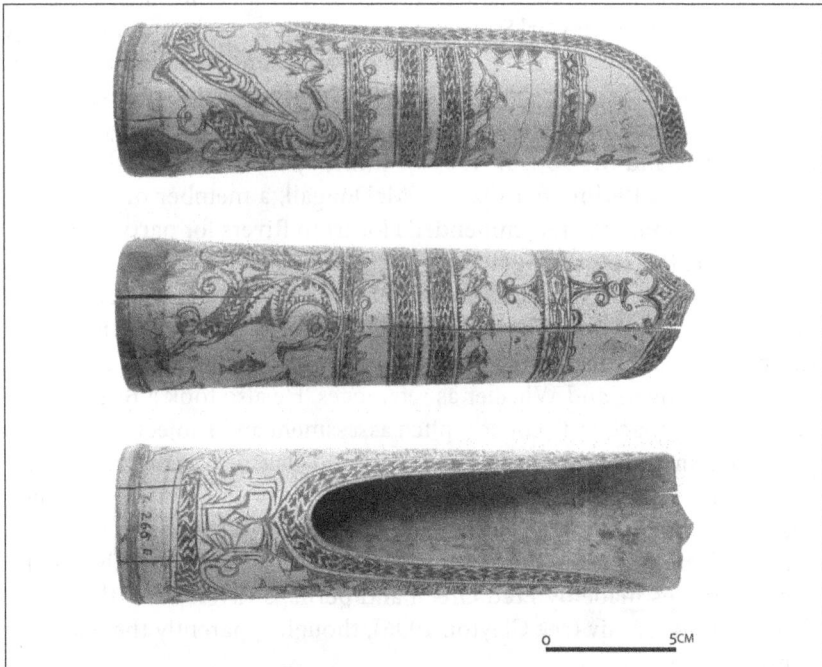

Figure 8.7: Bamboo water scoop, *pio*. Has 'R.374' pencilled on object referring to a page in Rivers's fieldnotes. This object was also drawn in pen and ink by Rivers (MAA z.265e).

The scoops were used to produce a sound that was thought to attract bonito schools, and are part of the rituals surrounding this form of fishing as described by Hocart (1935). Rivers also made drawings of these, and indeed some have pencilled references to pages in his fieldnotes written upon them.

Basketry

As noted above, Rivers made a study of the basketry techniques in use on Simbo – in fact it was one of the topics assigned him at the outset of field-work. There are twelve baskets and net bags from the New Georgia region in the collection, each illustrating different forms of basket and/or techniques of construction. Many were apparently collected by Rivers himself, though at least two were collected by Hocart and documented in his fieldnotes.

Musical Instruments

Musical instruments appear to have been of particular interest to Hocart, who, during his time studying psychology in Berlin (1906/7) also studied phenomenology under Carl Stumpf, an early instigator of ethnomusicology and originator of the Berlin Phonogramm-Archiv and musical instrument collection. Hocart's studies in psychology at Oxford included research on auditory perception, and he co-authored a paper with McDougall on the topic (Hocart and McDougall 1908) – this may have influenced his deci-sion to study in Berlin after Oxford. McDougall, a member of the Torres Strait Expedition, later recommended Hocart to Rivers for participation in the Percy Sladen Trust Expedition.

This background is reflected in the detailed notes Hocart took on music – his fieldnotes contain a record of local pitch classifications (which later transpired to be the names of flute fingering positions), using his own voice and those of Rivers and Wheeler as references. He also took a Boehm flute into the field for accurate concert pitch assessment and subject testing. His notes contain transcriptions of melodies and descriptions of how notes were produced from instruments, as well as the social context in which music was employed. Hocart also made sound recordings on wax cylinders and these were deposited in both the British Library Sound Archive (along with recordings made by Fred Green and perhaps Rivers) and the Berlin Phonogramm-Archiv (see Clayton 1996), though apparently the quality is highly variable.

The material culture collected perfectly correlates with these written notes and recordings, with the various instruments in question being collected in a variety of forms. Large 'bassoons' consisting of double lengths of bamboo blown to create polyphonic tones, and single flutes, are the most numerous musical instruments, though three Jew's harps and a conch-shell trumpet are also present.

Music was clearly one way Hocart engaged with local people, as referenced in a personal comment during a letter to Rivers written from Fiji:

> I met a Fijian in Suva who started talking Roviana [sic]; he told me my cook and brother was dead. A nice boy he was, and a precocious dandy, and eager to come to Fiji. I seriously thought of fatiguing him to have flute duets with him and keep a memorial of heathen Roviana but the financial difficulty was great besides possible legal ones.[17]

Food Preparation

Common domestic items were collected on most of the islands visited by Hocart and Rivers. Stone nut hammers, wooden mortars and stone pestles, as well as shell spoons and scrapers used in the processing of coconut and root crops, are present in the collection. However, there are few notes accompanying this class of object, perhaps reflecting the fact that both ethnographers' efforts were focused on matters other than food production. Indeed, several of the artefacts in this class are related to the ritual use of food, or are special purpose objects, somewhat different from items used during day-to-day food production and consumption.

Tools

The acquisition of tools was apparently guided by a desire to comprehensively document certain areas of production related to social institutions that captured the ethnographic interest of Hocart and Rivers. For example, four pump drills used in the production of shell valuables and the construction of sewn plank canoes were collected by Hocart, along with chert cores from which drill points were struck. Hocart and Rivers also made a study of house construction, and consequently there is a thatching tool in the collection.

A somewhat different case is presented by adzes. Rivers collected thirty-seven shell and stone adzes – his handwriting is the only script occurring in association with these artefacts. Such adzes were no longer in use by 1908 and may have been gathered up by local people when working gardens and so on. Many are heavily weathered, suggesting environmental exposure. It is likely that these were acquired as historical indices for comparative purposes, rather than for study of contemporary practice. As such they are part of Rivers's wider project of anthropological enquiry.

There are more generic items present in the collection, perhaps collected due to their apparent novelty – such as wood rasps made from stingray skin stretched over a wooden paddle. Torches made of resin wrapped in leaves are another example. On the other hand, there are also mundane items like sharpening stones – although these items are from Vella Lavella and have documentation associated with them giving Bilua-Simbo-English word equivalences, making the objects a kind of anchor for linguistic notes.

Botanical

Several disparate specimens of local plant material are present in the collection. One such example is a brown leaf bundle wrapped in red cloth, with a note from Hocart recording that it is 'Hambi Simbo', a plant apparently used for ritual purposes. Other items include fibres used to make arm bands worn during celebratory feasts (such as at the return of a headhunting party).

After returning to England, Rivers sent plant remains to the Royal Botanical Gardens at Kew for identification. Some were sent to him after fieldwork by Fred Green, but others were clearly collected during the Percy Sladen Trust Expedition proper. Although it is possible Rivers was acting to help establish biological reference collections, the majority of these specimens, like the artefacts, were requested because they related to specific charms, legends or practices in which he was himself interested (such as spells concerned with contraception and abortion; see Bayliss-Smith, this volume). Collecting flora and fauna associated with charms and ritual was a means of systematically reporting Latin species names in addition to indigenous terminology. But crucially, scientific identification enabled comparison across linguistic and cultural boundaries in order to draw connections and postulate relationships based on similarities in the way particular specimens were used.

Models and Drawings

The commission and collection of model versions of large cumbersome artefacts was an already established practice among European travellers by the time of Rivers's and Hocart's fieldwork. In his paper on canoes and bonito fishing, Hocart notes that 'Roviana canoes are to be seen in museums. A model made under our eyes in Eddystone has been deposited in the Cambridge Museum of Ethnology' (Hocart 1935: 97). Hocart took extensive notes on canoe making in the field, but the model (about 1.2 metres long), accurate in all its details, is partially completed with the caulking left unfinished, thus providing a view of the process of manufacture rather than simply the end result. Similarly, a wooden food trough, apparently collected by Rivers, is largely unpainted and unfinished but serves as a guide to basic form and decorative conventions.

A much stranger artefact is catalogued as a model skull house, made by Kundakolo and acquired by Rivers. It is constructed of two small pieces of Bristol packing crate nailed together and painted. The design is vaguely reminiscent of photographed skull houses, but is not much use as a guide to form or construction technique. Hocart did commission a small version of a wooden skull house, and photographed this as it was made (see Hocart 1922: figures 2 and 3), but the final object is not in the MAA collection, suggesting it was not transported.

These miniatures are the result of collusion between the ethnographers and local people, ending in a new kind of production. Similarly, Hocart also collected indigenous drawings of the legends and rituals he was recording.[18] Of particular note are six drawings made by Ango of Roviana in pencil on large sheets of heavy paper.[19] Hocart also encouraged depictions of modes of ritual ornamentation (Hocart 1931: 319) and the performance of ceremonies (Hocart 1931: 311). Like the models, these drawings are a new kind of artefact, a hybrid form emerging from a European mode of two-dimensional depiction (pencil and paper) and New Georgian agency and perceptions. Hocart was both cause and recipient of these artefacts – we might say that he elicited them for his own ends. But they also objectify the relationship between the ethnographer and his informants – they have dual origins, and index a new kind of social interaction in the region.

Miscellaneous

Some artefacts are difficult to fit within the previous categories, but deserve to be mentioned here.

Five limpet shells sent by Fred Green are referenced in the letter cited above: 'I have enclosed it [sic] one of the boxes the shells used for cutting to [sic] cord at birth you have a note about'.[20]

Several decorated pieces of wood, with unknown function or purpose, are present in the collection. This includes a wooden ornament carved in relief resembling a European mediaeval poppy-head finial. The flat reverse is decorated with an indigenous incised design infilled with lime. Another small rectangular flat piece of wood is incised with local motifs and is drawn and described in the early pages of Hocart's fieldnotes – he possibly used it to elicit local names for design motifs.

Photographs

It is difficult to give an overview of the photographic collection in a few paragraphs because it is rich and diverse. Nevertheless, we can group the images into four broad categories.

Portraits

Perhaps half the photographs are posed portraits of local people, taken mostly on Simbo. At first glance these conform to the conventions of anthropometric photography. Many are head-and-shoulder portraits of a sitting subject, taken in frontal and profile view. A light coloured canvas backdrop is draped behind the subject creating an ad hoc studio, isolating the person from their social, cultural and environmental context. These photographs were very likely taken during genealogical and anthropometric recording sessions. But cracks emerge upon closer inspection. Perhaps because Rivers made such detailed anthropometric measurements, many of the photographs lack a scale, and when one is present it is roughly drawn on the canvas, varying in placement and size. The people in the

Figure 8.8: Portraits of Njiruviri – right: quarter plate (MAA N.59587.WHR); left: broken half plate, standing in full ceremonial dress at Narovo bay foreshore with unknown male (MAA P.56032.ACH2). (By permission of the Cambridge Museum of Archaeology and Anthropology.)

photographs are not posed rigidly or particularly formally – they have relaxed into their own positions; some look directly into the lens, others look down or squint at the sun. Some are apparently simply presenting themselves in their finery to be photographed, though this is particularly the case with full length portraits.

Hocart recorded a few notes on local attitudes to photography: 'They liked to recognize someone, & when news spread abroad of Njiruviri's picture in 'The discovery of the Solomons' people were continually coming to see it. For portraits they had little interest & liked full length figures. They declared our half plate camera was good but the quarter plate was no good & it was with trouble that Njiruviri was induced to be photographed with the latter'.[21] The resulting head-and-shoulder and full-length portraits of Njiruviri (Figure 8.8) are made all the more interesting given this knowledge. In subtle ways, local people started to capture elements of the way they were depicted. It is important to note that almost none of the people in the photographs are anonymous – individual names are recorded on the glass-plate negative, its sleeve, and on the back of prints (as in Figure 8.9). These names can be linked directly to genealogies, and to texts describing ritual knowledge and so on. In effect, the images contribute to an almost biographical archive of the people of the day.

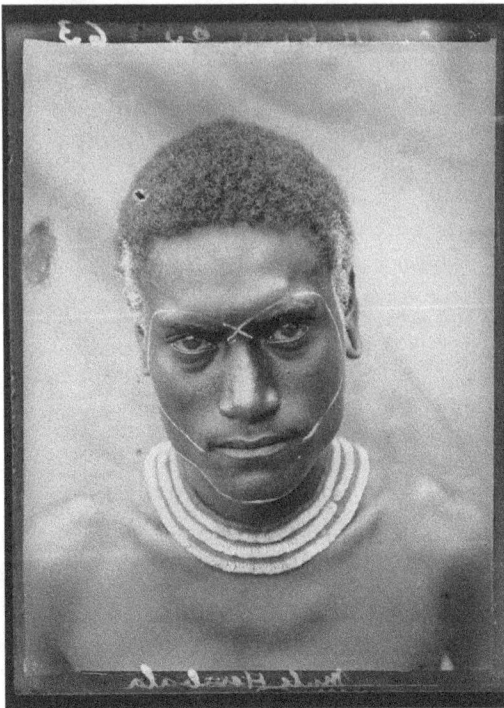

Figure 8.9: Portrait of Mule Hembala (MAA N.59482. WHR). On page 80 of Hocart's fieldnotes there is an annotated drawing of lime face paint as worn by 'Hembala son of Djoko', obviously supplementing this photograph and a corresponding profile view. Page 24 of the fieldnotes describes how Hembala applied lime to Hocart's own face.[22] (By permission of the Cambridge Museum of Archaeology and Anthropology.)

Other portraits are posed demonstrations of technique – such as the way a bassoon was blown, a shell ring drilled or barkcloth beaten (Figure 8.10). But images of people in more natural settings are also present, and several of these appear to be the result of fortuitous encounters, or are images taken during guided walks to particular sites.

Ritual Sites

Numerous photos of shrines were taken, representing the most complete archive of the variety of ritual sites during the period. Many of these are not successful images when printed at small scales, but examination of the glass-plate negatives reveals an enormous amount of useful detail, showing artefacts present, aromatic plants and shrine construction techniques and so on. In each case the location, function and name of the shrine is recorded. These can usually be linked directly to Hocart's published accounts of particular shrines. Shrines are usually presented without any people present, but at two locations there is a sequence of images showing the activities of a shrine attendant pounding puddings and making burnt offerings to the spirits. These are the only known images of such activities.

Figure 8.10: Pilu making barkcloth, Simbo (MAA N.59552.WHR). (By permission of the Cambridge Museum of Archaeology and Anthropology.)

Houses

Hocart and Rivers collaborated on the documentation of house-building techniques, though only Hocart's unpublished record is available.[23] This describes the occasion of a house-raising on Simbo in great detail, and in the margins of this document numbers referring to photographs have been added by hand. These correspond to negative plate numbers, and the relevant images are part of a long sequence showing all stages of the work. The photographer moves around the scene and accompanies the men during their work breaks, and we can effectively follow this path, giving a kind of documentary motion to the images.

Hocart then took this information in a comparative direction, taking photographs of numerous structures during his travels throughout Simbo, but also to Roviana and Vella Lavella. The annotations note differences in roof construction and awning style, and sometimes note who the house belongs to. Interior scenes are rare, though a notable exception is an image of a long decorated food trough hung up inside a canoe house in Roviana.

Other Scenes

Miscellaneous photographs were taken of outdoor meeting places, landscape features and village areas. The foreshore at Narovo bay is seen in several photos, and the hot springs and steaming soils of certain parts of Simbo were photographed on visits. There is a photograph of a man perched atop a fishing frame, and a sequence of images of men constructing a platform used to climb a nut tree during harvest season.

More careful research will be required to piece together whether both Rivers and Hocart were taking photographs and, if so, who created which images. Hocart's handwriting on all the glass-plate negatives is perhaps indicative that he was mostly responsible, but this may simply have been due to legibility issues with Rivers's handwriting. We can certainly assume with safety that the images taken in Roviana are Hocart's. Each photograph is numbered, and this numbering is sequential; thus it should be possible to reconstruct a timeline for the images, but this too will require further work.

Acknowledgements

I would like to thank the staff of the University of Cambridge Museum of Archaeology and Anthropology for their help during my 2012 visit. In particular, Jocelyne Dudding and Rachel Hand provided crucial assistance with the collections, and Anita Herle shared key information about Rivers.

Heather Donoghue was the perfect research assistant and collaborator. I thank Nicholas Thomas for suggesting my name to the editors for this chapter. Financial support for the research was provided by the University of Otago.

Notes

1. Gerald C. Wheeler accompanied Rivers and Hocart to the Solomon Islands and spent some time with them on Simbo before departing to conduct research in the Shortland Islands (see Hviding and Berg, this volume). His artefact collections are held at the British Museum, but have not been studied. A review of the British Museum online catalogue suggests Wheeler donated about forty-five items collected on Simbo.

2. Haddon also had a role in motivating the Percy Sladen Trust Expedition. In 1906, Haddon had spelled out a grandiose scheme to purchase a boat and conduct a long-term study of Melanesia (via a combination of survey and intensive fieldwork) with a team of anthropologists and other scientists. Notably he identified the transition from 'mother right' to 'father right' as being of particular interest, wishing to determine 'whether the passage has taken place spontaneously, or whether it is due to racial influences' (Haddon 1906: 157) – the very question that Rivers's 1908 expedition sought to address. In effect the Percy Sladen Trust Expedition was a shoe-string version of Haddon's proposal.

3. Green to Rivers, 16 November–2 December 1908, in Rivers, drafts of various articles, notes, drawings, correspondence, Turnbull Library, National Library of New Zealand, Wellington, Micro-MS-Coll-20–2621 (hereafter TL/R).

4. These are kept at the British Library National Sound Archive; see Clayton (1996: 74) and below.

5. See Urry (1972) for a history of this volume.

6. A striking passage occurs in an undated letter to Rivers (but which begins 'Re yours of 12/8/09') detailing edits to be made to draft versions of their planned books: 'I have been calling Mandegusu Eddystone for the sake of the vulgar who know none of its glories, glories which, alas, I am still sighing after, its unique profile, its reefs, its passages, its varied shore, the gliding canoes, the dense bush with its mysterious Skull houses & awful shrines of deities, & oh, those nuts & those Yamu'. Hocart to Rivers, n.d., Haddon Papers, Cambridge University Library, Cambridge (hereafter C/HP), env. 12081.

7. Hocart, Fieldnotes, unpublished manuscript, Turnbull Library, National Library of New Zealand, Wellington, p.504.

8. See Hocart, 'Trade & Money', unpublished manuscript, Turnbull Library, National Library of New Zealand, Wellington.

9. Hocart, Fieldnotes MS, p.1320.

10. Green to Rivers, 4 November 1910, TL/R.
11. See Hocart, Fieldnotes MS, p.53.
12. See Hocart, Fieldnotes MS, p.53.
13. Loose leaf drawing, C/HP, env. 12015.
14. Parker to Rivers, 29 July 1909, TL/R.
15. British Museum, registration number: Oc1914,-.311.
16. Hocart, Fieldnotes MS, p.814.
17. Hocart to Rivers, 27 September 1912, C/HP, env. 12019.
18. The practice of encouraging and collecting indigenous drawings had been pioneered by Rivers and Haddon during the Torres Strait Expedition.
19. See Hviding (this volume) for one of these drawings.
20. Green to Rivers, 16 November–2 December 1908, TL/R.
21. Hocart, 'Notes on Character &c.', unpublished manuscript, Turnbull Library, National Library of New Zealand, Wellington, p.3.
22. See Hocart, Fieldnotes MS, pp.80 and 24 respectively.
23. See Hocart, 'The House', unpublished manuscript, Turnbull Library, National Library of New Zealand, Wellington.

References

BAAS 1912. *Notes and Queries on Anthropology*, 4th edn. London: Royal Anthropological Institute.

Clayton, M. 1996. 'Ethnographic Wax Cylinders at the British Library National Sound Archive: A Brief History and Description of the Collection', *British Journal of Ethnomusicology* 5: 67–92.

Edwards, E. 2000. 'Surveying Culture: Photography, Collecting and Material Culture in British New Guinea, 1898', in *Hunting the Gatherers: Ethnographic Collectors, Agents and Agency in Melanesia, 1870s–1930s*, M. O'Hanlon and R.L. Welsch (eds), 103–26. Oxford: Berghahn.

Gosden, C., and C. Knowles 2001. *Collecting Colonialism: Material Culture and Colonial Change*. Oxford: Berg.

Haddon, A.C. 1906. 'A Plea for the Investigation of Biological and Anthropological Distributions in Melanesia', *Geographical Journal* 28: 155–59.

Herle, A. 1998. 'The Life-histories of Objects: Collections of the Cambridge Anthropological Expedition to the Torres Strait', in *Cambridge and the Torres Strait: Centenary Essays on the 1898 Anthropological Expedition*, A. Herle and S. Rouse (eds), 77–105. Cambridge: Cambridge University Press.

Herle, A., and S. Rouse (eds) 1998. *Cambridge and the Torres Strait: Centenary Essays on the 1898 Anthropological Expedition*. Cambridge: Cambridge University Press.

Hocart, A.M. 1922. 'The Cult of the Dead in Eddystone of the Solomons', *Journal of the Royal Anthropological Institute* 52: 71–117, 259–305.

_____ 1925. 'Medicine and Witchcraft in Eddystone of the Solomon Islands', *Journal of the Royal Anthropological Institute* 55: 229–70.

_____ 1931. 'Warfare in Eddystone of the Solomon Islands', *Journal of the Royal Anthropological Institute* 61: 301–24.

_____ 1935. 'The Canoe and the Bonito in Eddystone Island', *Journal of the Royal Anthropological Institute* 65: 97–111.

_____ 1937. 'Fishing in Eddystone Island', *Journal of the Royal Anthropological Institute* 67: 33–41.

Hocart, A.M., and W. McDougall 1908. 'Some Data for a Theory of the Auditory Perception of Direction', *British Journal of Psychology* 2: 386–405.

Langham, I. 1981. *The Building of British Social Anthropology*. Dordrecht: Springer.

O'Brien, A. 2011. 'Collecting the Solomon Islands: Colonial Encounters and Indigenous Experiences in the Solomon Island Collections of Charles Morris Woodford and Arthur Mahaffy (1886–1915)', PhD diss. Norwich: University of East Anglia.

O'Hanlon, M., and R.L. Welsch (eds) 2000. *Hunting the Gatherers: Ethnographic Collectors, Agents and Agency in Melanesia, 1870s–1930s*. Oxford: Berghahn.

Pinney, C. 2011. *Photography and Anthropology*. London: Reaktion Books.

Richards, R., and K. Roga 2005. *Not Quite Extinct: Melanesian bark cloth ('tapa') from Western Solomon Islands*. Wellington: Paremata Press.

Rivers, W.H.R. 1911. 'The Ethnological Analysis of Culture', *Science* 34: 385–97.

_____ 1912. 'Island-names in Melanesia', *Geographical Journal* 39: 458–64.

_____ 1914. *The History of Melanesian Society*, 2 vols. Cambridge: Cambridge University Press.

Rivers, W.H.R., and A.C. Haddon 1902. 'A Method of Recording String Figures and Tricks', *Man* 2: 146–53.

Rivers, W.H.R., and A. Hingston-Quiggin 1910. 'The Solomon Island Basket', *Man* 10: 161–63.

Somerville, H.B.T. 1897. 'Ethnographical Notes in New Georgia, Solomon Islands', *Journal of the Royal Anthropological Institute* 26: 357–413.

Stocking, G. 1995. *After Tylor: British Social Anthropology, 1888–1951*. Madison: University of Wisconsin Press.

Thomas, T. 2009. 'Topogenic Forms in New Georgia, Solomon Islands', *Sites: A Journal of Social Anthropology and Cultural Studies* 6: 92–118.

Urry, J. 1972. '"Notes and Queries on Anthropology" and the Development of Field Methods in British Anthropology, 1870–1920', *Proceedings of the Royal Anthropological Institute* 1972: 45–57.

Waite, D. 1984. 'The H.B.T. Somerville Collection of Artefacts from the Solomon Islands', in *The General's Gift: A Celebration of the Pitt-Rivers Museum Centenary, 1884–1984*, B.A.L. Cranstone and S. Seidenberg (eds), 41–52. Oxford: JASO Occasional Papers, 3.

_____ 1999. 'Toto Isu (Nguzunguzu) War Canoe Prow Figureheads from the Western District, Solomon Islands', *World of Tribal Arts*, Spring, 82–97.

_____ 2000. 'Notes and Queries, Science, and "Curios": Lieutenant Boyle Somerville's Ethnographic Collecting in the Solomon Islands, 1893–1895', *Journal of the Anthropological Society of Oxford* 31: 277–308.

Appendix 1

Unpublished Reports by W.H.R. Rivers to the Trustees of the Percy Sladen Memorial Trust Fund

◆●◆

Transcribed by Tim Bayliss-Smith

The following materials have been transcribed from the archives of the Percy Sladen Memorial Fund, held by the Linnean Society, Piccadilly, London. Appendix 1.1 is a three-page typewritten letter by Rivers to A.W. Kappel, secretary to the trustees of the Percy Sladen Memorial Trust, sent from Simbo, British Solomon Islands Protectorate, in 1908. Appendix 1.2 is a three-page typewritten letter by Rivers to the trustees of the Trust, sent from St John's College, Cambridge, England, in 1909. Appendix 1.3 is a five-page typewritten report accompanied by a handwritten letter from Rivers the trustees of the Trust, sent from St John's College, Cambridge, also written in 1909. The contributors to *The Ethnographic Experiment* are collectively very grateful to Mrs. Gina Douglas, Archivist at the Linnean Society of London, for access to the papers of the Percy Sladen Memorial Trust which the Linnean Society holds; and to the current Trustees for permission to reprint the reports of W.H.R. Rivers.

In the transcriptions that follow all of Rivers's original orthography has been retained. His spelling of place-names in particular does not always conform to modern usage.

Appendix 1.1

Simbo,
June 14, 1908
A.W. Kappel, Esq.,
Sec. to Trustees,
Percy Sladen Memorial Trust

Dear Sir,

Will you please lay before the trustees the following Report of the progress of the expedition up to the present time?

I first spent a month in the Hawaian islands, where I found the opportunities for anthropological work almost gone, but was able to collect a fair amount of material on kinship and marriage which I have embodied in a paper of which I have sent a copy to Dr Haddon. I then had a month in Fiji, passed almost entirely in the interior of the island of Viti Levu. There I was able to collect a large amount of new material, chiefly on kinship and totemism, the chief results of which I have recorded in two papers also sent to Dr Haddon. Only a few days were spent in Samoa and the Tongan islands, but enough to get a little work done. I reached Auckland on March 29 and left on April 4th on the Southern Cross, spending the following five weeks in the New Hebrides, Banks and Torres islands, the Santa Cruz islands and the Eastern Solomons. Though only a short time could be spent in each island at which we called, I was able to supplement the material collected with information given by natives who were travelling on the steamer and owing to the help of many of the missionaries who were travelling on the Southern Cross I was able to collect a large amount of material. I was able to work out about a dozen kinship systems, and to collect many quite new facts, especially from the islands of Mota and Raga.

On May 11th I was joined at Tulagi by Mr Hocart for whom the Trust have made the additional grant, and also by Mr Wheeler who has joined the expedition. Acting on the advice of Mr Woodward, the Resident Commissioner, I have now come with them to the island of Simbo or Narovo, where we have now been settled for a month. Circumstances have not been very favourable so far: the south-east season has been very late in setting in and in consequence we have had a great deal of rain; the people are very reticent and were at first very suspicious; the whole district is very unsettled, and all three members of the expedition have already had fever, but in spite of this we have done very well. The social organisation has been worked out to a great extent, though there is still much detail to fill in; we have collected a large amount of physical, technological and linguistic material and during the last week, we have begun to make a good deal of progress in the investigation of magic and religion, and the prospects for future work here now look very hopeful.

My present plans are to spend another two or three months with Simbo as our head-quarters, making during this time visits to the adjacent islands of Ranonga and Vella Lavella. After this I propose to return to the Eastern Solomons to continue the work I have already begun there, while Mr Hocart will probably go to the Shortland islands and other islands of the Bougainville Straits.

On the way home I hope to spend two or three weeks in the island of Mota in the Banks group, where I have been able to make arrangements to see some important ceremonies which are still being performed in those islands, ceremonies which were almost certainly practiced at one time in the Solomons, though they have now disappeared.

You will be glad to hear that Mr Hocart has fully justified all that was said in his favour. He is doing excellent work and gets on splendidly with the natives and I am confident that we have gained a most valuable recruit for anthropological research. I hope to be able to send a further report of good progress before too long and remain,

Yours faithfully,

W.H.R. Rivers

Appendix 1.2

St John's College,
Cambridge
Mar. 28, 1909

Dear Sirs,

I beg to present a second report on the work of the expedition to the Solomon Islands. My last report was written when we had been a few weeks on the island of Simbo in the Western Solomons. We stayed there till the end of August, altogether four and a half months and obtained a very complete account of the people. I then chartered a schooner and Mr Hocart and I spent a month visiting various places in the island of Vella Lavella where we found a culture resembling that of Simbo but of a simpler form and we were able in a month to obtain a fairly full account of the people. At the end of September I left the Western Solomons and, after a short time in the eastern part of the group, left on the Southern Cross and spent nearly six weeks on board travelling through Melanesia and continuing the work I had been doing on my way to the Solomons.

When I left Mr Hocart he went to Rubiana where he stayed for about two months and then returned to Simbo to clear up many points which had been raised by our later work in Vella Lavella and Rubiana. Then Mr Hocart took an opportunity which presented of visiting the island of Kulambangara after which he left for Fiji where he has taken a Government post which will give him opportunities of continuing anthropological work. Both Rubiana and Kulambangara were found to belong to the same culture as Simbo though specialised in different directions, and the experience here and in Vella Lavella showed that we had been right in our choice of Simbo as the chief field of our work, for it had been less influenced and was in a more suitable condition for anthropological work than the rest of the district.

As regards the form of the publication of the work of the expedition there are two alternatives; one to bring out the whole of the work in the form of Reports; the other to publish different parts in the form of separate books. We have so much material that it would probably not be possible to find a publisher for the Reports as a whole without making a contribution towards expenses while the size and cost of such a production would limit its circulation very greatly. I am therefore in favour of the second alternative and, if the Trustees offer no objection, hope to adopt it.

In this case the work of the expedition will probably be published in the following forms:

A book by Mr Hocart and myself on "The Western Solomon Islands", probably in two volumes;

A book by myself on "Kinship in Oceania";

A book containing numerous studies, chiefly from South Melanesia, which will probably be published in conjunction with the Rev. W.J. Durrad of the Melanesian Mission.

If, as is probable, there will not be room for the linguistic material in the book on the Western Solomons, this would be published separately by Mr Hocart.

The success of the work in the Solomons is largely due to Mr Hocart who has turned out to be an admirable investigator. He has sent me reports of his work after I had left and they show that this is very valuable and important. He has now taken a post in Fiji in which it is understood that he shall carry out anthropological work and there is little doubt that he will devote his life to work of this kind, a career of which the grant made to him by the Trustees will have furnished the starting point.

I am very greatly indebted to the Bishop of Melanesia for allowing me to travel on the Southern Cross. This enabled me to visit many places and to do much work which would otherwise have been impossible without a very great expenditure of money and I made a donation of £25 to the funds of the Mission in the name of the Trustees in addition to one from myself. Much help was given by various members of the Mission, especially the Rev. W.J. Durrad and the Rev. C.E. Fox. The expedition also owes much to the help of

Government officials, and especially of Sir Everard im Thurn and Mr Joske in Fiji and Mr Woodford in the Solomons.

I am glad of this opportunity of expressing my thanks to the Trustees for having by their grant made it possible for me to carry out the work of the expedition, the full results of which I hope to send as soon as they are published.

Yours faithfully,

W.H.R. Rivers

Appendix 1.3

St John's College,
Cambridge
May 4 [1909]

Dear Mr Kappel,

Here is my supplementary report. It is, I am afraid, not very full but it is very difficult to summarise the large mass of material on much of which I have not yet been able to work.

Yours sincerely,

W.H.R. Rivers

THE WESTERN SOLOMONS (The material obtained in the Western Solomons has been largely added to by Mr Hocart since I left those islands and only the briefest account of this has been received. The account of the work here must therefore be regarded as provisional)

Physical conditions. The people present a very difficult problem in physical anthropology for they are exceptionally black, probably the blackest of Melanesians, and yet their features are far less Negroid than the inhabitants of many other islands who are much lighter in colour and their hair is less frizzly and often only curly. If it had not been for their colour one would have had little doubt that there had been some Polynesian mixture which undoubtedly occurs here and there throughout Melanesia.

One feature of the physical work was that in every case where a person was measured his pedigree was obtained, so that it is possible to tell how far there had been mixture with the inhabitants of other islands, and this turned out to have been especially important in Vella Lavella where there had been much mixture with the people of Choiseul who differ from them decidedly in physical appearance. A series of measurements taken without this precaution would have been entirely misleading.

Further the knowledge of the relationships of those measured to one another will, it is hoped, provide a large mass of material for the study of heredity. Again in the island of Simbo the whole population was measured, men, women and children, thus providing data for the study of physical characters at different ages and in the two sexes which have hitherto been almost completely neglected by physical anthropologists.

Sociology. The people of the Western Solomons were found to have a very high type of social organisation, and all the institutions usually regarded as characteristic of Melanesia, such as female descent, the dual organisation and the secret societies were found to be absent. There was no trace of a clan organisation nor of totemism. The system of kinship was of a simple kind, almost as simple as that of Polynesia, and marriage was regulated entirely by kinship. Descent was entirely in the male line and there was a singular absence of any customs which might be regarded as survivals of mother-right.

There was chieftainship and in Simbo and Vella Lavella the chiefs seemed to have no great powers, but Mr Hocart has found that there was a more decided differentiation between the chiefs and the ordinary people in Rubiana. Formerly the lives of the people were devoted very largely to warfare and head-hunting and the methods and the ceremonial connected with this was very fully investigated.

Religion and Magic. The religion was of a relatively high order with various classes of sacred or semi-sacred beings, each with their shrines and ritual, the latter being of a simple kind. Of these beings the most important are the spirits of the dead whose shrines are the skull-houses at which offerings of first fruits and other rites are carried out. There is much ceremonial in connection with the events which occur between death and the placing of the skull in its skull-house and very definite beliefs about the future life. Another important class is formed by beings connected with anything mysterious in the environment of the people and in this class are included various animals. Other classes of sacred beings are connected with gardens and fishing, each having its appropriate shrine at which offerings are made on certain occasions.

A very important feature of the life of the people is the institution of taboo which has assumed among them a very special form, and in the island of Simbo alone there are over sixty forms of taboo as a means of protecting property, each with its definite ritual and formula; and the breaking of the taboo has in each case its special supernatural consequence for which there are remedies having an interesting relation to the measures by means of which the taboo was imposed.

Part of the magic is of a highly developed kind depending not on the immediate efficacy of the charms used or on that of the magician, but on the action of beings whose action is evoked by means of formulae and ceremonial resembling that of the strictly religious rites. This branch of the study of the people will furnish an interesting example of one state of the relations of religion and magic. In addition there were also magical practices of the more usual kind, and an unusual abundance of charms of various kinds.

Technology. In this branch of anthropology we have accumulated a large amount of material on such subjects as cultivation, fishing, house-building, canoe-making, etc.

The relation of this culture to that of the rest of Melanesia and the relations of the differing cultures of the different islands of the district is an extremely difficult topic on which at present I would rather not express an opinion.

THE EASTERN SOLOMONS

Here all that was done was to investigate the social organisation and the laws regulating kinship and marriage. These are very different from those of the Western Solomons and the conditions are far from being the same throughout this part of the group. In one part there is female descent with a clan organisation and a special form of totemism, while in another there is male descent with regulation of marriage by kinship. The systems of kinship, in which there is much variety, are all of a simple kind and in some parts, especially in Ulawa and South Mala, they have a simplicity equal to that of Polynesia.

There is little doubt that we have in the Solomon Islands the highest development of Melanesian culture, and that in the western part this has advanced so far that the Melanesian characters have entirely disappeared.

OTHER PARTS OF MELANESIA AND POLYNESIA

In Southern Melanesia attention was paid chiefly to kinship and marriage, especially in the Banks' and Torres groups and in the island of Pentecost in the New Hebrides. In the last was discovered what is probably the most complex kinship system hitherto recorded and its complexities can be clearly traced to the influence of marriage regulations which are now extinct. The systems of the Banks' and Torres groups and numerous customs which in those islands regulate relations of kin to one another provide important evidence in favour of a past state of communism. In the Banks' an account was obtained of many features of the ritual of the secret societies which have not hitherto been recorded and various other new customs were obtained here and in the Torres group.

A full account was obtained of the culture of the island of Tikopia. The people of this island are almost certainly Tongan emigrants and in their present state they show a most interesting simplification of Polynesian culture and there is much reason to believe that this simple character is not the result of their isolation but that they are a Polynesian offshoot which separated from the parent stock at a time when the social organisation was much simpler and more primitive than so far as we know it is elsewhere.

In Fiji my time was devoted almost entirely to kinship and this resulted in the discovery in the interior of Viti Levu of a form of kinship with far more complicated characters than that of the coastal tribes which had hitherto been the only form known.

The work in the Hawaiian islands was disappointing owing to the disappearance of nearly all the ancient culture of the people, but it was found possible to obtain some information on kinship and marriage which makes it probable that there have been grave misconceptions about the social relations of the people.

Among general results may be mentioned the demonstration of the presence of totemism in both Polynesia and Melanesia for which the evidence had been absent or doubtful. I propose to publish these results shortly as Dr Frazer is very anxious to make use of them in his forthcoming work on Totemism and Exogamy. Another general result is to show that Melanesian culture is far more varied in character than has hitherto been supposed, this variability applying not only to the different groups of islands but even to the different members of such small groups as those named after Banks and Torres.

It has also become clear that Southern Melanesia represents a far more primitive culture than that of the Solomons. My stay in the former has put me on the scent of numerous problems which I believe to be of the greatest importance for anthropology and it is my intention to return there directly I have finished the publication of the work done in the recent expedition.

[W.H.R. Rivers]

Appendix 2

Materials in Archives from the 1908 Percy Sladen Trust Expedition

◆●◆

Cato Berg

The chapters of this book draw upon a range of previously little known or little utilised sources in the history of anthropology. Since no general overview of these materials left by Hocart and Rivers exists, it is my purpose here to give in brief such an overview.

Much of what is left of the correspondence of W.H.R. Rivers is deposited in the Haddon Papers, part of the Rare Manuscripts Collection of the Cambridge University Library. Grafton Elliot Smith was Rivers's literary executor and, it seems, he passed on to Haddon some parts of Rivers's correspondence and notes, and after Haddon's death the Rivers papers were archived with Haddon's own material. Tim Bayliss-Smith found the original genealogies from Vella Lavella in these papers in 2004. The Rivers materials contained in the Haddon Papers are of various genres, from partial letters to Rivers (without replies), scraps of notes on various subjects, and notes that obviously stem from writing *The History of Melanesian Society* (Rivers 1914). The latter material is the fullest, and includes his original genealogies from large parts of New Georgia, and his later analytical notes about them. The Rivers materials contained in the Haddon Papers has not been catalogued in detail, and the contributors to this book who have used them – Bayliss-Smith, Bennett, Berg, Dureau, Hviding, Thomas – have restricted their use to the items directly relevant to their respective chapters.

Rivers carried out more work in Simbo and Vella Lavella than was previously known. His work on physical anthropology provides a grid for knowing whom he worked with at the time, as the measurements found in the Haddon Papers are all labelled with the name of the individuals measured, who are also identifiable from genealogies. Those genealogies that concern Vella Lavella are in Rivers's hand, while those that concern Simbo are in Hocart's hand (and are not included in the Haddon Papers). Both sets are attributable to Rivers and Hocart, respectively, from the small initials (WR, AH) on them. A small number of genealogies from Simbo are, however, originally recorded (and initialised) by G.C. Wheeler, and subsequently modified by Hocart. The latter are marked by the frequent crossing out of relations, and it does not seem that Wheeler (whose genealogical records seem to have been of poor quality) was able (or allowed) to do much of that line of work in Simbo. Even Rivers's own genealogies are clearly working versions, although they seem to have been edited to fuller versions already in the field. There are no differences between the genealogies used by Rivers to compute mortality figures for the volume on depopulation (Rivers 1922) and the original genealogies written down in the field. As far as I could ascertain, the only original, non-edited genealogies contained in the Haddon Papers are the ones from Vella Lavella (recorded by Rivers), while those of the other parts of New Georgia (recorded by Hocart) only exist in their annotated, calculated and further modified versions, perhaps contributed by Hocart after the fieldwork during his long residence in Fiji. The whereabouts of Hocart's original genealogies from Simbo remains unknown, but further investigation in the Turnbull Library in Wellington, New Zealand (see below) may clarify this.

In the collection of photographs from the 1908 fieldwork kept at Cambridge University's Museum of Archaeology and Anthropology (MAA), many images can be identified by name in relation to people and places. This composite set gives a brief but fascinating glimpse into the lived world of New Georgia in 1908 (see Thomas, this volume), a time of critical disruption (see Hviding and Berg; Hviding, this volume). In addition to the photographic collection, the MAA also has a collection of objects brought from the Solomons by Rivers, including tools, shields, axes, human skulls and so forth (Thomas, this volume).

The correspondence Rivers had with the Percy Sladen Memorial Trust is archived at the Linnean Society, London. As part of the joint preparations of this volume, Tim Bayliss-Smith located the correspondence and was permitted to transcribe it (see Appendix 1). This material gives valuable information on Rivers's objective with the expedition, as well as its rather substantial financial parameters, the total of which would, according to estimates, be equivalent to £30,000 (in 2010). Rivers's reports to the Trust also shed light on the progress of the expedition while still in the field.

By far the richest materials from the expedition are the unpublished notes and papers of A.M. Hocart, on deposit and on microfilm at the Alexander Turnbull Library, National Library of New Zealand, Wellington. This material is also the most well-known unpublished result of the expedition, and a number of scholars working on the Solomon Islands have been familiar with it for a long time. Indeed, the Hocart manuscripts are widely known outside these limited circles, including among islanders of the Western Solomons engaged in disputes over customary land. The microfilms contain Hocart's original and further processed fieldnotes on various categorised topics such as, 'Chieftainship', 'White Men', 'Money' and so on. Much of it is type-written with Hocart's hand-written annotations and corrections. Somewhat puzzling is the fact that the genealogical records (from Simbo, Roviana and 'Nduke' or Kolobangara) are all in Hocart's handwriting, despite Rivers being the acknowledged genealogical authority among the two. This may be due to genealogical work having been more demanding than originally thought, or that Hocart showed himself to be talented in this type of fieldwork (see Hviding, this volume). It is clear, moreover, that the genealogies from Roviana and Nduke (Kolobangara) are entirely Hocart's own, since Rivers did not work in these parts of New Georgia. Compared to the remaining materials from Rivers, Hocart's rich fieldnotes, like his published works arising from the expedition, give much more insight into the cumulative discovery process of the fieldwork, including copious comments as to the validity of individual informants' statements and the knowledge they were deemed to have of New Georgian ritual and social life. The Turnbull Library's Hocart manuscripts are unique in their capacity for giving a comprehensive view of early-twentieth-century life in New Georgia.

Glimpses of Rivers and Hocart also emerge in a variety of traders' letters and missionaries' and colonial officers' reports from the time. Although being aspiring anthropologists bent on living in the islands with local people, Rivers and Hocart were nonetheless part of the colonial scene (see Dureau; Kolshus, this volume). For instance, Rivers's name emerges from accounts of brief interaction with the Methodist missionary R.C. Nicholson on Vella Lavella, who even framed his own analysis of past life in Vella Lavella in diffusionist terms – thanks to Rivers!

The Percy Sladen Trust Expedition has not been given much weight by the official biographers of Rivers and Hocart, perhaps being better known from the fictional work of Pat Barker (1995). Against this enduring lack of attention to the events of 1908, the contributions to the present volume highlight the year as being formative for both of them. In this book, in-depth examinations of the somewhat mysterious archive materials are connected, for the first time, with the better-known published results of the Percy Sladen Trust Expedition.

References

Barker, P. 1995. *The Ghost Road*. London: Viking.

Rivers, W.H.R. 1914. *The History of Melanesian Society*. Cambridge: Cambridge University Press.

———— (ed.). 1922. *Essays on the Depopulation of Melanesia*. Cambridge: Cambridge University Press.

Appendix 3

Planning the Expedition

Letters Written Before the Fieldwork Began

◆●◆

Transcribed by Tim Bayliss-Smith

We know about the plans that Rivers made for his 1908 expedition from two sources. First are the documents kept in the Percy Sladen Memorial Fund archives at the Linnean Society, London (Appendix 1). Secondly there are two letters, one from Rivers and another written about him, and both sent to Charles Morris Woodford, Resident Commissioner of the British Solomon Islands Protectorate. These are preserved in the Woodford papers and have been scanned by the Pacific Manuscripts Bureau, Australian National University, Canberra (PMB 1290).[1] The original documents are now located in the Pacific Research Archives at the ANU. We are grateful to Kylie Moloney, Executive Director of the Pacific Manuscripts Bureau, for her help with access to PMB 1290.

Rivers first approached the trustees of Percy Sladen Memorial Fund for support on 30 May 1907 (Appendix 3.1).[2] Alfred Haddon, presumably at Rivers's request, had already sent the trustees a letter the previous day supporting the expedition and recommending Rivers as 'an ideal observer – patient, sympathetic, and absolutely efficient and honest' (Appendix 3.2). He praises Rivers's recently published monograph on the Todas, describing it as 'the very best socio-religious study of a native tribe that has yet been made by any field observer', and suggests that although his investigations had hitherto been conducted among peoples whose social systems were 'father-right', 'Dr Rivers now wishes to make an exhaustive study of a community still in the "mother-right" stage'.[3]

Rivers followed up his letter of 30 May with a formal application to the Percy Sladen Memorial Fund dated 13 June, in which he describes the project very briefly, but in words similar to those of his earlier letter. He writes in this application that his chief aim in the Solomon Islands will be 'to study the nature of social organisation based on maternal descent and the mode of its transition to paternal descent'.[4]

His subsequent letter of 10 July 1907 to C.M. Woodford confirms the evidence of these earlier documents (Appendix 3.3). It shows that from the outset Rivers had planned some relatively intensive fieldwork in the Solomons, residing in 'one or two limited districts' and with work lasting 'at least two or three months' in any one place. This letter shows also that he had not committed himself at that stage to any particular island or locality. Nor is there any mention of Arthur Hocart who, it seems, was only recruited by Rivers after the initial application to the Percy Sladen Memorial Fund had been made, and after the trustees had agreed to make him a grant of £400. Rivers made a further application in October asking for £300 to cover Hocart's expenses,[5] but in the event only a further £100 was granted.[6]

Rivers appears to have delayed choosing his fieldwork destination in the Solomons until after his arrival in Tulagi for discussions with Woodford in May 1908. It seems that initially Rivers was being steered by Cecil Wilson, the Bishop of Melanesia, in the direction of Santa Isabel (Bugotu). Wilson wrote a letter to the missionary Dr Henry Welchman at Maranatabu, Santa Isabel, saying that Rivers was soon arriving on the *Southern Cross* and requesting that Welchman 'look after' him. In a letter to Woodford dated 30 March 1908 Welchman refused outright to act in this way (Appendix 3.4). The Santa Isabel people were too civilised to be interesting, he wrote, being 'an Olia Podrida [incongruous melange] of speech, customs and clothes'. Rivers should go to some more accessible place in the Solomons, somewhere with 'more interesting and scientifically profitable peoples'.[7]

Welchman also hints at other, more personal reasons for his refusal to help Rivers. He wrote 'I am supposed to be useful as his Anthropological guide, philosopher and friend [but] he will be woefully disappointed and he had better keep away'. Welchman disapproved of the practices of his bishop – Cecil Wilson toured the islands on the *Southern Cross* and had never himself been a resident missionary anywhere. Perhaps Welchman suspected that Rivers was not only a friend of the bishop (they were both Cambridge men, after all) but also was some kind of anthropological tourist. Moreover, at this time Welchman was a sick man and did not have long to live – he died at Maranatabu in November 1908 aged 58, after twenty years of continuous service to the Melanesian Mission.

Perhaps as a result of having received Welchman's letter prior to the arrival of the anthropologists, Woodford advised Rivers, Hocart and Wheeler to do their fieldwork not in Santa Isabel but in the Western Solomons. In Simbo the English trader Fred Green became their local contact instead of the multi-lingual scholar Henry Welchman, with important consequences for the 1908 project.

Appendix 3.1

30 May 1907

Dear Sirs,

I beg to apply for a grant from the Percy Sladen Memorial Fund to aid me in undertaking a journey to the Solomon Islands for the purpose of making investigations in anthropology. I hope to be away from England for a year, of which I should spend at least six months in the Solomon Islands and shorter periods in one or two Polynesian islands, while, if possible, I would like to visit Lifu in the Loyalty Group.

I should endeavour while in the Solomons to obtain as complete an account as possible of the sociology and religion of the natives of two districts, one in which there is still a definite maternal system of society, and one in which this has been replaced by a system of father-right, my chief object being to study the mode of transition between the two states of social organisation. In addition I would hope to study the psychology of the natives, especially their senses, by experimental methods.

The shorter periods in the Polynesian islands would be devoted to obtaining the systems of kinship, on which subject I could obtain the information that I need in a few weeks.

I may mention that in the subjects to which I should pay special attention, the works of Codrington and others on the people of Melanesia give very little information.

My experience in anthropological investigations has been gained in Torres Straits and New Guinea as a member of the Cambridge Expedition to Torres Straits under the leadership of Dr Haddon, and in India which I visited with the aid of the Gunning Fund of the Royal Society. I have also done some work on the natives of Upper Egypt, and have examined in London parties of Eskimo and Pygmies, the latter as a member of a Committee of the Anthropological Institute appointed for that purpose.

In order to carry out the work I propose I should need a sum of £300 for my own expenses, but if a larger sum were available I should be very glad to take with me a colleague. I do not at present know of anyone who would be able to go with me, but if the necessary funds were available, I have no doubt I should be able to find someone who could work, either at natural history or at anthropology or at both.

I enclose a list of my chief publications in anthropology.

I am yours faithfully
W.H.R. Rivers

Appendix 3.2

Inisfail,
Hills Road,
Cambridge

29 May 1907

To A.W. Kappel Esq.,
Secretary to the Percy Sladen Memorial Fund

Dear Mr Kappel,

I understand that Dr Rivers is making an application for a Grant from the Fund, and I desire most cordially to support his application.

I have known Dr Rivers for many years, and have watched him at work in the field, and I have no hesitation in stating that he is an ideal observer – patient, sympathetic, and absolutely efficient and honest.

When on the Cambridge Expedition to the Torres Straits he elaborated an entirely new method of ethnological research, which has yielded the best results yet obtained, and his method must be adopted by all field students who desire to do their work thoroughly.

In writing up his results, he writes briefly and with the greatest candour, always pointing out where his information is defective, and he is very cautious in drawing conclusions. The result is that his work is to be depended upon absolutely, and nothing is slurred over.

His recent memoir on the Todas is, in my opinion and that of others, the very best socio-religious study of a native tribe that has yet been made by any field observer.

His investigations have hitherto been conducted among peoples in a state of 'father-right' – though the Torres Strait Islanders show traces of comparatively recent emergence from 'mother-right'. Dr Rivers now wishes to make an exhaustive study of a community still in the 'mother-right' stage.

The Trustees thus have the opportunity of sending into the field the best qualified Englishman, and the publication of his investigations will bring great credit to any Body that renders his researches possible.

I am yours sincerely,

Alfred C. Haddon

Appendix 3.3

St John's College,
Cambridge

July 10th 1907

Dear Sir,

You have probably heard from W. Read that I am hoping to come to the Solomons next year to do some anthropological work, and I shall be very glad of any help & advice you can give me.

I am thinking of leaving England at the end of the year & of travelling by way of America and the Pacific & I shall probably reach the Solomons about April or May. I imagine that from that time onwards would be not favourable for work so far as climate is concerned & I should be glad to know if from that point of view, there is any reason for arriving earlier. I suppose I can get direct to the Solomons from Fiji.

I may mention that my object would be to study anthropology & especially the social organisation, of one or two limited districts as thoroughly as possible & should not want to travel about but rather to stay in any one place for at least two or three months.

I was sorry to hear from W. Read that you are invalided in Sydney & hope that you are now quite well again.

Yours very truly,

W.H.R. Rivers

Appendix 3.4

Mara na Tabu
30 March 1908

C.M. Woodford Esq.
Tulagi

Dear Mr Woodford,
[the one-page letter concerns some financial transactions involving Lonsdale, Burrell and the Bugotu chief Soga, probably in relation to the schooner *Ruth*; also some oral history from Santa Isabel, in response to a query from Woodford]

With very kind regards, believe me yours sincerely,

Henry Welchman

P.S. I have just received a letter from the Bishop, since writing the above. ... [H]e tells me that Dr or Mr Rivers is coming down in the Southern Cross, and bids me look after him. That I cannot undertake. I do not know him and cannot write and tell him to keep away without seeming rude. Mara na Tabu will be deserted after the S.X. has left me, to allow of the peaceful arrival of a baby. I shall be away, and moving continually so that I cannot be at his call, and to tell the truth I do not think he will profit much by Ysabel. We are too civilised to be very interesting, and we are an Olia Podrida of speech, customs and clothes. Besides he would be very much out of the way of the more interesting and scientifically profitable peoples: once here he would find it hard to get away: we have so little communication with the rest of the group. I am supposed to be useful as his Anthropological guide, philosopher and friend: he will be woefully disappointed and he had better keep away. You will be far more capable of putting him in the right way of going about things. You have already got all that I know about Ysabel – little enough you will say. So it is. If you can put him on another route, you will be doing me a great kindness.

The jar came back all right: thanks for the information about the Huuhuu: it is a relief that my name will not go down to posterity linked with such a diabolical looking creature.

Notes

1. Pacific Manuscripts Bureau, Australian National University, Canberra: Woodford, Charles Morris, 'Papers on the Solomon Islands and other Pacific islands, 1879-1927'. PMB 1290, Bundle 24(2), 3/33 Folder 'Historical notes', Enclosure 2/59, handwritten letter on printed notepaper of St John's College, Cambridge.
2. Archive of the Percy Sladen Memorial Fund, Linnean Society, London: typed letter dated 30 May 1907, W.H.R. Rivers to Trustees of the PSMF.
3. Archive of the Percy Sladen Memorial Fund, Linnean Society, London: typed letter dated 29 May 1907, Alfred C. Haddon to A.W. Kappel, Secretary to Trustees of the PSMF.
4. Archive of the Percy Sladen Memorial Fund, Linnean Society, London: application form signed W.H.R. Rivers, St John's College, Cambridge, and dated 13 June 1907.
5. Archive of the Percy Sladen Memorial Fund, Linnean Society, London: typed letter dated 14 October 1907 from Dr W.W.R. Rivers and headed 'Application for an additional £300 to take an Assistant (A.M. Hocart)'.
6. Archive of the Percy Sladen Memorial Fund, Linnean Society, London: handwritten letter dated 18 December 1907 'on board R.M.S. "Adriatic"', W.H.R. Rivers to Mr Kappel, Secretary PSMT.
7   Pacific Manuscripts Bureau, Australian National University, Canberra: Woodford, Charles Morris, 'Papers on the Solomon Islands and other Pacific islands, 1879-1927'. PMB 1290, Bundle 24(2), 3/33 Folder 'Historical notes', Enclosure 2/60, typewritten letter from Henry Welchman to C.M. Woodford dated 30 March 1908.

Notes on Contributors

———— ♦●♦ ————

Tim Bayliss-Smith is Professor of Pacific Geography at the University of Cambridge and Fellow of St John's College, Cambridge. He has held visiting positions at the Australian National University, Luleå Technical University in Sweden, and the University of Otago, New Zealand. As well as in Solomon Islands, he has done fieldwork in Fiji, Papua New Guinea and Swedish Lapland. His books include *Islands of Rainforest: Agroforestry, Logging and Ecotourism in Solomon Islands* (with Edvard Hviding, 2000), *Rock Art and Sami Sacred Geography* (with Inga-Maria Mulk, 2006) and *An Otago Storeman in Solomon Islands: The Diary of William Crossan, Copra Trader, 1885–1886* (co-edited with Judith Bennett, 2012).

Judith A. Bennett is an Australian who lives in New Zealand. She is Professor of History at the University of Otago, Dunedin. Her main research has been in Solomon Islands about which she wrote a general history of trade and commerce and an environmental history of the forests, and edited an autobiography of a Solomon Islander of note. More recently, she has examined the environmental effects of World War Two on the Pacific Islands. She has also edited a book (with Tim Bayliss-Smith) on a the diary of a New Zealand trader resident in the Solomon Islands in the 1880s. Bennett is the author of *Wealth of the Solomons: A History of a Pacific Archipelago, 1800–1978* (1987), *Pacific Forest: A History of Resource Control in the Solomon Islands, 1800–1997* (2000) and *Natives and Exotics: World War II and Environment in the South Pacific* (2009); she is also co-editor of *Journeys in a Small Canoe: The Life and Times of a Solomon Islander* (with Khyla Russell, 2003) and *An Otago Storeman in the Solomon Islands* (with Tim Bayliss-Smith, 2012). She is currently editing a book with Angela Wanhalla on the histories of children of US servicemen and indigenous women in the wartime South Pacific.

Cato Berg is a Senior Lecturer in social anthropology at the University of Oslo and Associate Senior Scholar of the Bergen Pacific Studies Research Group. At the University of Bergen he has also held positions as a postdoctoral fellow and a lecturer in athropology. His research experience from Solomon

Islands includes fieldwork both in Honiara and on the island of Vella Lavella. He has recently studied how localised forms of hierarchy, kinship and land tenure are transformed in engagements with a Westminster-based legal system inherited from the nation's colonial past.

Christine Dureau is a Senior Lecturer in social anthropology at the University of Auckland. She is a historical ethnographer with research interests in the anthropology of Christianity, colonial cultures, motherhood, power and race, and she has conducted fieldwork on the island of Simbo in Solomon Islands. She is currently working on an edited version of A.M. Hocart's manuscripts, on a special journal issue on religion and the senses, and on an ethnographic account of early-twentieth-century Methodist missionaries in the Solomon Islands. Among her publications are the co-edited volume *Senses and Citizenships: Embodying Political Life* (with Susanna Trnka and Julie Park, 2013).

Annelin Eriksen is Professor of social anthropology at the University of Bergen, and director of the research programme 'Gender and Pentecostal Christianity: A Comparative Focus on Africa and Melanesia' funded by the Research Council of Norway. She has worked since 1995 in Vanuatu, first on Ambrym and in Port Vila. Her research deals with social and cultural change, Christianity and gender relations. Her publications include Gender, Christianity and Change in Vanuatu: An Analysis of Social Movements in North Ambrym (2008) and the co-edited volume *Contemporary Religiosities: Emergent Socialities and the Post-nation State* (with Bruce Kapferer and Kari Telle, 2010).

Edvard Hviding is Professor of social anthropology at the University of Bergen, Director of the Bergen Pacific Studies Research Group, and Coordinator of the EU-funded European Consortium for Pacific Studies. Among his publications are *Guardians of Marovo Lagoon* (1996), *Islands of Rainforest* (with T. Bayliss-Smith, 2000), *Reef and Rainforest: An Environmental Encyclopedia of Marovo Lagoon* (2005), *Made in Oceania* (edited with K.M. Rio, 2011) and *Pacific Alternatives* (edited with G. White, 2015). In 2010 Hviding was awarded the Solomon Islands Medal for his development of vernacular education programmes in the Marovo language. He has carried out fieldwork in the Western Solomons Islands regularly since 1986.

Thorgeir S. Kolshus is an Associate Professor at the Department of Social Anthropology, University of Oslo, and a commentator in the Norwegian daily *Aftenposten*. He is co-editor of a special issue of the *Journal of Pacific*

History on the Melanesian Mission and the Anglican Church in Melanesia, and author of a number of articles on the Melanesian Mission's influence on anthropology. He is currently finishing a monograph on Christianity on Mota (Banks Islands), examining the first self-sufficient Melanesian church.

Knut M. Rio is Professor of social anthropology at the University of Bergen, and is responsible for the ethnographic collections at the University Museum of Bergen. He has worked on Melanesian ethnography since 1995, with fieldwork in Vanuatu. His work on social ontology, production, ceremonial exchange and witchcraft in Vanuatu has resulted in journal publications and the monograph *The Power of Perspective: Social Ontology and Agency on Ambrym, Vanuatu* (2007). He has also co-edited *Hierarchy: Persistence and Transformation in Social Formations* (with O.H. Smedal, 2009), *Made in Oceania: Social Movements, Cultural Heritage and the State in the Pacific* (with E. Hviding, 2011) and *The Arts of Government: Crime, Christianity and Policing in Melanesia* (with Andrew Lattas, 2011).

Tim Thomas is a Senior Lecturer in archaeology at the University of Otago, Dunedin. He is working on several field projects focused on the New Georgia region of the Solomon Islands. Previous work on the material culture of late-prehistoric and early-contact-period Roviana has been followed by current research on the islands of Rendova and Tetepare, where he has been working with an indigenous conservation association to conduct archaeological and palaeoenvironmental surveys, gathering data to reconstruct the cultural history of Rendova and Tetepare and their place in wider Solomon Islands prehistory. He has co-edited *Lapita: Ancestors and Descendants* (with P.J. Sheppard and G.R. Summerhayes, 2009), and has published a wide range of journal articles and book chapters.

Index

———— ◆●◆ ————

www.ingramcontent.com/pod-product-compliance
Lightning Source LLC
Chambersburg PA
CBHW060025030426
42334CB00019B/2190